GRAINS OF TRUTH

Jack Webster was born in 1931 in the village of Maud, Aberdeenshire. As a child he suffered from a serious heart condition and there was no certainty that he would ever be able to work. But his determination to fulfil a boyhood dream of becoming a journalist overcame this problem and at the age of sixteen he started work on the *Turriff Advertiser*. He later moved on to the *Evening Express* and *The Press and Journal* in Aberdeen, before joining the *Scottish Daily Express* in Glasgow. After a highly successful period as a features writer with the *Express*, he is now a popular columnist with *The Herald*. Jack Webster lives in Glasgow.

GRAINS OF TRUTH

JACK WEBSTER

*To Douglas,
with best wishes
Jack Webster
Feb. 1996*

EDINBURGH
B&W PUBLISHING
1994

First published 1994
by B&W Publishing, Edinburgh
© Jack Webster
ISBN 1 873631 37 5

British Library Cataloguing in Publication Data:
A catalogue record for this book is available
from the British Library

PRINTED BY WERNER SÖDERSTRÖM

CONTENTS

A Grain of Truth

1	Come into the Garden	3
2	Main's Wooin'	10
3	A Buchan Sunrise	23
4	Philosophy and Fags	32
5	Wullie Lummies Galore	48
6	Haw-Haw, Hee-Hee	54
7	In Memory	71
8	From Whitehill to the White House	74
9	C'mon the Dons!	80
10	The Betty Hadden Mystery	85
11	The Turra Coo	93
12	The Rose that Faded	102
13	On Top of Her Ladyship	107
14	Aikey Fair	119
15	The Lifeboat's Over	128
16	Lord Jesus to Lord Boothby	137
17	From Maud to Moscow	144
18	On Board the Queen Mary	157
19	Chasing Charlie Chaplin	173
20	Hitler's Friend—and Mine	186
21	Foo's Yer Kweets?	193
22	The Hive of Honeyneuk	198
23	View from the Hill	207

Another Grain of Truth

1	The Way In . . .	213
2	The Roup	217
3	Champagne Breakfast	229
4	Roar Like a Dove	236
5	Like Robbie Burns	240
6	Greig and Grieg	246
7	On Mormond Hill	251
8	The Garden of Buchan	260
9	A German Provost	268
10	From Aberdour to ITN	276
11	Auld Meg Pom	285
12	The Buchan Tongue	290
13	There's Aye a Something	294
14	A Great Scot	297
15	Daughter of Grassic Gibbon	302
16	Trauchle and Triumph of Toulmin	310
17	The Scribe of St Combs	316
18	Moon Over Mormond	320
19	Gold and Silver	327
20	A Spurt of Oil	332
21	A Royal Day	338
22	Golden Age of Aberdeen	342
23	Granite City Growl	349
24	The Auld Hoose	358

25	The Queen and John Brown	366
26	The Mighty Monty	371
27	God Bless America	377
28	Fairy-tale of Forbes	382
29	My Heritage Trail	388
30	Back to Culsh	390
31	Rock of Ages	395
32	End of the Day	400

ACKNOWLEDGEMENTS

A Grain of Truth—My thanks for photographic assistance to:
Photo Service of Peterhead, Ian Hardie and Sandra Stephen
of Aberdeen Journals, George M Wilson formerly
of Fraserburgh, The *Scottish Daily Express*.

Another Grain of Truth—For permission to quote various items, I
would like to thank Colin MacLean of Aberdeen University Press
and the Charles Murray Trust; Nora Coutts, David Clark and the
newspaper empires of Geo. Outram, Thomson and the Express.
Thanks also to Messrs Aitken and Stone for the arrangement to
reproduce a passage from *The Kingdom by the Sea* by Paul Theroux.
Photographic assistance from George Dey, Leslie Yuill, Ken Melvin
of Glasgow, Scotpix of Aberdeen and Mrs Barnett of Strichen
Library was also much appreciated.

GRAINS OF TRUTH

By way of explanation. . . .

I wrote the first version of *A Grain of Truth* towards the end of 1963 (yes, we all remember what we were doing when President Kennedy was assassinated) but it didn't see the light of publication until Guy Fawkes Day of 1981.

By then I had reached my fiftieth birthday, a more mature milestone from which to look back nostalgically on my Aberdeenshire childhood and a subsequent life which had been more generous than I could ever have expected.

A Grain of Truth was published in hardback by Paul Harris of Edinburgh and sold well to its intended Scottish audience. Five years later, by which time I had wandered innocently into television and come up with the award-winning *Webster's Roup*, the chairman of Collins the publishers, Ian Chapman, was convinced I must have an interesting story to tell from that Aberdeenshire childhood and. . .

But the book had already been written, I said. It was called *A Grain of Truth* and, although they wouldn't have known much about it in London, it was a success in Scotland. However, there was no stopping Mr Chapman, whose family roots happened to be right there in the Buchan district where I grew up.

He would buy the paperback rights of *A Grain of Truth* for his company's Fontana imprint but he wanted to follow this up with a second volume. That was how I came to write *Another Grain of Truth*, which appeared as a Collins hardback in 1988 and as a Fontana paperback in the following year.

Ian Chapman, whose uncle and cousins farmed around Maud, New Deer and Strichen, then parted company with Collins and its new owner, Rupert Murdoch (his roots were also in Buchan), and established his own Chapmans Publishers of Drury Lane, London.

As one of his first commissions, he asked me to write the biography of Alistair MacLean, the former Scottish schoolmaster who rose to fame with books like *HMS Ulysses*, *The Guns of Navarone* and *Where Eagles Dare*. But that is another story.

Meanwhile the two *Grains of Truth* continued to sell into the 1990s. The notion of putting them both under one paperback cover was pursued by the enterprising Edinburgh company of B&W Publishing (the initials stand for the partners Campbell Brown and Steven Wiggins, who had met as students at St Andrews University in the 1980s). That is what you have in your hands right now.

As further evidence of their faith (or was it foolhardiness?) they decided to bring out another publication of mine on the same day—a celebration of my early journalism as traced through articles I was writing in the *Scottish Daily Express* during the Swinging Sixties. *The Express Years: A Golden Decade* complements the two *Grains of Truth* and brings irrefutable proof of a working lifespan which my boyish nature finds hard to accept.

But it is all here in black and white—and perhaps a few touches of colour as I unearth the canvas of my earlier life and presume to put it on display.

I

A GRAIN OF TRUTH

For my sons,
Geoffrey, Keith and Martin,
who inherit the tradition
—and remembering my beloved younger
cousins Greig Watt and Arthur Argo
whose lives were cut tragically short

CHAPTER ONE

COME INTO THE GARDEN

In the searing heat of 1947, that most glorious of twentieth century summers, they carried my bed to the front green of our council house in the village of Maud, Aberdeenshire, in the hope that it would hasten recuperation from a serious heart condition. I was just a boy in the sixteenth summer of life and there, under the cool of a garden shelter, I lay pale and limp, still smarting from the long series of cardiographs and blood tests, the shaking of heads and vague talk of leaking valves and murmurs which seemed like a fair concoction of doom. How psychologically damaging to discover that your life has apparently been defused before it has properly started; on top of which I was burdened with a painful stammer.

So there I lay as douce village folk came past and stopped for a cheery word; and when they had gone I would listen to that strange harmony of summer sounds which can swell a silence into an oratorio, and then I would drift into the daydream of a future that I had long envisaged. That future had now been cancelled, or so they said, as Professor Craig of Aberdeen looked down with kindly understanding and pronounced that I was 'a very tired boy'. If I were to work at all it would have to be behind an office desk.

That boyhood dream of being a journalist, which had lived with me for as long as I could remember, was now an option to put firmly out of my mind in favour of a job in an office. I gulped hard and felt an added weight descending upon an already over-burdened heart. But when the tears had been wiped away and a loving mother had given a glimmer of encouragement, there emerged a new resolution: If life ran the risk of being so limited then it had better be spent in the things I en-

3

joyed. 'No journalism' did they say? Ever so slowly a smile broke over a tear-stained face and I could swear that from that moment onwards, the good Lord put a healing hand on a faulty heart. . . .

The memory of it all was with me still, more than thirty years later, as I drove north towards Aberdeen on a journey which was filled with poignant expectation. For there I was, driving forward into the past on a mission of re-discovery, seeking to stand once more on the plains of North-East Scotland, at the place where I began, to take stock of the journey so far.

Since that summer of 1947 every day had been a bonus as skeely nature patched those cardiac cracks and enabled me to plod my way through the cherished dream of journalism via the varied empires of Lord Kemsley, Lord Beaverbrook and Willie Peters of Turriff.

That dicky heart had been put to the test in the chair of Chief Sub-editor of the *Scottish Sunday Express* and more strenuously in the varied wanderings of a writing newspaperman. As a features writer with the *Scottish Daily Express* I had dodged the bombs and bullets of Belfast, strolled among the Chinese hovels of Hong Kong and Singapore, slept rough in the jungles of Malaysia, walked rather appropriately with the afflicted to the shrine of Lourdes—and done some pretty banal and boring things as well. The pursuit of a life with a modest expectation had taken me across the Atlantic on the old *Queen Mary*, inside the White House of Washington and the Kremlin of Moscow, as well as face to face with a buffalo as I rode across the Badlands of the American Mid-West.

Fascinating hours in the company of people like Charlie Chaplin, Bing Crosby, Paul Getty, Mohammed Ali and Montgomery of Alamein (not to mention Shirley Bassey, Bill Haley and a few Prime Ministers!) may have seemed light years away from my thoughts as I sat back at the wheel of the motor car and sought to absorb every nook and nuance of landscape and emotion as they washed towards me.

4

Somehow the time had come to fit them all into the overall pattern of one man's life, however ill-matched some parts of that jigsaw may have seemed. Only then, having drawn all the threads together, could you step back and view the whole tapestry in perspective, giving yourself a therapy to clear the mind and fortify the soul. That was my mission on this northward journey which was already filling me with a mixture of excitement and a sense of well-being.

As the blue hills of Perthshire and the distant Cairngorms faded suitably away to the left I found myself pondering, a popular misconception that 'north' is Highland and 'south' is Lowland, whereas the division is much more east and west. For that very reason, Glasgow is arguably a Highland city and Aberdeen is a thoroughly Lowland one, the Aberdonians having driven out the Highlanders at the Battle of Harlaw and maintained a pretty cool welcome ever since.

So the high lands were taking their white caps and peaks into the mists and mysteries of a spacious west and leaving me to continue my journey over mild undulations by Forfar and Brechin towards that most distinctive of Scottish corners, the North-East.

Through Laurencekirk to the red soil of the Mearns and fresh excitement stirred my veins at the first whiff of the North-East atmosphere and the knowledge that the land of my begetting was racing towards me, mile by mile, minute by minute. Did she come with arms outstretched to enfold a returning son or with the rolling-pin of chastisement to scold a deserter?

That majestic sweep of land between the foothills of the Grampians and the Kincardineshire coast stirred nostalgic thoughts of my literary hero, Lewis Grassic Gibbon, the loon from Arbuthnott who made this land speak with a voice that was deep and warm and abiding.

That brought me to the lip of the gorge by which I must follow the path of a snake into the pit of Stonehaven, with its neat harbour and town square and sharply-rising mansions to the left. Now the road marched high by Portlethen and with the sudden flair of a magician unfolded the cloak of Aberdeen, that sparkling gem of British cities. There it lay in all its granite glory, sloping majestically towards the North Sea as the winter sun drew a dance of light from the rare reflection of the Rubislaw masonry.

An acceleration of pride was burning in my Buchan breast as I surveyed it on the downward drive towards the Brig o' Dee. Soon you lose the elevation and glide along the banks of the river by the football pitches, proud in a sudden awareness that this Granite City and its couthy hinterland are now well known around the world as more than just a hackneyed joke about meanness. For that of course we had to thank oil, which had put into the pronunciation of Aberdeen an international ring to compare with Houston.

As I drove up Holburn Street and down the grace of Union Street, I was struck by the humorous thought that my shrewd and canny kinsmen were sitting on a veritable fortune all that time (seventy-five million years at a rough guess) and didn't know it! How rough is the justice of the cruel, cruel sea, I was telling myself, as I passed C&A's at the top of Bridge Street and remembered that there had stood the queen of all Aberdeen hotels, the Palace, before it was burned down in 1941.

Imagine the effrontery of it that total strangers from alien cultures had managed to scoop up the prize of oil from under the noses of hard-headed people in whose company, it used to be said, the business-like Jews found it so difficult to survive that most of them fled the city a long time ago.

Then I had to drive on down King Street, across the Bridge of Don and out along the dual carriageway—or the double road, as we always called it—for my real destination was yet to come. They had improved the road to Ellon, long since cutting out that suicidal bend at Tipperty where incautious drivers were liable to make an involuntary call at the wee shoppie on the corner, across from the brickworks. So to Ellon, now a sprawl of oilmen's dormitories they said, and straight ahead at the roundabout where the Buchan boundary more or less begins.

The route past Arnage estate reminded me there was once a little boy called Donald Stewart who grew up in a cottage in one of the fields. He looked towards the imposing Arnage Castle and vowed to his widowed mother that one day he would own the place. Donald was as good as his word. By his early thirties he was a wealthy builder at the Bridge of Don and when he finally acquired the spacious residence he invited my parents and me to expensive parties where the adults drank and danced, children played games and we all gathered round to hear a virtuoso performance by a shy and elderly gentleman whose name was John Storrie. The particular fascination was that he laid across his knee an instrument which he then plugged into an electric socket before widening our eyes in wonder and twanging us from the cold Howe of Arnage to the heat of Hawaii with a sound I had never heard before. That was our introduction to the electric guitar, most of a generation before it became a weapon of assault upon the tenderness of the human eardrum.

But Auchnagatt awaited, not much of a place in size, but once boasting a flock of local farmers whose consumption at the Baron's Hotel would have drowned all other claims to alcoholic capacity. Past Nethermuir House, I turned right at the road sign which said 'MAUD 2' and embarked on that final drive along by places like Drymuir and Pitfoskie, where my uncle Jimmy still farmed. It was the most poignant stage of all as the road rose gently then suddenly presented you with the village of Maud below. There it was, spread out for all to see in the hollow valley, well off the beaten track of the tourist yet at the very heart of the area known as Buchan, famed for its beef cattle and broad humour and the barley which had ousted the great industry of oats.

You might well pass through it, unmoved, or miss it altogether if I did not pull you up by my side and let you into the secret of what it means to the eye of this particular beholder. For this Maud which gave me birth and a wealth of childhood memories may well be the last place on God's earth, as some uncharitable people have said; to which I can only reply the the good Lord kept the best until last.

I descended that last half mile into the village at the slow pace of reverence so that no part of the arrival would escape my senses. It was all so familiar that I might never have been away—Fedderate Cottages where I was born, the School, the old Poorhouse, the railway station now derelict; and the front green of 2 Park Crescent where I had lain ill that scorching summer. This was it. I was home in the place where I belonged, home in my own dour, rugged North-East corner of Scotland which has more romance in its story than many a distant place with colourful reputation.

As I gazed around and spotted the farm of Honeyneuk, I was reminded of an incident involving an eccentric acquaintance of my childhood, Willie Paul, who farmed there. Willie was a strange mixture of good heart and bad temper who would flare into a fearsome rage on occasion, with his bonnet stuck on at an angle to his nose. When a persistent taxman came round one day to make some tactful inquiry about a balance which was due to His Majesty's Inspector of Taxes, the doughty Willie got out his cartridges, pulled the double-barrelled gun from the hallstand and advanced upon the bowler-hatted bureaucrat as he came up the farm close, shouting 'Get oot o' here, ye bugger o' hell, or I'll sheet ye!' The inoffensive member of His Majesty's Inspectorate was last seen disappearing in the general direction of Maud, perhaps not fully aware of how narrowly he had escaped the discomfort of a shower of gunshot in his backside. Willie claimed that he had shot better rabbits than that.

When he died, my father borrowed enough money to buy Honeyneuk and a generation later there were new strangers wending their way in about the farm. This time they were not taxmen but mineral prospectors coming side by side with the oil explorers in the near-certain belief that there were commodities such as zinc to be found in that stretch of Buchan.

Mysterious helicopters buzzed overhead with detecting equipment, to be followed by men with persuasive arguments as to why my father should sell away the exploration rights of his two hundred arable acres for an annual retainer.

But North-East independence or shrewdness or thrawnness or whatever you care to call it will not be swept aside by the first influx of oil and mineral men. The divining rights of his land were to stay with my matter-of-fact father, John Webster, who simply raised his verbal shotgun, as opposed to Willie Paul's metallic one, and fired a Buchan broadside which was no less effective. In a changing and perplexing world I would lay a pound to a penny that one highly individualistic North-East character will do more to change the oil industry than the oil industry will do to affect the character of the North-East.

So the destination of the northward journey had been reached in my native village of Maud, twenty-eight miles beyond Aberdeen and perhaps marked 'Maud Junction' if your map precedes the surgery of Doctor Beeching. But that is not an end. In the contermacious ways of a Buchan man, let me upset the English dictionary by saying that the destination is just the beginning of our story. . . .

CHAPTER TWO

MAINS'S WOOIN'

The Buchan area of Scotland is bounded roughly by the towns of Peterhead, Fraserburgh, Turriff and Ellon and takes in one of the most intensively cultivated corners of the world. The fact that that is so is a memorial to the generations of decent, hardworking folk who have bent their bodies in sweated toil because Buchan, in all honesty, is by nature a sour and grudging land which has been tamed and cleared and ploughed and manured and nursed into a state of fertility which makes it one of the great agricultural romances of all time.

Out of it has come a breed of folk who have forged their own character, a quietly industrious people who have learned the lesson of making the most of what you have in this world and accepting that things might be a damned sight worse. Their unfashionable philosophy, were it more widely applied by mankind, might put the world in better heart. Such people are often the salt of the earth, developing their own dogged character and dry sense of humour with which they survey the urban scene with its ostentations and softer ways and pass some fairly harsh, but perhaps realistic, judgments. With the toil of their own hands, as I remember it, they ran their crofts and smallholdings and looked westward to Deeside and the aristocratic half of Aberdeenshire with a measure of tolerant disdain for the inbred lairds and their tweedy wives who came visiting to shoot the grouse, stalk the deer and fish the salmon before returning to the well-padded comfort of Eaton Square.

I grew up in a Buchan which thought less of such people than of the man who worked his own bit place and the cottar who raised a big family to provide the labour of the fields. I grew up with the broad rhythms of the land, the parks and the peesies, the smell of hot dung rising from stubble braes that surrounded our village of Maud which lay at the centre of it all. One half of it lay in the Parish of New Deer and the other in the Parish of Old Deer, which seemed an appropriate and comfortable place for a lady like Maud to lie. Eastward from the heights of Bonnykelly came the modest River Ugie which lapped its way round the village and ambled on between the historic Abbey of Deer and the hillside of Aikey Brae, which figures more prominently in the ramblings ahead. The valley blossomed out at Old Deer as the Garden of Buchan, for there at least you found an abundance of trees which were sadly absent from the rest of this highly-cultivated area.

Maud slumbered through each week till Wednesday when it stirred to become the biggest weekly cattle market in Britain, large floats careering down the country roads with load upon load of steaming livestock until you would think near all the beasts in Scotland were there, penned in the enclosures that stretched up and down the centre of the village, cattle lowing, sheep bleating and pigs skirling their various pleasures and protests. By ten o'clock the farmers had arrived in their hundreds, fine hardy chaps, ruddy from the exhilaration of outside work, puffing away at those short-stemmed Stonehives and greeting each other in twinkling but economic terms.

In the nineteen-thirties they came by bus and train and bicycle though today, with the trains removed and farming a more viable business, they flow in by motor car in an irregular progression which proves that, while they are perhaps the finest farmers in the world, they are without doubt the worst drivers. They seem to suffer from a curious notion that they have some kind of right of ownership to the public highway, particularly that half of it which comes in the opposite direction, and that perhaps explains the true story of the Buchan farmer who was charged with careless driving, having collided with another car while negotiating a local bend on the wrong side of the road. Scratching his head in puzzlement, he told the officiating policeman: 'Damnt tae hell, min, I've been gyan roon that corner the same wye for forty years an' I've never met anither car afore!'

The Wednesday morning scene would gain momentum, sharny-hipped bullocks and heifers, some fine and plump and some just shargers glad to be leaving the bareness of a sour croft, now driven on the hoof from nearby places, the fine rich smell of their bodies filling the nostrils with satisfaction. Less poetic roadmen who had to clean up afterwards said they were nothing but a skittery mess. As boys, we went down to the sale-ring and immersed ourselves in the babel of voices, farmers clustered round the arena, the blue-grey haze of cattle breath and Bogie Roll thickening in the shafts of sunlight which streaked in from roof windows. Through the fug it was just possible to pick out the auctioneer, rasping out his vocal shorthand from the rostrum, picking up winks and nods and veiled movements of the finger which were visible only to the sharp eye of experience. The man in the rostrum was my father, standing just where he had been when they brought him word one Wednesday morning that I had been born, a fact which was evidently absorbed with a perfunctory nod in the lull between a long-legged piner and a rough Irish stot.

The sale would continue well into the afternoon, with much coming and going of seedsmen and travellers and insurance lads till the attention which had been firmly fixed on pigs and stirks and farra coos was just as firmly transferred to the delights of Jimmy Henry's pub or the 'Refresh' at the railway station, which was run with maidenly care by the sisters Lil and Lena Murison. If the liquid lunch, which was always liable to extend beyond three courses, flowed out of control, a gig or hired Ford car was summoned to convey the casualty back to the farmstead. The Buchan farmer may not readily have admitted defeat but he had a special regard for John Barleycorn as a stiff opponent. Then the sun would stretch away across by Culsh, bringing the settled mellowness of late afternoon by which time the buses and trains had drained away the crowds, leaving our village and its five hundred inhabitants to relax once more into that six-day slumber from which they would surface next Wednesday and all the Wednesdays to come.

Life in a Scottish village before the Second World War was a placidly settled existence, with a firm base of family roots around the district and a predictable pattern of events in which the pace of any change, were it there at all, would have disturbed no-one. Everybody knew everybody else, from their pedigree to their pets, which explains the concern of one dear Buchan lady who was paying her first visit to London. In the uncaring bustle of King's Cross Station she spotted a poor stray cat and, turning to the relative who was meeting her, she inquired: 'Noo, fa's catty would that be?' Back home in Buchan it would not have been a ridiculous question.

Within that recognisable setting my own family tree had taken root, a story which is told upon the gravestones of neighbouring parishes like Aberdour and Gamrie, where every one of my forefathers for seven or eight generations had the name of John Webster. Whatever they lacked in the originality of choosing names they made good in honest toil. As the weavers of the Macfarlane clan they must have tired of the webs and turned instead to farming which had been their occupation for two hundred years or more. Their testimony, like that of their neighbours, lies in the fine arable lands of Buchan which they coaxed to fruition. But their plodding peasantry is short of drama, except for the extraordinary event of 1913, when my father's father contracted the animal disease of anthrax from one of his cattle and promptly died, leaving my father with the job of running the smallholding at Backhill of Allathan, New Deer, from the age of eight. Older men lent a neighbourly hand and marvelled at the enterprise of the child. As well as sorting the beasts he was soon working as a drover of cattle to the market and setting his heart on the ambition of his life—to occupy that rostrum in the mart at Maud. His aim was achieved in his middle twenties, before I was born, and John Webster

13

grew in both girth and stature as perhaps the most sound and sensible authority on the subject of Buchan farming. In the absence of a proper schooling, he not only taught himself everything from decimal fractions to land measurement but developed a gift for shrewd judgment which was close to uncanny, whether it concerned the quality of a beast or the honesty of a man. Embracing it all was a powerful personality which mixed great good humour with a ready temper and was fired by an engine room of energy which exhausted lesser mortals like myself, even in the observing of it.

He was well-built, with ruddy complexion and he embodied a talent for rural vulgarity which came so naturally that it caused little offence. He believed in calling a spade a bloody shovel and to hell with those who objected. His standard description of anything which was intolerably tough, for example, was to say that it was 'as hard as Hinnerson's erse' (Henderson's arse; Henderson being a North-East name for the Devil). If questioned on how hard 'Hinnerson's erse' was supposed to be, he would explain that it was ten times harder than flint, which surely made the point! If his pipe choked up and would neither suck nor blow he would fly into a rage at the confounded thing and declare that it was 'as ticht as a fisherman's erse—it'll naither let oot wind nor in water', which is just what a fisherman would need on a stormy sea!

As might be anticipated in such a man, the cultural realms of music, drama or literature were foreign fields into which he never ventured. The only concession he ever made to such wasteful pursuits was to give us a song which he learned at his mother's knee and which he intoned with a rare absence of anything resembling time, tone or rhythm. We would hide our amusement as he launched himself into his one and only song which went like this:

When I was a little wee pirn-taed loon
The ca'ed me 'silly little Jocky'

Ae day I was sittin' on ma granny's windae sill
Eatin' sweeties fae a grey paper pyokey

When by came a lassie and she offered me a kiss
I said 'That's a thing I never think o' scornin''
She bolted tae ma sweeties, ca'ed ma heid through the windae
And ma granny tellt me this neist mornin'

For it's aye said sayin' it's a bawbee for a bap
And a rosy-cheekit aipple aye lyin' on the tap. . . .

There ended the rendering, with a glow of pride that he had made his contribution to culture, while remaining blissfully unaware that the last verse was still two lines short of making poetic sense.

In the balancing ways of nature, such a man will almost inevitably marry a woman of a wholly different type and so it was with the ebullient John Webster, Buchan auctioneer. From the farm of Whitehill, several miles away, he met Margaret Barron, a fresh-faced country lass who harboured dreams of becoming a ballet dancer, and though that world was impossibly out of her reach in an Aberdeenshire backwater, she would pirouette and caper about the house and bicycle cheerfully along country roads with the wind blowing through her hair.

Her pedigree was not only different from that of John Webster but a rather unusual one in the Buchan setting. She was, in fact, descended from the family circle of Robert Burns, Scotland's national bard, whose grandfather, Robert Burness (that was the spelling) farmed at Clochinhill, near Stonehaven. Robert Burness had a brother William, a neighbouring farmer, from whom my mother was directly descended. Into that line of breeding, just two generations before herself, came another talented family, the Greigs, who claimed relationship with Edvard Grieg, the national composer of Norway, whose family was rooted at Rathen, near Fraserburgh, before his grandfather emigrated to Norway and changed the name from Greig to Grieg. Unlike the Burns connection, I cannot produce proof of a link with Edvard Grieg though the family themselves believed that they knew it. The focal point of the Greigs, however, was my great-grandfather, Gavin Greig, born in 1856, the son of a forester at Parkhill Estate of Dyce, near Aberdeen, a tall, lean and languid boy of great intellectual gift. As dux of his school he had also shown great promise as a pianist, organist and composer and the time spent on these other interests brought him the shame of entering the University of Aberdeen as fourth bursar instead of first, which was his proper intellectual measure. In those days there was little choice for a lad o' pairts in rural Scotland so he became a teacher, at the age of twenty-two the headmaster of the modest country school at Whitehill in the parish of New Deer, just three miles up the road from Maud, and there he settled in a job well beneath his capacity but with plenty of spare time to devote to his first love, which remained music.

Even at the end of the last century there was a great wealth of folk song being handed down by word of mouth but Gavin Greig realised that the habit was dying and that a whole field of Scottish tradition would be lost for ever. So he undertook what was to be the main work of his life, that of preserving in proper form the folk songs of North-East Scotland. Night after night he would mount his bicycle and scour the countryside, hunting out old men and women who recalled to him the versions which had been handed down to them. Sometimes there would be a variation, different words, a slightly different tune. All were catalogued.

At the end of the night the man of the house would escort Maister Greig to the road-end and there perhaps he would remember a verse which had eluded him by the ingle-neuk. So down they would crouch by the fun-buss, with the man humming above the sough of the wind while Greig was feverishly jotting down words or musical notes by the light of a storm lantern. The tedious process went on for years. Published in the *Buchan Observer* in Peterhead and later in book form, it is counted as perhaps the greatest collection of its kind in existence, safely housed in the library of King's College in the University of Aberdeen.

Those who know more about it than I do will confirm that it is a work of quite remarkable achievement, painstaking and thorough in its research and brilliant in its final sifting and presentation. Folk song is a branch of musical and poetic expression which needs to be fed and nurtured from a great depth of natural root and not everything which has been handed on as the 'song of the folk' can be regarded as entirely authentic and trustworthy. Down the ages there is many an ambitious versifier who has tampered with the originals and superimposed his own ego upon the true ancestry of the work. Perhaps it can best be said of Gavin Greig that he combined genius with honesty, a mixture which readily conveys itself to the human instinct. As a result, scholars have come from as far as America to study his work, sometimes with a sense of hero-worship and a gaze of reverence for his descendants, some of whom are not much acquainted with the collection and merely blush at the reflected glory.

Of the large family circle, my cousin, Arthur Argo, who became a producer with the BBC, had acquired the closest affinity with the mood and spirit of our great-grandfather's work. Folk song, in fact, had a lean period but Arthur Argo, with his inherited interest, was there at the beginning of the modern revival. In 1961, while in his mid twenties, he had taken leave of absence from his job as a reporter on *The Press and Journal* to tour the clubs and campus lands of the United States with not much more than a toothbrush, a guitar and a good Scots tongue. In the rovings of his six-month adventure he gathered friends and admirers with names like Bob Dylan, whose legendary status was still in the future. Back home, Arthur was already playing his major part in a folk revival, befriending young lads like Billy Connolly and Gerry Rafferty, and becoming in his own day one of Scotland's leading authorities on the subject of folk music.

But if the folk-song fame of Gavin Greig was strong in foreign parts, his reputation in Scotland during his own lifetime rested more on another activity, the one inherited from the Burnsian strand of his ancestry. As well as being a fine musician he had a keen observation, a sense of the dramatic and a true feeling for words. So in 1894 he produced something for the stage in a form which was not too familiar at the time. It was a play with music, a rural saga of the lives and loves of country people, their trials and troubles and the beautiful simplicity of their days. He called it *Mains's Wooin'*. It captured the imagination of its day and has been produced by local companies in many a school and village hall throughout the twentieth century. In 1954 there was a diamond jubilee performance back in the parish of New Deer where it all started and the chairwoman on that memorable evening was none other than Nellie Metcalfe, who had been the beautiful leading lady of that first *Mains's Wooin'* exactly sixty years earlier. Nellie had become the wife of Archie Campbell, farmer at Auchmunziel of New Deer and a well-known columnist in *The Press and Journal* under the name of 'The Buchan Farmer'. Nellie herself had become a writer of more distinction than Archie and together they produced a daughter, Flora, who combined their talents and became in more recent times one of the best Scottish poets of her day, under her married name of Flora Garry.

The jubilee performance of *Mains's Wooin'* was followed in 1963 by a mammoth production in the natural outdoor setting of the countryside with a cast of hundreds, including massed choirs and orchestra; and proving that Gavin Greig had captured something of worth in his play, the country folk came flocking to see it in 1963 just as they had done in 1894, recognising some basic thread of rural life which endures when other superficialities have passed away.

Gavin Greig followed up with a sequel, *Mains Again* and then with perhaps his finest musical creation of all, the operetta *Prince Charlie*. But the 'Prince' was a lavish production and, although it ran for a week at a time in places like Peter-head, the costumes had to be hired from London and there was a limit to the number of local societies which could afford the expense. He also collaborated in such notable musical works as *The Harp and Claymore* with that most memorable of Scottish violinist-composers, his friend Scott Skinner, and wrote four novels as well as the poetry which is represented in Edwards' *Modern Scottish Poets*.

In his introduction to Greig's poetry in 1884 (the poet was only twenty-eight), D.H. Edwards wrote: 'He is an accomplished musician as well as a tuneful and sweet poet, and although frequently urged to collect his scattered productions and issue them in book form, he has not as yet consented to do so. He looks on his poetical efforts as a mere mental recreation but the selections we give amply vindicate Mr Greig's right to be heard. His poetry is clearly the utterance of his heart. It is sustained by a sweet-toned fancy and is poured forth in natural gushes of feeling, clear and limpid as a Highland burn, and giving evidence of a rich mental poetical sympathy with the sights and sounds of nature.'

Gavin Greig was, of course, a product of the very soil from which the Buchan dialect of Scotland had sprung, not merely some intellectual who applied his curiosity to a quaint native speech but a man who had grown with it as naturally as the corn on the clay. His opening stanza on 'The Grampians' for example goes like this:

> Lat gentry chiels and ne'er-do-weels
> Gang owre the warld stravaigin'
> Syne rave an' write lang screeds o' styte
> O' foreign kintras braigin'—
> Het birstlin' clime, or realms o' rime,
> O' drouthy lands an' swampy anes;
> Here lat me bide nor budge a stride
> Frae Scotland and her Grampians

But his natural affinity with the Scots tongue did not hinder a brilliant command of the English language. His beautiful description of a Scottish Sabbath, written as a very young man, is too long to quote in full but you get the flavour of his mellow rhythms in the opening lines:

> It is the Sabbath morn; how still the day
> breaks on our native Scotland. Lo! it comes
> The deputy of Heaven, and freshly clad
> In all the mild authority of Peace.
> See how its advent chases every sight
> and sound suggestive of the secular world. . . .

So he proceeds to paint a word picture of the country worshippers wending their way to the kirk in the graveyard, some sitting on table slabs till the parson arrives, leading them to the pews and to a psalm of David:

> O'er the pews
> a rustling wakes, as on a quiet noon
> a leafy beech tree shivers and is still;
> For each is turning to the psalm announced.
> That duly found, the people turn to mark
> What tune the slow revolving placard tells;
> Some ancient melody, of style severe,
> Their fathers sang in old reforming days.

Tall and delicate and wearing a slight stoop by the time he reached his middle years, Gavin Greig surrounded himself with a wide spectrum of friends at the Schoolhouse of Whitehill, playing the organ and talking with a fluency and wit that drew intellectuals from all over the country. Their delight in his company was matched only by their surprise that such a being should bury himself in the backwater of Whitehill. But that was where he now belonged, where he fathered his nine children and where he was as genuinely at home with the local farm servants as he was with the visiting professors from Edinburgh.

It is also where you will find old folks even today who will glow with idolatory at the mention of his name. Despite his many fringe activities, he was also hailed as one of the finest schoolmasters in the land, admired, respected and sometimes feared in a smoking cap which offset his long, droopy moustache and the glittering ring which shone from a lean, artistic hand. Such a man was not robust. *Angina pectoras* had raised its restless agony and the news that a great war was breaking upon the world aggravated his condition and depressed his spirit. He foresaw such an upheaval in the affairs of the human species that he could hardly bear the thought of it. He did not have to. For he died in the month it began, August of 1914, a brilliant Scot still in his fifties with a lot of useful work to complete.

Among the young men inspired by his work was Alexander Keith, an Aberdeen graduate who became assistant editor and chief leader writer of the *Aberdeen Daily Journal* after the First World War. In 1925 he edited the ballad portion of Greig's folk song collection, which was entitled *Last Leaves of Traditional Ballads and Ballad Airs*, described by a leading American critic as the best book of its kind in existence. Alexander Keith, whose journalism appeared under the initials A.K. and whose books included *A Thousand Years of Aberdeen*, had this to say of my great-grandfather in his introduction to the 'Last Leaves':

> Had the accident of birth or the locality of his employment placed Gavin Greig within the notice of the London newspapers, there would be no need to write, at this date (1925), a tribute to his memory or to give an account of his research into popular poetry and the music of the people.
>
> Like most studious men, quiet work excluded both the desire and the opportunity for self-advertisement.
>
> As a recorder, especially of music, Greig was a master, for not only had he the knowledge of the art in very full degree, but he possessed also the extraordinarily percipient 'ear' which is sometimes, though by no means always, found in persons of high sensibility.

It is unfortunate that Greig did not reduce his conclusions into a complete and final judgment on the various problems of popular and traditional minstrelsy which cropped up to confront him during his investigations. Many of his theories were embodied in the lectures he delivered, some of which have been reprinted. But he had undoubtedly much more to say.

He carried his comments, as many a poor Scot had carried his library, 'under his bonnet' and death has obliterated the trace of them. Nevertheless, such opinions as he did commit to writing, combined with the range and interest of his collection, are proof of a remarkable penetration of research and soundness of reasoning.

So generously did he devote his strength and his abilities to his chosen subject that his epitaph may, not unjustly, be borrowed from Charles Murray's lines on the death of Heraclitus:

'Death that coffins a' the lave, your sangs can never kist.'

In the tragic pattern of those days, death had coffined some of Gavin Greig's own children before himself. Little Nellie, aged twelve, had gone to Crimond to keep house for her married sister, Maggie, who lay dying from consumption. But the child was smitten by the galloping variety and had to be taken to her grave at New Deer just ahead of her sister. The folk of those days were protected by a faith which somehow cushioned them from the overwhelming heartbreaks they had to endure. Maybe the faith diminished with the apparent need for it but it has left us pretty vulnerable, has it not, in our modern society which has found no substitute in times of distress.

CHAPTER THREE

A BUCHAN SUNRISE

In the days of Gavin Greig it was the survival of the fittest, and the genetic strength of his breeding had come first. His eldest child, Edith, who became my grandmother, survived them all and reigned into her nineties as the grand duchess of the family circle. From the Schoolhouse of Whitehill she had married Arthur Barron, a local farmer who took over the tenancy of Mains of Whitehill, and there they lived a hard and demanding life, wresting a bare living for themselves and their five surviving children, of whom my mother, Margaret Barron, was the eldest.

So the ebullient John Webster took his bride to the hotel at the Howe of New Deer and married her on a day of ferocious gales. As the small group of relatives sat down to the feed, douce and ill at ease as folk tend to be at weddings, funerals and other disturbing events, old Granny Webster had the benefit of a clear view up the village brae when she startled the gathering by jumping to her feet and exclaiming that a cartload of straw had been blown right over, farmer and all. There was a general scampering to mount a rescue operation for Buchan folk are not of the sort to let the minor matter of a wedding come between them and lending a hand to a fellow creature in distress.

With such an inauspicious send-off, my father and mother began their married life in a but-and-ben which still stands as a ruin at Mill of Bruxie, two miles from Maud, a place so riddled with vermin that my father spent his spare moments shooting rats from the kitchen window. By the time I was born they had moved to another two-roomed house at Fedderate Cottages in the village of Maud and it was there, in the front room, that I first saw the light of day on Wednesday, 8 July, 1931, a grand day to be born, folk said, though, despite a certain talent for recall, I am forced to admit that the experience escapes me!

By the time I was three we had moved into the more modern comfort of a council house at 2 Park Crescent and that was where my childhood came into its own. My father's personality as well as his job created a certain vortex of activity so it was a busy household with much coming and going of farm folk and martmen, everything leading up to the climax of the Wednesday mart then running down to the trough of the weekend and back up again. Dad went off to canvass for cattle at Fraserburgh on a Tuesday, while Fridays were spent in Aberdeen, where he auctioned at the mart's headquarters at Kittybrewster. The rest of his week was taken up with visits to Buchan farms to solicit cattle for the Wednesday mart, to arrange a displenish sale for farmers who were moving or a letting of grass for those with pasture to spare. In those early days there were three separate auctioning companies in the village of Maud, all competing for the livestock which would pass through their salerings. The two major companies were the Central and Northern Farmers Mart and the family firm of Reith and Anderson, neither of whom paid over-much attention to the minor competition from another family concern, which was Middleton's Mart. Indeed when my father became auctioneer to Middleton around 1930 he was sometimes struggling to muster six cattle for his Wednesday sale as against the massive numbers of his two big rivals. There was no contest. But he scoured the countryside on his motor-bike, seeking to establish himself as an honest man who knew something about beef cattle and was willing to learn the rest. Some bigsy farmers gave him short shrift and treated him rather shamefully but a few kindly men recognised his worth and good intentions and helped him to build up a clientele for Middleton's Mart. Week by week his figure rose till he became a major threat to the two big firms and brought himself a new respect among folk who knew the business. In time the three mart companies amalgamated and my father ended up as manager of the combined operation at Maud, never forgetting to return his thanks to the farmers who had given him a helping hand in those struggling days at Middleton's; and if the truth be known, he never quite forgot the ones who belittled him either.

All the time he was dispensing advice and help which became more and more eagerly sought by those who had learned of his instinct for a sound decision. All men were equal in my father's eyes and sometimes he would spot an able farm servant and encourage him to take the lease of a small croft as the first step on the road to becoming a farmer. The poor chap would shrink from lack of confidence but Dad would steel his nerve and offer him his first few cattle which did not have to be paid until they were brought back for sale, having been fattened to the butchers' requirements. Many a prosperous farmer to this day harks back to the time that my father bullied him into accepting the responsibility. He seldom had a failure. Widows or spinster ladies left to run a family holding would turn to him for help in stocking the place with cattle. One such lady, Miss Oliphant from Tyrie, was eternally grateful for his wise counsel. She was also distressed one day to learn that he had been laid low with measles and was in fact lying beside his pale-faced, seven-year-old son, a fearsome spectacle by contrast with a round red face resembling a harvest moon and covered in a most comical mass of scarlet spots. Father and son were feeling deeply miserable together when the morning post brought the sympathetic note from Miss Oliphant. I can still recall the occasion as he opened the letter and read it out in his deliberate, matter-of-fact tones: 'Dear Mr Webster; I am very sorry to hear that you are in bed with a measle . . .' The rest was lost in an explosion of oaths. 'A measle?' exclaimed my rumbustious father. 'Ah've thoosans o the buggers!'

Meanwhile my mother would busy herself about the house,

making cups of tea for Johnnie Ingram, the martman who would come hopping in with all the bounce of a bantam-cock, or Andra Forbes, the village bobby, who put his head cautiously round the sick-room door, gaped in amazement at the sight of my father's much-measled face and exclaimed 'Goad, what an ugly bugger!' before retreating in haste to a safer distance. Mam would conduct the business of the mart by means of the new-fangled contraption called the phone, which had recently come along to intrude on domestic privacy while giving you a certain exclusiveness in the village community; for it was not everybody who had a phone, was it? Even then she was struggling with chronic bronchitis which she used to describe rather graphically as having the taste of 'roosty nails'. She longed for the opportunity 'tae gyang doon wi' a barra and spad an' hae a gweed redd-oot.' (Translated from the Buchan dialects that means: 'to go down with a barrow and spade and have a good clean-out.')

But she was a brave and cheerful spirit and when the measles had subsided she and I would value the times when my father with his more oppressive ways was out of the house and we could turn on the wireless at high volume and cavort to the mellow tones of Harry Roy, Henry Hall, Roy Fox, Ambrose or Jack Hylton. At the same time my father was graduating from an old, dickie-backed car with a running-board and an outside battery to a green Austin 12 with the registration of RG 6502, which sticks with me to this day, when I would be incapable of telling you the number of my current car! In such new-found comfort we managed to drive to Glasgow for the Empire Exhibition of 1938, the biggest event ever held in Scotland, and there we found ourselves lodgings in Copland Road, just opposite Ibrox Park, and spent our days among the wonders of that spectacular show in Bellahouston Park. A miniature train transported you round the vast acreage of pavilions, which portrayed the life of the British Empire, and when the evenings came and the fountains and waterfalls were lit up in colour and the gigantic tower on the hill went soaring into the night sky, the crowds would link arms and dance up and down the terraced steps to the craze of the moment, which was 'The Lambeth Walk'. The effect on the child mind was inspirational. While in Glasgow for that first time, we joined a boat excursion to Clydebank and sailed round the hull of a massive ship which my mother explained would soon be sailing the high seas as the *Queen Elizabeth*. Thirty-five years later I was to commission a boat in Hong Kong Harbour to take me out to the bay where I sailed round that same ship, alas by then lying on her side, sabotaged and burned out in a heartbreaking spectacle. I had followed the great lady from her cradle at Clydebank to her graveyard in Hong Kong. On that occasion in 1938 we also visited Burns's Cottage at Ayr, feeling something of a family right to be there, and returning to Maud with a sense of having been on a world adventure. For travel was not the fashion of the day, except for those who went off to foreign parts and maybe never came back again. Anyone who had been abroad and returned was deserving of that curious interest which was later accorded to men who had been to the moon. Such creatures fell into two main categories: schoolteachers who had the time and the money to go during the long summer holidays and the ex-Servicemen who had been to France during the First World War. (It is now impossible to find a First War veteran who is under eighty and I find it sobering that I can remember them in their thirties.) A third category, almost beyond comprehension, had been policemen in faraway places like Shanghai or Hong Kong or tea-planters in Sumatra and some would come home with fine romantic tales of the East. But not all succeeded in making the impression they intended. One local adventurer home from his wanderings was holding court in the pub one night, extolling the benefits of travel as a means of broadening the mind and chastising the locals for their lack of enterprise. 'Be like me,' he counselled. 'Get out of this God-forsaken hole and see a bit of the world.' Old Geordie Bendie beheld him for a minute then said: 'Weel ye ken, Lord John

Sanger had a circus and in the circus there was an ass. Lord John Sanger took his circus a' roon the world an' the ass went too. But when the circus came back, the ass was still an ass. . .' As the locals shuffled their feet and chuckled quietly, a pompous gent was finishing his drink more quickly than he intended and making for the door in a huff!

So life in a Scottish village took on its own pace and pattern and the filterings of it are still strong with me now. In the wet plap of winter I can hear the early-morning rattle of bottles, with milk-boys whistling out of tune, an extra pint for Mrs Fyte; still dark with only a threatening glimmer of light in the east; now an early horse led by eident crofter was whinneying at the smiddy door and Willie Ogston handled it to a stall and gripped a hoof between his legs, having forged a shoe in a shower of sparks and cooled it in a sizzle of cold water. Then the day broke open and roadmen boarded a Leyland lorry to quarry stone from Aikey Brae. Country bairns, fresh from three-mile walks and shaming village laziness, came dysting in with piece-bags, fine ruddy cheeks and burning lugs well primed to hear the good sense of the three R's before returning to sort nowt and to bed themselves down on chaff. As the frosts came creeping up the howe, laying their crisp sparkle over ploughed park and grass, braeside croft or village dell, it was time for Christmas, tinsel wonder and kirk bells tolling for a simple service with candles and a fine warm feeling of neighbourliness and comfort and sureness. And as the snowdrift came creeping in the wake of the blast it was time to sledge clear parallel lines on virgin snow, fine moonlit nights with gay young voices echoing on distant hills then panting home, well past the hour, to the joys of deep sleep and the morning sorrow of thaw and brown slush, sandy water choking in the gurgle of drains, making a fair sotter of wonderland. Soon fresh winds were sweeping through the howe, clearing the last vestige of speckled white from the lithe of dykes; and days were waxing into Spring, the twitter of birds, bairns out to play beyond teatime and the bleat of a paraffin tractor telling of furrows that were spared the blast of winter and were only now folding over, one upon the other, in the neat harmony of Spring soil.

As crops were sown, a new crop of human flesh went fleetfooted to the excitement of Miss Catto's infant class, a world begun, of plasticine and counting beads, the smell of chalk and rubber and fresh exercise books, of slate and a one-third pint of morning milk and the exquisite reward for a week of diligent application—the Friday afternoon caramel. Simple days, simple tastes, lullabies and tender stirrings of love. Then the sun came higher in the sky and nights stretched through April and May to a sniff of summer that brought June on its wing, warm, steaming soil pushing up shoots of corn. June that brought holidays from school, an eternity that ended, sultry days of thunder-clapping and bursting rain and sun again and steam and cattle shows with animal breath and smell of skin and sharn, with crowds gathered at the ringside cheering hammer-throwers and Highland dancers, lustily taking sides in the embedded battles of tug o' war; great brosey chiels with names to terrify and at the end of the line an anchor-man of enormity, lying sodden with rope bound round his shoulders, determined not to yield an inch. The Bell family was the big name, all brothers and cousins from Tyrie, near Fraserburgh, welded into a leaden mass of brute force, heaving and checking to the command of their family head, Alex Bell, an auctioneer like my father and an irresistible force of heavyweight proportions, though short in the leg, filling the local church with as powerful a bass voice as there was in the land.

As the show days wore late the drunks were havering and slavering and tumbling in a world that would not stand still; the fiddles were tuning up for the marquee dance. Shy young deems and bolder ones, unable to get to the show during the day, came biking in from byre and bigging to cast themselves incautiously into the spinning-wheel of the Eightsome Reel, the Quadrilles or the Lancers, with hulking chiels fresh from hammer-throwing or whisky tent birling them off their feet, skirts flying out to uncover thighs of fiery flesh, an unco sight to blind the timid. The music and the heat and sweat and smoke fermented in a heady night that tailed off behind dykes and trees and left tired limbs for milking the kye or cutting the corn. And the golden rustle of hairst was here, binders whirring their tunes of glory, spilling out sheaves that were stookit and left to dry in the late summer winds. Horse and cart were yokit in a week or two, neighbours came to help with the leading, stooks were forked on to the carts and led to the cornyard where Grandpa's undisputed eminence as a ruck-builder with the eye of an artist came into its own. Rucks were thackit and tied against the wind and with the fields bare of all but stubble the triumphant cry of 'Winter!' went up and that was what was now awaited. The great joy of helping in the fields at hairst time was the arrival of the kitchie deem with the 'piece', the kettle of tea with the baps or plain loaf brought up from Morrison's Bakery and spread with home-made butter and syrup or raspberry jam (how much better does a mug of tea taste in the great outdoor, especially as a relief from hard toil). Then October winds blew cold and the long summer nights that had the sun no sooner ducking down than he was bobbing up again became long hours of darkness, with the great furnace shining his excesses on Australia and places like that with little wish for him. In the grey autumn, Granny Barron took the child on her knee and amused with rhymes like:

> Chin cherry
> Mou' merry
> Nose nappy
> E'e winky
> Brow Brinky
> Ower the hill and awa tae stinky!

Whatever the sense, it never failed to amuse and she prodded her tongue in the child's ear to heighten the climax. So we were back in the trauchle of dub and drudgery, grey dreich days that passed with a 'Losh aye, man, fairly that' or a spit or

a quiet laugh. And the milk bottles rattled in the village doorways and the loons were whistling 'Red Sails in the Sunset'.
But aye, there was a warm fireside.

CHAPTER FOUR

PHILOSOPHY AND FAGS

The trouble with the fireside of the nineteen-thirties was just that it resided in the kitchen or the living-room and on cold and frosty days and nights the rest of the house was fit for few but Eskimoes. How we survived in those days before central heating remains one of the lingering mysteries of my childhood. Mothers, being the dog's-bodies of the rural home, invariably got up first and lit the fire to bring some semblance of warmth before the rest of the family stirred. Yesterday's paper laid the foundation for a criss-crossing of kindlers and a mixed crowning of coal and cinders and if the confounded thing went out, as it usually did, you splashed it with paraffin which fairly made the lum rumble in a roar of flame and maybe set fire to the soot, sending a shower of red sparks and black yoaming reek to torment an early-morning washing. The dry lavvies which were often situated discreetly at the bottom of the garden were giving way to bathrooms in my young day but that was still a mixed blessing when a visit for the simplest call of nature meant that you ran a high risk of developing icicles where icicles were never meant to be. Undressing for a bath was such a nightmare that many people didn't bother. If the truth were known, many a country body of my acquaintance went through a whole lifetime without ever experiencing the shock of total immersion. Some took the view that even if cleanliness did come next to Godliness, there was no need to extend the thing to madness. In any case, a film of good clean dirt was maybe nature's best protection from germs, folk said, setting the invisible creatures to fight each other and leave a body in peace and good health. But there was one occasion at least when the feet, if no more, had to be solemnly washed and

that was the night before you went to Aberdeen for the day—
'just in case you get knocked doon wi' a tramcar and land in
the infirmary,' your mother would say. 'It wid be an affa disgrace if you had fool feet.'

My father, who was seldom stuck for a solution, had his
own particular way of combatting the cold houses before the
Second World War and indeed it was not an unusual one. He
simply slept in a big thick semmit, his shirt, long woollen drawers and socks, which would have armoured him for the Ant-
arctic and became such a habit that he saw no good reason for
abandoning it in the hottest night of summer. As a child I wore
'combies', short for combinations, uniting woollen vest and
pants in a garment which buttoned up the middle. To keep
away colds we were fitted out with iodine lockets round our
necks, totally unaware in those days that we were exposing
ourselves to the dangers of radiation. When it came to maintaining good health, however, Dad always believed that nothing much would come over you if you kept your bowels open
and your mind easy. It was his panacea for all ills and he did
not hesitate to say so, couching it in terms which were as graphi-
cal as they were unprintable! He backed up his theory with
splendid example, paying at least two and sometimes three
visitations upon the private room every morning before leaving the house. He swore absolutely by the power of prunes
and rhubarb.

But if we thought we were short of comfort in a village
house it did us good to visit the farmhouses of the day which
seemed pretty bare places in which to live. Red ochre walls,
paperless and featureless and lit by a bleak paraffin lamp
brought little cheer to folk who had bent their backs in toil
from early light till darkness. Up at Mains of Whitehill the
peat fire was the focal point of the evening, its shadows dancing on the walls with ghostly effect. Grandpa Barron would
sit reading his books, poetry and dirt like that, folk said, and
no one cared to speak unless they were spoken to. My uncle
Arthur would sit cutting out paper shapes of horses and a

most capital job he made of it too, him in his waistcoat and flannel shirt with stud but no collar; uncle Gavin would shave from a mug by the small mirror on the kitchen wall, scraping away a lather of soap with a cut-throat razor and revealing long furrows of bare skin with the same artistry that he would plough the stubble fields.

But the silent authority of Grandpa Barron belied the true heart of the man. Tall and studious, he had followed farming because it was the tradition and, through tradition, a passion of the blood, so he was a farmer by instinct. He tended his acres with motherly care, made two straws grow where one grew before and raised his children with love and discipline. I used to walk out with him from the farmhouse at Whitehill, through the dubby close to the bottom of the garden wall and there I would gaze up at him as he gazed out across his parks, his corn and his turnips, his grass and his cattle. There was a wistful look in his eyes which set me wondering what his thoughts might be. But they were private and sacred and not for the fathoming of a child. On occasion he would turn his hand to the writing of poetry and folk who read it and understood said it was grand stuff; fegs, the man shouldn't have been a farmer at all. Maybe his thoughts were of the life that might have been; then again they may have been his satisfied reflections on the life that existed, the real throbbing life of the land with its rhythmic pattern and pace, the golden corn stretching to the horizon by Hillies, broken only by the patchwork greenery of grass and neeps and the silver burn and the black stots. I think my grandfather perceived in his surroundings the basis of man's contentment, accepting the drudgery of the land as his price for living so close to the wonders of nature, privileged to a daily contact with God's own acre of poetry which was there for all to see and hear and smell.

Those visits to Whitehill were a particular joy, though my natural fondness for people and bustle brought a sense of the loneliness of country life when I went there for any length of time in the summer. Granny Barron would pad across the farm close with basins of milk in her hand and clods of boots on her feet, laced through hooks. One hook would catch on another and a piercing yell of 'Gweed preserve's!' would herald a slow-motion sprawl among the dubs, the milk overflowing in a tidal wave and streaking off as little white veins in a multitude of directions. Not that she was ever hurt for Providence takes care of drunk men, bairns and hapless grannies. In the hot sing of summer the smell of the farmyard, its hay and hen's dirt, the whirr of the cricket and the strut of the cockerel and the warm peace of the steading were a symphony of sight and sound to the soul of a child. Granny took pride in a self-confessed stupidity, on the basis that she didn't have enough sense to worry, a condition which served her well in a lifetime which stretched for more than ninety years, conscience-free and contented. Grandpa just supped his sowens and pease-brose and taught me to break oatcakes into a bowl of milk for what we called 'milk-and-breid' and, believe me, there was nothing finer.

In the loneliness of the farmstead the sight of a visitor was a matter of some excitement, though the only guarantee in the course of a day was the postman for, even if he had no letters, he would come pushing his bicycle up the road to deliver the Aberdeen *Press and Journal*, the daily paper of the North-East which brought all the local news. Every few weeks a fisher-wife would appear on the horizon with a creel on her back, a funereal figure in black dress and black shawl and smelling of kippers and yellow fish. These hardy souls came in family successions till their offspring were well known to the country customers. My granny knew the whole background of one particular fishwife and knew too that her daughter was expecting a child. Inquiring if the baby had arrived yet, she became engaged in the following conversation which is often recalled for amusement within our family:

> Fishwife: Oh aye she got her bairn
> Granny: And what did she ca' it?
> Fishwife: She ca'ed it Barty.

Granny: Oh, she ca'ed it Barty?
Fishwife: Aye, she ca'ed it Barty. But she might
        as well hae ca'ed it Farty for it's deid!

In the summer evenings folk would bicycle up the farm road and into the close for a game of croquet on the farmhouse green and they would play into the gloaming, tying white handkerchiefs on the hoops to guide a ball through the gathering darkness. They were evenings which swung from serious concentration to laughter and good fellowship but how strange that such an English game as croquet should have flourished in rural Scotland. Yet flourish it did and there were some devastating performers to prove it, not least Uncle Gavin and Aunt Betty who swung a mallet as some people swing a golf club.

When the hairsting was over it was time for the meal-and-ale, with all the folk who had neighboured to each other gathering to sup at a bowl of the strong stuff, a fine robust way to round off the in-gathering of the crop. Sometimes they would dance in the corn-loft or just adjourn to the parlour (it was always 'the parlour' on Scottish farms) to enjoy a musical evening which was as much home-made as the meal-and-ale. In the dim light of a paraffin lamp or the brighter glow of the new-fangled Tilley, and with peat reek yoaming up the lum, Uncle Gavin fitted his great clods of hands over the keyboard of the piano and drew out as sweet an *arpeggio* as a concert pianist, giving little hint that these same hands had been riving at frosty neeps or clearing a strang-hole not long before. Gavin's natural talent was unspoiled by tuition and you will find him, even today, still playing for the Macduff Strathspey and Reel Society, though his sight has now all but gone. Meanwhile Uncle Arthur would be tuning up his fiddle, joined by a cacophony of people from surrounding farms who had brought along their fiddles too. Aunt Betty gave a bit tootle on her flute and soon the general disorder was brought to a halt as my grandfather intoned from his favourite corner of the fireside: 'Weel lads, fit aboot "Stumpy"?' And away they went, a full-blooded orchestra cramped into the parlour of a farmhouse, swinging into strathspeys and reels and old-fashioned waltzes, the lilting melodies of the hills and howes and mosses, clear as the crystal of the burn, pure as the gold of the corn that had just been cut from the fields. One tune followed another, interpolated with the songs of Robbie Burns (we never called him Rabbie) or a more recent recitation from the North-East poet called 'Hamewith', whose real name was Charles Murray from Alford. There was a stop for a cup of tea and a dram then on again till the hour was late and the players exhilarated but exhausted. Then coats were fetched from the bedroom and the gas-lights were adjusted on bicycles before they set out upon their various directions, some in motor cars that had to be cranked with a starting-handle, and there was a final 'Gweednicht, folk, it's been a gran' affair' and my grandparents would call 'Hist ye back!' And back they would come on many another evening of joy and friendship.

Arthur and Gavin slept in the chaumer, which was normally the bothy of the work-folk, attached to the steading. They were typical of the farmers' sons who stayed at home to work if they were any use. If they weren't, they tended to be sent away to the agricultural college to take a diploma or a B.Sc. and to land in some advisory job with advice which their old father could no doubt have offered in the first place. One is reminded of Bernard Shaw's remark that 'he who can, does— he who cannot, teaches', though both Mr Shaw and myself are being a little facetious about a noble profession!

The wireless had not yet reached Mains of Whitehill so Granny and Grandpa travelled down to Maud to hear the broadcast funeral service of King George V when he died in 1936. They sat at the fireside and marvelled at the scientific wonders of the live transmission. My, whatever would they think of next? By the following year the conversation was dominated by talk of Edward VIII and a Mrs Simpson and folk were sharply divided. Some praised the uncrowned king for putting love before all else while others said he was simply under the infatuating influence of a bold hussy from America, a divorcee at that, who was clever in all respects except in her belief that the British people would accept her as queen. It was mostly above my head at the time, except that I had glossy picture books of Edward, Prince of Wales, and can still remember the linseed smell of the covers. His name was one of many which floated beyond the tide of understanding. Folk spoke about the Labour man, Ramsay MacDonald, and said 'A servant's bairn from Lossiemouth as Prime Minister? Lord, no wonder the world's in a mess!' They glowed with admiration and affection for Robert Boothby, a dashing young man with a shock of black hair who had exchanged the dust of Oxford for the sharn of East Aberdeenshire to sit him down in the House of Commons. And with growing alarm they talked about Hitler but that seemed far away and beyond my comprehension. I was safely cocooned within the gentle slopes which rose from the cavity of Maud and gave a microcosmic impression of the horizons of the world. I could encompass it all from a fence which overlooked the railway station, knowing for certain that England was down there beyond the Den Wood and that France lay just over the Hill o' Jock. Apart from England, France was the only foreign country I had heard anything about. Every 11 November we gathered in the gym hall of Maud School and bowed our heads in remembrance of men and things we knew not of. War, they said, the Somme and Ypres and Passchendale and I could only form my own imaginary picture of a clump of trees, like the one on top of Banks Hill, with men on horseback charging to a gory death.

Somebody said Amen and it was milk time, with cardboard top and a hole for the straw, then out we went to play tackie or cock-fighting and thought no more of the men and their war and their dying. Maud was my island, a self-contained paradise on which the few intrusions included the *Chick's Own* on a Tuesday and the *Dandy* on a Friday. When the adventures of Rupert became too juvenile then Korky the Cat became the fashion, while Desperate Dan convinced us that nothing was impossible. Hungry Horace was a kindred spirit, stuffing himself with all the things that were still available before wartime rationing. If Horace had stayed in Maud he would have been a regular customer of Lizzie Allan's sweetie shop, for Lizzie was the arch-priestess of the lollipop, goddess of gastronomy, who extracted the wonders of the world from secret holes of her poky little shop which was lit by a paraffin lamp that stank in every nostril. She was the magician whose wand could whip up an ecstatic galaxy of Mars and Milky Way, Aero, Sherbet and Cow Candy, striped balls and black-sugar straps. And Lizzie had no legs, not a toe to call her own. From early childhood two stumps had been her meagre standpoint but Nature, in the way that Nature does, paid compensation in the shape of a brilliant mind. She had had time to read and think and, legs or no legs, she had been able to travel to London in her younger day, wheeling her chair on to the guard's van of the King's Cross express, so that she could mix in the circle of sprouting Socialism.

In later years I was to discover that she dispensed politics with peppermints, philosophy with fags, never yielding a principle in the cause of business. Indeed, her main customers were the farmers on a Wednesday, buying their weekly supply of sweeties and tobacco, yet she would lash them for their wartime subsidies and fine motor cars and they would go away cursing 'that bloody Communist', determined that they would never darken her door again. But Lizzie, the reluctant capitalist, survived for more than forty years in that miserable shop and despite her enlightenment and visions of the future she never did concede to the comforts of electricity and modern living. She worked and slept in her shoppie, moving around in one of those old-fashioned basket wheelchairs which she pushed by the direct drive of her powerful arms. One day a crowd of mischievous youths were standing outside her shop when Tom Ogston joked to the others: 'I'll gyang in and tickle Lizzie's big tae.' Lizzie overheard and brought blushes by calling out: 'Come away in then, Tom, and have a try.' She was a noble spirit, a woman of wit and wisdom who bore her burden with a fine dignity. She had little time for religion, subscribing only to Shaw's idea of a life force, and expected to pass her eternity in oblivion. But for once she may have been wrong. I find it hard to believe that Lizzie Allan is not somewhere among the politics and the peppermints, even today, lecturing on the follies and fickleness of mankind, wearing the brown beret which was her companion for forty years and lighting a paraffin lamp at eventide . . . so that the good folk may see.

Lizzie was an essential part of our village scene, a vital thread in the pattern of permanency that gave us roots and a settled outlook on the world. Across the road from her wee shoppie in Timmer Street, Morrison the Baker made baps and butter biscuits (we called them 'hardies') which were unsurpassed in all the kingdom, while Chalmers the Baker along the street had his own distinctive delicacies. Down at the Square, Henry Panton the Saddler made harness for the horses and mended the canvas sheets for the harvest binders which cut the corn; John Grant the Miller ground your oats, Willie Ogston shod the horse, John Craig would mend your burst pipes, Hector Mavor was your joiner and told fine stories of his days in Chicago; Bob Sangster combined the skills of watchmaker and cycle agent and peered through his eye-glass surrounded by dozens of acid containers which were the wet batteries of the old wireless sets, in for charging; Alex Marshall delivered your coal but also obliged if you needed a hire, a hearse or a haircut.

Lizzie Allan surveyed it all from the confines of her wooden shop and kept up a fascinating range of conversation as she wheeled her solid torso from tobacco tin to sweetie jar, calling for the assistance of the customer only when the wanted item was totally out of her reach. I used to visit her every day, if only for my mother's regular packet of Players, which sold at $11^1/_2$d for 20 (slightly less than 5p in today's money) and stood side by side on the shelf with Gold Flake, Capstan, Kensitas, Du Maurier and the black cat of Craven A, not to mention the more modest Woodbine which could be bought in little paper packets of five. I learned a lot from Lizzie and once asked her to jot down a few recollections of earlier days in our village. Her short scribble came to light in a recent rummage through my old trunk and this is what she wrote:

In the early days the Market Stance, which I can see from my back window and is now covered with cattle pens, was an open meadow with lovely green grass right up to the cross-roads. Johnny Still, the martman, kept everything nice and trig. Even the dungheap had a classical look, so square and even. In the spring, when the farmers came with their carts to drive it away, I regretted seeing it disturbed. The grass was damaged and for a time the place looked untidy but Nature soon covered the scars and beauty reigned again.

Every summer people camped on the Stance. I have seen a dozen horse-drawn caravans at one time and it was fascinating to watch them draw in, select a site and settle down. The Market Stance was considered common ground at that time so they had plenty of freedom and made themselves at home. Horses and dogs were all over the place. They usually arrived in June but the height of their season was a week or two before Aikey Fair in July. They generally did their cooking on oil stoves but sometimes they formed a circle of stones and made a fire, over which they cooked a big pot of mystery which was dished out to the various members of the clan when they came back from their day's outing.

The men generally set out with shalt and float, taking a scythe as well. They brought back a load of grass, cut from the roadside, to feed their horses and sometimes they brought heather, which they fashioned into scrubbers. Meanwhile the women had set off with baskets on their arms to peddle their wares around the countryside. I remember especially one woman who could neither read nor write and who came in to me every year and got me to write out an order to a firm in Aberdeen. She listed all the goods and the price per dozen or gross and always she could tell me to within a few coppers what the cost of the order amounted to.

Then there was old Betty Townsley who wore an outsize in gold ear-rings. When she came in for half-an-ounce of tobacco she called down so many blessings on my head that I felt quite embarrassed. But we seldom have any gypsies in the village now. There is little room left for them to camp.

Another feature of village life which has gone is the feeing markets and I don't think anyone regrets their passing. The one held in May was not too bad as the weather was warmer but the one in November was a day to be endured. In order to keep warm the farm lads visited the whisky booths pretty freely, with the result that they were soon full of spirit in more senses than one. Many and varied are the arguments I have heard from my back window when the boys got het-up. Sometimes it was about who had the best 'pair' or who kept the cleanest harness or sometimes they had a heart-to-heart chat about the merits or faults of a lady they alluded to as 'the deem'.

I did not like the feeing markets. It seemed such a crude way of engaging a servant and at the end of the day there were many who were still not fixed up. They could do nothing to help themselves unless they joined the army, and the Gordon Highlanders pipe band was always in attendance to show what a glamourous life it was. Wright's Amusements or some other shows were always here for the market and at night the local people got a thrill from trying their luck at hoop-la or the shooting gallery whilst the children enjoyed the swings and merry-go-rounds or pestered their parents to knock down a coconut.

Something else which belonged to the past and lent a rustic air to the village was the number of little dairies in our midst—Kitchenhill, the Temperance Hotel, Mary Lamb, Bob Wallace, Andrew Hendry and others who kept a few cows—and in the summer evenings it was pleasant to watch them meandering along the village streets to the byres from nearby grazing. A little later you saw the housewives with their milk pails going along to their favourite source of supply and, while waiting for the milk to be measured, they had a fine opportunity to exchange any tit-bit of gossip they had gathered during the day. The village pump also served the same useful purpose. Now modern hygiene has swept away the little dairies and, with running water in most homes, it almost seems that the only outlet left to the ladies for a friendly chat is the W.R.I.

I greatly regret the disappearance of the horses which used to be seen on our roads. It was pleasant to hear the clip-clop of their hooves when the farmers drove into the village on market day. They were a stout people, the old farmers of a generation back; there they sat perched high on the seat of the gig with nothing to protect them from the wind or rain, although some did sport a luggit bonnet or a gravat in winter. On they passed with a wave of the whip and a cheery greeting to friends. After the horse had been stabled they joined their friends in the bar and had a glass of whisky to stimulate the circulation of their blood. And if, in the course of the day, a farmer overdid it with business drams, why worry? After the horse was yoked, friendly hands helped him into his seat, put the reins in his hands and, once headed for home, the horse took charge and delivered him safely to his family.

A winter scene I liked to watch from my window was that of the bakers loading a sledge when the roads were blocked with snow and vans could not get through. They started away early and always took a shovel in case they got stuck in a drift, also a flour-sack in which to carry bread to any farmhouse where the roads were too bad for the sledge to reach. I can still picture Jimmy Morrison, muffled up in a heavy coat, stamping around, flapping his arms and giving vent to his feelings with a few seasonable oaths. When these men set off amidst the falling snow I felt they were akin to Arctic explorers.

Thus, in the early nineteen-fifties, Lizzie Allan was putting down some of her memories of an earlier part of the century, intended for publication in *The Maud Review*, a magazine I had founded in my boyhood as a first outlet to the journalistic urge. Several of the features which cropped up in Lizzie's narrative were still very much in vogue within my own memory of the thirties. As well as genuine gypsies and hawker people, cart loads of tinkers would pass through the village, stop off for a drink and perhaps start a fight in the heat of the whisky.

As boys we gathered to watch the fracas, secretly excited by the prospect of some dreadful deed, but when it happened, with gory consequences, we ran for our lives lest the tinkers should close ranks and turn on us. There were poor bairns wrapped in shawls and sheltered by drunken women in the corner of miserable carts and one day the fighting factions charged off over the hill and down Broonies Brae, chasing each other with cries of vengeance. In the rabble and heat of the drink, a piner horse went over the dyke, taking cart and tinkers, women and bairns as well, and God knows what was the outcome.

Sometimes on a Saturday my parents would take me to the first house of the pictures at the Regal or the Playhouse in Peterhead, not that my father had much time for such doubtful pursuits. The talkies had arrived about the year I was born and the novelty had not worn off. Charlie Chaplin and Laurel and Hardy were still the rage, closely followed by Deanna Durbin's singing, Fred Astaire's dancing and Sonja Henie's skating. A band would play *Alexander's Ragtime Band* and the newsreel showed Amy Johnson flying across some distant water. *Snow White and the Seven Dwarfs* was a major event and when the picture was over we walked along the road to Luigi Zanre's for fish and chips to eat on the journey back to Maud. Somewhere about Mintlaw I would fade away, crunching at my second last chip, and hear only a half-world of adult voices and chugging engine till I was transferred to a warm bed, absorbing the mysteries and glamour of the Hollywood dream factory into the sub-conscious stream. But the talkies were not the only innovation of the thirties in our part of the world. All-in wrestling sprung into favour and every fortnight carloads of men would head off for Aberdeen to watch this or that grisly creature throwing his weight around the Music Hall. My father was caught up in the enthusiasm and came home with weird tales of a monster called Ali the Wicked, a fierce-looking Oriental who began his antics by praying towards Mecca before proceeding to commit all but murder, if the gyrations were to be taken as anything more serious than the comical gymnastics which they have certainly become in more recent times. At home I was fascinated by the one-man band who used to pass our way. With drum at his foot, tambourines on his knees, bells at his elbows, a melodeon in his hands and mouth-organ in his mouth, we gazed in wonder at the man's dexterity.

But undoubtedly the highlight of those pre-war days in our small village was the arrival of Dick's Circus. In fact I can think of nothing which enraged me at Hitler half as much as the loss of this notable event. As a small family circus performing in the open-air and without animals, it consisted mainly of acrobatics and clowning with every member playing a part, from grandfather down to the smallest child. Under arc-lights they swung from one high bar to another, balancing on each other's heads and feet, turning somersaults and bringing roars of approval from the village folk who were not over-accustomed to entertaining spectacles. Just as important, they brought swingboats and shooting galleries and roll-a-penny stalls, and they strung lights from stall to stall and round the circus ring, powered by a dynamo and illuminating a village scene which still awaited its electricity supply. Again it brought country folk together in a warm innocence, not yet troubled by the idiocies of a world that was just around the corner. Dick's brought light to our lives and so did another little circus, Pinder's, which was slightly bigger and could stretch to a tent with a sawdust ring, a few ponies and clowns and a menagerie.

It would not have looked much to town's folk but, all things being relative, it was a spectacular show on the Market Stance at Maud. I often wondered what became of these small family circuses for they did not reappear after the war, at least not as far north as Maud. I have found no trace of the Dick family, though I believe they were miners from Fife, but I did unearth one of the Pinders in a grimy tenement in the heart of Glasgow Gorbals.

By then, Leslie Ord Pinder was in his sixties and blind. There I sat in the cheerlessness of his flat, with the eerie echoes of Glasgow's slumland outside, listening to how at least one of those small shows began. The Pinder family had been in the circus business for two hundred years, Leslie told me. They travelled around Britain and the continent bringing delight to children who no doubt thought as much of their little villages as I did of mine. Then in 1905 the big Pinder's Circus broke up in a family row, the matter went to court and the outcome was that the Big Top was divided into three smaller tops and each group went its own way. Young Leslie Pinder had gone with his parents in the show they called Captain George Pinder, His Elephants and Ponies. In the dim light I could gain only half-vision of the rotund little man with the finely shaped head as he recalled their travels around the world. Yes, he remembered our North-East villages and knew all about local legends like 'The Bonnie Lass o' Fyvie' and 'Mill o' Tifty's Annie'. But the circus travelled beyond the bounds of Scotland and it was when it reached the Far East that young Leslie saw the depressing plight of the blind, for whom there was no provision other than the right to beg. He became absorbed in their misery and spent long nights in the caravan wondering how he could help. So he set to learning Braille and the art of punching out the symbols on those sheets of brown paper which were so well known to the blind. Then, with his knowledge of the East, he busied himself in endless nights of hard work and when he emerged again he had produced a Braille edition of the Koran, the Holy Book of the Islam. Now fate, whose hand can never be ignored, played just one more of her curious cards. Leslie Pinder, still an active trapeze artist, having graduated through the ranks from programme seller in the family business, was in the prime of life when he had an accident in the ring—and lost an eye. So he became condemned to the world of half-light and shadows and more deeply involved than ever in the work of the blind.

When I met him in the bleakness of the Gorbals he was

passing his days hand-punching Braille literature for any race or denomination so that they could read for themselves. He drew no financial benefit but a great deal of satisfaction from the gratitude that came to him from all over the world. Moslems knew him as Abdul Haque and wrote of him with reverence. Somewhere on the roads today there is still a Pinder's Circus for I came across their bills while motoring on the continent not so long ago.

CHAPTER FIVE

WULLIE LUMMIES GALORE

One of the excitements and minor terrors of my childhood was the sight of a formidable cart being pulled through the streets of Maud, not by a team of horses but a double row of menfolk, old and young, frail and fearsome, but all harnessed to long, strong ropes. They might be going to remove a load of dung or rubble or to help lay down the brand-new village bowling-green but whatever their purpose it was less important to us children than the fact that they were simply the Dafties.

The Buchan Combination Home in Maud was a refuge for the feeble-minded and helpless creatures of the area, sent from their various parishes, often enough because there was no relative to bear the responsibility. So they came from far and near and we would shout names at them and if one became incensed he would break away and chase us till a warder grabbed him and returned him to the yoke. But the Dafties were not all so daft. That outer crust of feebleness would often belie a keen perception from which emerged many a pure gem of philosophy.

At a higher level, one of the greatest North-East characters of all time, the inimitable Jamie Fleemin', jester to the Laird of Udny, was once being made a figure of fun by a superior gentleman in Edinburgh who, knowing full well his identity, asked Jamie who he was.

'Och, I'm the Laird of Udny's feel,' said Jamie, 'fa's feel are ye?' When he contemplated the eventual business of dying he made a special plea which became a legendary saying: 'Oh, dinna bury me like a beast.'

Maud Poorhouse was full of minor Jamie Fleemin's, oddities like Wullie Lummie (the Buchan version of William

48

Lumsden). In the days of the shalt and gig, Wullie was walking along bare, dusty roads in the heart of Buchan when a lady-like creature stopped to offer him a lift. Wullie accepted and felt obliged to offer something in return for the ride so he asked the lady if she would like to see a photograph of himself. She said she would be delighted and adjusted her bi-focals as Wullie turned out a grubby snapshot from his inner pocket. She blinked at what she saw then, recognising a familiar building, said: 'But this is not you—this is Strichen Brewery.' 'Aye,' Wullie proudly replied, pointing to the door, 'but I'm inside washin' bottles.'

Thereafter they took him to Maud Poorhouse and yet another character was removed from the public highway. But the stories persisted. On a visit to the inmates one day, Dr McLeod was confronted by Wullie who had a complaint about the food. Producing a whole pea from the previous day's broth, he said: 'Just see foo hard that is, doctor.' Dr McLeod took the pea between his teeth and agreed that it was impossibly hard. 'Ah weel,' said Wullie, 'that's just as it came through me!'

Worthies like Wullie were a common feature of Scottish rural life and not all were locked away in institutions. They roamed the land, often hairy and unkempt, some with settled abodes and others just vagabonds picking up a night's rest wherever a farmer would give them a corner of the barn to share with the rats. Jock Pom o' New Leeds and his sister Meg were still living legends in the nineteen-thirties and so was another female figure of black terror known only as Bleedy Heids. I can still relive the paralysing fear which gripped us smaller children at Maud School when some older girls in their mis-chief spread word one day that Meg Pom was coming to take us away. Jock Pom was one of the hardiest nomads, often tramping along in the snow, bare-footed, up in the morning and filling himself with water brose before setting off again on his morning rounds.

Those characters were relics of the nineteenth century but I had the good fortune to have personal contact with some of them. On my visits to Mains of Whitehill, Grandpa Barron was frequently in conversation with an oddity who was in the habit of breaking into a high-pitched laugh when no-one else could see what there was to laugh about. His favourite expression was 'Nae man, nae man,' and, although his real name was Johnnie Robson, we never knew him as anything other than Johnnie Naeman. I was unaware in those childhood days that I was in the company of one of the true characters of the North-East, widely known as the Carrot King because he was such a dab hand at growing carrots. Johnnie had plots of land here and there, including one from my grandfather, on which he grew his famous vegetables. He was industrious and well-behaved and at one time the Laird of Brucklay gave him a house and a piece of land, rent-free, at Oldwhat. Johnnie was also a man of music who could fair make the melodeon dirl and he and a neighbouring farmhand, Sandy Greig, who sang bothy ballads, made a glorious team. Just think what television missed. Such focus, however, would no doubt have swept away some of the native innocence which made those people the natural, unselfconscious beings they were.

I have only secondhand accounts of some of the others, who were either past or passing when I was born but Grandpa Barron had vivid recollections of some and an old acquaintance, James A. F. Murray, the Poor Inspector at Maud, told me of others. Not far from my birthplace there was the Hermit of Corsegight, Robert Henry Ironside, who lived in a lonely log cabin at the top of the hill. He went about without shoes or socks, straggly hair hanging limp over his shoulders, a forerunner of the hippies to come. But as a young man Robert had been a schoolmaster at Mountblairy, Alvah, and had given up convention apparently on account of ill-health. He sought the primitive ways of Nature, for which mankind regarded him as an eccentric. But he did not beg. He lived as God would provide and in pursuit of his hobby which was botany he made long journeys on foot in search of specimens. He was a man of undoubted mental ability, scientific in a way that was well ahead of his time. Yet he chose to live in this uninhibited way, not as a gimmick like some of the oddities of a later day but because he had re-discovered the essential goodness of life.

Then there was Deaf Davie, known throughout Buchan as the Smoke Doctor, because he had a great belief in his ability to find a remedy for a reeky chimney. In his thoroughness he would plague the housewife by sitting at a fireside for hours on end, watching the progress of smoke and noting the direction of the wind. But his gift for fascinating conversation made him a tolerable and even welcome visitor. Heather Jock was a Peterhead character of untidy habits who made and sold brooms but sometimes went to Greenland on local whalers. On one occasion he entered a draper's shop where he was confronted by a large mirror. Turning to the door, he was heard to mutter: 'It's time I was oot o' this. There's eneuch o' my kind here already.' Geordie Watson wore clogs in summer and winter and became known as Cloggie, travelling the countryside with a box but never pushing trade. The goods were there if anyone wanted them but Cloggie was more interested in the latest news of local and national affairs. He was short-sighted and reading newspapers proved something of a hazard. At a farmhouse one day he was given a paper to read, with pictures of fast-going steamships. Cloggie was reading the thing upside down for several seconds before he exclaimed to the farmer: 'There's surely been a lot o' shipwrecks last week!'

So the names come back to memory. The Braes O' Mar, an itinerant musician who delighted old and young alike with his concertina; Gadie, an abandoned bairn found on the banks of the Gadie, at the back of Benachie, who grew up to be a kenspeckle figure, selling everything from gingerbread and candy to yellow haddies. The whole change in the pace and exposure of human activity began to iron out the creases of character and folk were soon lamenting the disappearance of the old-time worthy. But the colourful characters had not disappeared altogether, even if their eccentricity had diminished.

In a rather different mould, a likeable warrior called John

Dickie Dempster was a regular visitor to our house at Park Crescent. With a wife who was capable of looking after the farm at Cairnbanno, Jock spent his days scouring the countryside, buying and selling calves or ponies and picking up the news of the day. As he dumbfounded some farmer with his latest titbit, the man would feel obliged to respond with some other piece of news which was added to Jock's repertoire. He would heave his large, rugged frame across our door-step at midnight and pour out the most varied conglomeration of news and gossip, re-told in a profusion of colour and native wit, till my father swore that on days that Jock Dempster came by there was no need for *The Press and Journal*. Jock was a big, unshaven hulk of a man, smoking one quarter of his cigarette, chewing another quarter and throwing away the middle half before calling to my mother in the kitchen: 'Lord, missus, have ye ony fags? I'm clean oot.' My mother would supply the fag or more often half a packet and say: 'Ye ken, Jock Dempster, ye wid be a richt handsome chiel if ye wid shave yerself!' and the big friendly bear would grin and blush and say: 'D'ye think so, missus?' Then he would sit into the small hours telling tales of 'yon crookit oolit o' a mannie, ye ken, John, him that sleeps wi' his brither's wife and breeds futtrats', or some lurid tale of 'yon bow-hyoched buggerick wi' the hubber an' the piner stirkies'. He could never remember the names but the description soon refreshed the listener's memory.

So Jock would arrive at a bewitching hour, perhaps with a salmon illegally extracted from the River Ythan that day, carving us a middle cut and regaling us with the news of Buchan till a calf would howl its boredom from his old black van standing outside and he would jump up saying: 'Gweed God, I've a calf to deliver tae yon weasel o' a wifie on the Hill o' Jock', and off he would go, his previous day's business not yet completed. Sometimes we cursed Jock Dempster for hours of lost sleep but he was a warm and entertaining character, an unspoiled individualist and we could not deny our affection for him.

My mother had to go for an operation and I was visiting her in an Aberdeen nursing home when there was a gentle knocking and who came sheepishly round the door but the rugged, masculine frame of Jock, shaven clean till we hardly recognised him—and carrying a bouquet of flowers. For a man who lived in a world of skittery cows and earthy talk it was the paradox to end them all. Jock sat himself down on a chair, gey ill at ease, handed my mother the beautiful bouquet, started to say something—and then burst into uncontrollable tears.

'I just canna stand tae see a body nae weel,' he sobbed as I led him out of the room and took him out of sight of my mother who had just had a major operation. I never saw Jock again. He drove off on one of his calf-hunting expeditions to the Highlands and stopped off for a cup of tea in Inverness. On the way back to the car he slumped against a lamp-post and, without time for an oath or a tear, just quietly died, a man still in his prime. Perhaps Jock and his kind were the latter-day characters, retaining that originality which is too readily smothered in our modern living. He was a native of the parish of Crimond, where they wrote the psalm tune. Nearby stands the old kirkyard of Rattray, which is now closed for burials. But they opened it up for Jock Dempster—a fitting gesture to a memorable character.

CHAPTER SIX

HAW-HAW, HEE-HEE

Among the popular lines of conversation which still linger with me from the thirties is the one which started with 'Have ye got the Grampian yet?' Needless to say, it had nothing to do with the television station of a later date. The 'Grampian' meant the brighter world of electricity which was spreading from a scheme of that name to replace the oil lamps and Tilley mantles which remained our main source of light in my childhood. There might have been a touch of old world charm but there was precious little light from the paraffin lamps which adorned our streets in those days. They were filled and lit and extinguished by the local leerie, Sandy Kelman, whose short, quick step was a familiar sound in the gathering darkness as he marched around the village with his little ladder over his shoulder, hooking it on to the collar of the lamp-post and scaling it, up and down, up and down, till the feeble flames were flickering in their glass cases and casting down a glow which was no more than a pool at the foot of the post. It was better than nothing but what I had forgotten, until Lizzie Allan reminded me, was that Sandy's paraffin lamps were lit on alternate fortnights—the first and last quarters of the Moon. The heavenly glow was supposed to light up Maud during its more potent fortnight though the powers-that-be seemed to take little account of the clouds which would regularly obscure it and leave us to grope along with torches or lanterns. You were more than likely to plunge into the puddles which were far too common in those days of poorly-made roads.

When the Grampian finally came our way I can still recall the thrill of the new illuminations, modest though they were in retrospect. Each evening at light-up time the children would gather beneath the lofty globes to await the magic moment, then stay to gaze in wonder at the miracles of modern science. But the years of the Grampian lights and the Dicks and the Pinders were all too short. After the arguments about Edward and Mrs Simpson the whole matter seemed to be resolved with a Coronation in 1937 when they presented us with mugs adorned with the pictures of King George VI and Queen Elizabeth. Folk spoke vaguely about the Spanish Civil War but that was overtaken as a topic of conversation by Chamberlain and his visits to Hitler in Munich. To the child mind there was a certain appeal in the gathering prospect of war though, if I had known that it meant the sacrifice of the circus, the Mars and Milky Way, the Cow Candy and the black-sugar straps, not to mention the oranges, bananas and melons, I would have been persuaded to take a more pacifist stand.

Events seemed to be coming to a head when my father declared that 'as sure as God made tatties, there's gyan tae be a war'. As sure indeed. In the last days of August an evacuation officer came round to tell my father and mother that they would be expected to take two boys from Glasgow to live in our house at 2 Park Crescent if the worst came to the worst. On Saturday, 2 September, there was a great stirring in the village as militia men and Territorials looked out their uniforms and said it wouldn't be long now. Jimmy Pirie was the first to come stepping down past our house, resplendent in his uniform, pausing for a cheery farewell and declaring that he was off to the war; the train would be arriving any time now. One by one the doors were opening and the men emerging with packs on their backs, relatives fussing at their tails, as we all began to gravitate to Maud Station, where there had never been such a stir, except on Aikey Fair days. Long trains drew in from Peterhead and Fraserburgh to link up at Maud and local lads had to be summoned from the Refreshment Rooms of Lil and Lena Murison on the station platform, stuffing bottles into their hip pockets. The married men took embarrassed goodbyes of blubbering wives and bairns, for the Buchan folk are ill at ease

55

with their emotions. But a dram helped to remove some of the inhibitions as well as blur the things that lay ahead. Single lads slubbered at their lasses and then an officer chiel from Fraserburgh, Captain Keith (who later turned up as my father-in-law!) came marching up the platform to say it was time now, time to steam away to war, to things unknown for these ploughmen and bakers, blacksmiths and vrichts, for most of whom it was an adventure to foreign parts with a purpose that was ill-defined. So they squeezed them into carriages and fastened the doors and through half-shut windows they roared their last messages to a waving, weeping crowd on the platform. The train gave a warning toot and drew slowly away, chugging up by the Den Wood and under the bridge of Old Maud Farm before turning out of our view. The folk stood there watching the smoke that hung on the distant trees and listening for the echoes which came resounding back long after it had disappeared. Then they looked at each other, said little and went home to their chappit tatties.

The void of the morning was filled in numbers at least by another train which steamed down the line from Aberdeen that afternoon. Curiosity brought out the crowds on this occasion as a horde of Glasgow children was disgorged on to the station platform in their escape from the danger of bombs in the industrial capital. Two hundred of the souls trooped off, some pale-faced and ricketty from their back-street hovels, some Irish-bred red-heads with twinkling eyes and pug noses that ran as fast as their feet. As they were marshalled into as much of an orderly column as you will achieve with industrial children, there fell upon our ears a language we had never heard before, unless we had been at the Empire Exhibition of the previous year.

'Goad, wha' a dump!' said one bubbly urchin.

'Hey Mac, whaur's ra flicks?'

We looked in dumb amazement, wholly unacquainted with the 'flicks' and such city jargon. They were marched to Victoria Hall with labels round their necks and some time after dark a car drew up outside our door and out spilled two boys, aged eleven and eight, a bit more refined than most, to be introduced as James Hyman Singer and his brother Myer from the Hillhead district of Glasgow.

Myer was a conventional little fellow but Jimmy was a strange and lonesome lad, fair-haired with prominent teeth and a filling of gold, quiet-spoken but expressing himself with long, artistic hands on which there grew at least one wart. He seemed a studious boy and if I dwell with that description it is because we could not have predicted what would come of such an extraordinary mixture. On the following week we all set-tled down together at Maud School, which had now doubled its roll, the Glaswegians having brought their own teachers as well as their own culture to our village scene. They were quicker and slicker in their movements having gained an agility, no doubt, from jumping on to tramcars, dashing across busy streets and running from their polis, as they called them. In Maud you heard a car at the other end of the village and had ample time to get out of its way. So the smarter city kids regarded us with some amusement, our slower country ways and speech, and they even had the audacity to mock at our dialect, appar-ently unaware of their own glottal sing-song. We divided into the Maud Hummlies and the Glesca Keelies, two warring fac-tions fighting out our own battles just as our elders were pre-paring to do in France. Each side had its own gang hut and its leader and sometimes we would join in fierce battle, the Maud loons ramming the Keelies' hut with a full-length tree-trunk which could have done mortal damage. But divine protection ensured that nothing much was to happen beyond a few black eyes and bruises.

In times of truce they would tell us of the River Clyde and the ships that sailed there, great hulking things that hooted in the fog; only months ago they had seen the *Queen Elizabeth* sail away from her launching berth, real proud they were. We heard of their flicks and fish-and-chip shops, their Rangers and Celtic, gangs and knives and bicycle chains, Barlinnie and

Auchenshuggle, trams, drams and trolley-cars; and it was time to fight again, the Maud loons led by Norman Rothney, a blond warrior of the heroic type, who was strong and courageous and used his fists in the cause of justice. Boys admired him, girls adored him and as he grew up he went to fell trees in the woods and came home with bulging muscles and a fine smell of resin. By seventeen he was married and beginning to father the first of his seven children and by thirty-four he was a grandfather. Norman could take on the Glesca Keelies two or three at a time if necessary and on one occasion there was a score to settle with Jimmy Singer, our gifted evacuee. My father proposed a proper bout with boxing gloves, so the kitchen floor was cleared and battle commenced. But the first round was still young when Norman landed a punch to the mouth which was followed by a metallic ricochet around the room and an agonising yell from Jimmy that he had lost his famous gold tooth. So father marched him off to Aberdeen next day for a replacement which cost him a guinea and he swore it was the best guinea's worth he could remember. My mother fell ill and with no bad grace the Singer boys moved in with Norman and his family. But Jimmy was showing the signs of a quietly troublesome nature and on one occasion he locked himself in an upstairs bedroom and Andra Forbes, the village Bobby, had to be summoned with a ladder to reach him through the window.

At Maud School, however, Jimmy Singer became the darling of the English teacher, Miss Cameron, for he was displaying a remarkable talent with words. She encouraged and guided him and was not mistaken in her declared belief that he had a future. Jimmy went back to Hyndland School, Glasgow, cut loose from a university education and began to gain a name as a poet, befriending men like Hugh MacDiarmid, Dylan Thomas, Louis MacNeice. Presenting himself now as Burns Singer, with his literary reputation on the ascendancy, he would return on occasions after the war to fawn over my mother, for whom he had a special affection, even though she had reservations about his stability and behaviour and used to express her fears to his mother.

Mrs Singer, a pale and delicate lady, could see nothing wrong in him and dismissed the cautions but was ready to acknowledge at a later date, when Jimmy had been in a variety of trouble with the Glasgow police, that my mother had been absolutely right. He was a mixture of kindness and courtesy, drunken moods and rudeness, but all the time he was writing poetry which was widely acclaimed, as well as a memorable book about the fishing industry called *Living Silver*. One day, back in Glasgow, he arrived at the family home in 9 Ruthven Street, just off Byres Road, to find his mother hanging by the neck and he faced the appalling task of cutting her body down. Life began to straighten itself out, however, when he married Dr Marie Battle, a famous American psychiatrist, but their happiness was shortlived. He collapsed and died from a thrombosis in his early thirties with his literary potential far from fulfilled. Years later I asked Hugh MacDiarmid what might have become of him if he had lived. Would he have compared with MacDiarmid himself, regarded by many as Scotland's greatest ever poet, surpassing Robert Burns? He pondered the question and said 'I think he might well have become a better poet than me.'

So Jimmy Singer and the rest of the evacuees drifted back to Glasgow. Our Stinker Burn was no match for their mighty Clyde with its *Queen Elizabeths* and *Queen Marys*. They missed their fish and chips and their flicks and the smell of the grimy tenements and bronchial back-streets. The fresh air and country food had added pinkness to their pallor but it was poison to their souls. They had come to us when there was little need to come, when the Phoney War was dragging on, and they went back in time for the bombing they had hoped to escape.

Meanwhile the war was warming up. The tragedy of Dunkirk had echoed in our North-East corner with its call for ships of any description to sail away to the evacuation. From

Fraserburgh and Peterhead they manned their tiny craft and headed off down the east coast on their way to France. In later years I was to meet a fisherman whose by-name was Daisy from St Combs and who became a legend in his lifetime for the part he played at Dunkirk. Daisy sailed his boat as near to the beaches as was possible then went ashore among the thousands of soldiers trapped with their backs to the sea. It was Britain's deadliest hour. The Germans were hot on our heels and desperate men were wading into the sea, pleading to be taken aboard some overcrowded craft. But even in dire emergency there are priorities and Daisy did not allow compassion to over-ride his main objective. So he ran up and down the beaches of Dunkirk, shouting at the pitch of his unmistakable Buchan voice: 'Is there onybody here frae St Combs, Inverallochy, Cairnbulg or the Broch (Fraserburgh)', and then, as an afterthought, 'And if there's ony room left, we'll tak folk frae Peterheid.' In the pure hell of Dunkirk, the local rivalries of the North-East fishing communities were given full expression, with the Blue Mogganers of Peterhead definitely at the end of Daisy's list! He filled his boat with room, I believe, even for a few unspecified creatures and sailed away with many a life saved. Daisy deserved his place on the roll of Dunkirk heroes.

And of course there was St Valery, high on the hill of that Normandy coast, which must for ever be a little part of Buchan and the North-East corner. For it was there that those men who drank their farewells at Maud Station and called their muted goodbyes fought their glorious battle as part of the 51st Highland Division, a losing battle that ended in death or the barbed-wire captivity of the German prison camps. News filtered back that they had crossed to France with the British Expeditionary Force early in 1940 to meet the mighty German thrust that was driving towards the Channel ports. The men of the 51st went into action at Abbeville but the Hun was in command, the line of retreat was cut off and a solitary division of North-East men was left to take on the whole German

Army. One of the three brigades formed an arc of protection to Le Havre but the other two were ensnared with their backs to the coast at St Valery. Back, back they went, fighting as only true Scottish blood can fight when your ammunition is no more, your casualties are colossal and those that remain are battle-weary and spent. Buchan folk don't like to give in but surrender was the only course as Rommel and his overwhelming numbers closed in. So arms went down and arms went up as they paraded away, heads hung low, to spend the next five years in German prisoner-of-war camps. It was a sorry day for Scotland with no blame attaching to the men who bore the burden. Those who defended Le Havre were successfully evacuated and became the basis of the revived 51st Division which trained for the challenge that lay ahead. By 1942 they were a vital force once more, ready to sail away that August for the start of the Desert Campaign.

Montgomery testified to their worth at Alamein when I met him in Yugoslavia after the war. Those fighting furies, bred from men who had left their fields in earlier days to draw blood as part of their land-rent, were now at war with a clearer purpose. Here was Rommel again, the man who had cut them off on the bare coast of France. Into battle they raged, guns blasting, bayonets flashing in the translucent desert light, bagpipes skirling in national fervour, with stifling sun and choking sand only minor hazards in the way of men hell-bent on winning a war. The nightmare of Alamein became the tolerable dream of Tripoli, Sicily and Italy, then it was back to Britain to prepare for the Second Front which was on everyone's lips. Off they went again that memorable D-Day of 6 June, 1944, back to the beaches of Normandy. The great drive to finish the German menace was on; and once they established themselves on French soil and took the offensive there was one object in the minds of those men from Maud and Fraserburgh and Peterhead and other North-East communities and farmsteads: St Valery. On they pushed, fighting for every field and cowshed, fortified with men and ammunition this time—and the memory of 1940. The Germans stuck grimly to their occupation of France but mile by mile they were blasted out of position till that precious moment arrived. Led by the men who had fought for their lives on that same coast, the Highland Division thundered into St Valery, back to settle a small account, albeit four years later. But the war had still to be won and they played a notable part in the rest of the drive through Europe and were the last infantry of the British Second Army to be in operation against the enemy. What a fitting operation it was. Near Bremerhaven they brought about the surrender of the much-admired 15th Panzer Grenadiers, their old combatants in North Africa. The account had finally been closed. Half-an-hour later, the Armistice terms were signed on Luneberg Heath.

Meanwhile Lord Haw-Haw (an Irishman called William Joyce who was working for German propaganda radio) was drawling out his regular bulletins in an attempt to undermine British morale. 'Gairmany calling, Gairmany calling' he used to begin, as we fiddled with the wireless knobs to make sure that we didn't miss his broadcasts. Almost invariably he was capable of shattering us with items of completely authentic news. 'The town clock at Forres stopped at one minute to midnight last night' was the kind of intelligence he was able to impart. 'Hitler will be in Scotland in time to perform the opening ceremony of the new bridge over the Ythan at Ellon.' Someone was obviously keeping him well informed and almost inevitably the word spread around that we had a spy in our midst. Everyone knew his name and he had a moustache and folk said it would just be like him to consort with the Nazis. Neighbours downstairs swore that they heard a radio transmitter in the room above but nothing was ever established and the man was probably completely innocent.

Churchill had made his famous speech about fighting them on the beaches and in the streets and I can still remember the confidence his voice instilled in the child. He may have been a man of many faults but forever after that he held the gratitude of children who felt that as long as he stood between them and Hitler no great harm would come. The way he spat out the word 'Nazi' left no doubt about his feelings, which were very much the same as my own child-like sentiments since the day I suffered from German measles. In addition to the strength of Churchill we were also blessed with the courage and fortification of the Local Defence Volunteers, later known as the Home Guard and the model from which the television people eventually gave us 'Dad's Army'.

Since my father had failed his medical for the forces he was a ripe candidate for the L.D.V. He was stout and suffered from a slight heart condition so they made him a captain. Death and insanity were the only possible grounds for exemption (not that you would always have noticed!), leaving a wide range of conditions for the ranks of the L.D.V. As my father rasped out his orders, a motley collection of mis-shapes who had come straight from field or work-bench jumped as near to attention as could be expected and off they would march in a zany column, with the left-rights about equally balanced by the right-lefts. There were the long and thin, the short and fat, the ploughman and the postman, the vricht and the grocer. But within such military inadequacy there was at least ample room for promotion. You could become a colonel with carbuncles or a lance-corporal with gout. They marched off on schemes, route marches and mock battles with camouflaged coverings that made them look like cows peering through a hedge. They would duck down behind ditches, reappear in a frenzy of battle activity and argue among themselves as to who was dead and who was not. Sometimes we boys would hide behind a dyke and call out 'L.D.V.—Look, Dook and Vanish!' and there was a stramash till we were hunted out like German snipers and delivered of a hefty kick on the backside. They built a pill-box by the village crossroads, at the top of the Bobby's Brae, with little holes through which they intended to shoot every German who came in sight. We were totally unfair to the L.D.V. of course, showing a cynicism which seems to thrive in Scotland, but I had an uncanny feeling that if the German invaders got as far as Maud they were unlikely to fail at the final hurdle of our fireside soldiers. Mercifully it was never put to the test and they remain but a memory, one of the many diversions which made the war years tolerable and sometimes even amusing. They had started with nothing but a forage cap and a khaki armband but soon they were fully dressed soldiers and, among my many souvenirs, I keep intact to this day my father's battledress with his three pips of a captain, a piece of moth-eaten nostalgia for a phase of history when the real and the unreal were never so closely wedded.

One of the attractions of the war to a country child was the unaccustomed bustle it created in places where visitors were about as scarce as hen's teeth. Great battalions of soldiers came driving in with heavy lorries and bren-gun carriers, and aerodromes sprang up at places like Longside and Crimond where sheep had grazed before, since we were the nearest point in Britain to Norway and the whole of northern Europe. The Russian convoys passed along our coast before heading out towards the Baltic and we would rush to the coast to watch this mysterious movement of ships, realising that we lived in stirring times. In Maud they commandeered Kerr's Hall and Victoria Hall, where they had held grand balls before the war and visiting repertory companies of professional actors used to present plays like *Alf's Button*. Now a thousand soldiers came to billet themselves in the village and at Brucklay Castle, two miles up the road—men of the King's Own Scottish Borderers who had come to prepare for the Second Front. What mattered more to me was that they had a pipe band. I had always wanted to play the pipes, ever since the days when the Gordon Highlanders had come on their pre-war recruiting drives, enlisting many a whisky-laden farm servant who had come to Maud with the innocent intention of taking a fee from a farmer and found himself next day with the arles of His Majesty and a posting to Gibraltar. I made myself known to Jock Gray from Kelso, who fair could make the pigskin skirl (he later moved to the Royal Scots Greys and formed the band which was to gain fame with *Amazing Grace*). Jock took me in hand in his spare time and taught me to play the chanter, which is the preliminary of the full-scale business of playing the pipes. You learn the fingering on the chanter, which is just a glorified penny-whistle with a reed giving out a mellow sound. Through the winter months of 1942-43 I deaved the neighbourhood with practice till I had a repertoire of three tunes, *Highland Laddie*, *The 79th Farewell to Gibraltar* and *The Green Hills of Tyrol*, before Andy Stewart gave it words and called it *The Scottish Soldier*. Everywhere the Kosbies went I was sure to go, striding along on route marches or church parades till the commanding officer did not have the heart to send me away. All the time I was helping in the kirk canteen, cajoling my mother to house the wives who came to visit their husbands and generally acting as mascot to the battalion.

On a glorious day in 1943 we had our one and only visit from Royalty, who would have little cause to pass our way at any other time. The KOSB had as their colonel-in-chief the Duchess of Gloucester, who arrived in splendour and inspected the children of Maud School in the village Pleasure Park before visiting her battalion at Brucklay. We followed her to the castle to share in the massive military spectacle, the like of which we had never seen in Buchan. The pipes and drums combined with the military band to give the most glorious musical performance and as I ran home late for my tea I can still remember pausing in the quiet of an April evening as the sound of the silver band came echoing through the Brucklay trees. The tune was Lehar's *Gold and Silver* and if there are moments in life which have the pureness of heaven on earth, which you try to fix in your consciousness because they will not come again, then this was one for me. I had my comfortable structure of life, easy and familiar and enriched for the moment at least by real, live soldiers and a Royal visitor and thrilling music. What more could a schoolboy want to fulfil his dreams of happiness?

Two weeks later the KOSB played for us again, this time in the village square, a full muster of bandsmen beating out the majesty of Retreat. Alas, it was to be the retreat from our village scene as well, a final tribute to folk who had opened their homes and their hearts to bring a touch of comfort to those Borderers, country folk like ourselves from the farms and mill towns at the other end of Scotland, who were now marching away to continue their D-Day training at Hayton Camp, Aberdeen. Trucks and bren-gun carriers led the way and, as the men stepped off on their twenty-eight mile march, a whole village turned out, every man, woman and child, to see them on their way. The bottom was about to fall out of my world. Once again I filed alongside the soldiers, the rich smell of their khaki tunics, their blanco and their boots, and marched till they were at Auchnagatt and the waves and cheers of the Maud folk had faded into the past. They fell out for a rest and when they formed up again Jock Gray put a hand on my shoulder and told me it was time to go home now or my mother would be worrying; big, friendly Jock, my wartime hero who epitomised the warmth and kindliness of Border folk. Yes, they would come back to see us and I would visit them in their part of Scotland when the war was over. So they formed up and, with a left and a right, they marched out of my life, these young soldiers, some of them never to come home from the battlefields of Europe. I stood there incapable of words, reminding myself that brave soldiers do not cry. I watched and waved, fighting back the lump in my throat, and they turned and waved back and when they were only a hazy mass on a distant horizon the bung dropped out and the tears came flooding to blur the final vision. I turned and ran back to the village and the wind dried the tears, leaving stains which told their own story.

Long after the war was over and they were back in their beloved Borders as veterans of a nightmare war that had now slipped away, they invited their Maud mascot as a guest at their reunion dinner in the Crown Hotel in Hawick. I was not prepared for a speech because that had not been the intention.

But the chairman asked if I would like to say a few words and I felt it in my heart to do so. It was a night of beer and bonhomie when speeches were regarded as something of an intrusion upon the revelry of the moment. But as I rose to survey the ranks of familiar faces, which time had altered with lines and specks of grey, there was a sudden shuffle of attention for the boy from Maud who had grown to a man with less hair than most of themselves. Straight out of the memory and the heart I took them back to those days in Maud, when they were in their twenties and early thirties, and gave them a sight of themselves through the eyes of a child. I could point to men I had not seen for thirty years and give them names and memories of their younger days which apparently touched them deeply and I could equally remember the ones who were gone. Suddenly I realised that the beer glasses were standing untouched on the tables and the men who were now in their fifties and sixties were silently engrossed in a bygone age.

Speech-making has never been a strength of mine but what I had to say was at least plain and sincere and I could see clearly that there were tears on many a cheek. So I finished abruptly and sat down and there was a pause of several seconds. Then those veterans of the Second World War, my young heroes of 1942, burst into a deafening applause and rose to their feet as a solid body to give the loon from Maud a standing ovation. It was a highly-charged moment and needless to say we delved deeper into the nostalgia, as well as the whisky bottles, before the night was out! Only the presence of Jock Gray could have made it better, but Jock was no longer with us.

By the time these men had marched out of my life in 1943 I had my own bagpipes and could play them, thanks to Jock, and when the war was nearly over and the L.D.V. (by then the Home Guard) decided that, in the absence of any Germans, it could now safely disband, I stepped out with another boy piper, Willie Stables, to lead them in their farewell parade.

Long before then, however, the routine of wartime had

become as familiar as the peace-time days of the thirties. Schooldays were joyously broken with air-raid drill, when Donald Murray, the headmaster, would blow a loud whistle and we would drop pencils and dash home, run once round the table and back to school. Sometimes the air-raids were for real as German bombers came trundling over Buchan, seeking out the Fraserburgh Toolworks or merely shedding their bombs as British fighters made chase to intercept. Their explosions blew craters in many a nearby field and on one occasion a plane of our own came crashing down in a field at Cairndale and we all ran up after school to see the burning shell. Farm children were allocated a village house as a refuge during air-raids and I was paired with Jimmy Allan from Bulwark, a droll lad with a long, solemn face but a quick mother-wit when he cared to speak. In return for the cups of tea during air-raids, he appeared at my mother's doorstep one Christmas morning with a turkey. Never a word was spoken as he held out the bulging bird. My mother, taken aback by the generosity, said: 'Oh Jimmy, this is surely nae for me?' Whereupon he surveyed her disdainfully and replied: 'Fa the hell ither?' Buchan drollness at its best.

At school we learned our three Rs, passing up the line from Miss Catto's infant class to Miss Duncan and Mrs Gregor, who had been coaxed out of retirement. The arrival of an auburn-haired lady called Miss Morrison was a fortuitous co-incidence with the stirring of interest in the fair sex. I can still remember her breezy walk, the toss of her head and the silk-stockinged legs upon which the boy could play out his first eager fantasies. Miss Auchinachie, with a bun in her hair, came to teach us music and a continental lady called Miss Feltges put us through dancing routines and thought that I was sufficiently well blessed with rhythm that I should demonstrate with Margaret Cassie, whose body movement was exquisite.

At home we listened to the wireless with its news bulletins brought by announcers who had to identify themselves for authenticity, in contrast to the earlier anonymity. So they began: 'Here is the news, read by Frank Phillips . . . or Joseph McLeod . . . Alvar Liddell . . . Bruce Belfrage. . . .' We listened to Reginald Foort at the BBC theatre organ, to *Band Wagon*, with Stinker Murdoch and Arthur Askey, as well as to *Happidrome*, with Mr Ramsbottom, Mr Lovejoy and Enoch singing:

> We three
> in harmony
> Working for the BBC
> Ramsbottom and Enoch and me . . .

And the talk of war wore on as the dominant theme of living, with every household pinning a map on the wall and moving little pointers which kept us up-to-date on the advances and retreats of the German and Allied forces. Arguments raged about who was going to win and how long it would last but I remember the general consensus was that it would run for all of ten years. 'It'll get waur afore it's better,' folk said with gloom in their voices. Well, it did get waur, as they forecast, but it did come to an end in six years instead of ten. And when the great upheaval ended and the crowds were thronging London to celebrate Victory in Europe, we had our own VE Night on the site of a burned-out garage, heaping old wood and tyres into a pile and enflaming it with paraffin till a glorious bonfire lit up the night sky of Tuesday, 8 May, 1945, and we celebrated the final destruction of Adolf Hitler. In no time at all the northern lights of the Grampian supply went up again and folk began to see a world they scarcely recognised. That bonfire glow which symbolised the end of Hitler was viewed with pensive gloom by hundreds of German soldiers, captured by the troops who went off to the D-Day invasion of France and sent back as prisoners-of-war to camps around our Buchan district. They worked on farms and we came to know them and to marvel at the fact that they were recognisable human beings, some just youngsters who had been conscripted into the Hitler Youth and sent off to combat the D-Day invasion when the fluff was scarcely off their chins.

Werner Hoffman had just started as a student at Heidelberg University when he was spirited off to battle, en route to captivity at Stuartfield. He was just one of several young lads—'They're a' somebody's bairn' as my mother used to say—who were welcomed to our house for tea on Sundays. Not all were disillusioned with their Fuhrer at that stage but we kept clear of the topic and treated them with courtesy and hospitality.

The British Government kept its prisoners till 1948, when we shook hands and wished them a better future. In the years between, I have motored a good deal across the continent and have never failed to call on Werner Hoffman when passing through the Heidelberg district, where he is a prosperous businessman with a charming family. He has entertained me to tea on Sundays, returning the compliment of my mother's table at 2 Park Crescent, Maud, and we have raised a glass of schnapps, agreed about the madness and futility of war and toasted the day when mankind will learn to live in peace.

CHAPTER SEVEN

IN MEMORY

Now that the war was over and the dust was settling, the kirk bells rang out one memorable Sunday, peeling from the Low Village right up through the quiet streets of Maud, beckoning old and young to gather round in memory of the men who had fallen. And in our quiet way we answered the call, near every walking soul of us, down to the granite slab that stood in the corner by the kirk. Its front was already well covered with the names of our village men who came to grief in what they called The Great War of 1914-18. There were not so many names this time for the total massacre was not so vast but the field of Flanders had broadened to take in the sands of the desert and the angry fathoms of the Atlantic. And we remembered. Sonny Barrie, who gave us lifts on the step of his bike that last leave before he rode away to his death; Patty Gordon, a studious boy who had been scarce away from Maud School when he was drowning at Narvik; Bertie Kelman who went down in the last weeks; Johnny Wallace, whose daughter Jean was left fatherless in my class, as we tried in our own awkward way to be kind. And the others.

We were a little village, just one of thousands whose dead were no more dead than the rest, but no less either, so we somehow embodied the whole tragedy of the situation, the price that was paid in simple human lives for the antics of a madman. A Union Jack covered the memorial as we bowed our heads and heard the minister say his say about our dear ones who had gone away without thought of self and had fought and died for the love of their country. You pondered the man's words and considered whether they had really gone with such patriotic purpose or whether it was more in the heat and spirit and compulsion of the moment, with the optimism which keeps most of us going in this bewildering world of ours.

So we sang a hymn and there was a scurrying as Mrs Chrissie Heddle stepped forward to pull the flag from the stone. She must have had her own memories for it was her husband, George Heddle, the local road surveyor, who mustered a company of our local county council roadmen to sail as a unit of the Royal Engineers for some secret destination abroad. Their ship, an old Egyptian tub called the *Mohammed-Ali-el-Kabir*, was somewhere in the dark Atlantic when it was torpedoed by a German U-boat which had waited until the escorting vessel was round the other side before piercing the troopship with a deadly weapon. Among the men who flailed about in dark and stormy seas was my uncle, John Argo, whose predicament was made worse when they threw down life rafts on top of the helpless soldiers and broke his back. Some were drowned and others maimed and the memory of it bore heavily on their leader who survived the war but died soon after.

We bowed our heads in prayer and I was back again in the infant class of pre-war days when we lowered our eyes for an Armistice Day that was vague and distant in its image. This time we knew more about the realities, about the men who had fought in the dubs and kyirn of the battlefield till they sweated the crimson sweat of death, a sweat that does not dry away but only hardens to a crust.

And there as they lay, with the blast of gunfire in their ears, the smell of cordite in their nostrils, I wondered if these men, who had thought little of danger when they rode off that September day and who were ill at ease with kirks and religion, came face to face with the truth of their plight, if they drew a lung-racking breath to utter from parched lips a prayer that was maybe their first and surely their last. And as the noise and stench of battle began to fade I knew that their thoughts would be with fadder and bridder in the parks of Buchan, pu'in' neeps in the wind and carting them to the neepshed with a curse for the bite of the blast or the sweirty of the horse. Or perhaps with midder washing eggs in the kitchen, little knowing that the son who tugged at her breasts those years ago lay dying in the helplessness of some foreign field.

Now the sotter of it all tore at the child heart as fadder and midder and bridder were seated in the glum silence of the next-of-kin, fighting back the tears that are seldom shed in Buchan. As the minister finished, a shrill wind blew up and darkness came early from Bulwark. Folk looked around and nodded one to the other in the silence which says so much in rural Scotland. So we went up the village that day, home to our little homes, leaving the cold grey granite with its poppies and flowers and black-printed names that are aye ready to tell a story to those who will pause and wonder.

CHAPTER EIGHT

FROM WHITEHILL TO THE WHITE HOUSE

At the country school of Whitehill my great-grandfather, Gavin Greig, had his share of natural talent but never one of such worldly promise as little Bertie Forbes, the baggy-breeked son of Robbie Forbes, the local tailor whose shop also dispensed the district supply of porter and ale. Out of poor and humble circumstances here was a rare talent which Gavin Greig set about fostering with tuition, books and encouragement. When the time came for Bertie to leave school, he told Maister Greig that he wanted to write. But the centres of journalism were far from Whitehill and the best that could be found for him was a job as a printer's devil on the *Peterhead Sentinel*, under the guidance of Dauvit Scott. He spent three years of typesetting there before joining the Dundee *Courier* as a reporter. When the Boer War advertised South Africa he landed in Johannesburg in time to team up with Edgar Wallace, the thriller writer, who was about to establish the *Rand Daily Mail*. At twenty-three he was the journalistic prodigy of the Veldt, worming out exclusives from important gold men, having eavesdropped on their conversations as he caddied on the golf courses of Johannesburg. Edgar Wallace allowed the young Forbes to write the Wallace column under the master's name, such was his regard for the Scots lad. He had already gone far since he walked from Whitehill School but his interest in the financial world of stocks and shares drew him inevitably to New York.

A growing reputation in South Africa, however, counted for nothing in America where it was fairly bluntly conveyed to him that the big financial dailies had little use for a Scottish country bumpkin who hardly knew Wall Street from Broadway. But the shrewd little Bertie, bumpkin or not, had the last word when he cunningly offered to work for nothing. Well, gee, there wasn't much to lose with a guy who worked for nothing and the New York *Journal of Commerce* unbent. After a week's work they made him a fifteen-dollar-a-week junior at the age of twenty-four and when Edgar Wallace offered him the London correspondent's post of the *Rand Daily Mail* six months later he had already made such an impression that the *Journal* gave him his choice of job. In his rapid promotion, he picked an important desk in the financial department and soon became editor. Bertie still remembered that the value of a dollar, like the bawbee he so seldom had to spare at Whitehill, depended on how it was spent.

In 1905, for example, he gave up his New York lodgings and moved into the old Waldorf Astoria, the meeting place of America's mighty men. While it cost him more than he was earning, it brought him an unrivalled amount of what the newspaper world calls 'contacts'. At thirty-two he was well settled in double anonymity as financial editor for the *Journal of Commerce* and editorial writer for the *Commercial and Financial Chronicle*. At that time the New York *American* was looking for a business editor and narrowed its choice to two men— both of whom turned out to be B.C. Forbes.

From there he began to make a deep impression on the business world of America, which had been accustomed to a form of journalism as innocuous as the business world wanted it to be. The dynamic Forbes demanded the right to express his personal view in the *American*, translating economics into the sort of copy which could have been understood by his old father at Whitehill. He shattered smugness, stirred the conscience of the moguls and became known as the humanizer of American business. He was now in such a position of knowledge and power that the next step seemed inevitable. Why not start his own business journal? So in 1917 the first issue of *Forbes Magazine* appeared on the stalls with the opening line: 'Business was originated to produce happiness, not pile up millions. Are we in danger of forgetting this?' It took the simple logic of a baggy-breeked boy from the backwoods of Scotland to drive home the lesson to the mighty men of America. In the same issue he flayed George Jay Gould, scion of Jay Gould's $80 million railroad empire, headlining him as 'A highly-placed misfit' and attributing the dissipation of the Gould system to George's 'narrowness of vision, unreasoning jealousy, distrust of both subordinates and rivals'. At the same time he offered a thousand dollars for the best essay on 'Who is the best Employer in America?' The magazine was not an immediate financial success and there were many Fridays when Bertie did not know where the wages were coming from. But he kept going with the determination which made Gavin Greig so sure that he had a winner in the class. The romantic stories continued, as did the windmill tilting in the classic Don Quixotic pattern. The boldest was the serialised searing of Henry Ford in 1927 ('Slave-driving in Ford Factories' etc). When some readers protested he wrote an editorial entitled 'Please cancel your subscriptions'. He then underlined the independent attitude with a rataplan of critical editorials about the R.J. Reynolds Tobacco Company, a crusade which lost him Camel advertising but left his self-respect intact.

Between issues he managed to write eleven books, to found the Investors' League in America and eventually to receive the recognition of an honorary degree from the University of Southern California and the Freedom Foundation Award 'for outstanding achievement in bringing about the better understanding of the American way of life'.

With his plush offices in New York's Fifth Avenue, Bertie Forbes had come a long way. But with the making of millions he never forgot the place where he began. Every two years there was a stirring of excitement in the parish when a chauffeur-driven Rolls Royce appeared over the horizon as Bertie and his entourage came home to visit old friends, having collected his surviving brothers and sisters on the way to share a few days at the scene of their youth. Bertie's Picnic became a major event, from the days of my mother's childhood, when they all piled into horse-drawn carts and journeyed to the beach at New Aberdour, where the sea smells better than anywhere else. By the time of my own acquaintance in the mid-thirties they were held in fields adjoining Gavin Greig's old school, where he had received all his formal education. There were races for children and adults alike, prizes and gifts for all and a word of encouragement from the man himself. He had a special affection for the Greig descendants and in the evenings of his visit he would entertain my parents and grandparents and other relatives to dinner at the Cruden Bay Hotel, which was the Gleneagles of the North-East in those days, served by a permanent way which its railway owners had laid from Ellon, as a tangent of the Buchan line. Sometimes I was allowed to join the party and to listen to the talk of a man who was on first-name terms with men like John D. Rockefeller and Frank Woolworth and who played Saturday night card games with George Gershwin's mother when the great American composer was just a lad about the house.

Bertie Forbes would encourage my interest in newspapers by telling me stories of his dealings with William Randolph Hearst, the most powerful newspaper owner in the world; of how Hearst had offered him a blank cheque to write for his empire and how he had assessed his own worth at a ridiculously high figure which was accepted without question. He was the first person we ever knew with a cine-camera and on the following visit he would show films of Hillie or Waulkie or the Miller running races and receiving their prizes and then, with a mischief which showed that he had not forgotten the value of a bawbee, he would reverse the reel and we saw the same people handing back their prize-money and running backwards like a lot of lunatics from a Keystone Cops adventure.

Since I was a direct descendant of his own boyhood hero, who had encouraged his career in journalism, he was by way of repaying a debt through an awe-struck lad who was only too glad to sit with his mouth open and savour that first rub with greatness. The name of Gavin Greig had hovered as an inspiration for as long as I could remember and now his pupil was adding a more immediate stimulus to the ambition which would lead me, surely, towards a writing career.

Bertie endowed his old school and the parish church at nearby New Deer. There are annual prizes of Bibles for children's attendance at the church, an encouragement in the ways of worship which were such an important part of his childhood at Whitehill. On his seventieth birthday he presented a baptismal font and was there at its dedication. It would be hard to forget the scene as he stood by the font, a powerful man of high places, and watched with tears on his cheeks as a humble child of his native parish was anointed with water from the same burn as his own christening water.

Who would know? Perhaps another lad o' pairts was on the way, for Bertie did not believe that the days of opportunity were over. His visits were always in the summer and he came again two years later. A further two years should have elapsed before his next visit but as December approached, word got round that Bertie Forbes was coming at Christmas, the first time he had ever made such a return to the old corner. No one knew why he came, only that he played Father Christmas and spoke to the children of the thrift and honesty and hard work that were ingrained in his Scottish character and which would enable them to lead happy, contented lives. Older men sensed that there was a longing in his eyes, that last embracing look at things which are of the beginning. Somehow the gloss of the big-time American with a life-long experience of Wall Street, the White House and the Waldorf Astoria peeled away and he became a child again, back at the Cunnyknowe where he was born, polishing boots for the local gentry, gathering peats and heading off to school and the strict discipline of Maister Greig.

Then his chauffeur drew up at our door at Maud, where he made his last call, and Bertie stepped into the limousine with his ever-faithful secretary, Gertrude Weiner, who had been with him since the very early days of *Forbes Magazine*; he bade us all a very thoughtful goodbye and rode away over the hill by

Old Maud, back to his adopted world of Manhattan. His instinct for life and death was as sure as his instinct for business because, just as he must have calculated himself, the daylight was running out. A few months later they found him slumped at his desk, having died in the way he had lived—with a pen in his hand. The financial empire is now run by one of his five sons, Malcolm, who was tipped as a future President of the United States during the fifties, when he rose to be the bright young hope of the Republican Party at roughly the same time as John F. Kennedy was blossoming for the Democrats. But it was the Irishman who strode on to become President while the Scot was turning to follow in his father's footsteps.

Malcolm Forbes has taken his father's foundations and extended them from the field of journalism into business ventures and land ownership of such a scale that Bertie Forbes could not have dreamed about. He has emerged as one of the richest and most extraordinary of American businessmen, world-famous as a hot-air balloonist and the owner of the Governor's Palace in Morocco, a massive chateau in France, Battersea House in London and a whole island in the Pacific, not to mention his own DC9 airplane and the biggest yacht in New York Harbour.

Bertie had invited my father and mother to the various anniversary gatherings of *Forbes Magazine*, including the thirtieth celebration, which was to act as a springboard for the Presidential candidacy of Thomas Dewey. However, a journey to New York seemed out of the question for folk from Maud in those days. But I vowed to myself that, at some time in the future, at least one member of the family would make a belated response to the invitation from the man who had finally inspired me on the road to journalism. The occasion lay many years ahead—but I had a good idea who that person would be!

CHAPTER NINE

C'MON THE DONS!

It was right in the heart of the Second World War that I savoured the true essence of Aberdeen when, on the basis of an I.Q. test, I was despatched for the purpose of developing an intelligence which was allegedly worth developing, though subsequent events were to cast some doubt on the theory. The choice was a straightforward one between Aberdeen Grammar, Lord Byron's old school, and Robert Gordon's College. The Grammar had the upper-crust image while Gordon's, with its bursaries and Scatterty Scholarships, was said to find a better social balance, mixing clever laddies from working-class city homes with the affluence of west-end fish and granite and the plain dyst of country loons.

So I strolled through the vaulted gateway of Robert Gordon's in Schoolhill at a time when Hitler was dropping his bombs on the major cities, into a world of black gowns and musty corridors, blue blazers and grey flannel pants, rugby, science and swimming, which was producing assorted heroes with names like Frank Thomson (later to become a controversial entrepreneur in the Highlands), I.D. Ewen, St Clair Taylor and Johnny Rose and had yet to produce an Olympic champion by the name of Ian Black. A jovial chap called John Smith used to hold court in the playground with all the assurance which later turned him into Lord Kirkhill; and among other contemporaries with whom I made my debut as an amateur actor was a solemn-faced boy from the Hilton district called Buff Hardie, later to gain fame as part of the *Scotland the What?* phenomenon.

Life at Gordon's was centred on a main building which had changed little since the butcher Cumberland billeted his men there on the march north for the Battle of Culloden and again on his way home, when he plundered and raped the city and citizens of Aberdeen in a most despicable manner. Robert Gordon had been a local merchant who made a fortune while trading in Danzig and who set up a 'hospital', which was a school for the poor boys of his native city, in 1732. The boys were known as Sillerton Loons. The centuries had turned the hospital into a great centre of learning, incorporating not only a day school but a technical college, art college and schools of architecture and navigation—and a boys' boarding-house which was called Sillerton House. So once again we were back with the original name of Sillerton Loons, of whom I became one, having been sent there after a spell in lodgings with Miss Stott in Elm Place, during which I had displayed a rare talent for putting football before fractions, pictures well ahead of Pythagoras. Snack bars and smokey cinemas, forbidden Woodbines and billiard salons (enriched by the coffee aroma from Collie's shop in Union Street) were much in vogue in the forties when the News Cinema in Diamond Street would provide, with commendable speed, a Monday showing of the Aberdeen football team's feats of the previous Saturday. Even with its immediacy, television can provide nothing of the atmosphere of those large-scale, ground-level projections.

The war was drawing to a close and big names of the thirties were returning to grace the turf of Pittodrie Park, which had been the home of Aberdeen F.C. since its inception in 1903. As I recall in another book, 'The Dons,' my wartime hero of the football field had been Johnny Pattillo, a bow-legged centre-forward with middle parting and lethal shot, but now he was being joined by players like George Hamilton and Archie Baird, two of the memorable thoroughbreds of football who had been employing their talents in more hostile pursuits these last six years.

Winston Churchill came driving up Union Street in an open car to celebrate victory over the Hun and to receive the Freedom of the City in the same month as the Dons carried off their very first honour at national level, the Scottish League Cup of 1946. It was a reflection of the farcical state of Scottish football that it had taken all that time for a single reward to get so far away from the Glasgow stranglehold of Rangers and Celtic. During the forty-three year period from 1904 till 1947 the Scottish League Championship was won once by Motherwell and on every other occasion by either Rangers or Celtic, with their large hordes of supporters who came to regard dominance as their birthright. How the game survived that appalling monopoly is more than I shall ever understand. Yet those old men who remembered the very beginnings of Pittodrie football would positively glow with happy recollection, if not of silverware success at least of great personalities who had graced the Merkland Road turf through close on half a century. There were names like Willie Lennie, Aberdeen's first Scottish internationalist, Donald Colman and Jock Hume, a famous fullback partnership to be followed by an equally effective pair in Jock Hutton and Matt Forsyth. There was that elegant member of the Wembley Wizards team, Alec Jackson, and a bouncy little Aberdonian by the name of Benny Yorston, regarded by many as the greatest Dons player of them all.

Brilliance continued through the thirties with men like the stylish Willie Mills and here we were in the forties, now coping with the turmoil and confusion of the world's most devastating war. From a football point of view the consolation for North-East people was that it brought some big names from the south to play at Pittodrie. In the great movement of armed forces, an airman billeted locally turned out to be Stanley Mortensen, later to become one half of a legendary partnership with Stanley Matthews for both Blackpool and England. During two seasons Mortensen was a guest player with Aberdeen, as was the habit of the time, scoring memorable goals and winning a host of friends in the North-East.

It was around that time that my mother and I were travelling to Aberdeen on the Buchan train one day in the company of Hector Mavor, the village joiner, who asked if I had ever been to Pittodrie. Youthful eyes glowed with interest for I knew the names and reputations though I had never been inside a football ground in my life. The soccer horizons had not extended beyond the Pleasure Park at Maud where some gory battles were fought out under the banner of the Buchan League. At least our village had contributed one player to the ranks of Aberdeen Football Club—goalkeeper Jimmy Henry, whose father owned the Station Hotel—but now Hector Mavor was offering to take me on my very first visit to Pittodrie while my mother went shopping, and she didn't have the heart to say no. So that afternoon in 1942 I set my disbelieving eyes on Pittodrie Park for the first time, to watch an Army select team playing Aberdeen.

But now in 1946, when a trophy had been won at long last, Aberdeen were poised to become an even greater force in Scottish football. Within a year they had done it again, this time going one better to win the more prestigious Scottish Cup. Only once before had they even reached the final of the national trophy. That was in 1937, when they were beaten by Celtic in a match which set an all-time crowd record of 146,433 for a club encounter in the British Isles. The disappointment of that result had been quickly followed by a tour of South Africa which brought the tragedy of Jackie Beynon, Aberdeen's popular outside right who was rushed to hospital in Johannesburg with an appendicitis—and died of peritonitis. The bitter memory of 1937 still lived with men like Willie Cooper, George Johnstone and Frank Dunlop, who survived to play again ten years later as Aberdeen embarked on another Scottish Cup competition. There was high excitement at Pittodrie with the first-round victory over Partick Thistle, gained by a last-minute goal from the veteran Willie Cooper, a loyal servant who was by then in his twentieth season with the Dons.

Come April of 1947 and we were delving into drawers to unearth any garment with red in it, for Aberdeen had reached the Scottish Cup final at Hampden Park, Glasgow, and the wartime austerity of clothing coupons was still with us. So my mother converted her only red jumper into a tammy with a tassle on top and off I went, an eager fifteen-year-old, to my first adventure as a Dons' supporter. Alas, as we boarded the special trains at the Joint Station that Saturday morning we knew that the Aberdeen team would be without the man who had made it all possible. Willie Cooper had been injured in the semi-final of the previous week. This was Willie's last chance to win any kind of medal and fate had done him an injustice. The opposition that day was Hibernian and after a disastrous start, in which they lost a silly goal in the first minute, Aberdeen came storming back to win by 2-1, little Stan Williams scoring one of the cheekiest of all goals.

As captain Frank Dunlop held the Cup aloft, Aberdonians in the vast crowd began to chant 'We want Cooper'. Willie was coaxed from his seat in the shadows to receive the acclaim of a grateful public. There he stood, a shy man near to tears, holding the Scottish Cup and absorbing a precious moment in football history. Those of us on the terracing with lumps in our throats had not yet formulated the thought. For sure, there had been a colourful and illustrious past at Pittodrie, with names to inspire an impassioned memory. But what we had just witnessed that April day in 1947 was the final arrival of Aberdeen on the scene of Scottish football.

CHAPTER TEN

THE BETTY HADDEN MYSTERY

During the Second World War Aberdeen was still a city of workhorses, pulling heavy carts up Market Street towards Union Street, which remains one of the most attractive thoroughfares in Britain.

Country folk would come into town for the Friday cattle market, the wives boarding a tram-car at the Kittybrewster mart and trundling down George Street to alight at the 'Queen' for a day's shopping while their farmer husbands sized up the shape and value of stots and heifers. Women folk would rummage in Raggie Morrison's, the best-known shop in Aberdeen, and treat themselves to a half-crown lunch at Isaac Benzie's, where digestion was ably assisted by the mellow tones of the three-piece orchestra. If there was time, they would take the tram-car back to Kittybrewster (later made famous as the home of Denis Law) to spend a couple of hours in the Astoria Cinema before their menfolks emerged from the Bogie Roll and bonhomie of the cattle ring or the public bar of the Northern Hotel.

As an alternative to the glamour of Hollywood, the ladies might steal away with some secrecy to Whitehouse Street, not far from the Grammar School, where a mysterious gentleman called Jimmy Birnie would read their fortunes and fill their heads with enough dreams of romance to brighten their trauchled lives and send them home to Buchan or Donside or the Garioch on a cushion of air which would sustain them till the next time they came to Aberdeen for the day. Not too many of them would admit to their visits to Jimmy Birnie's little shed in Whitehouse Street but they went there just the same.

Apart from the conglomeration of cinemas in Aberdeen, mostly owned by the Donald family, there was a most beautiful theatre, His Majesty's, which happily survives to this day, and there we would sample anything from the Shakespearean tones of Donald Wolfit to the rousing tenor of Richard Tauber, whose visit in 1941 still lingers with me as a memorable introduction to the world of theatre. Down at the Tivoli in Guild Street, near the station, the flavour of the old-time music hall was maintained by a motley range of comedians from Glasgow and elsewhere with their supporting casts and an orchestra conducted by Clifford Jordan, who later opened a hotel in Queen's Terrace with his wife Margaret and combined their two names to call it the Marcliffe Hotel.

I remember sitting in the Tivoli Theatre one night during the war, listening to a double act in which the husband, resplendent in bow tie and tails, sang in the most beautiful tenor while his wife accompanied on the piano. They were billed as Ted Andrews and Barbara and a small line beneath their names on the programme read '—and introducing Julie,' their little girl who was yet to become famous as the international musical star of films like *Mary Poppins* and *The Sound of Music*. It all came back to me vividly one evening in November, 1980, as I sat in a bar in Los Angeles, listening to the resident pianist. Suddenly a lady with a familiar face left her drink and crossed to the pianist to ask if she could borrow his piano. As she broke into a magnificent performance of Gershwin music I was in no doubt that this was Barbara Andrews and we ended the evening with a toast to those distant memories of Aberdeen.

Charlie Chaplin had appeared on the stage of the Tivoli in his early days as a comedian and it was one of the special pleasures of my life to take him back in his old age to see the place where he had tried out his baggy pants on an unsuspecting Aberdeen audience at the beginning of the century. But more of that later. So the smell of grease-paint still hung around Guild Street in those days of the forties and fish came strongly from the harbour as open-topped trams went shouding down to the beach from the Castlegate on hot summer days. In streets which fanned out from Castle Street you would find the Aberdeen version of a slum, with the odd drunken woman slavering with a fag at the corner of her mouth and offering herself for a packet of ten Woodbines, which seemed dear at the price. Boys intrigued by the conspiracy of sex would steal off to the Newmarket and mount the steps to the gallery where a pungent array of stalls included those which sold French Letters, or Frenchies as they were commonly called. If they could not be used for their intended purpose there was always the novel game of filling them up with water to see how much they could hold. I can report from experience that the capacity was absolutely staggering, as proof of a durability which went far beyond the possibility of human performance.

Sometimes there would be a dire event which would send us off with breathless tales on our lips. Such a day began with a grey, damp December morning as the city of Aberdeen lay fast asleep and a piercing shriek rang out over the harbour area to wake folk in nearby Torry. The hour was 2 a.m. But strange noises are not uncommon in the quayside clutter of gangways, sailors, pubs and women of doubtful morals. So those who were disturbed by the shriek turned over in their beds and dozed again till it was time to join the bustle of the fish-houses and the factories. Soon the tram-cars were clanking their way up and down Union Street, past grey granite buildings that stood aloof in the sparkle of first light. Heavy workhorses clopped up Market Street from the harbour to the main thoroughfares. Aberdeen had begun another day. But it was no ordinary day. Shortly after 9 a.m. an elderly man strolling on the foreshore by the mouth of the River Dee was searching for firewood when his eyes set upon an object which sent him gasping to the nearest telephone box to call the police. Later that morning, serious-faced detectives gathered round at police headquarters in Lodge Walk and pondered the mystery of the grisly object. It was a human arm, crudely sawn off,

87

with the fingers arched as if scratching at a killer in self-defence. To this day, more than thirty-five years later, detectives are still asking the question: Who killed Betty Hadden? To this day I sometimes wonder if I could have helped them.

The year was 1945. The great wartime offensive which had started with the D-Day landings of 1944 had reached its climax at Luneberg Heath in May when Victory in Europe was declared. By July the inspiration of that victory, Winston Churchill, had been discarded as Prime Minister even before the final victory over Japan. It was through that latter part of the war that I was one of the thirty-six boys at Sillerton House, where routine was strict.

Morning gong had us out of bed soon after seven o'clock and breakfast was followed by the mile-or-more walk down Carden Place, Skene Street and Rosemount Viaduct to school. The same distance was covered twice at lunchtime and again when school closed at 4.10 p.m. Tea was followed by 'prep' and by 9 p.m. boys of fourteen were heading for bed. Saturday mornings were for the rugby and soccer pitches and afternoons reserved for the cinema. After lunch we would line up in the common-room for the admission money then scamper off down Albyn Place to a seat in the stalls, to ride away in the excitement of the Wild West or swoon over Betty Grable or June Allyson. Occasionally the housemaster, George E.C. Barton, would concede to the attractions of First Division football but, even when he didn't, his eagle eye was still capable of spotting us on the terracings of Pittodrie from his own special seat in the grandstand.

On this particular Saturday afternoon, a cold, late-autumn day, Aberdeen were playing away from home and the choice of entertainment was to be the Odeon Cinema in Justice Mill Lane. Off I set down Albyn Place with two shillings in my pocket in the company of my friend from Buchan, Alastair Crombie, whose doctor father had seen me into the world. At the corner of Holburn Junction we were distracted by a call from a doorway. It was a sailor asking if we would care to earn a couple of bob by delivering a message. We would have to take a letter to a certain house, wait to see if there was a reply and bring it back to the same place at a given time. Swayed by the prospect of earning two bob instead of spending it (pocket-money at Sillerton was less than extravagant) we agreed and set out for a district which had a mixed reputation. Down Union Street we went and along George Street, branching into a housing area known as Froghall. It was a slum-clearance district, it seemed, but even then deteriorating into the sort of condition from which the inhabitants had so recently moved. We climbed the communal staircase, gripped by a sleazy excitement in this rather sinister setting so different from our own native corner of the county. Nervously we knocked on the door which was opened by a woman of brittle appearance who took the letter and disappeared inside. From the doorway, a couple of fourteen-year-olds, slightly apprehensive, could see and hear the revelry of a carefree household. The war was over and it was pub-closing time as drunken Servicemen lolled in chairs with women on their knees, exposing legs and thighs and goodness knows what. The woman who took the note returned to say that there would be no reply so we left and hurried back to Holburn Junction for the appointed hour.

The sailor, a smallish, dark, stocky fellow, was already there waiting. We gave him the news and never saw him again. We thought no more of the incident, not even on that December day a few weeks later when I bought an *Evening Express* from Patsy Gallagher's news-stand at the corner of Union Terrace and read about the severed arm. The police were baffled by the discovery. Whose arm was it? Superintendent John Westland, a man of instinct, ordered a check of finger-prints in the police records. It paid off. The prints were those of Betty Hadden, a seventeen-year-old who had once been in some minor trouble. A check at the home of her mother, a certain Kate Hadden whose name was not unknown in Aberdeen, revealed that Betty had in fact been missing from home for several days. But further checks showed that she had been seen at the city's Castlegate on the eve of the grisly find, only a few hours before the piercing noise that rent the northern air. She had been seen with sailors . . .

She had been seen with sailors and she had close friends in the Froghall district. A youth had been known to carry a message to her, apparently at a dance hall, and the police appealed to the youth to come forward. I knew that I was not that youth, though the description was similar, but from the hazy recollection of the name on the envelope, I had carried a note to someone who could have been Betty Hadden or a friend of hers who had an address in Froghall. The police were anxious to trace sailors and I had a clear picture of the one at Holburn Junction. The case was building up. Alastair and I sat on our secret, nervously protecting ourselves with silence. To admit that the route to the Odeon Cinema that Saturday afternoon had been exchanged for what was possibly an involvement in the prelude to a ghastly murder would have been the likeliest of all short-cuts to expulsion from Sillerton House—and my academic performance was already deteriorating from a starting-point of mediocrity. So the silence was maintained while sailors on boats were followed to the ends of the earth.

No clues were found. The killer of Betty Hadden, it seemed, had done his job quickly, clinically and cleverly. He had probably disposed of the body in a trunk but was unable to tuck in the surplus arm. So he sawed it off and carelessly disposed of it in the river. There were those who believed that the murderer was a local person who knew the lie of the land, a quiet inhabitant of Torry who continued perhaps to live out his life with an air of respectability. The file on Betty Hadden is still there in all its macabre mystery and covered with question marks at Grampian Police headquarters in Queen Street, Aberdeen.

The severed forearm was bottled and labelled for posterity by Professor R.D. Lockhart at the anatomy department of the University of Aberdeen. Several years after his retirement, however, the arm was thrown out in a general disposal of materials at the department, an action which surprised many people, not least Professor Lockhart. It was the last link with the good-time girl with the long, dark hair who will take her very special place in North-East criminal history.

The Press was full of it, of course, and by then I was so intrigued by newspapers that I would stand outside the offices of *The Press and Journal* in Broad Street and gaze in wonder that such a plain and shabby building could house the names and traditions of one of the oldest publications in existence. At that time the *Evening Express*, published in the same building, was running one of the most controversial columns of its day, a page of snappy snippets, informative, critical and provocative under the name of Jack Adrian. There were few people in the North-East at that time who did not know of Jack Adrian, whose real identity turned out to be Edward F. Balloch, a Turriff boy who had started his journalistic career with *The Banffshire Journal*, under a noted editor of the day called Dr Barclay, before joining Aberdeen Journals, which was owned by Lord Kemsley. Heading off to London, Eddie Balloch had become the blue-eyed boy of the Kemsley reporting team, covering major events around the world and risking his neck on at least one occasion in order to get his story back to London ahead of his rivals (in those days before television the newspaper 'scoop' mattered a great deal more than it does today). He was following the Duke of Windsor and Mrs Simpson across Europe on one of those interminable train journeys when he tumbled upon a story which had to be despatched at great speed if it was to catch the morning paper. Faced with several hours before the next stop, he jumped from the moving train and ended up with a variety of cuts and bruises—and a proper scoop in the following morning's paper.

In his mid-thirties he was back in his native North-East, apparently being groomed for the top job at Aberdeen Journals, at that time occupied by a wily old bird called William Veitch, who had been a well-known Parliamentary correspondent in his day. In the event, Balloch did not wait for that promotion but all this information was to come my way a few years later when I followed my own determination in defiance of doctors and went in pursuit of my cherished ambition—a job as a journalist.

CHAPTER ELEVEN

THE TURRA COO

That troublesome heart condition had brought a shaking of heads and second opinions, cardiographs, blood tests and a year of idleness during which I lay helpless in that blistering heat of 1947. The medical message was clearly that, if I were ever to work at all—and that was doubtful—it would have to be in a sedentary position. My own view was simply that, if life was to be as short as all that, I must spend it in the journalism which had been my only choice since childhood.

Glamorous figures like Eddie Balloch had become my heroes but their glossy world of the thirties had been replaced by a post-war austerity in which openings were practically non-existent and firms were struggling to re-employ journalists for whom there was nothing to do because of the newsprint crisis and the consequence of four-page papers. But the *Turriff Advertiser* needed a boy and the persistent pesterings of a loon from Maud, which were already well known to every newspaper in the land, were finally conveyed to the proprietors by John Hardie of *The Press and Journal*.

After months in bed it was a distinct pleasure just to walk again, to breath in the tang of the land and even to raise a protective collar against the Nor'east blast which swept mercilessly over the plains of Buchan and did something to the human character.

The sheer joy of being alive was intensified that March day of 1948 by the prospect of gaining a toe-hold on the profession which had stirred within me dreams of glass palaces. But the Beaverbrooks, Northcliffes and Kemsleys were a distant cry from the joiner's yard which served as the editorial entrance to the *Turriff Advertiser*, through which I passed en route to the most important interview of my life, having travelled the fifteen miles across Buchan by bus. Through the doorway I surveyed an old flat-bed printing machine upon which a chase was being laboriously shuttled back and fore, inking itself on virgin sheets of paper which were in turn whisked into a neat pile by a fly-leaf. There I gazed upon the fundamentals of printing and from there I was directed upstairs via a wooden contraption which opened on to the composing room, where one man sat at the solitary type-setting machine. Two others were picking type from boxes, as we had done as children, and spelling them into words in slotted handgrips. There was an atmosphere of molten lead and slow but certain industry as setting got under way for the weekly issue on Friday. One small corner was partitioned off and marked 'Editor' though I hesitated to enter in case it was merely his W.C. Much as I wanted to meet the gentleman, I preferred to start the interview unflushed! The room was of appropriate size, with one seat and an abundance of paper but it was nevertheless the editor's room, his inner and only sanctum, strewn with papers and proofs, paste and scissors, a cold cup of tea and an ashtray of dottle. From the midst of the clutter there emerged the editor, his eager eyes popping out of thick glasses as he focussed on the intruder who had disturbed his daily doze. He turned out to be an Englishman with a fine moustache, a dainty wife and new-born twins but the power of hire and fire lay with the proprietor, William D. Peters, who strode in with brown hat squarely on his head, pipe just as squarely in his mouth and bree oozing freely from the weeks.

'Ye're wantin' a job?' he confirmed gruffly. 'Can ye dae shorthand?' I had to confess that I couldn't. 'But I'll soon learn', I replied hopefully. A laconic exchange ended in a mixture of pathos and comedy with the old man turning to his son Bob, a delicate man who had crept unnoticed upon the proceedings, and saying: 'Well, what dae ye think?' 'Oh, I suppose he'll dae a' richt,' was the opinion which summed me up as a definite risk but one which could, with a little daring, be taken. Persistence pays off in this life so I landed the job and travelled back to Maud, elevated out of my skin to a cloud of joy, which says a lot about my condition considering I was travelling in one of Burnett's old buses. I wouldn't have called the King my cousin. 'Foo muckle are they gyan' tae pey ye?' was my father's first question, having never regarded it as anything but 'a damned tippence-ha'penny bugger o' a job' at the best.

Pay me? Nobody had mentioned paying me anything but what was money anyway? The world was obsessed with it. Well, for a start it was the stuff you paid landladies with and that taught me a fundamental lesson in life—that there is nothing like hard economics for bringing a man to his senses.

That Sunday night I settled in the household of Jim Anderson and his wife Mary at 31 Woodlands Crescent, Turriff, and felt that the world was not such a bad place after all. Mary was a homely woman of ample girth and rosy cheeks from being brought up on the Hill of Tollo, where only the hardy survived. Jim was one of a breed, lean, pale and wiry, a man of considerable knowledge and intelligence who should have been in a job of some responsibility. Instead he was a labourer, sometimes digging roads, sometimes in the harvest field, but ill at ease with his lot and finding some consolation in the *Daily Worker* which he read avidly. He was also a keen betting man, in common with many other people in Turriff, which was surely one of the most gambling-ridden towns in the land at that time. Jim would place a regular and judicious bet and make knowing forecasts that a fourteen-year-old apprentice jockey by the name of Lester Piggott was going to be one of the greatest riders of all time. Whatever one might have said about the *Daily Worker*, there was no denying the skill of its racing tipster. Jim's enthusiasm, however, was no greater than that of his wife who knew a horsey better than most. She depended on more Right Wing sources for her information, thoroughly disapproving of her husband's interest in the 'Worker'.

On my first night, Jim and I settled down at opposite sides of the fireside to take a long, broad look at the world. Real chief-like we were with our grand gestures and sweeping statements and me, at last, a worker with sixteen years of life behind me and therefore equipped with all the answers to life's problems (the doubts come later). We involved everyone from Jesus Christ to Robert Burns in establishing the brotherhood of man, which was coming yet, for a' that and a' that, and it might have seemed only a matter of time before we raised the Red Flag on the Braes of Turra. But the revolution never did materialise and all that happened was that W. D. Peters looked round the door of the editorial doocot and said that he had not mentioned pay but he would wait until the end of the week to decide what I was worth. That attitude, however bluntly put, was wholly in line with my own idealistic view that a man's reward in life should be linked with his value to society. If I were ever tempted to desert a noble opinion it was at the end of that first week when my worth was assessed at thirty shillings, less 1s 11d for National Insurance, which left 28s 1d to pay Mrs. Anderson (35s), bus fares home at the week-end (2s 6d), not to mention pocket money. It took no great feat of accountancy to deduce that I was a pound out of pocket before I started, which could hardly be described as nature's incentive to personal saving. But my father, whose hard head was offset by a generous heart, undertook to make good the deficit and I was soon immersing myself in the life of a country newspaper with the financial problem at least temporarily solved.

Ronald Scott Hutton, the editor, found me a willing worker, running round the town, upstairs and downstairs as often as Willie Winkie, eagerly ferreting out the items which made up the *Turriff Advertiser* every week. If I should be found lacking in a knowledge of death or whist drives (is there a difference?), police courts, Women's Guilds or cattle shows then it was not for the want of experience. On my first week Ronald Scott Hutton sent me to collect some details about an elderly gentleman from Duff Street who had been called to higher service. A kindly lady showed me into the best room in which the dim light from drawn curtains was made even dimmer by the fact that I had just come in from the sunshine. As she went to fetch a closer relative I leaned gently against the sideboard and hastened to readjust my eyes to the light in the room. One by one I picked out the dining table, tea trolley, pictures, sideboard . . . *sideboard*? I was leaning on it was I not? My sudden swerve of verification was met by the waxen face of a man I had never seen alive but who was finding it not too late for a faintly amused smile at my expense. In the lily-white calm of his coffin he must have seemed just that degree nearer to life than the chattering object which shot out to the lobby to be met by a bewildered relative, who had all the details jotted down on a piece of paper. I left with scarce a word of thanks and returned to our editorial doocot, a trembling slip of a boy, having learned a little sooner than I would have chosen that life on a newspaper is not all gloss and glamour. Hawking the town and countryside for twelve or fourteen hours a day, however, was mainly a joy, even at the subsidised level of thirty bob a week.

Ronald Scott Hutton spent his time in the office, writing feature material but in between times he would break off to relate some of his weird experiences in the East during the war, which was nearly three years past. He would tell of terrible things that happened at the docks when ships came in and there was the tale about the donkey in the Middle East and off I would go on my rounds, bewildered by some of his fantastic stories.

But a most unholy row blew up one Saturday morning between W. D. Peters and Ronald Scott Hutton with the result that the little editor made such a hasty departure that I never did see him again. It took time to dawn on me that following Monday when I turned up for work that I was now, to all intents and purposes, the editor of the *Turriff Advertiser* at the age of sixteen. Among the pleasurable discoveries I had made in my short time at Turriff was that the Balloch family had a financial interest in the paper and that Eddie Balloch's mother, who lived in the town, was proud to open up her scrapbook to show me the evidence of her son's escapades. From the distance of Aberdeen he himself proceeded to bolster my juvenile editorship by supplying some splendid material to help the family out. He sent a provocative series about bygone days in the town, written in longhand, with a note of guidance and encouragement. When the reality of my new-found status finally dawned, I was not averse to stretching back on a chair, putting my feet on the desk and drawing heavily on an imaginary cigar. I would emphasise a point to my sylph-like secretary and summon one of my lackeys from the far end of the room to fly to Foggieloan (all of seven miles away) on a dangerous assignment. It was a creditable performance but the show was soon over when I realised that I had an admiring audience of two office girls at an upstairs window across the lane. Reporting duties of the Hutton era were now extended to feature writing and sub-editing. On publication night, which was Thursday, I stayed behind to help fold papers as they were churned from Robbie Cameron's flat-bed machine. When the process ground to a halt in the dead of night and Turriff folk were dreaming about who would win the 2.30 at Newmarket, I tramped round the streets in the cold, dank hours of Friday morning, leaving bundles of 'Advertisers' at shop doors. Then I would head home to Mrs Anderson's in Woodlands Crescent, drop into bed and hardly have time to reflect on this tough but exciting life before drifting into the blissful sleeps of youth.

The big event in the social calendar was the Turriff Show, one of the biggest and best agricultural events in Scotland. It took place, and still does, on the first Tuesday of August when the cream of cattle, horses, sheep and poultry would gather from far and wide to be groomed and pampered, judged and paraded for all of 20,000 people to see. Stock pens were ranged on one side and rows of agricultural machinery on the other and throughout the forenoon the bustle of activity would rise with the morning sun, stockmen in their white coats holding high the aristocratic heads of Aberdeen-Angus bulls which would collect their pedigree prizes, to be proudly displayed alongside other 'firsts' collected at New Deer or Tarland or even the Royal Highland Show, and would surely go on to complete the triumph at Keith on the following Tuesday. By now the town's folk and villagers and others whose knowledge of the finer points of animal progeny was confined to a fillet-steak on a dinner plate came trekking down the brae to the Haughs, which was a splendid natural setting for a public spectacle. They would come in time for the parade of prize-winning stock, great cumbersome beasts swinging their virility from side to side with total lack of modesty or inhibition. Then the sports programme got under way with the travelling circus of heavyweight athletes throwing hammers, putting shots and tossing cabers, decked out in obligatory kilts and semmits and emitting great grunts of effort and satisfaction as their implements took off in various directions. Side by side with brute strength, little madams in kilts and ruffles stepped on to a board supported by lemonade boxes and competed for Highland Dancing medals, all very colourful and coquettish and entertaining if you like that sort of thing but conducted with a deadly seriousness which was almost frightening, especially if you were a judge and fell foul of some of the mothers. They tended to be a toughish breed from down-town Aberdeen who found it hard to accept that their dancing darlings might possibly have been out-done by some other fleet-footed flinger.

Turriff Show, like its neighbouring rival at Keith, was a place for horse-racing, not exactly within the rules of the Jockey Club but fast and exciting nevertheless with fearful rivalries among owners who roared terrifying threats at horses and jockeys as they spun around the limited showring circuit. Then there would be novelty displays by trick cyclists and historical pageants presented on moving lorries by ladies of the Womens' Rural Institute; tug o' war teams arrayed their muscular force at either end of an unsuspecting rope and heaved and lifted to the roars and counter-roars of partisan spectators. So there would be cycle races and slow cycle races and musical chairs for car-drivers, then as the day wore late and folk gathered up their belongings and meandered up through the braes of Turriff the scene was left to the younger fry to fill the large marquee at night. There they would dance till the floor-boards dirled to the beat of a thousand feet and the beer would flow and here and there a fight would break out. But at the end of it all, Nature worked her skeely process of human selection and young folk made the excuse of a warm night to wander off, two by two, along the banks of the Turra Burn to kiss and cuddle and God knows what.

I had been there as a child in the thirties and now I was there as a reporter in the late forties, recording one particular show which was washed out by the most torrential summer rain the North-East had seen this century. Bravely the organisers carried on through a limited programme, led by the stout heart of Niven Paterson, but it was an impossible task. The sheer misery of the day was perhaps best conveyed by my father, who was never short of a descriptive phrase and who recalled of the occasion that 'the watter wis rinnin' oot the erse o' ma breeks'. In those days Turriff still had an abundance of witnesses to the most notorious incident in the whole history of the district, the story of the Turra Coo, which put the name of Turriff in newspaper headlines around the world. I had the good fortune to hear it from Bertie Reid, a local auctioneer who had left school in time to become orra-loon at the farm of Lendrum, helping with the job of looking after the famous cow.

It happened in 1913, after Lloyd George had introduced National Insurance to the British public. Robbie Paterson, the farmer at Lendrum, near Turriff, and a man of some substance, felt that the new insurance should not apply to farm servants and he made his stand by refusing to stamp the card when it was presented by one of his employees. The law stepped in to impound some item which could be sold to raise the money which Robbie should have been paying and they settled on his distinctive white cow. Foolishly, they took it to the town square of Turriff and offered it for public auction, a much publicised event which drew out large crowds and offered a splendid opportunity for a riot. That opportunity was not ignored and in the ensuring disorder the auctioneer was pelted with a hail of divots and assorted missiles, the police sergeant was struck on the eye with an egg, fireworks were let off and the bewildered cow released to run free.

Finally, it was taken to Aberdeen and sold through the auction ring but a group of farmers traced the animal and brought it back to the town square of Turriff, where the riot had taken place. Headed by the Turriff Brass Band playing 'Jock o' Hazeldene', the cow was paraded before a crowd of 4,000 people, with anti-Lloyd George slogans on its flanks, and there it was handed over to Robbie Paterson by Archie Campbell of Auchmunziel as a gift of appreciation from his fellow-farmers. The great Scott Skinner wrote a tune called 'The Turra Coo', for that was how it became known, the most famous cow in the world, even if it was not much of a milker, living out its days in peace and distinction till it died in 1919 and was buried at Lendrum where its memorial stands to this day—a memorial not only to a cow but to the North-East farmer who made a notable stand against bureaucracy.

CHAPTER TWELVE

THE ROSE THAT FADED

In the still of a summer's day I travelled along the road from Turriff to Fyvie, ten miles away, to interview the head gardener at Fyvie Castle about the abundance of flowers that year. Fyvie Castle was one of the fine baronial halls of Aberdeenshire, the home of Sir Ian Forbes-Leith, a much respected laird and aristocrat. As the gardener conducted me from one profusion to another the conversation strayed to the family and I happened to mention a legend about the Forbes-Leiths which I had heard from older people. The tale was told that a curse had been spoken by a witch-like creature that no direct male heir would succeed to the title. Subsequent history had, alas, borne out the tale. For several generations, succeeding wars had played a part in ensuring that the eldest son had not, in fact, followed his father. But surely, I said in my suspicion of old wives' tales, this was a matter of pure coincidence. Before the gardener had time to air his views, if indeed he intended to do so, we stopped in our tracks as a man in his early twenties came striding down the path towards us, tall, dark and strapping in the Forbes-Leith tradition, as handsome a fellow as you would find.

'Here's young John, the laird's son,' the gardener said hastily.

'The heir?' I queried.

'Aye. The elder of two sons. There are daughters forbye.'

The man around whose head an evil legend hovered was now beside us, with a courteous acknowledgement of the stranger and a warm word of farewell for the gardener. Then he passed on down the garden, followed by the gaze of two

above: Gavin Greig, my great-grandfather, who became Scotland's greatest ever collector of folk songs.
below: The Marchioness of Aberdeen opens a fete at Brucklay Castle, Maud, in 1934. I am in my mother's arms on left.

left: Coronation Day 1937. In the f
dress parade at Maud, my rajah c
takes second place to the red-whi
and-blue of Sandy Duncan, now
local butcher.

below: Bertie Forbes, the New Yor
millionaire, with my parents.

above: As a young reporter on the *Turriff Advertiser*, with the proprietors, W.D. Peters and his son Bob.
below: Fun at marquee dance after the 'wash-out' Turriff Show of 1949 — with my editor, Donald Noble, brother of Sir Fraser Noble, Principal of Aberdeen University.

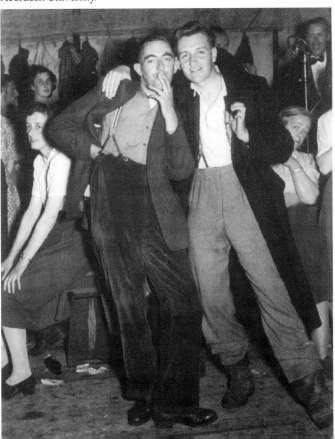

above: My father as thousands remember him, selling cattle at Maud Mart.

below: Honeyneuk Farm, Maud, which my father bought in 1952.

above: My farewell night at Aberdeen Journals, February 1960.
below: A jolly night at the fabulous Forbes party, with the Vice-President of the United States, Senator Hubert Humphrey, Agnes Baird and Gertrude Weiner.

above: With Bing Crosby at Turnberry Hotel.

below: The KOSB reunion in Hawick, with soldiers I had known in 1942-43.

above: The day I brought Mohammed Ali to the Express editorial conference–and he took over from editor Ian McColl.

silent people. As he disappeared through a gate at the bottom, the gardener was telling me: 'He is with the Guards in Malaya. That was him saying "cheerio" afore he goes back the morn.'

No more was said, and perhaps no more needed to be said, as I hurled back in the bus from Fyvie to Turriff that afternoon. A few weeks later I boarded that bus again, back through the Howe of Auchterless and up the brae to Fyvie Parish Kirk, scarcely heeding the view that spread to the gardens of the castle. For I was back with my Bible to attend the funeral service of John Forbes-Leith of Fyvie. Off he had gone that next day as planned, back to the heat and scent and song of the jungle, to a Malayan land which was deep in the throes of guerrilla warfare. And there, of the bullets and grenades which could have found target on so many thousands of British soldiers, there was one which was labelled for the future laird of Fyvie. From foreign fields they brought him for burial to the land of his fathers, where crofters and labourers joined with the rich and aristocratic to pay their last respects to a fine young man. As the great gathering in the Auld Kirk bowed its head in prayer I raised mine and surveyed the scene. Who would have dreamt of it those few weeks ago? What cloud could possibly dim the sunshine of a perfect summer's day, the joy of a godly garden? I slipped quietly away from the kirk to walk alone to the garden of Fyvie Castle, there to stand on the spot where I had stood before. It was as if time had lost its regularity and I was standing there as though never before, with the earlier visit but an imaginary figment rising now to torment and perplex. There was little knowing and even less understanding of the quirks of fate. But the blooms had faded in that bountiful garden and the wind that blew from a chill airt through the howe came echoing like the eerie call of a witch in the night. At such a time you hardly dare wonder if that evil spirit has had her way once more.

In this day and age when everything is scientifically recorded and computerised it is hard to believe that there were elderly people alive not so long ago who were by no means certain of their precise date of birth. Until the middle of last century they were less particular about birth certificates and the matter was made plain to me when I went to visit Mrs Mary Macdonald at Roseacre Cottage, on the outskirts of Turriff, a splendid old lady who reckoned that she had lived on this earth for a hundred years. Her centenary was naturally a matter of interest to the *Turriff Advertiser*, with telegrams from King George VI and so on, and there she sat with a remarkable clarity of mind recalling details of everyday life in the eighteen-fifties. In a memorable hour of her company I became vividly aware of the day-to-day continuity of time which swept away notions of barriers between the ages and turned all history into a throbbing excitement of the things that happened the day before the day before. . . .

One particular incident of her recollection entranced me more than anything. Mrs Macdonald told me of her grand-uncle, whom she remembered as an old man when she was a schoolgirl. He used to take her on his knee and tell her about his travels which took him to the Battle of Trafalgar in 1805 and there he had actually been present at the death of Nelson. Here was a man who had lived at the same time as Robert Burns, our national Bard, with vivid memories of the seventeen-hundreds, and there was I, talking to someone who had had personal contact with such a man. That simple experience gave me a whole new perspective of time. But the natural instinct of a reporter was not satisfied with the situation of a lady who genuinely did not know her own age so I made some inquiries at the appropriate quarter in Edinburgh to see if there was any trace of her birth being recorded. Indeed there was. Mrs Macdonald had, in fact, passed her hundredth birthday on the previous year and was now into her 102nd year! Taking the precaution of all good journalists, I put a pang of guilt behind me and prepared her obituary notice, believing that she would not have many more summers this side of eternity. I tucked it in my wallet in readiness for the day; but I was on holiday in London when I received word of her passing, which could not have been more untimely. I was crossing Westminster Bridge that afternoon when I paused and extracted the final tribute from my wallet. On this same spot, I recalled to myself, Wordsworth raised his head and saw a sight so touching in its majesty. I lowered mine and dropped the tattered little note over the parapet, down, down to be carried off by the gilded waters of the Thames. I permitted myself an ironic smile as it drifted away, like the lady it described, to the great unknown.

Stories like that of Mrs Macdonald were always good for regurgitating to the national daily papers where lineage payments could put a fresh complexion on the personal economics. My connections were with the *Daily Mail* and *Daily Record* but it was from the *Mail* that I gained a lesson which remains of paramount importance to every budding reporter: check your facts. I had not been conscious of any particular lapse when I received a letter one morning from their head office in Edinburgh which said, in effect: 'When sending us items of local news please see that they are not copied directly from local newspapers without checking for accuracy.' I was puzzled. Why tell me this? There was nothing for it but to ring the *Mail*'s office in Aberdeen to see if they could throw any light on the matter. I spoke to Stanley Maxton, a quiet, languid fellow, shrewd observer and fine writer, who merely chuckled at the other end of the line as he began to ease my dismay. That same letter had gone out to all local correspondents and he went on to tell me the delightful story behind it. Evidently some overzealous fellow, in scanning local weekly papers to find material for the *Mail*, had tumbled upon a most human and touching story which was worthy of prominence in any national paper. What a shame, he thought, that such a gem should be confined to the columns of a small-town weekly. So he dutifully removed it from its local setting and re-told it to the *Daily Mail*. It concerned the town bell-ringer who had faithfully rung the bell for most of his life and had become a well-kent figure to generations. But times were changing and the town had decided that it could no longer afford his services. With regret it was terminating his appointment. A lifetime of duty and devotion was coming to an end. However, the old bell-ringer belonged to a generation which cared less about money than about a job well done and he came forward, cap in hand, and offered to continue ringing the bell just for the love of it. The editor of the *Mail* could hardly believe his luck at landing such a wonderful scoop from under the noses of the *Express* and other popular papers. He was not so charmed with life, however, when he learned the real story. Certainly the old gentleman had done all that was said of him. Certainly there would have been no harm in the enthusiastic reporter taking the story from the local paper. But it would have helped to simplify matters if he had noticed that the column in which this human tear-jerker appeared was headed: ONE HUNDRED YEARS AGO.

CHAPTER THIRTEEN

ON TOP OF HER LADYSHIP

I had now lived through that early post-war period when food was still rationed. Sir Stafford Cripps, a brilliant man in many ways, had become the symbol of miserable austerity in his roll as Chancellor of the Exchequer. Everything was under the strictest control. Motor cars were of the pre-war vintage and I can remember the excitement in the streets of Turriff when someone acquired the first of the new Jowett Javelins. A world which had been hemmed in by the most appalling war in all history and an aftermath of depression was crying out for an escape to freedom. Back in Turriff old Willie Peters had his own minor economic dilemma; by 1950 he was due to pay me the princely sum of £3.00 a week but that was the starting-point for income-tax so he came up with the ingenious solution of paying me just £2.19s. In that way, he said, I would lose nothing and he would save the shilling which would normally have been paid to the Inland Revenue. All was well. But at the age of nineteen and after two-and-a-half years in Turriff I was now ready for the wider world of journalism and that meant turning my eyes once more to the offices of Aberdeen Journals which, despite their dingy appearance, represented the urgency and excitement of the daily paper. There was a fine sense of history about the building which housed *The Press and Journal* and the *Evening Express*, the creaky staircase and the musty smell of the old library and the fact that Robert Burns himself had once visited the place. Side by side with the past came the modern bustle and energy, the daily need to write tonight what would be read in the morning. The corn might still be growing out of my ears but I was filled with a new-found enthusiasm.

The essence of Aberdeen had already been absorbed during

my days at Gordon's College—the cold welcome of the granite; the noble sweep of Union Street, its imaginative construction on top of arches putting Aberdeen a century ahead in town planning; the thin voices of the waitresses, the waft of fish from the market and smoke from the Joint Station; the adjacent array in Rosemount Viaduct of the Public Library, the South Church, His Majesty's Theatre and the old Schoolhill Station, more easily remembered as 'education, salvation, damnation and railway station'. Aberdeen was clean and clinical. Its hospitals were set where hospitals ought to be set, in their own grounds and far from the sort of muck and pollution and noise which must have made places like Glasgow Royal Infirmary something of a doctor's dilemma. *The Press and Journal* was set in Broad Street, which happened to be one of the narrowest streets in the city, but even Aberdeen must have its little jokes.

I found myself part of a reporting staff which was a good mixture of experienced older hands like John Dunbar, energetic ones in their twenties, like George Hutcheon, Jimmy Menzies, Jimmy Lees and Ethel Simpson and a few chaps just down from university like Peter Chambers and John Lodge, who was to become a special friend. One fellow asked me where I had come from and when I said Turriff he looked at me as if I might be the Turra Coo itself and said 'Good God, another junior? It's experience they're needing here'. I cleared my throat of a turnip and apologised for the straw in my left lughole. His long scarf, I may say, was dangling invitingly near his thrapple; but mercifully he was an exception.

At *The Press and Journal* and *Evening Express* there was such an array of talented and experienced sub-editors as has ever graced a British newspaper, men of the stature of Sandy Meston, Jimmy Gilchrist and Jimmy Grant, intellectual self-educated giants like George Ritchie and Andrew Ingram, a man with a fine bald dome who had worked in India at the time of Eric Linklater and who taught me once and for all the essential difference between my split infinitives and my

108

dangling participles. They were men who shaped a newspaper with speed and efficiency, gaining the final accolade as Scotsmen extraordinary by working through Hogmanay Night up to the midnight bells, laying down their pencils to rise and shake hands and wish each other 'A Happy New Year' before resuming work on the issue of January 1, which was still a publication day in those earlier times. At quieter moments in the dead of night they would stretch back in their chairs and recall great events and memorable men who put them into words. There were stories of many a notable reporter who would spend his life between the office and pub, including one John Sleigh, who dressed immaculately in black coat, tie and bowler and never failed to add the final glow of perfection from within. No one knew for certain how long John had been in newspapers but his working years had certainly stretched back from the Second World War to the Tay Bridge disaster of 1879 and maybe further. Much whisky and soda had flowed under the bridge since he first put pen to unsteady paper. His timelessness was once reflected by a colleague who wrote a parody of John Sleigh to the tune of 'John Peel'. A typical stanza ended:

> And when the Ten Commandments got their first big shak'
> He gave Moses half-a-column in the mornin'.

John was tailor-made for society weddings and funerals. On one occasion he was sent to report on the burial of a well-known aristocratic lady from Deeside whose age had long remained a mystery. John was despatched with express instructions to glance at the coffin lid which, in Scotland, had always carried the name and age of the deceased. But John had adjourned to the local hostelry before the interment and was amply lubricated before joining the mourners at the graveside. He was idly listening to the words he had heard so often before, when the finality of 'earth to earth, dust to dust' jogged him into the hazy realisation that he had not looked at the coffin lid. Elbowing his way through the assembled dignitaries, raising his bowler hat in apology, John got down on hands and knees to peer into the grave. It was at that moment of poignancy that John Barleycorn tipped the balance for John Sleigh and sent him toppling headlong on top of her ladyship in her last resting place. The living were appalled and there was, to put it mildly, a sequel back at Broad Street. Canny Deeside folk were thoroughly amused, however, and some winked and said it was the first time her ladyship had ever had a man on top of her; such a pity the opportunity had arrived when she could no longer respond. Older men swore the tale was true and they proceeded to tell another which proved that John Sleigh survived his premature entry to the grave, even if it brought him deep disgrace. Once again John was despatched to Deeside, for a society wedding this time, and not seeking to break the habit of a lifetime he topped up with some human anti-freeze before adjourning to the church. But nature has its necessities and John had to decide which side of the church the bride and her father would traverse when arriving for the ceremony. Having decided, he then chose the opposite side as the venue for his relief. But alas the judgment was at fault. As the bride walked sedately with her father along John's side of the kirk, the inimitable journalist doffed his bowler hat as a mark of respect and an attempt at camouflage and there he stood, eyes fixed ahead, with the dignity of a soldier holding to his post in the face of adversity. Nothing finer had been seen since the Relief of Mafeking.

But the characters of journalism had not all passed away by 1950 (if indeed they have passed away even now) and it was my great fortune to have close encounter with at least one of them. You reached him in a glory-hole into which no light was allowed to penetrate, a dingy, mysterious room piled high with papers and reference books, galley proofs and a general disorder that had the pungent smell of age. There he sat, a fine Dickensian figure, his bulky outline slumped in a chair, long straggly hair sprouting over his ears and disappearing over the collar of an old raincoat which he wore incessantly, or so it seemed. His name was Allan Taylor and it saddens me to think that it will mean little to any but a few. For if Robert Boothby should have been in the thick of world politics, Allan Taylor should have been one of the legendary columnists of Fleet Street or editor of *The Times*. Here was a great conglomeration of humanity built into one man, the shrewdest brain I ever encountered, keen, perceptive, with a mischievous sense of humour, a resounding voice and a large face which the world would have judged as ugly but which was such an adventure of character elements as to make it a study in itself. But it was the wisdom of that head which intrigued me most of all, the brilliant thoughts which leaped out through an eloquent tongue, not only for the benefit of men like Boothby, who valued his opinions more than most, but for young reporters like Jimmy Kinnaird and myself.

If we worshipped at his feet it was because we knew we were unlikely to meet his kind again. A fondness for the bottle had blighted his early career and there he was, not in the higher echelons of Fleet Street but in the comparative obscurity of Peterhead, that wind-blown town on the North-East coast where the choice of Scotland's criminals are sent to cool off for anything up to a lifetime. His job was the editorship of *The Buchan Observer*, a journal he enriched with a standard of writing hardly known to any other local paper in the land. That the powerful prose of such a mind had to share pages with whist drives and fish prices, circulating to a few thousand people in one small corner of Britain was ludicrous. All Britain should have been sharing in his puckish humour, every politician exposed to his analyses and proddings of pomposity. He was as much at home with politics and philosophy as he was with music, art and the dramas of Ibsen but the subject above all which fascinated him as player and writer, as it did Neville Cardus, was cricket. He perceived in the game a whole range of standards and qualities which he could portray as a basis for living. Allan Taylor was the son of plain folk who apprenticed him to a lawyer's office in Aberdeen as the best they could do for a clever boy. In his musty den he would tell me of a peculiarity that dogged his early life. Even great men must have their phobias and his was a totally irrational horror of being 'tagged'. His lawyer bosses thought he could go far in law but he dreaded being known as 'Taylor the lawyer'. He might have chosen any one of many careers but each one carried a tag and that somehow tethered his spirit. Ironically, the label he dreaded most of all was 'journalist' yet that was what he became, working in Laurencekirk before moving to Peterhead in 1926. There, alas, people were more inclined to discuss his alcoholic than his mental capacity though he mastered the former in the twilight of his days.

He was an elderly man before I knew him well enough to impose upon his time but I sought his company unashamedly in the hope that contact with his electricity might conduct even a modicum of his power into my own being. The opportunity to do so came at the age of twenty when William Veitch asked me to take charge of the Buchan district office of Aberdeen Journals at Peterhead. With the help of two other reporters, Andrew C. Buchan and Gordon Argo, I covered the local scene from councils and courts to football and fish prices, working till all hours and sometimes tailing off a long day in the office overlooking the Broadgate, eating a fish supper from Luigi Zanre's and listening to Pete Murray on Radio Luxembourg. As often as not, however, you would find me in the company of Allan Taylor. There were nearly fifty years of difference in our ages but the power of his personality overcame all, the vast geography of his face creasing to reveal a few decaying tusks, his eyes dancing with original mischief. He would tell great tales of local political battles in the twenties and thirties, of the coming of Boothby and the antics of the foxy little Socialist, Max Schultze, a brilliant man of German birth who found himself, invidiously, in the role of Peterhead's Provost in 1939 as we went to war with his native country. (His herring-curing family, disliking Prussian militarism, had moved from

112

the Baltic to live in Peterhead about 1885 and the richness of his culture came partly from his grand-aunt, Malvinia von Meysenbug, the poetess who befriended Richard Wagner and was buried in Rome beside two more of her friends, Shelley and Keats.)

Then Allan Taylor would go farther back to his days at Laurencekirk when he had travelled by train to Stonehaven to attend courts and council meetings, returning in the late afternoon. One aspect of those days stuck firmly in his mind. On the return journey, schoolchildren from Mackie Academy used to join the train and drop off at their various stations. Often they would share his compartment, joking, jostling youngsters always up to their tricks. But in the melee there was one boy who was noticeable as the outling, the quiet one who did not enter into the fun. So he became the butt of many a prank and other boys would hold his head between his knees all the way from Stonehaven to Fordoun. Allan Taylor took special note of the quiet boy who accepted punishment with such good humour, smiling philosophically as if he had some hidden advantage over those bantering youngsters. The lad had big ears and seemed to have them poised for the sounds around him, listening and absorbing. Then a compositor would burst in with an interruption and we changed the subject.

'Why have you never written a book?' I used to challenge him. 'You have so much to offer and your style of writing is so readable.'

'I've tried my hand at plays, three-act ones,' he would say, 'but I can never get past the second act.'

'But the novel,' I said. 'This area is crying out for a book. Why don't you write it?'

He leaned back heavily in his chair and surveyed me as if I had just unveiled one of his secrets.

'I haven't told many people but I did once begin. Yes, I thought I was writing rather a good book about this North-East corner; a novel it was, just the sort of thing you have in mind. That was back in the early thirties, just about the time you were being born, laddie.'

'And what happened to that?'

'Well a peculiar thing happened. I was just about finished when a new book appeared on the market, a novel about the North-East of Scotland. It was called *Sunset Song* and it was written by Lewis Grassic Gibbon. Well man, I read that book and I read it again and I realised that everything I had been trying to say about the North-East had now been said a great deal more eloquently by Grassic Gibbon. So I tore up the manuscript and I've never tried writing another novel.'

I was pondering the misfortune of one brilliant writer having unwittingly thwarted another, when Allan Taylor was speaking again. 'Man, there was just one thing I forgot to tell you. Remember the boy in the train, him that was aye listening and watching? Well I did take the trouble to find out his name. It was James Leslie Mitchell and I need hardly tell you that that turned out to be the real name of Lewis Grassic Gibbon.'

Sunset Song had been followed by *Cloud Howe* in 1933 and *Grey Granite* in 1934 and by the following year, while barely thirty-four, Grassic Gibbon was dead, having failed to rally from a stomach operation. So a great voice of Scotland was silenced for ever, except for an echoing legacy of words and story which the public is only beginning to elevate to its proper place in literature. Allan Taylor's story sharpened my interest in the North-East's greatest writer. Apart from reading his books I came to know his widow, Rebecca, his brother John and several of his friends. Not least, I went on a private pilgrimage to Arbuthnott Kirkyard with his old schoolmaster, Alexander Gray, who, just as my own great-grandfather had fostered the talent of Bertie Forbes, encouraged the young Mitchell when he showed signs of a talent for writing. He was just the boy from the little croft of Bloomfield up the road, come of hard-working country folk who were hewers of wood, drawers of water but seldom readers of books. Old man Mitchell had been scandalised that a son of his should want to write for a living instead of following the tradition of the land and doing something useful. But Alexander Gray took me back to his own house in Stonehaven and turned out a school exercise book which he kept to the day he died and which showed clearly that there were no two careers for James Leslie Mitchell. He was only twelve when he wrote this piece of description in an essay. Little wonder Alexander Gray blinked when he read it: 'What an irresistible feeling of power comes when, on a calm clear night, you gaze up at the millions of glistening worlds and constellations which form the Milky Way. 'Tis then, and then only, that one can realise the full power of the Creator and the truth of the wild dream of the German poet. There is no beginning, yea, even as there is no end.'

The words of an untutored country loon aged twelve! Gray took pride in giving the boy the books which would help develop his talents and took equal pride in telling me about the success of his old pupil. Away he had gone from school to be a reporter in Aberdeen and Glasgow. But his interest in prehistoric times led him into the forces so that he could travel to the Middle East. Years of obscurity at least gave him time to ponder the past and study the relics and finally to turn out a dozen books.

Grassic Gibbon returned to his native North-East and had a reunion with his brother John, a man of no literary leanings at all who chaffed him about his writing and threw out a challenge which can hardly be discounted in any appraisal of Scottish letters. 'With all this damned writing you do, Leslie, why don't you write about your own homeland?'

Leslie just laughed and said aye, maybe it wasn't a bad idea. Whether or not he had it in mind already, he went straight back to his base in Welwyn Garden City and turned out *Sunset Song* in six weeks. It became the first part of the now famous trilogy called *A Scots Quair*. He was already the acquaintance of men like H. G. Wells and by 1934 was making his way as a successful writer. That summer he came north for what was to be his last visit to his native land. By now he had a car and his father's disgust at a son who had chosen a worthless career now turned to sarcasm about 'getting up in the world', with a fine motor car and rising above his old father. There was no pleasing old Mitchell so Leslie spent much of his last visit with Mr and Mrs Gray, who had now moved to Echt, and there in the schoolhouse garden, during that fine clear summer of 1934, he put the finishing touches to *Grey Granite*. Sitting in a deck-chair out on the green he closed his notebook and said, 'Well well, Mrs Gray, that's the end of *Grey Granite* but I dinna expect you'll think as much o't as you did o' the other two.' He drove off back to London with his friend Cuthbert Graham, later to be features editor of *The Press and Journal*, back to his publisher and back to a stomach operation which seemed like a routine matter. Tragically, he did not regain consciousness on the operating table. They brought his ashes back to Arbuthnott Kirkyard, just down the road from the school where he had shown that first glimmer of genius, and there we were, the dominie and I, standing at the headstone and reading the epitaph:

> The kindness of friends
> The warmth of toil
> The peace of rest

words from that closing passage of *Sunset Song* which can move a man to tears. Scottish poetess Helen Cruickshank was there that cold bright burial afternoon in February, 1935, and she described how she looked around at the farming folk who had come from all over the Mearns to see Leslie's ashes interred, wondering whether they would ever understand him as he had understood them. She looked at his father 'with a face like Saint Andrew of Scotland' and his mother with her lined face working nervously, conquering her tears, and she thought of them going home to unyoke the shelt, milk the kye, feed the hens and 'to know the balm that is released from the soil, without knowing that they knew it'.

I am told that old Mitchell realised only when it was too late that he had sired a genius, perhaps Scotland's greatest-ever writer, and he broke his heart as privately as a dour North-East man must, and did not long survive his loon.

From Grassic Gibbon's own place of the sunset Mr Gray turned his gaze across the steaming soil of the Mearns, with its parks and peesies, the folk still working their crofts and the hills beyond. His pupil had given voice to them all. As I followed his gaze across the land so still and enduring I was thinking too of Allan Taylor, himself now gone from a life that had endowed him with gifts but little luck, a life that burned brightly with joy and humour and humanity as a life must if it is to shield itself from hardship. His wife Phyllis was stone-blind but to the end of his day he had cared for her and her house-work with devotion, lightening her days and softening the memory of the brilliant daughter they had bred and reared to academic glory before she wandered one day to a tragic death on the rocky coasts of Buchan. When his blind widow was left alone and helpless she came to live in Maud Hospital, which looked after the aged and chronic sick. I went to visit her regularly, feeling that the little attention was at least a token return of the debt which could never be repaid. One day, breaking off from reminiscences of her childhood in Egypt in the eighteen-eighties when her father was helping to build the Suez Canal, she gripped my arm and said she had never visited her husband's grave. On the following Sunday I drove up to the hospital and said we were going to Peterhead. With a firm grip of Allan Taylor's silver-topped walking staff she seated herself in the car and we motored the fourteen-mile journey to the cemetery. Alas, I was to discover that, among all the headstones and fancily-carved memorials to so many ordinary mortals, there was none to mark the last resting place of Allan R. Taylor. Such is the way of things. But a helpful attendant consulted the record books, led us to the appropriate pathway and then, pacing so many steps forward and so many to the left, said: 'He should be just about here.'

Phyllis Taylor knelt down on the dewy sward and held her own communion with the man who shared those turbulent years. When the two of them had had their say she plucked some greenery from the plot and we formed a posy of flowers and weeds which I had gathered around the cemetery; and there we left Allan Taylor to his anonymity and walked arm in arm, feeling it some consolation perhaps that, in the spreading forest of granite slabs, a great man should be in death as he had been in life—so different from the crowd, so free from that dreaded tag which might have labelled him as lawyer or politician or journalist or even as 'deceased' on a headstone. Such rare human beings do not die while there are those with a moment to remember them.

CHAPTER FOURTEEN

AIKEY FAIR

When the Government engaged Doctor Beeching to apply a surgical knife to the railway lines of this country they went a long way towards cutting the heart out of our village life. For the station was so often the focal point of local activity, the main artery to the outside world. Five trains each way per day brought papers and post, commercial travellers and lowing calves, all in the name of the London and North-Eastern Railway. There was a bustle and excitement at train times for Maud was the junction where the carriages from Aberdeen split into two sections, the one heading for Peterhead and the other for Fraserburgh. Porters would dyst along the platform, calling 'Maud, change for Fraserburgh', and checking carriage doors which were marked 1st and 3rd, for these were deemed to be the classes of rail travel in the days of the steam engine. The fireman sweated black rivulets as he shovelled coal from his tender into the furnace on the footplate to keep the train in steam, while the driver, with an air of adventure about him, leaned nonchalantly with an elbow on his side-vent, winking to folk on the platform and cracking a joke before whistling a blast of steam and pulling his locomotive into a laboured movement which gradually gained momentum till it was scudding round some distant bend, sending back hoots of joy and abandon.

Along those parallel lines, as we have seen, the men went off to war and the wounded came back; children came from Auchnagatt to Maud School and farmers were transported to Friday markets in Aberdeen. Out of it all grew a folklore about the 'Buchan train' which was taken as a synonym for slow and leisurely movement though, heaven knows, in my young day it covered the twenty-eight miles from Maud to Aberdeen in a comfortable fifty minutes, which was fast enough even by much later standards. One of the great characters of the nineteenth century, a man of athletic prowess called Francie Marcus, once challenged the new-fangled contraption to a race and, while he did not exactly win over the full distance, he vowed afterwards that, 'gin I'd gotten her in the Moss o' Byth, I'd hae gi'en the bugger a red face.' (Thereafter Francie devoted his remarkable energies to the fathering of illegitimate children, being called upon by many a farmer with an unmarriageable daughter to sacrifice himself to the duties of human stallion, in the belief that the lassie could only improve the stock with a sire of such admirable physique. Buchan folk, as I have already indicated, are nothing if not practical.)

Of the stories which grew out of the Buchan train, there is one in particular which tells much about the local character. A commercial traveller from England arrived at the Joint Station in Aberdeen one Friday afternoon, en route for Maud. With time to spare, he boarded the Buchan train, found an empty compartment and placed his brief-case and rolled umbrella on a corner seat before withdrawing to the station buffet for a cup of tea. When he finally returned to the train he found to his surprise that it was now jam-packed with brosey farmers on their way home from the Friday mart. Furthermore, his particular compartment was fully occupied with solid men of the soil, his brief-case and umbrella now dismissed to the rack above. Pulling himself up with controlled indignation, but still as polite as the English tend to be, he said, 'Excuse me, gentlemen, when a man puts his brief-case and umbrella on a seat it rather indicates that he has reserved that seat—at least in the part of the world where I come from.' Whereupon the Buchan farmer in the corner, taking his pipe out of his mouth and surveying the Sassenach with measured disdain, replied: 'Ah weel, my mannie, in this pairt o' the world it's erses that coont!'

So the village life revolved around the railway station, with its John Menzies bookstall and refreshment rooms where you could eat or drink amidst the general buzz of activity. The complex of railway lines spread wide into goods sidings, which came into their own on a very special day during the summer holidays every year. That day was Aikey Fair—the first Wednesday after the nineteenth of July—when all roads led to the wooded hillside called Aikey Brae, two miles out of Maud on the way to Peterhead. Aikey Fair was a piece of local history on which I was first instructed by my mother one steaming hot day in 1935 when she took me for a picnic on the embankment overlooking the station. As we tucked into the delicacies of the picnic basket, we watched wave after wave of Clydesdale horses with foals nibbling at their sides as they trekked round the hillside into the village and up the short incline to the station below us. There were scenes of frightening excitement as porter billies, more accustomed to spouting Labour politics than handling animals, struggled with beasts that were sweir to surrender their liberty to the claustrophobic trucks which would take them away to the south. I learned from my mother that they had just been sold at Aikey Fair and I learned, too, the fascinating legend of how it all began.

Somewhere in the mists of history, the story went, a packman was crossing the River Ugie as it flowed from Maud to Old Deer when his foot misjudged a stepping-stone and splash!— he was as far up to his neck as the Ugie will take you. 'A day's business lost,' he cursed as he emerged from the burn like a drookit rat and spread out his wares, as well as his own clothing, to dry. Then country folk came passing along the dusty track nearby on their way to this place or that. When they spotted the packman they stopped for a chat and a view of his colourful wares, for it was not in the nature of those times to pass a man by without at least a greeting, unless he belonged to the horde of beggars who roamed the countryside and terrorised decent folk in those days. Far from being a beggar, he was a genuine trader, perhaps the grand-forefather of the highpowered salesman. As the crowd grew and grew that fateful July day he sensed a most capital opportunity for business. It is said that he sold and sold till, dammit man, he sold his own wheeling drawers before gathering up an empty pack and announcing that he would be back next year, same time, same place. He was as good as his word and, without the preliminary of a dooking, spread out his wares for another day's lucrative business. Word spread from parish to parish in the way of those times and as more people came to buy, more came to sell. It extended up the hillside, known as Aikey Brae (Oakey Brae, the Scots word for 'oak' being 'aik') and soon became an annual fair of increasing importance, the occasion for buying and selling everything from horses to hairpins, settling accounts, taking a hairst fee and clinching them all with a dram. By the middle of last century a short corn in the cap or button-hole had become a sign that a man or woman was out for a fee, with men capable of scything or stackyard work being engaged for the harvest at a substantial £6 to £7, women to gather at £3 to £5 and stout lads to ca' the carts up to £5. Where the crowds would gather you were sure to find the showman so the serious business became levened with all the fun of the fair. Aikey grew to be one of the biggest horse markets in the land, attracting dealers from far and near and there I was, hearing the tale of its beginnings and watching the wise, melancholy creatures being cajoled into their trucks and away to some alien place in the south.

But the story of Aikey Fair does not end there. For many years the show people had arrived on the previous weekend to set up their stalls and amusements in preparation for the Wednesday and, just as those country folk of olden times had gathered to see the packman, so did a later generation roll up to watch the show people at work. Then one Sunday in 1926, an astute showman (perhaps a descendant of the old man?) started up his merry-go-round to test public reaction in an area which had a fair respect for its Sabbath. The crowds stood abashed at first, some edging back lest they be drawn into a desecration of the Lord's Day. But the young, not so conscious of their Maker and itching to have a spin on the roundabout, gave it a second thought and finally threw in their lot with the Devil. Aikey Sunday was born in an instant. It ran side by side with the Wednesday Fair till the workhorse population began to fall away and the emphasis moved more and more to the preceding Sunday. It became known as Scotland's most notorious continental Sunday, totally out of character with its setting in a land of Sabbath faces and all the more intriguing because of it.

Looking back on those Aikey Sundays before the Second World War, I remember especially 1939 when the speak was of Hitler and the young farm servants thought it would be a braw idea to enlist or join the Territorial Army in preference to taking a hairst fee. Older men just shook their heads and said they remembered overmuch about the last time, the million dead and the terrible sights they saw in France. The sun brought a sinister warmth to Aikey that faraway Sunday as I made my way round the hill with my father and mother. We could hear the noise of the funfair before we left the village and as we reached Aikey Brae there was a hot and feverish excitement that such an appealing decadence could so invade our pastoral peace. There were the merry-go-rounds and the gypsy fortune-tellers, dark, knowing ladies in long ear-rings, holding a key to the mysterious future; there were chair-o'-planes and buskers, music blaring and petrol engines spluttering out fumes that rose with the smell of fish and chips and Broch candy and mingled with the purity of parched grass and the scent of heather on the hill. Over the face of the brae a few tink pipers were swigging at bottles and squeezing the pigskin in weird echoes that rang out across the howe till it near minded you of Auld Nick in the Kirk o' Alloway. Nearby a group of evangelists, complete with tracts and megaphones, were in feverish condemnation of this whole dreadful deed, this vulgar insult to the Lord's Day, till they hardly left the Devil with a leg to stand on, poor man. For sure, they said, we were all on the low road to hell when up piped a dry-humoured farm servant and said 'Weel weel man, we're gettin' a gran' day for't'. I could hardly contain my excitement at the rare sight of it all. Down in the howe the whisperings of the River Ugie were drowned for a day and across on the other side, where the childe St Drostan had come to preach, there lay the Cistercian Abbey of Deer, which had fallen into disrepair before being taken over once more by the Roman Catholic Church in 1930. In the gaunt shell, the derelict walls now kept their secrets like silent nuns, calm in the consuming wonder of time, frowning perhaps at a pagan festival across the burn yet conceding that there was something to be said for a gathering which somehow strengthened that continuing thread of rural life. How fitting that men and women should come again on some appointed day to the place where their forefathers joined in revels before them, to keep tryst with the spirit of the land and the people that were of it.

The emotional effect on the child was strong as the day matured and the great red sun was rolling down on the surrounding woods, trimming the firs before drowning in the horizon beyond. It was time to forsake the hillside for another year and make for home, so we gathered our stuff and joined in the general exodus and, as a last glimpse of Aikey, we stopped to catch sight of a young man whose name had a ring of magic, Benny Lynch. All Scotland loved little Benny, the boy from Glasgow Gorbals who had so recently been flyweight boxing champion of the world before losing his title through overweight. Benny had started as a slogger at fairgrounds and on the way to the top had gathered too many hangers-on who quickly landed him back where he began. But Benny had spirit. That sunny day at Aikey Fair he sparred forty-eight rounds with Freddy Tennant and at the end of the day, as we started for home, he was calling defiantly to all who would pause and listen: 'I'll be back—and if I get to the top I'll stay there.' But Benny returned to his back-street slums and chums, never to see the top again and to die a few years later, down-and-out and penniless. So the crowds went home that night, fine and red and sonsy and contented, home to milk the kye and bed

124

down for an early start to the moss, there to cut and set the peats for winter's fuel. It was part of a familiar pattern that had known little change for generations.

But Aikey Fair was only weeks past when Hitler's hell broke loose and the crowds did not gather on the hillside again until 1946 when, despite the great rift in tradition and the gloom of austerity, the farmers still came cheerfully with their horses on the appointed day. But the tractor was now dehumanising the farmstead, ousting the Clydesdale from its place of dignity, and the end of Aikey Wednesday was surely in sight. In 1950 I was there as a young reporter to find that the gathering of horses was down to a mere hundred. The following year it had dropped to sixty. I should have been better prepared in 1952, for the end came more suddenly than anyone expected. Back I went with my notebook and pencil to find that no-one had yet arrived except Peter Grant, the hotelkeeper from Old Deer who was also the feuar of the Aikey land. His refreshment tent was already in position, stocked for a moderate day's business. A few buyers arrived from the south on the forenoon train to Maud and came on by hired car to Aikey Brae. Policemen turned up to regulate the traffic, as had always been the custom. Ten o'clock became eleven o'clock and by noon only one piebald pony had been presented for sale. It came from Willie Barber of Aberdeen and it was sold to another well-known horsey man from Aberdeen, George Ross, for £21.10s. In such ludicrous circumstances and after centuries of high spectacle the great Aikey Fair came abruptly to an end.

But it was a warm day and a man's mouth was for more than speaking with so the small gathering repaired to Peter Grant's tent. Big Sandy Wilson from Strichen was there and that was a joy in itself for Sandy was another of the notable characters produced by the Buchan district. In his varied interests and activities, he had been mainly a horse dealer, on such a scale that he once paraded a hundred horses at Aikey.

'What are ye for?' I asked Sandy as we gathered at the bar counter.

'Man, I'm nae in a drinkin' humour—I'll just hae a rum,' he said.

'Rum for Sandy,' I ordered, reaching for the ginger bottle. 'D'ye want something in it?'

'Aye,' said Sandy. 'Mair rum.'

So a large rum it was and he opened his mouth and filtered it straight down his thrapple before I had time to feel grateful that this wasn't one of his drinking days.

Sandy went to Canada on one occasion to visit relatives and regarded the event as no valid reason for depriving the inner man of his liquid comfort. In a state of advanced inebriation he looked up at the moon one night and convulsed his Canadian hosts by declaring 'Man, that's helluva like the Moon we hae in Buchan.' Then back to his beloved Buchan and down in the fishing town of Fraserburgh one Saturday night, he joined the throng in the Broadgate as the pubs were closing. Like many communities that live by the sea, Fraserburgh was given to periodic outbursts of evangelism and there on the plainstones a Salvation Army girl was fair giving Aud Nick a bad name. She testified to her own wickedness before that wondrous moment when she saw the light and some farm servants, down for their Saturday night out, nudged each other and said dammit man, they would rather have known her before the light appeared. If she was half as fervent in the dark she would still have been a fire risk to the haystacks! Her blousy bust gave rhythmic counterpoint to her rantings as she reached a fine and holy climax with the ambiguous declaration 'Tonight, my friends, I am in the arms of life; tomorrow I may be in the arms of Jesus. . .' when up piped Sandy Wilson with fruity voice and rekindled spirit of youth to inquire: 'And what might you be doin' on Monday nicht, lassie?'

But here we were in the dying minutes of Aikey Fair. One piebald pony. The old fair that had started with a footless packman had taken centuries to turn full tilt but now it had served its purpose and was passing just as swiftly as it had come. Those of us present tidied up the loose ends of history

126

and drank a final toast. The Sunday fair still survives and draws upwards of 10,000 people on that Sunday in July but as I walked away from Aikey that Wednesday in 1952 I felt that I had left something of myself on the bareness of a Buchan brae, the part that belonged to older times. As I turned back to gaze on the desolate scene I knew that I was witnessing a poignant moment in local history, for we would never see its like again. Such a moment is hard to crystallise in the hour of its happening. Time alone can give it perspective.

CHAPTER FIFTEEN

THE LIFEBOAT'S OVER!

You are not long in the company of an Englishman before you know his whole story, unabridged, unexpurgated. Not so the Scot, least of all the rural Scot and if there is anything less than least it will be the hardy chaps of the North-East. In their granite towers of dumb caution they are dourly suspicious of gab in all its forms. There is the story of the bowler-hatted commercial traveller who boarded the train at Maud and entered a compartment already occupied by two Buchan farmers. In the breezy manner of the highway, the man raised his bowler and said 'Good morning, gentlemen.' The two worthies exchanged looks of contained amusement and merely took another puff at their pungent Steenhives. The commercial did not intrude on their silence for the rest of the journey and settled diligently to his *Scotsman* crossword. When he came to his destination at Ellon, he gathered his briefcase, opened the compartment door and, with normal courtesy, raised his hat again and said: 'Well, . . . good morning, gentlemen.' Still there was no acknowledgement and when the man had finally departed, one farmer turned to the other and summed up the creature with unmistakable disgust: 'A gabbin' vratch!'

Economy in words, economy in most aspects of life, thus the reputation for thrift and the legion of international stories about the mean Aberdonian, most of which originated in Aberdeen itself or twal' mile roun'. But it was based on thrift, not greed, a conviction that a man must make the best of what he had, springing no doubt from the earlier life on a grudging land that had to be farmed with good care and good sense, leaving no room for waste. The whole conditioning of the species made for a certain dourness but it found its own natural outlet in hard work and dry humour and did not swell into a social problem on a psychiatrist's couch. However, for those who might be intent upon probing the inner thoughts and feelings, even for those like myself who grew up with it, there were daunting problems.

Take the religious and political standpoint, for example, and you would soon find out what I mean. On paper the religious position seemed plain enough. The people were mostly on the roll of the Church of Scotland, the doughty Aul' Kirk which stood bare and forbidding on every parish heath. Their visitations upon the building might be twice a year, at the May and November communions, or if they wished to minimise the shock effect of their rare appearances on the poor brute of a minister they might well attend on the preceding Sunday as well. They would tell you they learned the Catechism at school, though they were damned if they could recite it now, and the man body would stump into the kirk like a tethered tup, solemn-faced and slow with the ill-gait of a man entering a place of infamy where he would rather not be seen. His red-faced wife, tight-lipped and douce, would be left to bring up the rear, which might amount to half-a-dozen bairns, to raise her tones at hymn time, bow her head at prayer time and maybe open her purse at collection time. And when it was all over Jeems would dyst his way to the door muttering that it would have been a grand day for riddling tatties. If it had been communion and the wine was served in the microscopic glasses which became the fashion, he might nudge a neighbouring farmer and crack: 'We could hae been daein' wi' something stronger on a caul' day like this.' Then he went home to his chappit tatties and thought little about God or religion till the next communion or the one after that if he was not burdened with one of those unreasonable ministers who threatened to cross him off the list. Of course he would give Jesus Christ innumerable mentions in the interval but seldom in the Biblical context. The trouble with Jeems and Dod was that they distrusted holiness as much as they distrusted gab. They saw it as a doubtful element and would judge harshly any neighbour who dared to profess openly his belief in God. Such a soul was suspected of brain impairment and promptly dismissed as having 'gone all to hell with religion'. Those brave men who took to the ministry in places like Buchan deserved either danger money in this life or a special corner of Heaven thereafter, or both. From the start they were social outcasts, unworldly creatures who would not be much good at pulling neeps, figures of good-natured ribaldry who were the better accepted if they took a dram, in which case they were likely to be voted most capital chaps, 'just nae like a minister ava' ', which was taken to be a recommendation.

Perhaps it was the bi-annual tirades about non-attendance which drove people away from the Church of Scotland, for the Scot does not care to be too forcibly reminded of his misdemeanours. But who could blame a minister who preached for fifty weeks in the year to a handful of converted pandropsuckers if he grasped at the chance of a little straight talking when suddenly confronted by a houseful of half-kent faces? Then again it may have been the severity of the Aul' Kirk service that set the Buchan folk back on their heels—the plain, unpadded pews that would give a man corns where corns were never meant to be, the stark walls and windows and the long theological sermons that too often meant little to hard-headed folk. I can think of Kirsty leaving the kirk one dry summer Sunday when Dr M. Welsh Neilson, the minister, had preached a wise and well-considered sermon on the theme of 'Always keep a well in your own backyard'. He related it to the current drought as a worldly illustration of his real message, which was about the wisdom of keeping within one's self a spiritual well from which to draw strength in times of need. When Granny Barron commended the sermon to Kirsty she responded enthusiastically with the comment 'Aye, Mrs Barron, it is richt handy when ye've a drappie water aboot the back door.' Alas, the spiritual analogy had evaporated in the reigning pre-occupation with a shortage of water.

Yet the severity of the service was in keeping with the character of the area and its people and perhaps there was something to be said for the Aul' Kirk form of worship. It may have been stark but wasn't there something wholesome and roundly satisfying about a minister who mounted the pulpit steps and without palaver summoned his flock with 'let us worship God'. That was basic.

Sundays in the thirties were usually spent at your grandparents, in my case at Mains of Whitehill, four miles up the road from Maud. At the foot of the farm road stood the old Kirk of Whitehill, which had been an important place of worship before the motor car took people to village kirks nearby. But it was still in use on one Sunday of each month when neighbouring ministers took the chance of addressing an old sermon to new ears. On the preceding week my grandfather, Arthur Barron, who was in such close harmony with his land, took a pride in seeing that the place was cleaned and made decent for the service, as if seeking to repay his Maker for the many debts of life. Sometimes I was sent along to lend a hand and on those occasions I grasped at the chance of exploring the in-timmers of a kirk when the minister was not there. It was something I had always wanted to do, just as I liked to sneak into my father's rostrum at the mart and pretend that I was selling cattle. When I tired of scrubbing and polishing I would steal away to the pulpit, mount the steps with due pomp and, having set my Bibles round their various positions, proceed to deliver an imaginary sermon to an imaginary congregation before being hounded by a most unimaginary command to come out of there at once and not make such a din in the Lord's house.

It was in the Kirk of Whitehill that I gathered my first memories of preachers. One in particular I recall for he fair could make the rafters dirl as he laid forth about Moses and Abraham and lots of folk I had never heard of. By the sound of them I had no real wish to further the acquaintance either. Yet, looking back, there was a good deal to be said for those spiritual scrubbings. He spoke of hell with absolute authority; indeed, had it not been so far away, I should near have sworn that the man had been there, so clear was his account of fire and furnace. At times its warmth may have caused envy in the cold air of the kirk; but without doubt it had a sobering effect on the potential sinner. It was a brave heart that would have considered anything but the straight-and-narrow in the face of such fiery threats, such technicolour, wide-screen projection of Auld Nick's Palace of Purgatory. Psychologically, the message would not have been uplifting to any but hardy North-East folk, for it labelled them with sins they did not know they possessed and held out a pretty slender hope for improvement. But his congregation was made of steely stuff and he knew that they would not readily give up the ghost, particularly the Holy One, and that they would strive to live, if nowhere else, at least on the lesser slopes of sinfulness. Today the Kirk of Whitehill is no longer a kirk. It became, as I recall it, an enormous henhouse with tier upon tier of clucking, laying hens. In an atmosphere so charged with the power of hell's generators, I am willing to bet there were no more righteous hens in Christendom, laying eggs of golden purity and ne'er coveting a neighbour's nest, nay, nor casting a lustful eye upon a neighbour's cockerel.

But if the rural folk of the North-East had an apparent indifference to religious matters it may simply have been that they felt little need to show it, having been fired by the essence of Christianity for longer than anyone knows. Their code of honest, decent living may well have stretched from prehistoric times when a great Maglemosian horde is believed to have come from southern Europe to settle in the land we now know as Scotland. They were a peace-loving people, we are told, with the basic ingredients of true civilisation, men with a lesson in living which became lost in the developing process of land division. That was before the age of the Savage but, alas, the lesson has yet to be re-discovered. We pride ourselves in our progress as human beings but have we really come so very far from the ways of the jungle? In a few odd corners of the world you can still find remnants of the old civilisations and the North-East of Scotland could well be one of them. It is just a thought.

How strange that the fisher folk in places like the North-East could march side by side with their rural kinsmen and yet remain a race apart in so many ways. In places like Fraserburgh, Peterhead and St Combs they spoke a language which was scarcely intelligible to farming people just a few miles inland. Their religion was a more complex matter than that of their farming neighbours but much less of an inhibition too. Living by the sea with its attendant dangers had made them more aware of their Maker and the possibility of meeting Him a little sooner than the dysting ploughmen who turned over the fresh soil of inland parks. So the men who sailed away in their fishing boats to reap the harvest of the sea came home on a floodtide of evangelism which found expression in a baffling diversity of religions. In towns like Peterhead and Fraserburgh, with populations around the 12,000 mark, you would find not only four or five Church of Scotland buildings and Roman Catholic and Episcopal ones as well but a whole choice of Baptist, Methodist, Pentecostal, Christadelphian and Salvation Army persuasions, not to mention the Brethren, which divided itself into separate shades of Open and Close and what more I cannot tell. I have sat in some of those places and listened to fishermen and their families give testimony to the day they saw the light and there was no doubting their sincerity. I merely marvelled that people from my own North-East corner, so near to the reticent folk of the land, could speak so unashamedly about their God. Religion was a more conscious matter in the fishing towns and villages where their gable-ends faced out to the mysteries of time and tide, and the tang of the ocean could lure them in search of a lucrative living or just as swiftly despatch them to a watery grave.

I had some first-hand experience of their homes and their

hearts one February day in 1953, a few months after I had been asked by William Veitch to move the Buchan office of Aberdeen Journals from Peterhead to Fraserburgh, a town which was then outstripping its local rival in prosperity.

The great January gale of that year had blown itself out just nine days earlier, leaving wreckage everywhere, and the skies had opened to the sparkling clarity of a premature Spring. Overhead a few white wisps of cloud were drifting to nowhere in particular and Fraserburgh was having its after-lunch nap. But far away in the North Sea the storm was still churning up the waters and rippling its effect across a hundred miles. Yawls had sailed out that morning to bring in fresh catches of white fish when suddenly they were caught up in a dangerous swell by the inshore regions. Fraserburgh lifeboat went out to shepherd them home and, with the last one over the harbour bar, coxswain Andrew Ritchie turned his lifeboat back towards port. Skippers know how to ride those rough seas but the great swell which echoed that distant storm was suddenly to throw up a freak sequence of wave movement which could not have been anticipated. Up came a lump of water and tossed the Fraserburgh lifeboat over on her face, trapping the seven crew members inside.

Within minutes the cry had spread through the town: 'The lifeboat's over!' And instinctively a whole population seemed to be running for the shore. Fraserburgh had lost a lifeboat before (and was to do so again) and year by year those people knew the agony of giving up a few of their fishermen to the mysteries of the deep. I am sometimes even today haunted by the plight of those townsfolk as they reached the shore to witness one of the most ironic dramas ever enacted. There I stood among them, the local reporter and one of the first to see crew members fighting for their lives within a few hundred yards of their own firesides. Frantic sons and brothers and fathers had to be restrained from jumping into the boiling surf to reach out a helping hand. The sea was in command that day and would take any other victims who cared to come. In the gurgle of their upturned boat the men tried to swim down and out beneath but their lungs choked up with the water, their bodies were battered in the rage and now those of us who were so near and yet so far could only stand and shout our encouragement. 'Come on, Andrew, stick it, man, stick it!' Andrew Ritchie, coxswain and powerful swimmer, reached out with his great arms and thrashed his way towards his wife and young family, driven to the limits of his remaining stamina. The cheering rose to crescendo as if for a sporting achievement, with victory now seemingly in his grasp. Then up bobbed a piece of flotsam, knocking the very last ounce of strength from his body—and we watched, helpless, as a brave man went under for the last time. Five others went the same way and only young Charles Tait survived. Folk ran this way and that in the general upheaval, relatives pumping dear ones in the faint hope of life's glimmer. But the cruel sea had struck again.

That evening I had the melancholy task of visiting the homes of the dead to collect photographs and biographical details for the next day's *Press and Journal* and there I was introduced to the philosophy and steadfastness of the fisher folk's religion if I did not know it before. Though young Charles Tait survived, his father was drowned and it was to old Mrs Tait that I made my first call. There she sat by the side of the coal fire, gazing into the flames that danced their evil round the room. With a heavy heart and eyes fixed on the fire, she spoke quietly and sensibly about the whole disaster. In the sorrow of losing her life's partner she was able to point out the blessing that it was the father and not the son that had been taken. She was an ageing woman whose burden might be burden enough but how much worse it would have been for the young Mrs Tait with her children to bring up. We had to count our blessings, hadn't we? A week later they called a meeting to enrol replacements in the lifeboat crew, for a town could not afford to be without its mercy ship when the livelihood depended on the sea. There was no scarcity of volunteers. Leading the queue was Skipper Joe Ritchie, offering to take the place of his brother

Andrew. The survivor, Charles Tait, had brought along his younger brother who wanted to take the place of their father. It is the way of things when the sea runs wild in your veins and there is a job to be done, a tradition to follow. What can you say of such people?

We packed the Old Parish Church for the funeral service and suddenly the great variance of religious interests channelled themselves into one remembrance, thanking God for the courage and resilience that sent men down to the sea in little ships; giving thanks too for the wives and families who waited and worried, knowing that the friendly waters which lapped their doorstep at the sunset glow of a still evening could just as quickly whip up a furious floodtide of sorrow. Country folk came in from their farms and villages, glad to pay tribute to the neighbours they knew so little but respected so much. I like to think of them together, these two factions of the North-East scene—the pride of the sea, the salt of the earth.

CHAPTER SIXTEEN

LORD JESUS TO LORD BOOTHBY

If it was hard to plumb the spiritual depths of the North-East, the task did not become easier when you tried to gauge the political temperature. By tradition, I suppose my ancestors and most of their neighbours were Liberals, sending to Westminster such distinguished men as Fred Martin, the blind M.P. from Mintlaw. But when the party lost its fire, they could find no clear affinity with either the class-consciousness of the up-and-coming Labour Party or the upper-crust image of the Tories. Instead they settled for a new phenomenon called Boothbyism. In their moment of need along had come a handsome young man with an Oxford degree, a good Scottish background, a golden voice and a personality which disarmed the men and captivated the women. At twenty-four, Robert John Graham Boothby, only son of a comfortable Edinburgh family, was heading for Westminster, the brightest prospect on the political scene, soon to become Parliamentary Private Secretary to Winston Churchill, set fair for unlimited possibilities. A few Aberdeenshire farmers, headed by Baillie Booth from Peterhead, had gone to Orkney to buy some bullocks—and brought back Robert Boothby as an unexpected piece of livestock. They had gone along one evening to listen to the young man as he fought an unsuccessful campaign with the Liberal. The men of East Aberdeenshire liked what they heard and judged rightly that he was a man of such independent thought and action that he would represent them with good sense and conviction, even if it ran against the grain of his party, which happened to be the Conservative Party. In other words, he would reflect their own distinctive character.

Some of my earliest memories concerned the name of

Boothby, pronounced with a great many more o's than it was spelled and spoken with a reverence by his local adviser, the late hammer-throwing champion Archie Campbell, who was sometimes in the company of my grandfather and who wrote popularly under the name of 'The Buchan Farmer'. About the time I first remember him, Mr Boothby was wedding himself to Lady Diana Cavendish, from the well-known Devonshire family. A few years later that marriage was dissolved and the folk of East Aberdeenshire winced but granted that his private life was his own, even if divorce was hardly known among the farming fraternity of Buchan at that time. Irreconcilable couples tended to thole each other, no matter how deep and interminable the misery, rather than be dragged into the shame and prominence of the Court of Session. About the same time, when war was breaking over Europe, the so-called scandal of Boothby's connection with Czechoslovakian assets in this country exploded as a storm of international proportions and there, prematurely and tragically, a career at the top end of politics where he most properly belonged was no longer a prospect. In backing a move for Czech assets in this country to be frozen and paid to those exiles whose assets had been confiscated by Hitler, he failed to declare a personal interest in the matter. (It was later discovered that he was not obliged to.) Political opponents did not pass up their opportunity and Parliament ruled that he had brought the House into disrepute. Boothby protested his innocence of any shady work and convinced many people in high places as well as his constituency party, who met him at the height of his crisis with the full expectation of parting company. But the doubt was cast and Churchill, who had seen such great things ahead for the young Boothby, cut him adrift and gave him no further support for the rest of his political life.

It was a sad and saddening experience and left Boothby, whose good nature held little room for bitterness, with some harsh things to say about his old master. If ever a man was destined for Number 10 Downing Street it was surely Robert

Boothby. He had many of Churchill's qualities—mental and physical capacity, vision, courage, the power of language; he had perhaps an even more engaging personality than Churchill and was one of those rare beings whose very presence would charge the air with an electricity. Great men can sometimes be a disappointment in the flesh. I remember once losing my way in the House of Commons, finding myself alone in a remote corridor and suddenly coming face to face with the aging Winston Churchill. The whole of his legendary life came flooding in, from the Boer War and the Siege of Sidney Street to his immortal years of the Second World War, his sayings and doings. I was seeing it all in the history books, being read a hundred years ahead by people who would speak of Churchill in the same breath as Cromwell and Pitt and Gladstone. Yet there, in a lonely corridor, it was hard to condense that legend to a size which would fit inside the mortal frame which approached me now. Boothby was a more flamboyant personality than this. Perhaps he lacked stability.

So the forces of history worked against Robert Boothby and the nation's loss became East Aberdeenshire's gain. He spent his days fighting for the fishermen of Peterhead and Fraserburgh, their minimum prices, their grants and loans, and fighting just as hard for the Buchan farmers, their oats and beef cattle, their subsidies and deficiency payments. He made his mark at the Council of Europe but eventually accepted a knighthood and later a baronetcy, which made him Baron Boothby of Buchan and Rattray Head (the land and the sea), still a powerful voice but confined to a roll in public life far short of what it should have been.

As a journalist, I attended the dinner held in Aberdeen to celebrate his knighthood. His old friend Compton Mackenzie was the main speaker, who kept the company in stitches for half-an-hour with a speech that might have been matched only by Boothby himself. Then, his audience soft with laughter, he drove home a telling jab at the 'farce' of the Czech affair. The man who should have been at that moment Prime Minister of

Great Britain had become a public entertainer, empanelled on the cheapness of television games. On that night in Aberdeen and on subsequent occasions when I have sat with him at his home in London's Eaton Square, I could not but reflect on the cruelty of fate. The man himself would take it all philosophically.

When the baronetcy winged him off to the Lords, he left a vacuum which was to become a whirlpool of political trouble in East Aberdeenshire. At first, the constituency, so long accustomed to the uniqueness of a Boothby cult, had to refresh its memory on the party to which he himself belonged. That they would, in tribute, elect a candidate of the same party went without saying. But in the late fifties there were no Boothbys on the political horizon. If they had not already thrown away the mould then men of that rugged ebullience were finding their niche in life outwith the spectrum of politics. East Aberdeenshire settled for an upright young man from one of the aristocratic homes of the district, Patrick Wolrige-Gordon, whose mother was a daughter of the colourful Dame Flora MacLeod of MacLeod, Clan Chief and hostess to her worldwide flock at Dunvegan Castle in Skye. Young Patrick was virtually unknown on his own native heath, having been educated, like most of his aristocratic cousins, in England, treading the familiar path from Eton to Oxford. When the time came, he left a degree unfinished to come back to the land of his birth as Conservative candidate. Out of the speculation as to who would be chosen came this political sapling, introduced to the people by one of his neighbouring aristocrats, Major David Gordon of Haddo, who was later to become Lord Aberdeen. Everything smelled of roses, or so it seemed. Patrick Wolrige-Gordon won the by-election caused by the departure of Boothby and consolidated his position at the General Election of 1959, which followed soon afterwards; then his troubles began to brew, not because the fishermen thought he was not fighting their cause, not because the farmers were dissatisfied or the general mood was turning against him.

140

Trouble was coming from the source which had introduced him, from the upper crust of his committee, from Major Gordon of Haddo and even from his own brother who was now laird of the family home at Esslemont, near Ellon. The folk who had worked to bring him in were now working just as hard to get him out.

The Tories had run into a wave of national unpopularity, by-elections were bringing disastrous results and the call had gone out from London to the constituency chairmen to make sure that their houses were in order. There was a general casting of opinions, followed by rumours of hush-hush dinner parties for the hierarchy of the East Aberdeenshire Tories. The outcome, as later revealed: Patrick Wolrige-Gordon, recently elected M.P. for East Aberdeenshire, no longer held the confidence of some of his constituency bosses as the man to retain the seat at the next election. Executive meetings were organised to bring about his rejection as candidate and, on the surface at least, it seemed just as simple as that. But as the whole fester began to erupt it became clear that another issue was involved, though no-one was keen to admit it. Young Patrick was now courting Anne, the beautiful daughter of Peter Howard, author, playwright and leader in Britain of the growing Moral Rearmament movement. In higher circles there were people who still thought of M.R.A. in terms of Fascism through the founder, Frank Buchman. Patrick was said to be spending too much time on Moral Rearmament and not enough on his constituency though he had previously met his executive and thrashed out that matter. Was there, then, a rooted objection to the fact that he was connected with M.R.A. at all? That was what no-one would admit.

The ordinary folk of East Aberdeenshire were not much concerned about Moral Rearmament, accepting Wolrige-Gordon for what he was—a decent young fellow who was doing his best to learn about the problems of the constituency and was prepared to work hard for his people. The plain fact was that very few Buchan folk had any notion of what the initials M.R.A. stood for and when they discovered, they were more than outraged that a young man should be persecuted for what they were convinced were his high moral aspirations, especially at a time when the Government he served was on the verge of acute embarrassment at the hands of the whores and pimps of the Profumo Affair. There were rowdy meetings and much writhing and wrangling but the outcome of a neck-or-nothing showdown was that Patrick Wolrige-Gordon carried the people with him. It was a hazardous business for a sensitive man still in his mid-twenties, enough to shatter his confidence for years to come. Perhaps it could be said that he had enough moral armament to see him through—though goodness knows what part the ordeal eventually played in his political destiny. The rumpus coincided with his wedding which was attended by a trainload of well-wishers from Buchan, who travelled to Anne Howard's parish in the south of England and joined with people from many walks of life. Patrick and Anne were to find that the loyalty and sense of justice which are built into the Buchan folk would sustain them in their plight. Without the personal support of plain country bodies they could not have survived. Politically, Patrick Wolrige-Gordon continued as an industrious Member of Parliament throughout the sixties but he perished in the spread of Scottish Nationalism which ran down from Moray and Nairn through Banffshire and into Aberdeenshire in the early seventies. I shall leave the political pundits to analyse the root-cause of that particular phenomenon.

Among the Buchan folk I was never aware of any deep allegiance to one political party, except the Liberals in earlier times. Boothbyism had taken care of itself; Socialism was regarded as fine for railway porters and Fraserburgh toolworkers but seemed to suffer from a suspected affiliation with the Devil; and in the general search for an alternative I suppose Nationalism looked as safe a compromise as any. It gave expression to that minority of Scots who held genuine aspirations for self-government and enabled bankers and schoolteachers and people like that, for whom political posturing was a risky business, to take up a stance of some sort. But I doubt if there is a party which can face a General Election in Buchan with feelings of utter safety. Dogmatic doctrine does not exactly clink with the native character.

CHAPTER SEVENTEEN

FROM MAUD TO MOSCOW

By the time of the Wolrige-Gordon rumpus I had not only moved back from Buchan to the Broad Street headquarters of Aberdeen Journals, having enjoyed the three years in my native corner, but had also moved south to explore the deeper jungles of journalism. I have long wondered what takes us from one place to another in this life. Is it a restless pursuit of money, position, adventure? Are we guided by instinct along the road of a pre-destined fate? Or are we simply the aimless creatures of circumstance? Few of us have more than a hazy notion but for my part I became aware that the time had come to move from Aberdeen if I ever intended to sample the working world beyond.

I had spent the latter part of the fifties as a sub-editor on the *Evening Express*, laying out pages, writing headlines and generally trimming other people's writing to fit the spaces. Broad Street was a busy, exciting place, part of the massive empire of Lord Kemsley (his daughter married the Marquis of Huntly) but soon to pass into the hands of Roy Thomson, an unknown name from Canada who suddenly appeared on the British scene, bought up *The Scotsman*, set his sights on Kemsley's network of regional newspapers and gained the franchise for Scottish Television, drawing upon his experience of television in Canada to declare that he had just been given a licence to print money. How right he was.

Most of my colleagues of the early fifties were still there, some of whom I was only now getting to know. There were able journalists like the red-headed Donald Thornton from Arbroath and his wife, Helen Fisher, daughter of a former Broad Street character, Pat Fisher; there were breezy young men like

Kenneth Peters and Bob Smith and sages like George Fraser and the lonesome Cuthbert Graham who, when you could penetrate his painful shyness, would fascinate with tales of his friendship with Lewis Grassic Gibbon and how they had driven south together on that occasion in 1934 after Gibbon's very last visit to the North-East, the handwritten manuscript of *Grey Granite* now in his pocket for a final revision before going to the publisher. When I met him in his mid-forties, Cuthbert Graham was little known to the public, apparently happy to remain a studious backroom boy of journalism which suited the physical handicap of a badly crippled leg. But his vast knowledge of North-East history, its castles and its folklore, gradually built him a reputation through the sixties and seventies, when he charted them all in the weekend review of *The Press and Journal*. Like all the best developments, his stature grew slowly but it was well rooted and bound to blossom in time. In an age of vanity, when pomposity seems to score over real worth, how splendid that a man as modest as Cuthbert Graham should finally be dug out of his cocoon and marched high upon a dais at the University of Aberdeen to be publicly declared an Honorary Doctor of Laws.

So Cuthbert was there but some of the other personalities had gone, notably George Rowntree Harvey, who was not only a fine poet and playwright but widely regarded as one of the finest critics of music and drama in all Britain. Like many another journalistic genius, Rowntree Harvey had a fondness for the bottle and during my early days in Turriff I had watched, fascinated, as he slept through an entire performance of *The Messiah* in St Ninian's Kirk—and then produced a brilliantly-constructed criticism in the following morning's issue of *The Press and Journal*. When you remembered that he had seen *The Messiah* eighty-five times it was less surprising that he found consolation in a good dram and an even better sleep. George Rowntree Harvey belonged to that breed of Bohemian bachelor, bow-tied and theatrical, warm, wayward and untidy, a home-bred Aberdonian with cosmopolitan overtones who was equally at home in obscure conversation with learned professors and in unpatronising patter with the cleaning wifies at *The Press and Journal* office. He was the brilliant wit and mimic who became the inspiration of a lively student life at the University of Aberdeen immediately after the First World War. George Fraser told me later how Rowntree Harvey had attended university by day and worked full-time as a sub-editor by night, never asking for a single evening off, not even for the final examinations which were to bring him a first-class honours degree. His name was soon legendary far beyond his native land and when it came to his funeral at Kaimhill Crematorium, the amazing breadth of his circle was truly reflected in the assorted gathering of human beings.

Among the missing faces when I returned to Aberdeen from the Buchan office was that of Ian Howard, a quiet, lanky lad who had come north from the tenements of Glasgow to learn his journalism in the calmer pastures of *The Banffshire Journal* before transferring his genius as a lay-out expert to the *Evening Express*. Ian and I had shared an attic room at an hotel in Albyn Terrace and generally engaged in adventures both journalistic and otherwise. One night Ian vowed that he could lure the highly popular Beverley Sisters, who were appearing in town, from under the chaperoning eye of their father. It was regarded as an impossible feat but these were a speciality of the persuasive Howard. The fact that we ended that evening with the Beverleys on our knees, driving along the Prom in an old Morris car driven by George Chrystal (better known as cartoonist Chrys, the creator of Wee Alickie) is more than just a pleasant memory. It told me something about the quiet determination of Ian Howard which was to make him one of the most significant journalists of his day.

He had long since returned to his native Glasgow to make his mark on the *Scottish Daily Express* when I received a message one January day in 1960 that he wanted to see me immediately in the City Bar, across from *The Press and Journal*. He was asking me to join him as a sub-editor at the *Daily Express* in Glasgow at a salary of £25 a week, which seemed like a fortune in 1960. I was earning £16 a week in Broad Street at a time, before inflation, when salaries of £25 belonged to another bracket. What's more, a job on the *Express* was the envy of almost every journalist in that era. It was the paper with flair and excitement, created by men like Lord Beaverbrook and his famous editor Arthur Christiansen. The reign of Christiansen in London had run parallel for twenty-five years with that of Sandy Trotter as editor of the *Scottish Daily Express*, the sister paper, but both were now drawing to a close. A fiery Sassenach called Roger Wood had taken over as editor in Scotland and one of his first tasks was to build up a depleted sub-editing staff, thus the instruction to Ian Howard to find new blood. His first step was to the familiar territory of Aberdeen where he sought to recruit Duncan Macrae and myself.

Four years earlier I had married Eden Keith, whose father was headmaster at Strichen, and she required no persuading that we were on our way to Glasgow, perhaps en route to Fleet Street. I left Aberdeen Journals in the time-honoured fashion of a drunken presentation, filled not only with whisky but with an enthusiasm for the wider world, yet harbouring a mild regret that I would not be savouring the full flavour of a Broad Street tradition which had stretched from the John Sleighs to the Rowntree Harveys, the Andrew Ingrams, the Cuthbert Grahams. Where again would I find such men? Where would I find a caseroom with such intellectual giants as George Dunn? (It says a great deal for the Thomson Organisation that they spotted the talent of that humble craftsman and eventually made him managing director of their publishing centre at Withy Grove, Manchester.)

On Leap Year Night of 1960, having travelled down on the train from Aberdeen, I mounted the stairway of Lord Beaverbrook's glass palace in Albion Street, Glasgow, to present myself as a sub-editor of news stories, an area of 'subbing' where I had very little experience. Secretly I was hoping that I could pick it up quietly before they decided I was not worth my new-found wealth!

The editorial floor of the *Express* was a large, open-plan system so different from Aberdeen, where reporters and sub-editors had worked on separate floors and even in small compartments. Here was a free-ranging hive of activity, buzzing with the kind of vitality which seemed to typify the spirit of Glasgow itself. Shirt-sleeved executives on the news desk conducted a kind of frenetic performance of new gathering which owed at least something to Hollywood and must have done more for the adrenalin than it did for the nervous system. Along another side of the vast area, sports phones were ringing and confusion was reduced to a semblance of order by a splendid man called Bruce Swadel, who wore formidable boots and looked less like a sports editor than a baillie dysting down the byre to muck the nowt. At least that reminded me of home and so did the voice of the chief sub-editor, Ronnie Sangster, whose father was a butcher in Aberdeen.

Across the editorial floor the familiar faces of the day would flit. John Mackenzie was called the 'Voice of Football', blossoming in stature with the kind of confidence which the *Express* could instil in its writers; Kevin Fitzgerald was known as 'Scotia', the best racing tipster in the land; Magnus Magnusson would drift over from the features department, sporting an image which was much less staid than that which turned up in his later days as a television pundit. But the hub of a national newpaper is the sub-editor's department where the whole assorted mass of news, sport and features is drawn together and shaped and chiselled into the final production of next day's newspaper. It was around that horse-shoe formation that I settled myself on a February night in 1960, feeling my way quietly into the atmosphere of the great *Daily Express* on a nightly routine which ran mainly from 6 p.m. till 2 a.m., with a canteen break at 9 o' clock.

It was a bustling, tiring, smoke-filled night which hovered forever between excitement and hysteria as editions were either caught or missed. A murder trial in Glasgow would mingle with a Free Kirk row in Skye, a beauty queen elopement in Dundee and the fish prices from Peterhead. And when the frenzy of the night's production had died down we would put on our coats and step out into the smoggy air of industrial Glasgow, sometimes walking all the way home in the hope of clearing the head of smoke and noise and restoring a normal blood pressure before going to bed.

Such was the reputation of Glasgow in those days that I chose to walk home only if there were two or three of us going in the same direction for our route to the South Side took us through the Gorbals, where close-mouths were worth a careful glance in the passing, or so it seemed. By chance I had found myself a bungalow in Burnside, which still reeked of the mass murderer Peter Manuel, for it was here that he had so recently massacred the Watt family on his way to becoming Scotland's most notorious killer of all time. Oddly enough I had seen Manuel in Peterhead Prison in the early fifties when he was serving a sentence for a previous rape. But I paid less attention to him than to people like Johnny Ramensky, the notorious safe-blower who interrupted half a lifetime in Peterhead with a distinguished wartime career when he was parachuted behind enemy lines to use his delicate expertise in the blowing of safes and the stealing of vital documents.

While the feeling was still fresh, I absorbed the true essence of Glasgow through the filter of my senses—Glasgow, that great conglomeration of villages, city of golden hearts and stainless steel razors that guarantees to kill you, with kindness if not with cutlass, city of tongue and twang where even the church organs are liable to have glottal stops. To this great parish pump, far from the fresh fields of Buchan, I took my ploughman's stride, a motion which starts somewhere in the marrow of the bone, and there I ploughed an uncertain furrow through streetfuls of ricketty, bow-legged men and fat, asthmatic women, gravel-voiced beer-barrels and pint-sized nyuchs who would raise hell in the name of the Pope or King

Billy yet never enter a church or think of religion as anything but a noble pretext for a 'square go'.

As nights wore on, I applied myself diligently to the fashioning of other people's writing, feeling that the raw copy of the *Express* reporter fell short of the standards on *The Press and Journal* and *Evening Express*. So I would re-write it to my own idea of clarity and extend that principle to the *Sunday Express* for whom I worked on a Saturday night. I thought I was doing no more than an average sub-editor should; but here again, the standards of an Aberdeen training stood me on good ground. I was asked to become Chief Sub-editor of the *Sunday Express*, on top of my daily duties and I ran a dual role through the middle sixties.

But there is a limit to the satisfaction of polishing other people's prose and soon I was submitting the occasional article to the features department and finding myself with a by-line on the pages of the *Scottish Daily Express*. One day I noticed the features boss, a blunt but breezy Dundonian called Drew Rennie, pacing up and down near my desk. It was much later I discovered that he was trying to pluck up courage to ask if I would write an article based on a news story of that day. The story was about a soldier being court-martialled for desertion and the explanation in his defence was that he had a bad stammer and fellow-soldiers were making his life such a misery that he could stand it no longer. What were the agonies of having a stammer? Since the verbal banana-skins had plagued me since early childhood I was well qualified and perfectly willing to write about it, so Drew Rennie could have saved himself the embarrassment. It was at that point that Ian MacColl, an outstanding editor of the *Express*, suggested I should make my choice between a sub-editing career and a writing one. I jumped at the latter and embarked upon the most exciting period of my whole life. The bulk of the work as a features writer, I found, was in Britain but every so often there was a trip abroad, fitting in with my ambition to see the world. So, in a sense, the *Express* became a vehicle on which to fulfil some personal ambitions.

I had no sooner come under the brilliant leadership of Drew Rennie than he told me one December morning in 1964 to get myself to Italy as quickly as possible and to make contact with Helenio Herrera, boss of Inter Milan and the greatest football coach in the world. Glasgow Rangers had been drawn against his team in the European Cup and, in a familiar *Express* tradition, we would want to 'ghost' a series of articles about Herrera and his views on Rangers, Scotland and football in general. It was my first professional experience of grabbing a passport and some currency and catching a plane to a foreign country at short notice. Inter Milan were playing Fiorentina on the Sunday so I flew via London to Rome, drove once round the Colosseum in the airport bus and caught a train to Florence.

Herrera was the biggest name of his day in world football and just how powerful a figure in Italy I was soon to discover. Without a word of Italian I had difficulty in finding where he and his team were staying for the match with Fiorentina. Finally a taxi-driver took me on a run into the country and deposited me in pitch darkness at a mansion where, he understood, the Inter Milan party were staying. It turned out to be the Villa la Massa, a fifteenth century castle converted into a hotel, and there I verified the presence of Herrera and booked myself in. Having been surveyed with curiosity, I was further baffled in the baronial dining-room that night to find that there was one long table for the Inter Milan party and a small table for me, without another soul in sight. When Herrera's men boarded their bus for the match next day, the entire staff of the hotel were packing their bags to leave as well. Then it was explained to me that Villa la Massa was a seasonal hotel which opened for one night of winter, recalling its staff for the sole purpose of accommodating Herrera and his national heroes. My attempts to sign him up for an *Express* series, which included an invitation to visit Glasgow, were met with a command to appear at his home in Appiano Gentile, north of Milan, on the Monday morning. As a dictator in football, his authoritative manner tended to spill over to private conversation.

I duly appeared on his doorstep on a dull, foggy December morning and negotiated a deal in a form of pidgin English which left me wondering if I had unwittingly committed the *Express* to paying a fortune. Among the lessons I had learned in those three days were how to find your way about a foreign country when you don't know the language, and what to expect from a razor-sharp brain in a business transaction. I also learned that I could go all the way to Italy with a lucrative contract for Mr Herrera—and he didn't even ask me over the doorstep for a cup of tea or glass of vino or whatever they drink in Milan. They would have had better manners in Maud!

The involvement of Rangers in another European football match—the Cup Winners' Cup Final in Barcelona—set me off on a mission to Moscow to see how the other half lived, the supporters of Moscow Dynamo who would not be able to join the 20,000 Rangers fans at the Spanish stadium. Anxious days of pleading and persuasion at the Soviet Embassy in London (and some personal advice from Sir Alec Douglas-Home) produced a last-minute visa and I was on my way to Moscow, via Copenhagen, in a big Ilyushin plane.

The flight into Soviet territory began with the chilling instruction over the intercom to put away your binoculars. Once more without the language, I was busily engaged with the phrase-book to ensure that at least I knew the difference between 'da' and 'niet'. When I found that the Russians put 'c' when the sound is 's' and 'p' when they really mean 'r' then I gave up trying to understand their hieroglyphics and ordered myself a double vodka. The only piece of verbiage which seemed to make sense was the word for brassiere, which is pronounced 'lift-chick', and that at least proved that the Russians are not without a sense of humour!

When the Ilyushin touched down at Moscow Airport and unloaded its luggage, the Russians were covered with embarrassment that they had mislaid my travelling bag in Copenhagen. While they sorted out who was due for a long stay in Siberia, I sauntered out to the taxi rank, minus razor, toothbrush, pyjamas or a clean shirt, and hired a car to take me to the flat of a journalist in Kutuzovsky Prospekt. That was when the Russians lost track of me. Firmly seated in the back of a Communist cab, I absorbed my first impressions of life in the Soviet system. By the light of early evening women were still toiling in the fields as we passed that memorial point where the invading German armies of the Second World War were finally turned back to perish in the freeze of a foreign field.

I spent the next few days at large in the Russian capital, taking in the breadth and beauty of that impressive city and finding out about how the people live. It was a unique opportunity, enriched by the help of a splendid interpreter whom I managed to engage for the duration of my visit. Through her I was able to meet scores of people and to learn about their lifestyle as they went about their daily routines. At the end of the working day it seemed that regimented hordes would all flock in one direction to the large departmental store known as GUM, near Red Square, before flocking off again towards the Underground warrens which would lead them home. I found that, when Ivan had reached the large block of flats which was home to most people and had consumed his beetroot soup and sliced sausage, the chances were that he would turn his thoughts to football.

Outside the Dynamo Stadium I met large groups of supporters just standing there, like cloth-capped Scots of the thirties, discussing the merits of last week's match and the prospects for the one to come. When they discovered where I came from, they gathered round to give my interpreter the busiest hour of her life. She was intrigued to be in the middle of such a frank exchange of views, so clearly a rare experience in a Communist country. My attempts at finding out about them were more than balanced by their own attempts to learn about life outside the Soviet Union. Their ignorance of basic facts was quite pathetic and what a pleasure it was to enlighten them, even a little, about the way we live. They were delightful people, eager for knowledge and friendship (and perhaps freedom) and it was sad to think that such a minor encounter had been like a major event in their lives. But heavy-jowled men appeared on the fringe of our gathering and for the future safety of my interpreter I bade my Russian friends farewell and beat a hasty retreat. Their parting handshakes and smiles and wistful looks still haunt me to this day. I watched them in greater mass at the Lenin Stadium, where the Central Army was playing Kiev Dynamo and found that football supporters behave much the same the world over. Any notion that Ivan on the terracing is a dour comrade in long coat and dumb emotions can come only from the imagination of a moviemaker. As they bawled abuse at the referee it came clear to me that this was perhaps their only opportunity to kick against authority without risk of a train-ride to Siberia.

This was a Moscow where no one could own his own house, where they joined long queues for food—and where they still took out your appendix with a local anaesthetic. Surprisingly, it was a Moscow with a serious beer-drinking problem, a fact which was confirmed as I left the Lenin Stadium that evening. No alcohol was permitted inside the football ground but they made up for it at the beer stands on the approach roads where the gutters were lined with drunks, left to sober up in their own good time, I was told.

A journalist friend put me right on the private enterprise ventures which manage to survive in Moscow. For example, if I were waiting for a bus and an unmarked car drew up and offered me a lift, it would be quite safe to accept. I would merely give the driver a rouble (about fifty pence at that time) and he would take me anywhere in Moscow. He would simply be a worker driving a State-owned car across town and taking the chance of some pocket money en route. Sure enough, it happened as the man said, convincing me that capitalism is not dead in the Soviet Union.

Back in Red Square, where no traffic is permitted, the crowds paid homage by the portrait of Lenin and the golden domes of the Kremlin shone out a reminder of another age. Earlier in the day I had walked through the walled enclosure of the governmental seat with a keen awareness of the dictatorial oppression. Now five illuminated ruby stars stood out as an impressive contrast to the night sky and, from the dining-room of the National Hotel, which looks across Revolution Square towards the Kremlin, I surveyed it all with a deep sense of the history. So much had happened in that astonishing country in the 800 years since the Kremlin *was* Moscow.

In a city which was geared up that night for the visit of President Nixon, there was an air of anticipation at the National Hotel as Russian families joined gaily in an evening of food and good fellowship. A bell rang out across the moonlit city and the little orchestra struck up 'Midnight in Moscow'. Another day had ended in the Soviet Union. Tomorrow it would be time for the homeward journey, my notebook filled with interviews and impressions. I had met such men as Lev Yashin, Russia's World Cup goalkeeper who was coaching Dynamo under the direction of another football legend, Konstantin Beskov, remembered as the dashing inside-left of the famous Dynamo team which played Rangers in a memorable game in 1945.

When I arrived at the airport for the journey back to Scotland, via Paris and London, I was suddenly confronted by grim-faced officials who bundled me into a cell-like interrogation room and demanded to know where I had been. I should have been staying at the official tourist hotel and they had lost all trace of me. Well that was their bad luck. I had had a marvellous time in Moscow. What's more, my bag had now turned up so I would be able to shave and wear a clean shirt. With bad grace, they finally escorted me out along a red carpet and drove me to a waiting plane, through massed ranks of Soviet soldiers and military bands. I thought they were really over-doing the ceremonial—until I remembered that, as I flew out, President Nixon flew in!

Back home, the career of Ian Howard, the man who took me to the *Express* in the first place, had rocketed to high success before disintegrating into a series of disasters in his private life. He had been to America and back when he phoned me one day from a Glasgow hospital to ask if I would visit him. His marriage was broken, he had few friends left and he had just suffered his sixth heart attack. Ian Howard should just have been approaching the prime of a brilliant career but the bloated wreckage I found at the hospital that night was merely struggling to stay alive. Recollection of our early days in Aberdeen produced the boyish laughter I had known so well and we spent a happy hour together. My plans to help in his rehabilitation were superfluous, however. Ian died a few days later.

CHAPTER EIGHTEEN

ON BOARD THE QUEEN MARY

The three familiar funnels of the old *Queen Mary* rose above the dockland clutter of Southampton Harbour as my taxi headed towards the greatest ship that ever sailed the seas. I was on my way to America for the very first time with plans to interview people like Richard Rodgers, composer of some of our greatest musical shows, and Lester Pearson, Prime Minister of Canada. The visit was partly professional and partly private but it was really sparked off by the news that Malcolm Forbes, son of Bertie, was planning a sumptuous celebration to mark the fiftieth anniversary of *Forbes Magazine*. I had vowed all those years ago that I would become a writer—and that I would attend one of the big whingdings at *Forbes*. It had been too far for my parents and grandparents when they were invited by Bertie himself but there would never be a better occasion than the Golden Jubilee dinner. I was turning it into the central feature of a prolonged stay in the United States, at which I would represent the corner of Scotland where the whole romantic story of Bertie Forbes began. What's more, I was going to do it in style. While there was still an ocean liner to float you over the Atlantic there was really only one way to travel on your first visit to America. Compared to the six-hour flight in an airliner the five-and-a-half day voyage to New York was just about right for a gradual adjustment to the cultural shock.

So there I was, about to board the *Queen Mary* on her third last trip before she was sold off by Cunard to take up some static position at Long Beach, California. Stepping out of the taxi, I stood in disbelief at the size and scope of that magnificent lady, her black outline soaring to the heavens and dwarfing all around her. Slowly I made my way up the gangplank and disappeared into a different world—a floating island of fun and fascination, of good companionship and the most gracious living. In the gathering excitement of impending departure, people found their cabins, explored the vast avenues of the ship and gathered on deck as the crowds on the quayside waved and cheered. At the end of an era they would not see this sight too often again. As the tug-boats guided us down the channel towards the open sea, the burning torch of Fawley oil refinery lit up the night sky then faded into a distant spark as Britain sailed out of our reach and we entered the dark and lonely acres of the ocean.

To walk inside the *Queen Mary* was like entering the largest and most luxurious hotel in the world, where there was so much to do and absolutely no obligation to do it. You could walk up spacious staircases, surveyed by the portrait of *Queen Mary* herself, flit from games deck to the cinema or the swimming pool or simply drift from the Verandah Grill to the Midship Bar, strolling, jogging, dancing, drinking, talking, according to the mood of the moment.

But the centre-piece of that magnificent ship was the main lounge, more elegant than any hotel I had seen, high-pillared and wood-panelled with an air of majesty which summoned up an age that was gone. Amid the tinkle of afternoon tea-cups, leisured ladies did their crosswords with only a gentle grind of vibration to remind them that they were somewhere in mid-Atlantic and not in Mayfair. On a flower-decked stage where Henry Hall was once the maestro, a small string orchestra of bow-tied gentlemen was gliding into the honey-toned melodies which lent the final touch of Palm Court atmosphere to a scene of pleasant anachronism.

In the gathering momentum of night-time the revelry became fast and furious, music filtering from every deck and echoing across the churn of the Atlantic Ocean. Day by day the air grew warmer till the crew changed into white tunics and you sensed the gradual approach of the New World. In the moonlit cool of late evening I would walk out on deck and survey the splendid isolation of our ship at sea, appreciating the soothing therapy of simply taking your time on the way to America. (What an eerie business it was on the Sabbath of our crossing to hear the church bell peeling out across the parish of the Atlantic.) Back inside, the bars were filled with people exchanging stories of where they came from and why they were going to the States. Everyone had a story, whether it was a British couple going to visit their exiled relatives, a shrill American lady who had just done Europe, or an idle roué, complete with gin and tonic, who had been on this ship so often that he couldn't remember if he was coming or going. Having stood with Captain Treasure Jones on the bridge of the great ship, I then accepted an invitation to his cocktail party, a semi-formal occasion which more than lived up to its reputation. At meal times you kept to the same table where eight or ten of you were liable to form a lasting friendship. And so it was on that auspicious voyage when my companions included Professor and Mrs Harry Barth from New York, a delightful couple with whom I still correspond.

The last night on board ship is always a gala occasion. After dinner Mrs Barth persuaded me to join in the last session of bingo, a pastime which I had strenuously resisted till then. We arrived in time to collect the very last card in the very last game. Such was my ignorance of this idiotic pursuit that Mrs Barth had to instruct me on the most basic of rules. When I had run through all the shouted numbers she propelled me to my feet to call 'Bingo!' I felt ever such a fool as I was ushered to the dais by a red-coated gent amid a flourish of musical chords. However, I felt less of a fool when he announced that I had won the week's accumulated jackpot of 160 dollars. That was my first and last game of bingo and it heralded such a night of champagne as to put us in poor shape for a clear-headed arrival in New York.

Nevertheless, by 5 a.m. we were all on deck with a bleary-eyed sense of anticipation, wrapped up in sweaters as the first cold light from the east revealed a shadowy land-mass ahead of us. Distant lights began to twinkle out of the dawn and a cigar-smoking American drawled the information that these were the lights of South Brooklyn, yeah man. Closer and closer it came with the rising light when, out of the haze, grew the Verrazano Bridge, the longest suspension in the world, bearing its early morning traffic on the way to work. It was just another Tuesday as the great *Queen Mary* slid under its girders. The sudden appearance of the Statue of Liberty to the left brought us clustering to port side. Then just as suddenly we headed for the bows as the mighty skyline of Manhattan peered through the morning mist and rooted us to the spot like mesmerised rabbits as we silently beheld one of the legendary sights of the world. We just stood there with our own thoughts, striving to fit the reality into the framework of a long-established image and allowing the magnetism of Manhattan to pull us close to her warm and welcoming breast. Even when you are near to the lower end of the island and the skyscrapers are clear and close, what strikes you most from the estuary is the utter silence of the noisiest city in the world.

It was H.G. Wells who said that the view of New York from a distance was not so much that of a city but of a collection of boxes from which a city might be unwrapped. Well, as the *Queen Mary* finally edged into her berth on the Hudson River, New York unwrapped itself all right, the teeming noise of the city suddenly breaking over you like a tidal wave in a cacophony of dockside din, hooters blaring, porters shouting and yellow cabs screeching to a halt. The farewells taken, the baggage gathered, I turned for a last look at the Grand Old Lady of the Sea and hailed a taxi which drove me down Broadway and along 42nd Street to the Tudor Hotel, which was close to the *Daily News* building, where the *Daily Express* had its office.

The Forbes celebration was several weeks away so I settled myself in with the *Express* staff and went out to explore this intriguing island which the Dutch originally bought from the Mana-Hatta Indians for a few ribbons, beads and trinkets

160

worth twenty-four dollars. They called it New Amsterdam but the British captured it from the Dutch and it became New York. Then the Americans captured it from the British and it became neurotic. Some dismiss it as a concrete jungle but New York is a wonderfully vibrant, exciting city, dramatic in its broad avenues running down the island and its gently undulating streets running across it. I steeped myself in the atmosphere, walking, talking, exploring and absorbing till I was totally ensnared by her alluring charms. Just to stand in Park Avenue, outside the Waldorf Astoria Hotel, and to consider that the glass mountains around and above you are man-made is one of the bewildering experiences of a lifetime.

My first interview in America was with one of those legendary figures whose name and music had reverberated around the world so long and so powerfully that it was hard to imagine him as a recognisable human being. To meet Richard Rodgers I took a lift to the fourth floor of an office block in Madison Avenue where I was shown into a well-appointed suite, hung with framed mementoes, a typical business office in midtown Manhattan except for the grand piano which stood out as a clue in the corner. The muted noise of traffic rising from the street below was the nearest thing to the sound of music I could hear as we settled down to talk across a desk. Could the small, dapper, unimpressive figure really be Richard Rodgers, composer of as great a wealth of popular melodies as one man has ever produced? It was hard to fit someone so unassumingly ordinary in appearance into the legend which his talent had created, yet it taught me the lesson that greatness burns quietly in the heart or soul or mind of a human being without regard to the wrapping. I turned it all over in my mind as we talked—the memorable pre-war partnership of Rodgers and Hart which was followed, on the death of Lorenz Hart, by an even greater partnership of Rodgers and Hammerstein. That second period alone had given the world an array of musical plays which ranged from *Oklahoma* and *Carousel* to *South Pacific*, *The King and I* and *The Sound of*

Music. Richard Rodgers looked every inch a business man, adding to the picture by travelling to his office most days from either of his homes in Manhattan or Fairfield, Connecticut.

I found Rodgers a difficult man to interview. For someone who had cascaded with beautiful melodies for half a century he seemed strangely short of emotional content. His answers were clipped and measured and precisely to the point and he insisted that his output had nothing to do with inspiration. He merely wrote according to order, providing appropriate musical sounds for the mood of the story presented to him. I still refuse to believe it but this was how Rodgers himself explained it to me:

> 'I am not the kind of composer who wakens up in the middle of the night with an idea and springs out of bed to put it down on paper. I have to sit down and concentrate—and work. It begins with the idea of the play, the situation and the character. If I have a lyric I can go ahead and write the music. Sometimes I do the music first but the important thing is the situation and the character. And that is usually provided by someone else . . .'

The 'someone else' who inspired the melodic genius of Richard Rodgers to reach its heights was, successively, Lorenz Hart and Oscar Hammerstein, the men who wrote the words. Both were gone by then and, since Hammerstein's death in 1960, Rodgers had written *No Strings* which was a success in America, and *Do I Hear a Waltz?* which was a failure. He never did find a third partner, nor was that surprising since he had already had the good fortune to attract two of the greatest lyricists of all time.

Richard Rodgers, son of a New York doctor, had amassed a fortune which at that moment was being expanded by the cinema success of *The Sound of Music*. He was astounded to hear that it was still running in the same Glasgow cinema after two years and nine months and that encouraged him to speak warmly of his visit to Scotland in 1930 for the opening of *Evergreen*. Gradually it became clear that the cool manner was simply the nature of a genuine and modest man—and that the measured speech may well have another explanation. I braced myself to ask the delicate question at a time when cancer was even more of a forbidden subject than it is now.

'Yes, it is true that I have had cancer. I have not kept it a secret,' he told me. 'It was in the jaw. But that was twelve years ago and I was cured. I had a check-up for it yesterday and I'm all right.'

I thanked him for revealing so much of the character and humour of the American people. In plays like *Oklahoma* I could instantly recognise the country folk of a land I had never seen as being the same country folk of my own native corner.

I told him that the wind which swept down the plains of Oklahoma blew just as surely in the far corners of rural Aberdeenshire where my own mother went about her housework on the farm, whistling a happy tune which could originate in a Manhattan skyscraper but struck a universal chord in Maud, Milan and Melbourne. Through an unchanging expression I knew that he was deeply moved by the tribute. As we shook hands I knew too that I was leaving a lonesome man, one who had taken us through a chorus of tunefulness from *Blue Moon* to that last song which he and Oscar Hammerstein sat down to write together, *Edelweiss*. His consolation was that his music was capable of cheering so many millions of people. His last words to me were: 'Yes, I would like my music to live.' And who can doubt that it will?

As I flew north from Chicago to keep an appointment in Ottawa with Lester Pearson, the Prime Minister of Canada, all eyes were on the main headline of the day—the downfall of the previous Prime Minister, John Diefenbaker. Not only had he been voted out in favour of Pearson but he had now been kicked out as leader of his own Conservative Party. The big showdown had just taken place at the party convention in the Maple Leaf, Toronto, and this was surely the end for

Dief. There was a note of regret all round for, even if his career had gone sour, Diefenbaken was still regarded as one of the greatest Canadians of the century. I changed planes at Toronto Airport and hurried across the tarmac to take up the last remaining seat in an extra flight to Ottawa. Having fastened my seat-belt, breathless from the rush, I sought to regain my composure in the silence around me. Once more all heads were deep in the newspapers. 'Dief the Chief—it's the End' they said. Casually, I glanced across the narrow passageway and who was sitting next to me but Diefenbaker himself, gazing into space with the heavy eyes of private grief, his wife Olive resting a consoling hand on his arm. The Press had been pursuing him at Toronto and they would be waiting for him again at the Canadian capital but here I had him to myself, practically sitting on my lap! Was it prudent to intrude on his privacy at that moment? Should I try to interview him there and then? I decided to await our arrival in Ottawa, spending my time observing at close quarters the emotions of a great Prime Minister in this hour of personal defeat. I smiled respectfully and kept close on his heels as we left the plane and crossed the tarmac to a waiting battery of Press and television men.

The Press corps of Ottawa were obviously in a sympathetic mood as he paused to give his obligatory few minutes of general interview.

'What do you plan to do now, Mr Diefenbaker?' asked one reporter.

'Well, I guess I'll go out West and do a bit of fishin',' he replied.

As he answered further innocuous questions it struck me that, in his moment of uselessness, he would relish the opportunity to get his teeth into something positive.

'Mr Diefenbaker,' I began. 'As a visiting journalist from Great Britain, can I ask if you have anything to say to the people of the Old Country in this, your moment of departure?'

The big issue of the moment was that appalling speech by

President de Gaulle in which he had called out to his French-Canadian audience '*Vive le Quebec libre!*' It was a mischievous call for a split in the nation.

John Diefenbaker turned slowly and said: 'Yes. Yes, I do have something to say to the people of Great Britain.' Cameras whirred, pencils hovered over notebooks. 'I want the people of Britain to know that, even if I am no longer at the centre of Canadian politics I shall fight till the end of my life to preserve a one-nation Canada.' And from there he launched into a major speech, short but snappy, which gave the old warrior an escape from his grief. There was spirit in him yet and when he finally stepped into his limousine to be driven away, hard-bitten journalists put down their gear and gave him a spontaneous round of applause. He rolled down the window and said: 'Gentlemen, you don't know how much that means to me.' Tears were streaming down his cheeks. What a poignant moment in Canada's political life I had just witnessed. Since I had sparked it off, the journalists crowded round to thank me for putting in the vital question. That night it went out across the nation on radio and television. Next morning I had an appointment with Diefenbaker's successor, the very different personality of Lester Pearson.

After a night at the magnificent Chateau Laurier Hotel in the Canadian capital (Ottawa has something of the atmosphere of Edinburgh) I walked to Parliament Hill and was guided along a corridor to the Premier's office. Lester Bowles Pearson was the fourteenth Prime Minister of Canada, variously regarded as informal, friendly, complicated and a master of dignified protocol. Moreover, he had taken on a kind of balancing role between Britain and the United States. As an international figure of significance he was playing host to the world which had come to join in the massive world exhibition known as Expo 67. All this coincided with the centenary of Confederation for Canada as well as with his own seventieth birthday.

But if ever I needed a lesson that great men are really very ordinary mortals at heart it came to me in Lester Pearson's office. For there he sat, with the pin-striped appearance of a local lawyer, drinking coffee out of a blue and white mug that you would find on any working man's table. He swivelled in his big leather chair and began to question me about my late boss, that remarkable Scots-Canadian Max Aitken, better known as Lord Beaverbrook. I took my cue from Russia's Jacob Malik who once said: 'I always listen when Lester Pearson speaks', and we got on like a house on fire. The former history professor talked historically of how Canada had lived under the shadow of Downing Street in the early days and latterly of America.

'Our way of life became North American and, in some ways, quite indistinguishable from the United States, except in Quebec,' he said. 'Now we realise in this centennial year that it is a great thing to be a Canadian and we have learned for the first time how to celebrate Canadianism with a kind of nationalistic fervor. One of the reasons why we have suspected patriotic breast-beating in the past may have been that the Scottish element is so strong. By tradition the Scots don't go in for that. Their emotions run deep and do not readily show. So we were more reserved and there was a stability and dignity of life. But this has changed and I believe it is for the better.'

In the wake of the de Gaulle speech we were able to talk about the problems of the two-language nation and a wide variety of other subjects. One of the pleasures of interviewing the really top people in life is that there is practically no question which cannot be asked. They will give you an answer of some sort.

Pearson drank his coffee as we looked out towards the Mounties parading before Parliament Buildings. Visiting heads of state were there for the Canadian celebrations and a tap on the door reminded him that he was running behind time. Mr Pearson apologised for the hustle and, as I was shown out, the President of Italy was shown in. Another busy day was under way in the Canadian capital. The work of a nation awaited.

The strength of that Scottish influence which the Prime Minister had mentioned was all around in evidence. Indeed is there a family in Scotland today without a branch in Canada? In my own case the Canadian relatives now outnumber the Scots with the majority in the Toronto area. In the familiar fashion it happened around 1910 that Uncle Jimmy Barron, a brother of my grandfather, set out from the North-East with his wife and ten children for a new life in a new world. Prospects for country folk in Scotland in those far-off days must have seemed as bleak as the Hills of Fisherie, making the very name of Canada sound like a romantic escape from drudgery. So they sailed away from Greenock, out across the bare Atlantic on such a rough and miserable voyage that they vowed they would never set foot on a ship again—and they never did. From the St Lawrence they had to find their way to Guelph, Ontario, where a small farm awaited their attention. When they got there, I am told, Uncle Jimmy put down his case, surveyed the new abode with a scratch of his head and said very little. His children casting anxious eyes on their father could only guess at the thoughts running through his head.

Nearly sixty years later I was now walking up that same farm road to meet Uncle Jimmy's children, by then in an age range from 58 to 80, and putting myself in the boots of that Buchan man arriving there in 1910 with all those children and responsibilities. I could have a fair guess at those thoughts which were passing through his head. Roughly speaking, he must have been questioning the sanity of coming all those thousands of miles for this. Canada, a land of opportunity, ready to flow with milk and honey? That small-holding on the plains of Ontario looked just like a thousand other bare bit places on the grudging clay lands of Buchan. But with a stomach and an equilibrium sorely turned upside down by that nightmare voyage, the destiny of Jimmy Barron and his wife and ten children was there in Guelph, for better or worse.

And there they settled down and made the best of it, in all truth not much better than they would have done at home.

His remains had gone to dust long by now but bachelor sons still farmed the same land and the others were clustered around the area. True to the vows of 1910 not one of those elderly Barrons had ever set foot on a ship—nor a plane for that matter—to see their mother country and my arrival was a matter of great curiosity and even celebration for I was the very first relative from Scotland they had seen in all those years.

What a marvellous moment it was as I approached them outside the farmhouse where they had all been children together. All except one of the ten were there, lining up as a kind of guard-of-honour, and there I was, walking up the line shaking hands with people I could have picked out of a multitude as being blood relatives of my own. Mary was just Auntie Annie all over again. John Barron was just another version of his namesake cousin back home.

Inside, the kitchen was just like an old-fashioned kitchie on a Buchan farm, made all the more quaint by a stove in the middle of the room with the lum going up through the ceiling. Having known I was coming they had baked a cake, suitably inscribed, and their children and their children's children gathered round and we had a fair old party. Outby in the fields they seemed to scrape a living which could never have brought them riches. And in one corner of the barn lay an old-fashioned trunk with the initials M.B. It was one of the kists which had brought their worldly belongings on that journey from Scotland. Such was the pattern of immigration. In this simple way the Scots had been taking their families and their skills to foreign lands for hundreds of years. You marvelled at their sense of adventure and indeed that very quality, allied to their energy and desire to create a better life for themselves, must surely explain the prosperity which came to so many of their adopted lands.

When the acquaintances had been soundly forged, the greetings and memories exchanged and the food and the drams well and truly consumed, I was on my way to further travels in North America. As I headed for the troubled city of Detroit with its streets aflame in the race riots of 1967, the Barron family were still there at the door which had given them a childhood home all those years ago. The umbilical cord of a family stretches across oceans, a fact which came clear to me as I turned and waved and felt the sharp sting of a lump in my throat.

So I journeyed on through the North American continent, sampling their motels and their hamburger stalls and attuning my heathery lugs to a language which seemed to have a recurring rota of words and phrases like 'Huh', 'Right', 'You're welcome' and 'It's bin nice talkin' to you'. There were Bar BQs and even Car BQs (were they selling cars or turning them on a spit?) and there was a gradual acceptance of the American people for what they are. And what are they? They are a serious-minded, hard-working and hospitable people so blessed with both the energy and naivety of youth that they never know when they are beaten, so they never are. They may create a farce like their early attempts at launching a rocket from Cape Canaveral but they pursued the problem—as they do with all their problems—until they finally beat the Russians in the race to the moon.

An obsession with health means that everyone knows his calorie intake; an obsession with education means that everyone seems to have graduated from one college or another though, in all truth, their basic instruction falls far short of what we learned at Maud School. Nevertheless the American talks with a freedom and confidence which makes him sound a great deal more educated than he is. A Buchan loon might know a damned sight more but he won't say it half as well! The travels and the interviews and the general intake of the American life were building up to the grand climax of my main purpose in coming to this great land in the first place.

As a preliminary to the gigantic party which would celebrate the fiftieth anniversary of *Forbes Magazine* I walked down Fifth Avenue, central artery of Manhattan island and one of the most impressive streets in the world. There is Tiffany's and the Empire State Building and a mixture of people and cultures, sights and sounds, yellow cabs screeching, lights which say 'Walk'—'Don't Walk', feathered flunkeys, dull-eyed junkies, high-stepping ladies, low-shuffling beggars, the famous, the forgotten, the has-beens and the never-weres, all contained in the kaleidoscope of human flotsam which makes up New York. Down Fifth Avenue towards Greenwich Village my eyes settled upon a building which set my heart beating just that little bit faster. Above the flutter of the Stars and Stripes the name was emblazoned for all to see: *Forbes Magazine*, headquarters of an organisation which owed its very existence to a lad from a country cottage in Aberdeenshire.

Bertie Forbes was gone but his creation lived on, housed in a building of neo-classical charm and character which was formerly the headquarters of the Macmillan Publishing Company. Macmillan's had built it, they said, from the profits of H. G. Wells' *Outline of History* and Wells himself was among the visitors, along with Sean O'Casey, James Mitchener, Kathleen Windsor and Margaret Mitchell, the creator of *Gone with the Wind*. It was here that a brash young editor asked Kathleen Windsor if *Forever Amber* was based on her own bedroom experiences. 'No' replied Miss Windsor. 'If it were, I never would have had time to write it.' It was a building of marble staircases and chandeliers while next door stood a magnificent town house which Bertie's son Malcolm used for the entertaining of distinguished guests.

Malcolm's own home, however, lay across the Hudson River and out into the rural peace of a New Jersey estate called Timberfield. On the big night I was driven out to the Forbes home in a gleaming limousine, along with Bertie's loyal secretary, Gertrude Weiner, and his niece from Glasgow, Agnes Baird. Security officers vetted the arrivals at the gateway while inside, private airplanes were touching down on a specially-laid airstrip, bringing four hundred of America's business and political leaders and their wives to what was generally acclaimed as the biggest spree that that great nation had seen for a generation. Every president or chairman, from Coca Cola to General Motors, was there filing through the Forbes mansion for a personal introduction to the guest-of-honour, the Vice-President of the United States, Hubert Humphrey.

Thereafter we sauntered out to the lawn for cocktails in the warm air of a September evening, the ladies attired in the very best that America's richest men could buy. But darkness came early to the peace of the Timberfield valley which dipped below the lawn and as cocktail glasses clinked and moguls dangled at the end of outsized cigars there came a sight which startled even the most blasé out of their cynicism. Suddenly the gathering dusk became a glitter of floodlights and across the valley from the trees beyond came a hundred pipers playing *Scotland the Brave*. Lips which spell out million-dollar deals fell apart as those giants of Wall Street took in the incredible spectacle and confessed that, while they had seen just about everything in this goddam life, they had never seen anything quite like this. Hell man, this sure was something. Up they came to the manicured lawns, this parade of exiled pipers, a rousing echo of dear auld Scotland, forming a guard-of-honour for the guests as they trooped into the massive marquee where the anniversary dinner was being held. It is a well-worn joke about everything being bigger and better in America but the joke is on those who don't believe it. All the superlatives could not do justice to the fabulous events of that evening which began with the mellow strings of a massive orchestra performing on a stage bedecked with a plane-load of heather flown in from Prestwick.

We ate and danced and drank far into the night, Hubert Humphrey and I sharing a joke that we were the only two people there who were not Presidents! More chillingly, and in the light of recent events in Dallas, Texas, he could have been said to be just one shot away from being President of the United States. But this was a night for warm celebration in which Humphrey made a memorable speech, paying tribute to Bertie Forbes, the boy from the Cunnyknowe who took the standards of an Aberdeenshire cottage and used them as the yardstick by which he judged the shadier sections of business behaviour in his adopted land. Thus he became known as 'the great humanizer of American business', honoured by universities and respected all the way from the cottar houses of Buchan to the White House of Washington. It was a long way from New Deer to New York but that was the journey which little Bertie Forbes had taken so many years ago. He had encouraged me into journalism and here I was, amid the music and champagne and general euphoria of a special night in American history, rubbing shoulders with the mighty and reflecting on a scene which could not have been further removed from the origins of that romantic story.

It was indeed a far cry from the plains of Buchan as I turned it all over in my mind on the journey back to Manhattan. Dawn was already breaking over the skyscrapers of New York as the Cadillac delivered me in full evening dress to my hotel in 42nd Street. With the time difference, they would already be half way through a morning's yokin' in the hairst fields of Buchan, with little thought or caring for a fancy spree in a far-off land. Yet, to the extent that this had been Bertie's night, it was their night too. At the centre of the top table that evening had been Malcolm Forbes, carrying on the tradition of his famous father, just as he carries on to this day the magazine column which Bertie made popular on Wall Street and which is headed with a text he took from his days in the family pew at New Deer: 'With all thy getting, get understanding.'

CHAPTER NINETEEN

CHASING CHARLIE CHAPLIN

From the Atlantic to the Pacific I had seen that great American continent in the turmoil of a social revolution which ranged from the black uprisings of Detroit to the drug-assisted love-ins of the Flower People by the Golden Gate Park of San Francisco.

Back home in Britain the Rock 'n' Roll explosion of the fifties, which had blown sky-high the reigning standards of restraint and discipline, had given way to a more sophisticated social order which was generally described as the 'Swinging Sixties'. It was a stimulating decade, made all the more so in my own case by the range of people I came to meet. Even before that spell in America I had come in contact with a man who was to become the best-known name in the world, Cassius Clay, later choosing to call himself Mohammed Ali. He had already set the boxing world alight with his destruction of Sonny Liston and everyone was talking about this phenomenal fighter.

My encounter with Ali came about because I had some experience of the art of ghost-writing. That simply means you interview someone then write the article in the first person as if they had done it themselves. There is nothing dishonest about it. You are merely absorbing their thoughts and feelings and putting it all down as they would wish to express it. The first book I ever wrote was a 'ghosting' job, the autobiography of the immortal Jimmy Johnstone of Celtic, a football genius whose talents would never have extended to writing his own book. So I did it for him and the formula has become commonplace in modern times, especially among sports books.

The *Express* had signed up Mohammed Ali for a series of

first-person articles during his visit to Britain and I became the ghost-writer, travelling with him, eating with him, staying close enough to see and hear what was happening yet keeping discreetly in the shadows at the proper moments. With his regular flow of language Ali was, of course, a ghost-writer's dream, pausing from time to time to rattle off the kind of phrases which were unmistakably his own. In his build-up for an exhibition fight at the Paisley Ice Rink he travelled around like the celebrity he already was, meeting a bewildered public, signing autographs and generally playing the role for which he was to become even more famous.

His interest in verse prompted a visit to Burns's Cottage at Ayr and as we browsed round the little, white-washed house, Ali marvelled at the poetic creations which had sprung from such a humble base. He drew his hand over the bed clothes, turned the spinning wheel and fell into an unaccustomed silence from which he emerged to say: 'Man, I was feeling 'way 'way back in time just there. It does you good to pause sometimes and think about these things.'

The highlight of his day came when he sat in Burns's own chair, made out of the printing press which turned out his early editions. The Muse was not long in alighting on his broad shoulders for soon the Heavyweight Champion of the World was starting to reel off those verses which, even then, were coming to him so naturally. They came in odd scraps like:

> Now this man Burns lived far out of town
> It wasn't always easy to get around
> He began to find he'd plenty of time
> So he sat right down and started to rhyme. . . .

Then he was entertaining a growing band of admirers with frivolous stuff:

> I've heard of a man named Burns
> —supposed to be a poet

But if he was, how come I didn't know it?
They told me his work was very very neat
So I replied: 'But who did he ever beat?'

It was all carried out in a spirit of great good humour. But the most touching moment of my time with Mohammed Ali came at the MacDonald Hotel, on the south side of Glasgow, where he and Sugar Ray Robinson and most of the American boxers have chosen to stay down the years.

We were sitting at lunch one day when a little black nurse appeared at the dining-room door, shyly indicating that she wanted to speak to Ali. She was being given precious little encouragement until Ali sensed the situation and beckoned her in. The little lady introduced herself as Jen and recalled that she was one of the kids he used to play with in their back-street days in the state of Ohio. Of course! He remembered her well. So a chair was pulled up and Jen was invited to join us for lunch as the two of them delved back into their childhood days in less affluent surroundings.

It transpired that Jen was training as a nurse in Glasgow, still at the bottom end of her profession, when she announced to her superintendent that she knew Cassius Clay—and that she would ask him to come and visit the children in the Western General. There had evidently been explosions of disbelief and amusement at the claims of this little Miss Nobody. How could she possibly know the Heavyweight Champion of the World and how would he ever agree to interrupt his busy schedule even if she did? Well, can you imagine the scene as Mohammed Ali and I showed Jen into our classy limousine and drove up to the superintendent's office? Yes, yes, it was all true. Jen was indeed his childhood friend and he was delighted to come and visit the sick children in her hospital.

When Jen's superiors had managed to close their gaping mouths and rub the disbelief from their eyes, they led the Heavyweight Champion on a round of the wards where he played games, signed plaster-casts and kept up a non-stop patter which delighted his young audience. In the midst of it all he pulled me aside and said: 'This is the sort of thing ah like to do for ma people. Just think what this will do for little Jen.' There was no doubt that her achievements of that day had given her a new status. Her superiors were looking on her already with fresh respect and I always cherished the thought that the confidence which blossomed before our very eyes was the starting point for a successful career in a noble profession.

Wherever he went in Glasgow, into shops, banks or walking on pavements, traffic came to a halt and there was minor pandemonium. He accompanied me to the *Express* office and took over the daily editorial conference from Ian MacColl, the editor. Then he would withdraw to his hotel room and dial Los Angeles for it was the mid-sixties and there were race riots in the Watts district of the city, in which he showed a keen interest.

Street riots in America seemed a far cry from the more orderly ways of Britain at that moment but I was soon to learn that we should be careful about smug comparisons. Before long, the *Daily Express* was running a headline which said: '*Express* men caught in gas attack'. Imagine the horror of my father and mother in Maud as they read that their only loon had struggled to a telephone, suffering from a bellyful of the Army's notorious C.S. gas, to report the news that all hell had broken loose in Belfast, with gun battles, bomb explosions and the dead and injured lying everywhere. It was early days in the modern upheaval of the Ulster people but that particular night was to become known as the most violent in fifty years of Irish troubles. When the dust had settled and I had cleared my lungs of that fearful gas, I gathered my thoughts to write an article for the *Express*, from which this is an excerpt:

By the time I got to bed on Saturday, five people lay dead— two of them snipers gunned down by the Army—and dozens more, including 19 soldiers, were injured. All this in a land whose coastline at its nearest is just 13 miles from Scotland.

The first essential in a situation like Belfast is to sort out the niceties of noise, the crack of gunfire from the light boom of the gas grenade and the heavy thud of a bomb explosion. We had them all.

Then you learn the geography of the city in terms of the Catholic and Protestant areas, and the history in terms of the Unionists, Republicans or Nationalists and their multifarious offshoots.

Beyond that, there is the constant interpreting of events—why the stones, the barricades, the burning buses? Until you get to grips with the Irish position at close quarters the bald events can be oddly meaningless.

The weekend stones began to fly because the troops went in search of guns in the houses of Balkan Street. In one of the houses lay the corpse of a teenage girl and the menfolk didn't like it. That was when we began to dodge a hail of bricks and bottles.

The soldiers countered with C.S. gas and that was the moment when I did not require a second telling to beat it, running left and right in a blind agony of burning eyes and choking throat.

A kindly old lady called out 'Here me boy, dip your hanky in this and soak your face.' I did and found enough relief to see that most other people were in the same predicament. That antidote to C.S. gas was vinegar, supplied in bowl or bucket on window sills for everyone's use.

As the troops withdrew, a bulldozer came roaring round the corner with a scoopful of bricks, dumping loads at every street-end. The people of the Lower Falls were storing up their ammunition, some of it paving stones dug up with a pneumatic drill in readiness for a night of trouble.

They hi-jacked local buses and pushed them across the entrances to their symmetrical little streets to keep out possible attack from Protestants.

I found myself behind these barriers and soon up against a wall being closely questioned by a group of vigilante youths as to why I was there. Scottish journalists were not high on the popularity list and the situation looked ugly before I was finally cleared of suspicion. Some were for 'taking him inside' and I could only plead that I was a personal acquaintance of Jock Stein, whose respected name was plastered high on a facing wall.

And with darkness came the bullets, a full-scale shoot-out between the British troops and the stray gunmen of Albert Street, Servia Street, Leeson Street.

Down came the curfew in which everyone was ordered indoors except for a brief outing to collect milk and essential supplies. The people were allowed out again to church and Curfew Town came suddenly alive. The nightmare of bullets and bombs was over, for the moment at least. Now it was time to dress up in their Sunday best for Mass.

Children came out to play with the Army sandbags, finding some consolation for their weekend of bewilderment. Older folks said they could not remember anything like it, even in the 1920s. At lunchtime hundreds of Catholic women, singing cheerfully, came marching down the Falls Road from other districts with loaves of bread and bottles of milk to hand to their friends and relatives inside the curfew area.

Meanwhile the soldiers counted up the haul of captured arms—52 pistols, 35 rifles, six automatic weapons, 100 incendiary bombs, 25 pounds of explosives and 20,730 rounds of ammunition, enough to supply a battalion.

In the midst of a Belfast battle scene the incomer does not stop to question the insanity. He accepts it at face value—and runs like hell.

That was just the start of my encounters in trouble-torn Ulster as I proceeded to dodge the bombs and bullets on many a frightening night. Perhaps the most hair-raising took place in the Turf Lodge district of Belfast when I was travelling with an Army patrol inside an armoured car (known as a pig). The rattling of dustbin lids was the way of spreading the news that the Army was here and we were soon under ambush from a hostile crowd who finally exploded a nail bomb beneath where

I was seated. The tragedy of Northern Ireland has continued to plague us in an age of scientific wonders when mankind has come to expect that there must be a solution to every human problem. Whatever expedients may be found by the politicians, I would offer the depressing postscript that the troubles of the Emerald Isle may prove to be without any real solution at all.

On a lighter note, there was another insoluble problem of that period: trying to interview Charlie Chaplin. I had been trying repeatedly to make contact with the great actor, intending to visit him at his home in Vevey, Switzerland. But protective secretaries merely confirmed what was already well-known about Chaplin—that ever since those McCarthy days in America, when he was the subject of a witch-hunt for his allegedly Left Wing views, he would have nothing to do with Press interviews.

After five-and-a-half years of pursuit I was ready to give up, believing that there was a limit to the endurance of the most persistent of journalists. Then I heard that Chaplin and his wife Oona, daughter of the famous writer, Eugene O'Neill, were to take a holiday in this country, his first visit to Scotland in fifty years. It was too good a chance to miss. Somehow I had to find him and talk to him. My only clue to his whereabouts was a rumour that he would spend a night at the Torna-Coille Hotel, Banchory, but the receptionist there had been suitably briefed to keep the matter private. I knew by her reaction, however, that he was definitely coming so I booked myself a room and prepared to wait until Chaplin arrived. I then posted myself in the reception area, casually drinking cocktails and coffee and with one eye on a book and the other on the door. I did not have too long to wait. On my second day at the hotel a sleek limousine drew up at the doorway of the Torna-Coille and out stepped the greatest cinema legend of all time, a stocky little man of eighty-one, a raincoat hanging unbuttoned and a soft hat on top of his white hair.

I kept my distance, observing the check-in procedure, the

disappearance to a private suite and the re-emergence at the cocktail bar, where the Chaplins chatted happily with mine host, Matthew Armstrong, and other guests. I dined at the next table that evening and sat fascinated by the gestures and mannerisms of a man who still bore the unmistakable trace of his great days on the screen. He still tilted his head in that bashful way of making an overture to a lady, in this case his beloved Oona, his fourth wife by whom he had eight children and with whom he had found his deepest serenity.

It was not until later that evening when he had gone up-stairs that I made my introductions to Oona, explaining the innocence of my purpose—simply to talk to the great Chaplin and then write about him in the most affectionate way. The days of witch-hunts were surely gone and would he not accept at face value a Scottish journalist whose motives were strictly honourable?

Oona understood and promised to put the proposition to her husband, though she explained that he was extremely tired. She would bring his reply in the morning. I was already in position in the foyer when the Chaplins came for breakfast but her news was depressing. Regretfully, Charlie would not break his rule about interviews and there was no more she could do; she was sorry. I thanked her and knew that, as they prepared to leave after breakfast on the next stage of their holiday, my one and only opportunity in a lifetime to make contact was slipping away. There was just one chance left. I had brought along my copy of Chaplin's book, one of the finest autobiographies ever written. Would he sit down and autograph it while Oona went back to gather their bags?

He agreed and I helped him into a low sofa from which his aging bones might feel less inclined to emerge as soon as the signing was over! As he wrote—and to my astonishment—he began to answer my questions about the life which had taken him from poverty in the East End of London to great fame and fortune as the king of comedy. Was there a child in the world who did not regard Charlie Chaplin as a friend?

He had known every famous figure from Caruso, Valentino and Rachmaninov to Churchill, Einstein and H.G. Wells. We talked . . . and he sat . . . and we talked. At one stage I noticed that his nose had begun to run and he searched in vain for a handkerchief. Quickly I produced a clean one and he wiped his nose with that old familiar twitch. I asked him to keep it but he insisted in handing it back and we played out a short comedy routine reminiscent of his old films. 'Nowadays I live in Switzerland,' he said, 'and Oona and I go on holiday to Africa. But this year I said "Let's go to Scotland." Now we are heading towards Aberdeen and the south.'

Aberdeen? How would he like to see the old Tivoli Theatre where he had performed in the early years of this century? That familiar smile broke over his face. Yes, he would rather like to see the place again. Well, I would lead his chauffeur from Banchory to Guild Street for a brief stop before he headed south. It was all fixed. I made frantic contact with *Daily Express* photographer Ron Taylor who would record the precious moment at the Tivoli.

And so it happened. The chauffeur-driven Daimler drew up at the Tivoli door and out stepped the legendary Chaplin to pause with his memories of sixty-five years earlier. The entrance still beckoned you to 'Fauteuils and stalls' but now the show inside was bingo, not music hall. 'I used to come here both before and during my Fred Karno days,' he told me. 'In fact I was only about fourteen or fifteen at the time. I came to Scotland with "Sherlock Holmes" and we played here and in smaller towns like Dumfries and Dunfermline. I had a clear impression of Aberdeen and I did so want to see it again,' he added. And he marvelled at the beauty of what he had managed to see.

By now word had spread that Charlie Chaplin was here and within minutes a crowd had materialised. 'Good old Charlie', they called. As he glanced from side to side I half expected to see the little tramp accelerate round the corner, tripping the pursuing mob one by one with the crook of his stick. Instead he smiled, patted heads, signed autographs and realised in a heartwarming moment that there was a whole new generation of kids in this age of television to whom he meant just as much as he had done to their fathers and grandfathers. We took our farewells and I conveyed him back to his Daimler.

It had been a memorable episode and now he was seated in the back beside Oona, the woman who took his attention, as he said himself, 'with a luminous beauty, sequestered charm and gentleness'. Together they drove off, smiling and waving to the large crowd. I knew then the legend of Charlie Chaplin would never die. And that, having brought me the rarity of an interview with the man himself, my patience over five-and-a-half years had been well and truly rewarded.

The Chaplin experience taught me a lesson in perseverance which served me well in a similar pursuit of the richest man in the world, Paul Getty. Time after time I had sought an interview with Getty at his magnificent residence of Sutton Place, the stately home in Surrey which he had bought from the Duke of Sutherland. Getty, of course, was an American domiciled in Britain and owing his massive fortune to an uncanny nose for oil. His millions outstripped even those of the mysterious Howard Hughes.

Such men are generally hard to pin down and harder still to question about the secrets of their wealth so it came as no surprise when I was regularly passed on to a gentleman called Mr Wallace, who was never blunt enough to close the door completely but was always advising another call in about a month's time.

Patiently I followed the instruction, not just for two or three months but for *eighteen* of them! On that eighteenth call I asked as usual for my Mr Wallace and the girl on the Sutton Place switchboard plugged me into an extension. When the voice answered I said, as always: 'Is that Mr Wallace?' 'Mr Wallace?' queried the husky voice at the other end of the line.

'No, you've got the wrong extension. This is Mr Getty speaking.' 'Mr Getty?' I exploded in disbelief. 'Oh, it's really you I want to speak to, Mr Getty. As a matter of fact I've been trying to speak to you for the past eighteen months but I can never get past Mr Wallace. You're always too busy.'

I explained my journalistic mission, with particular reference to North Sea oil, in which Getty had a mere £100 million investment, and he replied: 'And you have been trying to talk to me for eighteen months? Well just you call back Mr Wallace and tell him to give you the first available appointment in my book.'

With a fluster of thanks I rang off and re-called the same number (for once in my lifetime blessing the error of a switchboard operator) and asked for Mr Wallace. As he began the familiar routine of calling back in a month's time I was able to say, with the greatest of authority: 'Mr Wallace, I am not asking for an appointment this time. I'm telling you! On Mr Getty's instructions, find me the first available appointment.'

'Mr Getty's instructions?'

It did not take long to convince him that I had spoken to the man himself—and within a week I was driving out into the Surrey countryside in a taxi and presenting myself at the first hurdle of security for the richest man in the world. Any notion that money means freedom takes on a farcical aspect when you find yourself passing through a system of electronic gates and being cautioned by a guard that you cannot walk in these grounds alone for fear of being savaged by the dogs. They snarled from every enclosure along the way to the mansion which was set within a massive acreage. To gain some impression of the scale of Getty's home you had to consider, for example, that the front lawn was fifteen times the size of Hampden Park. The rest of his life was built to match.

By a chain of aides I was conducted through this sumptuous mansion, which was built by Henry VIII for one of his knights, until we finally reached a rather modest-looking den where I was left alone with Jean Paul Getty. The picture was rather a pathetic one. For the man who counted his millions by the hundred was sitting alone with his shoe and sock off, nursing an agonising foot which all the money in the world could do little to ease. He apologised for the indignity of the situation but soon adjusted his mind to the matter of North Sea oil and began to answer my questions with a measured judgment which gradually revealed the tremendous depth of the man.

Greatness comes in a variety of guises but Getty seemed to feed your questions into a computer where a vast mechanism of knowledge, experience, instinct and wisdom produced a print-out which told you clearly that there is no substitute for the supremacy of human genius. He himself had bought up plot after plot which spurted oil with remarkable regularity. In 1949 he drew forecasts of bankruptcy when he bought the rights to a stretch of the Arabian desert which seemed like an endless waste of barren sand. In fact it turned out to be one of the most valuable oil properties in the world. Getty had a natural instinct for oil and helped me to put the North Sea saga into perspective by illustrating that there was a single oilwell in the Middle East which had more reserves than the whole of our Scottish waters put together.

It was springtime in the English countryside and together we looked out upon acres of daffodils as he contemplated a life which had been filled with the tragedies which so often beset the rich. His eldest son George died of an overdose of drink and drugs. The young son of his fifth marriage, whom he adored, took a brain tumour and died when he was twelve. There had been family rifts and finally there was the kidnapping of a grandson whose ear was chopped off.

Paul Getty, a man of deep culture, turned slowly to me with a wistful look in his eye and said: 'But I am an optimist. You have to be. There is no room for pessimists in the oil business.'

He bade me a courteous goodbye and invited me to come again. I turned on leaving the room and found him waving a frail old hand. The richest man in the world was not just alone but lonely.

I had come to know people like Bing Crosby to the point of exchanging Christmas cards and found the Old Groaner by far the easiest man in the world to interview. Once again it was a case of penetrating the barrier of protectors, often self-appointed, to find that the man himself was as free and amenable as one could wish for. Meetings with Crosby became as regular as they were delightful. He would tell me stories of the great American composers who were a particular interest of mine—the Gershwins, Berlins, Kerns and Porters. Having recently spoken to Irving Berlin and marvelling that he was writing popular songs in 1906 and was still doing so more than sixty years later, I appreciated one of Bing's tales in particular.

Irving Berlin made a point of keeping the copyright of everything he did, which showed that his business sense was as sound as his melodic inventiveness. Bing told me about the big musical they were making in Hollywood, featuring Berlin's music. In one particular song they needed to change key in the middle, a modulation which required the insertion of one single note. But it wasn't as simple as that. The director had to call in Berlin's lawyer to explain the situation. There was deep discussion and furrowed brows till the lawyer finally agreed to get on the phone to Mr Berlin in New York. Having fully explained the situation he waited for the master's permission to insert that vital note. There was evidently a long pause while the composer pondered the copyright position. Then he permitted himself a slow and cautious reply. 'Yeah,' he said. 'Yeah, I suppose that will be all right. But remember—it's *ma* note!'

CHAPTER TWENTY

HITLER'S FRIEND—AND MINE

Adolf Hitler and I had one thing in common—a mutual friend whose name was hardly known to the general public but who must rank as the most intriguing of all the people I have ever interviewed.

In the bid to play down the Hitler era after the Second World War, the German people had conveniently forgotten that Dr Ernst Hanfstaengl ever existed. But I had heard of him and managed to track him down at his villa in an exclusive suburb of Munich where he had lived for most of his extraordinary career as Press Chief of the Nazi Party and close friend and counsellor of Hitler, with a totally unique insight into the character of that fiendish man. It was Putzi Hanfstaengl (that was his popular name), the semi-aristocrat of big, broad build and charm to match, who took Hitler from the beer-halls of Munich and introduced him to the culture of the Hanfstaengl home, where the politicians, artists, writers and other influential people had a habit of gathering.

It was Hanfstaengl, himself taught by a pupil of Liszt, who became Hitler's favourite pianist, summoned from his home by car on many a night to play lullabies for the Führer when he couldn't sleep, which was often. It was Hanfstaengl who brought Hitler and Churchill to within a few yards of each other in a Munich hotel before the Nazi leader chickened out of an encounter which might have done wonders for world history. It was Hanfstaengl who came to know so much about the sexual deficiencies of the shrill little monster who had long pestered Mrs Helene Hanfstaengl (daughter of a German American businessman) with his amorous attentions. Finally it was Hanfstaengl who fell foul of his leader in 1937, escaped an attempt to assassinate him and fled to Britain where he was interned at the start of the Second World War. During the war he was transferred to the United States and became adviser to his old Harvard Club friend, President Roosevelt, on political and psychological warfare against Hitler.

The stories of this colourful career, verified by several of the Nazi war criminals, became a special fascination to be savoured over a period when I was a regular visitor at his charming home in Munich, the same house where he had entertained the Nazi hierarchy and where he would point out that Hitler used to sit there and Eva Braun there, and Goering and Goebbels over there, during their vigorous days of the twenties.

There we would talk into the night in a dimly-lit studio-room, piled high with musty books and magazines, still laden with an atmosphere of power and lingering evil—and finally enriched by the music which flowed from his old grand piano as he sat himself down on Mozart's own piano stool and ran his masterful fingers along the keyboard.

On one of our last evenings, when we had decanted an impressive array of wine bottles, he was full of nostalgia for an America which had given him not only his mother but firm friendships with people such as Roosevelt, William Randolph Hearst, T.S. Eliot and Walter Lippmann. He had, in fact, just returned from the 65th anniversary reunion of his Harvard classmates. His original arrival at Harvard in 1905, at the age of eighteen, had brought him to a country familiar not only because of his mother but because the family business of art reproduction had by then a branch on New York's Fifth Avenue.

His college days over, he stayed on to look after the branch, suffering the sticks and stones of anti-German feeling during the First World War. By 1921 the call of the Fatherland took him home to a Munich already embroiled in the ominous rumblings of Communism and other political agitations. Then one day he had a phone call from Warren Robbins, another ex-Harvard contact who worked at the American Embassy in Berlin, to say that he was sending down an attache to assess the on-goings in Bavaria and he wanted Hanfstaengl to introduce him to the right people. The attache arrived—Truman-Smith was his name, a Yale man but not a bad fellow for all that—and spent a few days summing up the situation before returning to take his leave of Hanfstaengl. 'I met the most remarkable fellow I've ever come across this morning,' he said. 'Adolf Hitler is his name.'

Hanfstaengl, who knew everyone worth knowing in Munich, looked blank.

'Are you sure you don't mean Hilpert, the German Nationalist?' he queried. No no, it was Hitler; and he was to be holding a meeting in a beer-hall that evening for which there were placards saying 'No entry for Jews'. Truman-Smith had to return to Berlin but he wanted Herr Hanfstaengl to attend the meeting and report his impressions to the American Embassy.

So he went along to the Kindlkeller beer-hall that evening, asked someone to point out this fellow Hitler—and suddenly clapped eyes on the unknown figure who would one day change the course of civilisation. Evidently Hitler gave a well-reasoned speech, with all the marks of a great orator and Hanfstaengl told me how he had gone up to the platform at the end to introduce himself. Hitler grasped at the chance of an entry to the Hanfstaengl home with its social graces and valuable contacts. Being himself ill-acquainted with the world outside Germany, he would come to rely on Hanfstaengl for guidance in that and many other respects. He wanted to know about America. He admired the Ku Klux Klan and Henry Ford (because of his allegedly anti-Semitic tendencies and also because he might be a source of funds).

Putzi Hanfstaengl used to play him stirring American marches from the days when he was taken along with the Harvard football team to rouse them to action before a game. He composed some himself. 'That's what we need for the movement,' said Hitler; and in his old age Hanfstaengl would cringe at the thought that it was one of his own compositions which was played by the Brownshirt columns as they marched through the Brandenburg Gate on the day that Hitler took power in Germany.

So the connection grew, at meetings in the Cafe Neumaier or back at Hitler's dull little room at 41 Thierschstrasse, with its threadbare rugs where he would pad around in braces and no collar, and where his collection of books ranged from *A History of the Great War* to the *History of Erotic Art*. He disliked Bach and Mozart but was always delighted when Putzi would sit down and play him the prelude to Wagner's *Meistersinger*. Gradually Putzi Hanfstaengl was able to unravel the mystery of Hitler's sex life and to come up with the intriguing and probably accurate theory about the connection between his hysterical oratory and his sexual deficiencies. The beautiful Mrs Hanfstaengl, who had had to fend off his persistent infatuation, told her husband that the Führer was in fact a neuter, neither fully homosexual nor heterosexual and suffering complexes from the time he caught syphilis in Vienna in 1908.

To Hanfstaengl his speeches were akin to the work of a great orchestral conductor. But he once wrote this interesting observation: 'It was gradually being borne in on me that Hitler was a narcissus type for whom the crowd represented a substitute medium for the woman he did not seem able to find. Speaking, for him, represented the satisfaction of some depletion urge and to me this made the phenomenon of his oratory more intelligible. The last eight to ten minutes of a speech resembled an orgasm of words.'

Hanfstaengl became the man above most who could say almost anything to Hitler and get away with it. Standing tall and impressive outwith the immediate political circle, he occupied a unique position as friend and counsellor, link man between Hitler and the world's Press, as well as pianist, sparkling conversationalist and high-class court jester. Disdainful of some of the human trash who surrounded the Führer, he raised jealousy and suspicion among them, a special position which he relished. Moreover—and only Putzi could have achieved this—he claimed that he never did join the Nazi Party! He did, however, become deeply involved in such ploys as the notorious Putsch of 1923 and had to flee for his life when it came unstuck. Hitler fled one way (to Hanfstaengl's wife at their country home in Uffing) while Hanfstaengl himself crossed to Austria and visited some of Hitler's relatives in Vienna. These included Hitler's niece, the ill-fated Geli Raubel, whom he took to the opera, not knowing that she would later come to Germany, become the object of Uncle Adolf's amorous approaches and finally commit suicide, an incident which seemed to divert him to an even more resolute course of savage behaviour.

Hanfstaengl crept back to Germany in disguise but Hitler was caught and jailed at Landsberg, where he gathered his thoughts for his book, *Mein Kampf*. On the day he left prison he went straight to the Hanfstaengl house at Pienzenauer Strasse in Munich for a celebration dinner of turkey and the rich Austrian pastry which Hitler loved so much. The inner circle was meeting at the Cafe Heck in Munich's Galleriestrasse—and the course towards eventual power was resumed.

It was in the early 1930s, when Hitler was heading briskly towards his dictatorship, that he came to within a few yards of Churchill, the closest the two men ever came to actually meeting. Hanfstaengl was dining with the Churchill family at the Hotel Continental in Munich, to which he had been asked to bring Hitler along. But the latter made his excuses and Putzi had to go alone. As the dinner conversation wore on, he realised how vital it could be to bring the two men together. He told me: 'I excused myself from the table and went off frantically to reach Hitler by telephone to see if he would change his mind. Lo and behold! There he was in the hotel lobby, in his dirty white overcoat and green hat, taking his farewell of a Dutchman. Here was Hitler in the lobby and Winston Churchill in the restaurant and me in the middle failing, I'm afraid, to convince Hitler of the need to come in for a chat. He was unshaven and, in any case, he had too much to do, he said. So I had to go back and put a good face on it. But what an opportunity lost.'

Putzi Hanfstaengl, a man with an enormous capacity for living, became more and more distressed at the trend of Hitler's thinking and concerned about the influence of men like Rudolf Hess, who was later to rot out his days in Berlin's Spandau Jail. Hanfstaengl's attempts to moderate the course brought him into conflict with the hell-bent aims of his leader and the crisis had to come.

Sitting in his Munich study one February day in 1937, preparing a speech for the 205th anniversary of George Washington, Hanfstaengl had a call to say that Hitler's pilot was coming to collect him. The mission was to go to Spain to complain to Franco about the lack of facilities for German correspondents covering the Spanish Civil War. It was an unusual errand but he complied. On the flight the pilot, who he happened to know, tipped him the wink that this was an assassination bid. There was no intention of landing in Spain. The Gestapo were on board and Hanfstaengl was to be conveniently 'dropped'. Instead, the pilot obligingly brought the plane down with some engine trouble and enabled Putzi to make his getaway across the Swiss border. It was his fiftieth birthday.

It seemed that Hitler's fury had boiled over at tales of Hanfstaengl's criticism, carried to him by Miss Unity Mitford, the British girl who had hopes of becoming Hitler's wife. So began the exile in Britain and America. Lord Beaverbrook took a special interest in his arrival in Britain for Hanfstaengl had once successfully sued the Beaver for £10,000 in the London High Court over a defamatory item in the William Hickey column of its day. But Ribbentrop, who was German Ambassador in London at the time, advised Hitler to prevent the money from being uplifted because of Beaverbrook's immense influence in political affairs. It would do Germany no good at all. So Putzi had to do without his money and now found himself at the mercy of the British when war broke out in

1939. He was first despatched to Beaverbrook's native land of Canada and then to America and it was ten years before he would see his beloved Germany again. When he did so, he gradually settled to a life as quiet as a man of such large personality and joyous extravagance of living can have.

A Germany so anxious to forget its Hitlerism soon managed to obliterate Hanfstaengl from its memory. But having once unearthed him in his secluded setting I continued to visit him more or less every year, taking my wife and three sons for whom it was a fascinating encounter with the reality which had already found its way to the forefront of their history books at school.

We would stroll through the French windows to the lawn or repair to the den with its grand piano and books and lingering sense of the Nazi hierarchy. There Putzi would sit, recalling it all with the aid of expressive hands, a full crop of hair crowning a noble head, the deep voice alternating with a comic falsetto as the jester jested. He would talk and fill up the wine glasses and put it all to music on that fine old piano. I tried to freeze the moments and absorb Putzi Hanfstaengl as a piece of living history, a likeable rascal in his own right, a vital witness to the character of a madman who wrote the blackest chapter of all in the story of man's inhumanity to man.

CHAPTER TWENTY-ONE

FOO'S YER KWEETS?

It is one of the abiding joys of my life that I have been able to carry the boyhood enthusiasm for journalism right through to middle age. The early gloom about my health has added an edge of appreciation to the experiences of life and encouraged me to wring a maximum of satisfaction from all I do. The excitements of famous people and faraway places have been more than I had any right to expect; but now I was putting it all behind me for the moment and looking again at the place where I began with its steady ways and customs, its particular rhythms and very distinctive form of speech.

Robert Louis Stevenson believed that the local dialects of Scotland would more or less die out in his lifetime. Certainly he was still in early middle-age when he died suddenly in 1894 but even if he had lived a normal span he would still have been mistaken in his judgment. As I have already mentioned, the Doric play which my great-grandfather wrote in the year of Stevenson's death survives into the latter part of the twentieth century. Nearly ninety years after Stevenson I would not dare forecast that the rich, expressive dialect of the North-East will disappear in my lifetime nor in that of my children; and that allowing for the fact that it is under its most serious bombardment of all time from the neutralising effects of television.

But if the language survives it is undeniably in the process of dilution, not so rapidly in the accent as in the substitution of the anglicised word for the dialect one. In the thirties, for example, the day after Monday was Tyesday and two days after that was Fiersday, as surely as your ankles were your 'kweets', the hooping-cough was the 'kink-host' and children learned to count in 'een, twa, three, fower, five, sax, seiven, acht. . . .' You might 'tak a muckle clort o' a deem in yer oxters' and regret it at your leisure but the language on which I was weaned was a colourful expression of human thought, with many a word or phrase so hopelessly irreplaceable by an English equivalent. I knew these words because I had heard them in everyday use among the country folk of my childhood. But I do not use them widely now, except as a recollection, and my vocabulary does not compare with that of my grandfather and my own children's knowledge of Scots words will not match my own; so the inevitable conclusion must be that the words will eventually disappear, except as objects of scholarly study. Stevenson was mistaken only in his time-scale.

Yet those words express something deep and eternal in the character of the people who were bred from them and they are readily recognised when the occasion arises. I cannot recall that any of my friends would have claimed the slightest interest in the works of Burns when we were teenagers. That was exclusively for the decrepit. Yet in 1976 I attended the 150th anniversary dinner of Peterhead Burns Club and there, around the table, proposing toasts and drinking to them and generally acclaiming the genius of a master of Scots language, was an array of kent faces from my own generation, now solid, middle-aged citizens steeped in the glories of a man they would not have acknowledged thirty years earlier.

There is another glimmer of hope. In the lifetime of television drama it has become acceptable to parade the accents of London, Wales and the West Country, Liverpool, Geordieland and even the slovenly English of Glasgow. But somehow the richness of the North-East dialect of Scotland was considered too obscure to be intelligible. That insult to a fine native tongue was finally quashed when that brilliant BBC producer, Pharic MacLaren, decided to televise Lewis Grassic Gibbon's *Sunset Song* and proved that the rhythms of Aberdeenshire could be understood and enjoyed not only across the breadth of Britain but over the entire American continent as well.

It was a significant step, giving rise to more television exposure of Grassic Gibbon's work as well as that of other North-East writers like Jessie Kesson (*The White Bird Passes*) and the Buchan fisherman James Duthie (*Donal and Sally* and *The Drystane Dyker*). Interest broadened and the poetry of people like Flora Garry and the prose of that delightfully unspoiled farm servant David Toulmin took on a fashionable mantle.

Their speech was part of that eternal thread of Scottishness which draws us together as a recognisable people and was the firm foundation of my village childhood, where everything was sound and settled and permanent and you were not disturbed by the constant irritation of change for change's sake. Life was based on a fabric of people whose families had been there for as long as your own and whose inter-relationships were bluntly frank. Nobody rose too far without the decided risk of being forcibly brought back to earth with the traditional Scottish leveller of 'Ah kent yer faither'. My own native village of Maud had produced one of the best British playwrights of this century, Lesley Storm—her father was minister at Maud for thirty-five years—but through all the fame and wealth which she gained with plays like *Black Chiffon* and *Roar Like A Dove* she was never known as anything else but her real name, 'Mabel Cowie, the minister's dother'.

In that setting there was a dogged determination towards hard work and good learning and maybe they knocked the stuffing out of us in a pattern of life which left little room for anything that was not worthwhile. Folk who went gallivanting away on holiday were as little regarded as a man who wore suede shoes or yellow gloves. Sex was all right as long as you didn't enjoy it. My father was capable of hard judgments in his earlier days and the maddening thing was that his verdicts on individual worth so often turned out to be justified in the end. My mother on the other hand would take a more liberal view of life and question the devotion to hard work and sensible attitudes as a worthy cause in its own right. Her romantic dreams beyond the bare boundaries of Buchan would have made her suspect in some quarters but she stirred in me a craving for the brighter lights and exotic excitements of a more glamorous world. Washing off the Imperial Leather soap from her face and sitting down to spread witch-hazel jelly on her chappit fingers she would long for the opportunity to dance through the Vienna Woods to the rousing waltzes of Johann Strauss or Franz Lehar. She had never seen an opera in her life but that did not prevent her from memorising every note of *Cavalleria Rusticana* or *Carmen* or a dozen others through listening to the wireless and she could tell me in plain Buchan tones the merits of *Ave Maria* from the pen of Schubert as opposed to the Bach-Gounod version. She was a disciple of the Russian composer Katchachurian thirty years before the public discovered his name from *The Onedin Line* and she would caper around the living-room to the rousing waltz from his *Masquerade Suite*.

So culture came into our house at 2 Park Crescent more or less by the back door and took its place among the homespun life and language of an otherwise average Buchan family. Sometimes the matter-of-factness of our rural ways would spill over to a coarseness which was less than attractive. I can think of the feet-washing, for example, that strange ritual which preceded a marriage and brought out some of the rougher edges of the North-East character. It was counted as a manly act for a whole gathering of weighty chiels to capture the bridegroom on the eve of his wedding and subject him to a rough-and-tumble in a large zinc tub. If his bride could be lured to the scene then she, too, was manhandled to the ceremony and some rugged chap, with the help of a woman body, would unhook her suspenders (who had heard of tights in those days?) and remove her stockings for the fray. It struck me as a cowardly exercise, alarming enough for the spectating child let alone the poor victims. Any pretence of giving the feet of the betrothed a clean start was usually destroyed by the subsequent extravagance of blackening them all over with boot polish. Many a bridegroom went to the altar with skin that was hard-scrubbed and raw from the last-minute attempts to remove some grimy application. A relative of mine became so distressed by the vulgar display that he grabbed his double-barrelled shotgun and threatened to shoot the lot of them and I must say I had some sympathy with him.

The sickening excitement of those feet-washings in the farm kitchen was matched by another local horror from time to time on a Sunday when a dentist came from Aberdeen to hold surgery on a kitchen chair and friends and neighbours came nervously to have their rotten teeth extracted and to spit volumes of dark blood into a white enamel pail. Dentistry has come a long way when I relate my own experience to children who now undergo the most sophisticated treatment, with high-speed drills and orthodontists to straighten their teeth. In 1938 I was laid flat on my back on the kitchen table by Dr Crombie—yes, a doctor, not a dentist—who proceeded to cover my nose and mouth with the terrors of a chloroform mask and tell me to count sheep. I counted close on a hundred of the damned creatures before finally succumbing to the choking sensation of the mask and for the next half-hour he used a pair of glorified pliers to pull seventeen of my first teeth, during which my mother was cooking the mince and tatties through the scullery door. Such was the level of sophistication in the thirties.

But all things are relative as I thoroughly conceded when Granny Barron gave me proof beyond all doubt that it could have been worse. As a young girl she had had her tonsils removed without any anaesthetic at all. The doctor simply turned up at the Schoolhouse of Whitehill one day and told her to lean back on the settee and open her mouth. Without more ado he put a knife down her throat, cut out one tonsil then gave her time to clear the blood and gather her remaining strength and courage. 'Now we'll do the other one,' he said and the performance began all over again. So there is something to be said for modern medicine and methods after all, even if it has to be recorded that Granny Barron nevertheless lived gloriously on to be ninety-one.

CHAPTER TWENTY-TWO

THE HIVE OF HONEYNEUK

As I cast back over it now I can still recapture the sense of that childhood and youth which had taken me through the thirties into the Second World War and out of it to a world of atom bombs and austerity, bread units and clothing coupons; but it was drawing to a close with the approach of my twenty-first birthday in 1952.

By then a man I was later to know as Bill Haley was formulating a new sound in music which was to hit the world as Rock 'n' Roll and set off a whole new trend in the public behaviour of human beings. The mood of the thirties had carried over to the post-war era, a little threadbare and erratic in its pace, with the Ruritania of Ivor Novello still maintaining its glorious illusion on the London stage. In Scotland a new race of comedians like Stanley Baxter and Jimmy Logan was emerging to extend the tradition of Tommy Lorne, Harry Gordon, Tommy Morgan, Dave Willis and others. But there was a feeling of suspension as if the whole structure might soon collapse and be replaced by something new; and that happened in the early-to-mid fifties when Bill Haley and Elvis Presley in America and Tommy Steele in Britain threw wide the floodgates of a new and more energetic order. The world had at least come alive again, with whatever mixture of consequences.

Before that youth finally slipped away from me, however, my father was casting his eyes upwards from the council house in the village towards the farm of Honeyneuk, just half-a-mile up the brae on the way to Brucklay. For long he had dreamed of owning his own farm and Honeyneuk in particular, for it sat on a picturesque slope with a windmill and encompassed the whole valley from its front lawn. The boy who had become the mainstay of his mother's smallholding at the age of eight would indeed have arrived at the peak of his ambition if he could lay hands on Honeyneuk which was then, at that moment in 1952, on the market for sale. Two hundred acres of it and some was stony land, they said, which played havoc with your ploughshares. But he had plans for blasting the boulders out of existence and turning it into as fine a farm as there was in the district.

John Webster had been a wage-earner all his life and was not a man of capital, but he did possess those incomparable assets of a sound knowledge of his subject, a reliable character and a determination to succeed; in short, he was a bank manager's dream and that was why he had no difficulty in borrowing the thousands necessary to bid for Honeyneuk. It was not my mother's idea of joy to exchange her village home, where the neighbours dropped in at any old time for a fly-cup and a blether, for the greater solitude of the farmhouse. By nature she was a gregarious creature who thrived on human contact but there was no possible hope of thwarting my father in his treasured ambition. He surveyed the broad acres with a stick and a dog and was in no doubt that this was the place for him. So the bid went in and the farm was his and to Honeyneuk they went and there my mother would turn up the volume of her beloved radiogram, which now augmented the wireless, to give full flavour to Dvorak or Tchaikovsky or Strauss and she would gaze wistfully down the brae towards the village where she had spent her happiest years. In place of the ready neighbour she would spend her time in the company of Albert Ketelbey and the glorious sound of his *Sanctuary of the Heart* or *In a Monastery Garden*.

As further consolation she had the company of Nigger, a most extraordinary dog who was half a collie and half a Black Labrador but he was almost wholly a gonner one day in 1949 when my father arrived at a farm on the Red Hill and found the man on the verge of shooting the poor brute. 'Na, na, ye canna dae that,' said my father as Nigger pleaded with his big brown eyes. 'Ah'll tak' the beast hame.' Thus Nigger moved from the edge of death to a fulness of life which can hardly have been surpassed in canine history. He became the Websters' dog, surrounded by affection and proving himself a beast of such uncanny intelligence that my mother swore he was human. On his first Christmas morning he returned from a furtive adventure and produced from the tenderness of his Labrador mouth a little chicken, alive, unmarked and terrified. He laid it on the mat between my father and mother, guarded it with one paw and looked up as if to say: 'It's not much but here is a token of gratitude for saving my life.' We discovered that the bird had come from the hen-run of Ann-Jean Stephen, an elderly spinster not exactly famed for her sociable habits. Dad had the devil's own job to slip the chick back where it belonged before the dire deed was discovered! Nigger moved from the village to the farm with the flitting of 1952 and lived on to the ripe old age of sixteen, constantly repaying his debt with an utter devastation of the rat population at Honeyneuk. When he finally died, poor brute, Dad dug him a decent grave at the garden gate and there his bones lie to this day, marked by a few rough stones of remembrance while his soul must surely rest in that corner of the Hereafter where the good Lord keeps his kennels. I can vouch for the fact that there will be no rats in heaven for as long as Nigger reigns.

Meanwhile, my father had set about the blasting of the Honeyneuk stones though he had scarcely embarked on the task when he was overtaken by the notorious January Gale of 1953, the worst in living memory, when houses were blown apart, people lifted off their feet and carried away and the northern half of Scotland was left bare and devastated. That frightening day of 31 January was to carve its own memorial in the clumps of trees atop the Scottish knolls. They stand even now with slanted posture, like ballerinas wilting with outstretched arms, their leafy cloaks in rags and the power to generate their greenery sadly depleted. Everybody had a story to tell, sometimes an exaggerated one, which would illustrate the force of the fearsome blast but few surpassed the one told by my father, who had been trying to explain to another farmer the strength of the wind which had howled around Honeyneuk. 'Ach, that's naething,' said the other chiel. 'We had sic a force o' wind that oor dog opened his mou' tae bark—and farted.'

Indeed the man's story might well have been true for that same gale took hold of the Honeyneuk steading roof, lifted it off its supports and swept it up, up and away, across the woods of Brucklay estate, which lies adjacent, and we never saw it again. With some help from a relief fund my father put on a better roof, believing it was an ill wind that did nobody some good, with windows brought from the derelict remains of Brucklay Castle to filter God's light and to brighten the winter munchings of the beef cattle which were the mainstay of a farm like Honeyneuk. The basics of a Buchan farm were much as they had been for generations, except that the traditional crop of oats, which gave us our porridge and brose and fed the livestock, was giving way to barley which could either feed cattle or be sold to the distillers for the commendable cause of making whisky. But the farm life which faced my mother in the fifties was a vastly different business from that of her mother in the earlier part of the century. Almost gone were the hens which had scratched about the farm-close at Mains of Whitehill picking up Nature's protein and turning out eggs with rich red yokes which tasted like eggs. The big combines had moved into the trade by then, mass-producing the eggs from hens in solitary confinement, encouraging the birds to grow for an early death with injections of stuff which was said to endanger a man's virility. God preserve us! By then, too, my father had decided that it was better to dispense with the farm cow and to buy milk from a travelling dairyman. An older generation would have turned in its grave but this was what the world called progress and maybe it was and maybe it wasn't. For certain the world was changing at the time of our arrival at Honeyneuk.

Was it then that I severed my ties with a Buchan childhood and youth or was it not until some time later when the telephone rang one Saturday morning in my Glasgow home? However it may sound in cold print, there was nothing callous in the introduction which greeted me as I answered the call from my father. 'Well Jack, fit like?' 'Oh nae bad Dad.' 'Well, mother passed away at nine o'clock. . .' Thus a Buchan man will announce the death of his wife to their only child and thus a Buchan loon will discover how swiftly the world can become a duller place to live in. The gaiety of spirit had finally been worn down by the hazards of a crippling and chronic bronchitis, that taste of roosty nails, as she had described, which she wanted to tackle by going down 'wi' a barra and spad tae hae a gweed redd-oot'. As the auctioneer's wife she had answered the phone, taken messages and offered advice to most farming folk in Buchan for she had acquired a sound knowledge of my father's business and was blessed with a clarity of explanation which eluded my father.

If I seek the source of my journalistic interest I need look no further than my mother who was a natural reporter. Long after I had left Buchan she kept me fully informed on local life with a weekly bulletin which was a model of keen observation and brilliant description. People felt the better for talking to her and they did not forget. When we held the funeral service in New Deer Church, where she had first joined as a girl along with my father, they said there had never been a turn-out of folk to match it. Eight hundred flocked from all over Buchan to pack out the downstairs of the kirk and none deserved the tribute better. Her dreams of being a ballet dancer came no nearer than a single visit to a performance of *Coppelia* at His Majesty's Theatre, Aberdeen, but she had enriched her life with the joys of music. If I had failed in my promise to take her to Vienna one day there was some consolation in the fact that I had taken her to meet her operatic heroine, Joan Hammond, when she was staying at the Caledonian Hotel, Aberdeen, as well as Max Jaffa, Reginald Kilby and Jack Byfield who were among her other favourites. Through all the music she had absorbed from the wireless there was one particular piece which emerged as her eventual choice above all others.

'Dvorak's *New World Symphony*,' she would tell you. 'I want it played at my funeral. Tell Johnny Walker, the organist.' And so it was. When the time came, Johnny Walker was told and the eight hundred souls who flocked into New Deer Church that cold January day were greeted with the strains of 'Going Home' from the Dvorak symphony. Mam was going home all right, much too soon for one who had enlivened all that she had touched; gone with so much left unsaid by a careless son. In the manner of a country funeral we raised our voices and sang *Crimond*, composed just a few miles away by Jessie Seymour Irvine, who sang in her father's church choir along with my wife's grandfather. Then came that other favourite hymn, 'The Day Thou Gavest, Lord, is Ended', before we proceeded up the main street of New Deer to the kirkyard on the Hill of Culsh, a high point from which you could survey the whole of Buchan. And there we laid her to rest as the minister raised his hand in benediction and the wind blew cold over Culsh's brae. I raised my head and saw in the distance Mains of Whitehill, the small farm where she had been born. Half a mile below us was the village of New Deer, where she had gone to school, and further down the naked plain of Buchan I could see Maud, crisp and clear, where she had spent her married life from 1931 to 1971.

'Lay me against the cemetery dyke so that I'll be sheltered on windy nights,' she used to joke; she was one layer short, as it turned out, and there we left her to the gathering darkness of a winter's night with a wind rising snell by the monument of Culsh and a sore tugging at the conscience about leaving her there alone. I like to think that the January blast was of little consequence in the haven of her journey's end and that the hot sing of a summer's day was the climatic background to a Dvorak symphony which would leap and linger to her eternal pleasure in the auditorium of the golden sunset.

We gathered back at Honeyneuk for a dram and had a sandwich and saw folk we hadn't seen for years; it was a time of happy recollection, of good fellowship in the way that funerals tend to be. People are drawn closer in a greater dependence and an unwillingness to part. The women-folk served tea in the best room where the radiogram and the records still lay and where Mam herself had lain till that very day. Then one by one folk left for home till there were only Dad and myself.

Next day I was to drive away south and the parting was bound to be hazardous for two Buchan men, father and son, whose tradition gives them little practice in the art of communication, especially on tender matters. So we stood in the farm-close, awkward and embarrassed, neither knowing what to say to the other. Emotionally, we had been strangers, my father and I, uneasy with each other's company but now, in the very moment when we had lost our common bond, forced into the contact of two little boys who had suddenly been orphaned. In the platitudes of goodbye, we fell into a silence, standing side by side, then as if jogged by the woman who was gone we acted in one movement and clasped each other by the hand. It was hopelessly out of character, daft-like and bizarre for Buchan men, and I wondered when I had last as much as touched my father's hand for it was not in the nature of the creatures to do so. There we stood without words but not without tears till we had regained our composure and self-respect, for Buchan men do not cry.

Thus I stepped into the car and drove out of the farm-close towards Aberdeen and the south, leaving behind the place of my roots and deepest affections and knowing in my heart that it could never be the same again. The setting of my childhood was there before me in all its familiar landscape but suddenly its meaning and its bare beauty had drained to a deadness, for landscapes and what they mean to us live mainly by the people who inhabit and enrich them. Whoever created the cliché about no one being indispensible must surely have forgotten about mothers.

Well into his sixties, my father was still planning the future of Honeyneuk with a stretch of vision and anticipation which pre-supposed a lengthy stay on this earth. With a keener aware-ness of life's limits, my mother had poked fun at his sense of immortality and chided him for not drawing in his horns. But Dad would seldom take a telling. Lack of a father may have given him an early independence but it left him without a check-ing influence. His enthusiasm for the single-minded pursuit of farming had, indeed, given him a sense of immortality, as Mam had said, but a couple of minor dwams at the mart at Maud were Nature's hint and the next time I was visiting him he casually mentioned that I should carry on the farm 'if onything ever happens tae me'. It was the first time he had acknowl-edged the possibility, however remote, but his instinct was sure once more. The gradual clogging of a cerebral artery became complete in one day and the life of John Webster, dynamic, good-humoured, quick-tempered Buchan farmer and auction-eer, virtually ended on that Burns' Day of 1976. He never made another decision, though he lingered on for sixteen months of predictable decline until the night in May, 1977, when a fur-ther stroke put him into his final hours.

I arrived at Honeyneuk in time to wipe his fevered brow and, as I did so, the black crow of death came settling on the window-sill as an omen of the inevitable. I would not have believed that such things really happen. Whatever he knew or could see or hear or think in those fading hours we shall never know for he was gripped in an involuntary rhythm of heavy breathing, like the bellows which once blew his mother's peat fire into life or out of it. This time there was no choice and I knew that I was about to witness the moment of death for the first time. The bellows-breathing ended and the upturned eyes reverted to a normal setting but the head came forward in a jaw-jutting determination to live. In the very throes of death and with the doggedness which sustained his character, John Webster was not prepared to go without a fight. A last gesture of defiance then death came down over his face like the final

205

curtain of a theatrical production, leaving no doubt that the performance of life was over. John Webster: 1905-1977. So that was how, in the briefness of a few seconds, a human life comes finally to a close. The moment itself seemed unworthy of the wealth of time and experience and effort which had gone before.

Outside on a fine Spring night his cattle munched at lush grass on the land which he had made his own, fields which he had cleansed of the inhibiting stone through fifteen years of relentless blasting and turned into rich acres of fertility. A tractor bleated on a distant hill and raucous laughter came through the still air from the village below, loud and uncaring, to prove that life will go on as ever. But at Honeyneuk, the farm which he had longed for those many years ago and had finally acquired and tended and loved with an unspeakable devotion, the maister was at rest for ever. Charlie Fraser, the grieve, came up and so did Jimmy Mutch, the baillie, and tea was brewed for the gathering relatives by Mrs Mutch and Helen, who had been there in domestic service with my mother since she left school. Eric Simpson the joiner, who had been at school with me, came with his quiet efficiency and took charge of the arrangements (as he had done with my mother) though he himself, poor lad, did not have long to live. Dad's immortality had ended, as Mam said it would, and there was only a sheet to pull up and a dram to pour and a quiet prayer to offer in the stillness of the Buchan night.

CHAPTER TWENTY-THREE

VIEW FROM THE HILL

Essentially I am a peasant, rising from the stock of the land, so it has been no surprise that I have wandered the world and felt an affinity with bedouins in the Sahara Desert and innocent tribes in the thickets of the Malayan jungle. A man can escape from the confines of his beginnings and take on layers of sophistication but he cannot escape from himself. When you peel away the veneer of our civilisation there are bonds which are as old as time itself and which tie us without yield to the places of our sunrise.

So I have come on this sentimental journey to look again on the soil which gave me roots and what better night to come than Hogmanay, a watershed in the Scottish psyche? Outby the night is crisp and clear, half-lit by a moon which casts its glow o'er parks and crofts and village houses down below, a world that hovers between reality and fantasy and makes a man stop to wonder where the known might end and the unknown begin. Here I am on Banks Hill, at the other side of the valley from Honeyneuk, with an elevated view of the village of Maud. Down there lies Fedderate Cottages, where I was born in the front room of a but-and-ben those many years ago, and just behind it No.2 Park Crescent, which is filled with such happy memories. There is the path which led us to school and the playground where we jostled at cock-fighting or tackie or football and keeked over the wall as Doris or Mary or Margaret skipped and played rounders and squaries. Over there lies the Market Stance of the feein' markets and cattle floats and Dick's Circus; down to the right the station where I first watched the horses coming round from Aikey Fair and where we waved goodbye to the men who were off to war. Now a solitary engine hoots a plaintive call as a hundred years of bustling history comes sadly to an end. Down farther to the right the Low Village and the war memorial, where moss is gathering on those clear black names of yesteryear. Along to the hospital, or the Poorhouse as it was in those earlier days of the Dafties who slaved so hard.

On the grey horizon of a vanishing light, the Monument of Culsh points its fingers in the prayerful direction of heaven and beneath it now, ice-cold and still, lie the two who once found warmth and joy in my conception. Up here on Banks Hill those forty year ago we sledged on clear frosty nights like this and felt no need to contemplate a world that was heading for war and strife. This was our rural enclosure and we were safe and forever; and even when you flee the nest and come back again it seems as if you might never have been away. Was it all a dream? A fantasy? Did the Kremlin and the White House and the heights and the hovels and garish excitement of Hong Kong really exist? If so, they did nothing to break the thread of continuity which runs through the fabric of a people and will do so for as long as human beings will breed their own. Is it just my imagination or do I hear an organ playing quietly in the kirk below? Either way, I cannot but be stirred with love for my native soil as country voices soar into the heavens in plain sincerity. Perhaps it is in the singing of a simple hymn that people are drawn closest together, lifted out of themselves to a height of noble harmony which is beyond worldly explanation.

From the moonlit pool beneath comes the maudlin call of a Hogmanay drunk and a reminder that it is time to suspend the reverie and to stride down again to the maelstrom of living. The voices from the kirk come louder to meet me:

> A thousand ages in thy sight
> Are like an evening gone;
> Short is the watch that ends the night
> Before the rising sun

Time, like an ever-rolling stream,
Bears all its sons away;
Then fly, forgotten, as a dream
Dies at the opening day

O God, our help in ages past
Our hope for years to come;
Be thou our Guard while troubles last
And our eternal home.

By the iron railings of the kirk I pause to listen and to glance at the memorial in the corner. The spell is broken once more by a worldly wail of 'Nelly Dean' and the hooching and thumping in the village hall as mundane spirits cast themselves upon the helter-skelter of the eightsome reel. Yes, it is Hogmanay, an end and a beginning. A cursory glance around ensures that nobody is looking as I lunge my boyhood fervour at a well-shaped pebble which ricochets from kerb to dyke and back again, its echoes ringing eerily up the street and through the Bow Briggie.

Thus a Buchan loon embraces the scene of his childhood and finds a new warmth in the place where he began. Once more in the cradle, the wandering bairn drifts happily to sleep.

II

ANOTHER GRAIN OF TRUTH

To the folk of Buchan,
whose life and language, rich and expressive,
have compelled me to write about them
over the years.

CHAPTER ONE

THE WAY IN . . .

On a wild November afternoon of 1981 I drove up from the south and out through Aberdeen towards the Buchan fishing port of Fraserburgh, a town in which I was far from being a stranger.

I had grown up in that North-East corner of Scotland, just fifteen miles inland, but now I was back as an author for my first real encounter with the 'signing session', that precarious adventure in book promotion which can boost your sales and morale at one deft stroke or send you scurrying for a hiding-place with a colourful attack of embarrassment.

Vivid in my mind was the day I accompanied the American best-selling author, Burt Hirschfeld, to a signing session at which not a single soul turned up. The bookshop manager was reduced to dressing up his staff in overcoats so that they could masquerade as customers and avoid the worst rigours of a total fiasco.

Having driven into the hard blast of an early winter's day in Fraserburgh, where the wind has a habit of reaching parts too private for words as well as comfort, I warmed myself with a plate of Willie Bannerman's broth at the Alexandra Hotel and wondered who would be foolhardy enough to venture out on a day like this for the dubious privilege of attaching my undistinguished signature to their copy of a book I had just written.

Still worse in this moment of self-doubt, what right did I have to expect that there was even a market for this particular type of book, which was, after all, no more than the reminiscences of an Aberdeenshire country boy? I had called it *A Grain of Truth* and publisher Paul Harris had travelled north to Fraserburgh (or the Broch, as I had more commonly known it), anxious to gauge the potential of this sort of literature.

When the broth and the brisket had been well and truly digested we ventured cautiously round the corner of Mid Street in the direction of Mrs Maitland's bookshop, there to behold a sight which did our hearts a power of good. For the queue of customers was already out through the shop and into the winter bleakness of the street. Within the next few hours I had signed no fewer than 270 copies of *A Grain of Truth*, drawing to a halt only because there were no more copies there to sell. We fixed a date for a second session at the same shop, convinced at least that our modest little adventure was not without its public demand.

But commercial considerations were furthest from my mind that memorable afternoon as people came by with stories to tell, sometimes of my own childhood and even that of my parents. By the time I had completed the signing circuit, taking in my native village of Maud and the nearby town of Turriff, where I had started my newspaper career in 1948, I had been through an emotional wringer in the most pleasurable of fashions.

Within those columns of familiar Buchan faces there was the lady who remembered my father, the ebullient John Webster, as a schoolboy pursuing his ambition to be an auctioneer, standing on his mother's kitchen table at the farm of Backhill of Allathan, rouping everything within sight—including his own mother!

There was the formidable daughter of Robbie Paterson, owner of the legendary Turra Coo, who stalked in to say that, along with every other person who had written about that notorious creature, I did not get the story quite right. I met former schoolmates, girl-friends and dancing partners as well as elderly ladies who remembered me in my pram. At Fraserburgh there was the lady who thrust into my hand a snapshot from 1927, when she was a nurse at the City Hospital, Aberdeen, and there I beheld a cheery group of her fellow-nurses which included the carefree and unmistakable figure of Meg Barron, my late mother. That choked me up for the moment and, as the lady too bit back a tear, she turned and vanished before I had time to know her name.

Touching incidents had been happening from the day we launched *A Grain of Truth* at the Aberdeen Art Gallery, where the company included Miss Catto, the infant teacher who welcomed me on that very first day at Maud School in April of 1936, and her colleague, Miss Morrison, who took over in my primary years. It was not an occasion for fancy speeches, but on the spur of the moment Miss Morrison, now Mrs Reith from Banchory, rose to say a few words that were simple and sincere, observing that her former pupil 'has inherited his mother's sentiment and romance and his father's determination'. It was a fair assessment.

The author and one-time farm servant, David Toulmin, was among others who helped to launch *A Grain of Truth* on that Guy Fawkes Day of 1981, a date which prompted the wish that the book might rocket to success rather than fizzle out as a damp squib. I need hardly have worried. The second print had to be ordered before publication day was over, and soon there was not an unsold copy to be found.

In time it gave its title to an award-winning television film, produced by the BBC, and that, in turn, set off a demand for another book. In the avalanche of letters which descended on my desk after two showings of the film, there were some which blossomed into verse, like that of Mrs Ruth Gatt from Bagrae of Alvah, Banff, whom I had once known as Ruth Brodie from Balthangie.

Summing up the essence of the mail in general, she wrote: 'We left our television sets in silence, a lump in our throats, yet proud to belong to that part of Aberdeenshire called Buchan.' She closed with these lines:

> As journalist and North-East loon
> Ye're bra well kent for miles aroon
> Ye've interviewed baith great an' sma

Seen Honeyneuk fit deep in sna
'A Grain o' Truth' ye've written tee
—An' it taks pride o place wi me—
So creep in tae yer ingle-neuk
An' write for's a'—anither beuk.

I have laboured into the night at that 'ingle-neuk' (now fired by gas instead of peat); but if the effort can bring some warmth to the caul blast of a winter's evening, I shall not have gone unrewarded.

CHAPTER TWO

THE ROUP

When the cameras stopped whirring and the last of the folk
had drained away from the farm-close of Honeyneuk that calm
summer evening, I wandered round the back of the steading
for one last look across the valley of the Ugie towards the
woods of Brucklay.

At last I was alone on a day of torn emotion, the day I
had finally sold off my father's farm in the heart of that Aberdeenshire cattle country known as Buchan and witnessed the
dispersal of his livestock and implements to the winks and
nods which he himself would have been the first to detect, in
his eventful career as one of the best-known auctioneers in
Scotland.

The BBC had chosen the occasion to make a television documentary film of the roup (a Scottish term for an auction sale)
and the presence of the camera crew was to add an extra di-
mension of drama to a day in my life when that commodity
would not have been in short supply in any case.

Having long since left the rural scene of my childhood, in
physical terms at least, I was back this day to conclude an
agonizing decision and to be invited in for my tea at a farmhouse table where my mother had long been the welcoming
mistress and my father the indisputable master.

As the new owners of Honeyneuk's 200 acres, Jim and
Belinda Muir had already moved in, having uprooted themselves from the Orkney island of Shapinsay and boarded a
lorry, together with their two children, dog, cats, hens, bees
and assorted goods and chattels for the crossing to the Main-
land of Orkney and thereafter for the longer voyage to the
landfall of Scotland. That family adventure of a lifetime had

217

brought them through Aberdeenshire and finally into the heart of Buchan, to which many an Orcadian farmer and his family had drifted before them, attracted by the proximity to suppliers and markets and the educational opportunities of which their children might wish to avail themselves in years to come.

So the Muirs had ventured through the front door of Honeyneuk, a house left gaunt and empty with my father and mother both dead and gone, but once a bustling hive of activity, well charged with the power of John Webster's personality and the warmth of my mother's welcoming fly-cup, not to mention her music which pervaded every corner and filtered down the half-mile distance to the village of Maud below.

From that same front door, the Muirs would look beyond the rooftops of Maud and absorb their first exhilarating view of that valley of the Ugie which curled its way from the back of Honeyneuk, round by the Buchan railway line and on towards the Garden of Buchan at Old Deer, eventually to the North Sea at Peterhead.

This was their new beginning in an alien part of Scotland which was to me as familiar as the back of my own hand, the shallow valleys where I had grown up all those years ago, without knowing that I was amassing a wealth of experience, physical, emotional and artistic, which would one day leave me the residual inheritance of my best memories.

Such memories were vividly with me now, in the summer of 1985, as I faced the fact that, for the first time in my fifty-four years, I did not have a place to lay my head in the *quoad sacra* parish of Maud, where I was born.

Jim Muir and his family had settled into the farmhouse of Honeyneuk, just as my parents had done in 1952, and Willie Paul had done before them and the Raes before that, stretching back to the Galls, who had lived in the old farmhouse (later a henhouse) before they built the present one in 1910. Old Sandy Horne from the village would wander past and tell us of how he had been a mason at the building of our substantial dwelling in those early years of the century. Snapshots at the time of building show a bare landscape, as yet without the benefit of nature's artistry which would in time paint in the trees and hedges and terraced garden to make it an enclosure for rhubarb and rhododendrons, kail, cabbage and croquet— and the little summer-house where my mother could toss back her hair, turn her face to the sunshine she adored and dream the dreams which spilled from her romantic nature.

As my former schoolteacher, Miss Morrison, had said at the launching of *A Grain of Truth*, I was a mixture of my mother's sentiment and romance and my father's down-to-earth determination. Paradoxically, the former qualities had encouraged me to retain Honeyneuk on the death of my father, though I knew I would never return to farm it, and the latter had counselled me to sell it in the light of depreciating land values.

It was an agonizing decision, guaranteed to have rattled the rafters of heaven as a point of contention between my parents, but the decision was mine alone and I knew it would have the full support of my mother, who would have accepted the wisdom of realizing my asset, especially when a lack of interest in farming had taken me away from it in the first place.

To distance myself from farming, however, was not to be confused with any lack of feeling for my native Buchan, a passion of love which bit deep into the marrow of my being and had become the quintessence of my soul.

But a Buchan love is an unspeakable one, quiet and dour, bound by native restraint and forced to find an expression in outlets which can run to the bizarre. It remains for me a ruling passion of my blood, a romantic link made the stronger because it has never been capable of fulfilment. An uncaring visitor might tell you that Buchan is a bare, bare place, but nakedness has a charm of its own. To me, she lies with all the allure of a temptress, her beacon head resting on the rocks of Kinnaird, surveying the comely bust which blossoms over Mormond and dips to her navel at Old Deer, before the fair lady spread-eagles herself to the toe-holds of Turriff and Slains, promising, but cool and untouchable.

Those feelings for my native corner of Scotland had to be kept in further check that summer day as I drove in about to Honeyneuk, prepared to meet the folk who would come from far and near for the occasion of my father's roup; for it was much more John Webster's roup than mine. I was the only son who had gone away from it all to the south to make a life of my own, much to the disbelief of my father, who firmly believed that God's handiwork was centred on Buchan and that His world began to go wrong somewhere to the south of Stonehaven, before slithering towards London and into the fiery depths of Hell altogether.

He had spent his entire working life as the Buchan auctioneer, based at Maud, which was a village of only a few hundred people yet could claim to be the biggest weekly cattle market in Britain, the heartland of Aberdeenshire beef. His role as the boss gave him a status to match his expanding girth, and there, with all the fire of good humour and quick temper, he went rollicking along for forty-five years, steeped in the selling of cattle on a Wednesday, measuring land, valuing crops, dispensing sound advice and getting to know the worth of every man and beast within a radius of twenty miles.

But his eye was always on the nearby farm of Honeyneuk and when the laird of Brucklay decided to sell it in 1952, he borrowed every single penny of the purchase price and bought it, moving out with my mother from their council house at 2 Park Crescent, in the village of Maud.

To that furrowed land of Buchan in general, and Honeyneuk in particular, he became wedded as firmly as any man to his wife, a land so sour and grudging those 200 years ago but tamed now and caressed into a fertility which makes it as rich a cattle country as you will find in the kingdom. In so doing, my forebears and their neighbours forged a character that was hard-working, good-humoured, kindly and damnably thrawn.

Their descendants, still sketched by the same sure hand of heredity, came up the Honeyneuk road that day, caught spontaneously by those television cameras which had come to capture a depiction of rural life. Some were encased in motor cars, others came dysting on foot, and there was even the quaint arrival of a figure in shalt and gig, who might have been an Old Testament prophet or a fugitive from the hairy sixties. In fact, he turned out to be David Watson Hood, an artist who had settled at Overhill Smiddy Croft, near my mother's birthplace at Whitehill. His arrival, unplanned and unannounced, came fortuitously to the camera lens to give a weird sense of the continuity which threads itself through the fabric of Scottish rural life.

As those cameras panned across the landscape, I took up the commentary about how the farming life of Buchan had revolved around the village of Maud and particularly its livestock mart, all lying twenty-eight miles to the north of Aberdeen and fourteen miles inland from Peterhead. It was there, in a front room of Fedderate Cottages, that I was born on a July day in the decade of national depression, they say, though to the country child of the thirties it was more of a golden haze of harmony and mellow foxtrots. This was the centre of my universe, bounded by Willie Ogston's smiddy, Lizzie Allan's sweetie shop, the River Ugie and the railway line, Bank's Hill and the Peershoose, Kitchie's Dam and the Creeshie Raa.

Maud Station was the heart and soul of our existence, the junction where the train from Aberdeen split into two sections, one for Fraserburgh (or the Broch, as we knew it) and the other for Peterhead, better known as the Blue Toon. Porters puffing at their Steenhives would dyst along the platform, calling out 'Maud, change for Fraserburgh', and the steam engines would hoot and whistle and thrust themselves into motion, weaving symmetrically outwards from our spacious junction, two halves of a locomotive worm, one heading down through Brucklay, Strichen, Mormond, Lonmay, Rathen and Philorth to the Broch and the other ploughing through the Garden of Buchan by Mintlaw, Longside and Inverugie to Peterhead. This Buchan line had scythed its way through the cornparks of the North-East since 1865, but the infamous

Doctor Beeching put an end to all that in the centenary year of 1965, and here, as I strode along the platform that June day of twenty years later, it was hard to believe that such a life had ever existed.

Yet weird images arose before me now to confirm that this had once been much more than a station platform in one small corner of the great railway network of Britain. It was our platform of life, our chance to gaze at the in-coming stranger, to sense the ebb and flow of a throbbing world that lay out yonder.

By this gateway to the rest of the world I had stood as a little boy that September day of 1939, when the Territorials came streaming out of doorways all the way up the village and headed down the Bobby's Brae to join that train to war. Our little station was grand enough to have a John Menzies book-stall, run by Tibby Bruce, who was blind as a bat, and a Re-fresh which was leased by Lil and Lena Murison. From within that modest hostelry, young men stuffed gill bottles in their pockets and put on a brave face for the adventures ahead. Buchan folk are ill at ease with their emotions, but solid coun-try men and women let slip a tear as that train drew out for a destination unknown, a foray over the neep parks of a foreign land from which many would not return. They steamed out towards Aberdeen, and as I stood there now, re-creating the vision of that September day when war broke out, I could see again their flailing arms, waving from the distance of the Den Wood, and hear their farewell calls, echoing back through the cutting of a line now derelict and overgrown and left behind in the name of progress.

In time, I too had left all this behind and headed off to be a journalist, in Turriff and Aberdeen and then in Glasgow, where you would find me as a sub-editor on the *Daily Express* before branching out as a writer, travelling the world and coming in contact with Prime Ministers and Presidents, inter-viewing the stars, from Charlie Chaplin, Burt Lancaster, Bing Crosby and Bob Hope to James Mason, Ginger Rogers and

Sophia Loren. Not much of that impressed my matter-of-fact father until the day I could tell him that my income had surpassed his own. My spirited mother, warm and understanding, noticed a quiet change of heart, even a pride in the fact that 'the loon's daein nae bad for himsel'.

From the station I wandered along to the mart which had been my father's place of work for more than forty years. Daily day he tramped these floors from which the prime beef of Buchan still finds its way to the top hotels of London. This was his store-cattle ring where, as a boy, he had envied the auctioneer in his rostrum, the central performer in a weekly agricultural drama.

Dad was a crofter's boy from Backhill of Allathan at New Deer, but his father died of an anthrax infection when the boy was eight and there he strove to look after his mother, younger brother and their few beasts, and eventually set out as a drover of cattle to the mart. But his aim was always that auctioneer's box and, in time, he was given the chance to canvass for cattle on his motor bike. By the time I was a child he had graduated to a dickey-backed car with a spare wheel up front and a battery on the running-board.

His ambition achieved, he worked at a dynamic pace with a sense of immortality which amused my mother. 'Ye winna stop for yer ain funeral,' she would chide. But he did. Since 1977 I had carried on his beloved farm, albeit at a great distance and not with the interest and commitment demanded of modern farming. So I made the decision to sell, and there, as I stood in his own rostrum at Maud Mart and heard the echo of his powerful voice, I could not but reflect on the irony that the notice board which had once announced other people's displenish sales had something now to say about John Webster himself.

Just last night, within this very auditorium, the furniture and household effects which had seen my father and mother through their eventful married years, had been put under the hammer of my father's successors. Tomorrow. Tomorrow his implements and most of his cattle would follow suit.

In distant places where folk had furs and jewellery and never fouled a hand in honest toil they had their theatres and opera houses and fanciful entertainments. In a place like Maud they mainly sublimated their dramatic instincts in 'The Roup', an amphitheatre of cut-and-thrust with all the fascination of the chase, the competitive bidding, sometimes to land you with what you wanted and sometimes to make sure Mrs So-and-so didn't get it. Up there in his box my father was the ringmaster, cracking his whip this way and that, teasing, encouraging, cajoling, challenging.

Among the household goods of my childhood, the chanty was always guaranteed to bring some comic relief to the more serious nature of the occasion. 'Come on noo, Mrs Duguid,' my father would rasp out, picking on a lady of vulnerable proportions. 'This should jist aboot fit you!' There would be great guffaws as a willing audience released its imagination on the prospect of one fat lady arranging herself on the limited scope of an enamel chanty. This was Sotheby's with sharn on your boots, a real-life drama for rural folk whose uncompromising life had fashioned them with a steady gait, a kindly heart, an eye for observation and a dry and biting wit.

But the main disposal of John Webster's effects was at Honeyneuk that summer Saturday of 1985, and now that a crowd of 1,000 people had congregated round the tool-shed door, Charlie Morrison, the auctioneer, was calling them to attention to announce the conditions of sale before bursting into that rhythm of rouping in which my father had been the acknowledged expert.

Of smaller build, Charlie Morrison had picked up the art to fine effect, beating out a rataplan of rhetoric which may have been commonplace to the folk of Buchan but was a revelation to the television million, who were captivated by the big tackety boots as they broke into a disco-like accompaniment to the quest for bids. A box of nuts and bolts, with a potential of no more than ten pence, was given as much enthusiasm as a trac-

224

tor costing thousands. I stood on the perimeter of it all, trying to absorb those elusive nuances of a memorable occasion and casting an eye round the faces, some of my father's generation but others of my own, men grown into the mould of their begetters, with all the skeely tracings of nature, sure and dependable as the night that follows day. Old or young, they came up to tell me what a grand chap my father was, how he had helped them with sound advice over the years. Often enough they were crofter folk, not good with words of gratitude, they said, but maybe I would know what they meant; and they walked away with a silent nod and I knew well and lo'ed them for it.

Those auctioneers who had grown up under the shadow of my father were taking it in turn to preside over a decent dispersal. Norman Law, Ian Emslie, Norman Murison, Charlie Morrison. From the tool-shed door, eident hands kept up the flow of goods for sale, hands that were gnarled from years of work at Honeyneuk. I could not have carried on the farm since my father died had it not been for the two men who worked the place for me. They say the good farm worker is a memory from a bygone age, but that would insult men like Charlie Fraser, my grieve, and Jimmy Mutch, the cattleman.

There was Charlie now at work, surrounded by his three sons, boys in the splendid mould of their father, who would have turned to the land if there had been work for them to do. And there was Jimmy Mutch, who followed his father as the baillie at Honeyneuk and had qualified for the Highland Society's medal for thirty years' service by the time he was forty-nine. It is no condescension to say that these men are the salt of the earth, honest, decent country folk who would put most of us to shame with the effort and integrity which they invest in their daily darg. Another time and my father would have encouraged men of that ilk to become their own masters, such was his belief in the right of the farming folk to benefit from the ownership of their own few acres. Rising costs put that out of the question, and agriculture became the poorer for it; but the downward trend in land prices during the 1980s may well have prefaced a modern revolution in the use of our soil and—who knows?—the small man might well come into his own once more in the new century.

Buchan had always been the working end of Aberdeenshire, championed by that great Parliamentarian Robert Boothby, their MP who happened to be a Conservative but would have been elected no matter his persuasion. Somehow he symbolized that rural culture to which we had belonged for countless generations and from which there was no ready route of exit, even for those of us who had physically separated our daily lives from the tilth of our beginnings.

Disposal of Honeyneuk may have been a sensible decision, but there was no escaping a tug of conscience and a speculation of what John Webster would be making of it this day when 1,000 Buchan folk were milling around his beloved farm in such a gathering as Honeyneuk had never seen. That distant rumbling was a clap of thunder, I hoped, and not the vibration of my father turning in his grave up there in the Kirkyard of Culsh, as a preliminary to stalking down upon this intrusion of his property and scattering them back to their own bit biggings.

Round in the implement shed, Beatrice Cardno, who feeds the farmers on Wednesday mart days, was filling her mince baps and Buchan folk were downing a dram in the warm camaraderie of a country roup. Within their own company, conversation comes easily, free and frank and gloriously good-humoured. I met people like Ian Will, whom I had not seen since the day I left Maud School. Where had we been since those wartime years? Boys grown to men in a world which guarantees little but change; change in our surroundings, no doubt, but change most of all in ourselves.

While Charlie Morrison the auctioneer gyrated on the outside, his namesake, Charlie Morrison the cashier, was gathering in the proceeds of the sale in that old farmhouse of Honeyneuk. All that my father had created in his vision of building a lasting entity of farming was dissolving into liquid cash at the hands of what some would no doubt see as the worthlessness of his wastrel son. When Dad finally accepted that he was not destined for an immortal life, a matter about which he seemed unconvinced for most of his days, he made known that he would like the place carried on. In his heart of hearts I think he knew there would be a limit to that possibility, though he never spoke about it. A blockage of the brain on Burns Night of 1976 put him out of touch with reality in the matter of a minute. He was seventy. He lived for another sixteen months, and I had lingered with the ownership of the farm for another eight years. But now it was time to turn my back on Honeyneuk, with all its memories and associations, and to hand it over to Jim and Belinda Muir, the kind of hardworking couple of whom my father would have thoroughly approved.

Folk carted away their day's purchases, most of it practical (for Buchan folk are nothing if not practical) but some of it just a souvenir of John Webster; then they came past to say their goodbyes. Now the fields and the byres and the shelves of Honeyneuk lay empty, and an eerie silence was creeping in with the shadows of evening.

How odd that I should speak so much about my father, because, much as I admired him, I was very much closer to my mother, about whom I have said very little. Before I would break this tangible link with Buchan, however, there was one more call to make on that perplexing day. As I have said, my parents lie there in the Kirkyard of Culsh, near the neighbouring village of New Deer, my mother having gone there much too soon for one who so enlivened everything she touched. Through her grandfather, Gavin Greig, she was closely connected to the families of both Robert Burns and Edvard Grieg, whose ancestors went to Norway from Buchan.

It is appropriate that my parents should lie there at Culsh, for they both grew up and lived their entire lives within three miles of that final resting place. The relatives and old neighbours from Maud and New Deer are all there together, including the remains of Gavin Greig and my young cousin, Arthur Argo. From such a place of peace I can gaze out over the Buchan landscape and conjure up pictures of a childhood that pulsated with love and laughter, hard work and good fellowship. When the furrows of spring had produced the corn of late summer, the stubble of autumn and the joyous cry of 'Winter!' when the last sheaf had been forked, it was time for the meal-an'-ale and the bothy ballads.

But my mother's horizons stretched far beyond the cornfields of Buchan. From her wireless, she was just as much at home with *The Sleeping Beauty* of Tchaikovsky as with *The Barnyards of Delgaty*. Among her favourite pieces of music was Dvorak's 'New World' Symphony. 'I want it played at my funeral,' she used to joke. 'Tell Johnny Walker, the organist.' So we did. And the strains of 'Goin' Home' from that Dvorak symphony followed her up the brae to Culsh, strains which linger with me even at a time when I have cut my ties with Honeyneuk and seek out this very special panorama from the heights of the kirkyard. From here, by the Monument of Culsh, I can see Mains of Whitehill, where she was born, and the route she had taken to the school at New Deer. Down the brae to Maud, just two miles away, she had gone to spend her entire married life, in the village itself and later at Honeyneuk.

As the day draws to its close, I can just see the sombre outline of the farm steading, brooding in the last of the evening light. All around me is peace and contentment. In spite of the perplexities of the day, there is a sense of embracing the world in one wide sweep, suddenly identifying its multifarious elements in a pattern that begins to make some kind of sense. In microcosm, I suppose, that wider world is represented here within the landscape spread now before me. As that Dvorak symphony swells once more in haunting harmony and I stand here alone in soliloquy, I must surely know now, if I didn't know it before, that I am a Buchan man for ever.

CHAPTER THREE

CHAMPAGNE BREAKFAST

On the morning of my fiftieth birthday I had wandered along to Fedderate Cottages, in the village of Maud, and presented myself at the door of Bill and Isobel Clark, who had been well forewarned of my mission.

I had come, complete with bottle of champagne, for the sentimental ritual of standing in the small front room where, exactly half a century earlier, I had been born at a quarter to nine on a Wednesday morning, an event of such insignificance that my father could not have been expected to disturb his weekly routine of selling cattle at the local mart.

For Wednesday was the big day of the week in Maud (some might say the only day of the week in Maud), and John Webster was the central figure in that conglomeration of cattle, sheep and pigs being bought and sold in front of a couthy congregation of Aberdeenshire farmers, who brought with them to the village thoroughfares all the dysting gait of the plough-rig and the warm aroma of the Bogie Roll which came yoaming from their Steenhive pipes to mingle with cattle breath and turn the atmosphere of the sale-ring into a steaming, blue-grey concoction.

News of my birth that morning in 1931 was carried to the edge of the auctioneer's rostrum by a neighbour's daughter, little Elma Craig, and my father paused just long enough to absorb my grandmother's note before proceeding with the sale of the next bit sharny-hipped heifer.

Fifty years later, it happened to be a Wednesday once again and down the village streets came the corresponding parade of Buchan cattle, driven by the sons and grandsons of that earlier generation, creating an illusion that very little had changed in the intervening period, and indeed, in the more subtle areas of our existence, maybe very little had.

At a quarter to nine I stood four-square by the corner of the room where my mother had undergone the agonies of child-birth, before being rushed off to the City Hospital in Aberdeen where she had once been a trainee nurse and left at the end of the ward, in an expectation of the early death which came almost invariably to sufferers of peritonitis in those distant days.

Gritting her teeth in a determination to return to the new-born child, she drew back from death's door after weeks on the threshold, and the surgeon came to see us many years later, still marvelling at the will power which alone had pulled her through.

So there was no doubt about the subject of a silent toast as friends dropped in to share a glass of champagne that Wednes-day morning and to exchange stories from our village life of fifty years before.

When the ritual was over, I stood at that cottage door and mused over the mileage I had covered since first I ventured down the steps of Fedderate Cottages, the bank of experience I had built up, the people and the places, the joys and the heartaches.

I had come back to my very first reference point of exist-ence, to the room where I had gasped the first burst of air, peered out at the opening glimmer of God's light and taken those first faltering steps on the journey of the unknown.

On that same day fifty years earlier, according to the local daily newspaper, the Aberdeen *Press and Journal*, King George V was holding a glittering reception at the Palace of Holyroodhouse; Oswald Mosley was leading his New Party of five into the Commons, to the jeers of the ruling Socialists from whom he had just broken away; the weather forecast was predictably middling; and Raggie Morrison's shop in St Nicholas Street, Aberdeen, was selling leatherette coats at 6s 6d (thirty-two and a half pence).

In Aberdeen, the famous comedian Tommy Lorne was appearing at His Majesty's Theatre, the mysterious Doctor Walford Bodie from Macduff was performing his electrical feats at the Tivoli and the inimitable Harry Gordon was starring at his Beach Pavilion, with Flanagan and Allen among his supporting acts.

On the National Radio programme, Henry Hall's Gleneagles Band was playing from 11 p.m. till midnight and *The Press and Journal* gave highlights of twenty-nine foreign stations, from a Beethoven concert on Algiers Radio to the waltzes of Vienna Radio.

Nearer home there were more mundane matters like hoeing matches at Lumphanan, Monymusk and Vale of Alford and a bowling match at Maud, where the local rink of Hector Macphail, Hector Mavor, J. G. Morrison and James Murray were beating the Causewayend Old Boys of Aberdeen.

If that decade of the thirties had ushered in a national depression then the folk of Maud would be less affected than most, for they had long survived on a staple diet of meal, milk and tatties and were perhaps no better or worse off than they had ever been.

Material hardship and deprivation had long been the accepted lot in this cold shoulder of Scotland, the land of Buchan which cut inland from the Moray Firth by the holy place of Gardenstown, down through Turriff and round by Methlick to Ellon and eastward to the great North Sea.

Whereas the Lord in His infinite mercy had given lush land to those who languished in places like the Lothians and down through the English countryside, he proposed a stiffer examination of character for his Pictish peasantry in that North-East corner of Scotland called Buchan.

Not for them the soft meadows of the south, the willing tilth that surrenders to the first hint of proposition from a ploughshare with all the haste of a whore.

Instead, there was bog and whin and peaty moss, moraines of long stony ridge and barren hill, defying all but the

231

sternest effort of mankind's best specimens to wrest it from sour intransigence and turn it into something that might pass for cultivation. The folk who have farmed that land of Buchan since the time of Prince Charlie have created their own living monument to the limits of human endurance, the fortitude of ordinary men and women challenged to a survival that might have seemed of such dubious nature as to make it hardly worth the effort.

That monument is writ large, not on slabs of granite but in mile after mile of fertile field, barley and oats, turnip and potatoes, the rich green of pasture and, in this late twentieth century, the mustard yellow that might once have been taken for the weed of skelloch but is now the profitable crop of oilseed rape.

The epitaph to generations of hardy Buchan folk who broke their backs and maybe their spirits is there in the black and white of well-fed cattle, in the neat trim of drysteen dykes and the undersoil network of drainage.

My own forefathers were of that breed, not least Grandpa Barron, my mother's father, who made his own contribution to the improvement of the land, once he became the tenant farmer at Mains of Whitehill, but who could recall the customary discomfort and health hazards of the halflin, which he suffered in the last quarter of the nineteenth century, when he slept in an open bothy above the horse-stalls.

Grandpa Barron would wander across the brae to the farm of Atherb for a news with a man for whom he had the keenest admiration. John Milne was not only an improving farmer but a man who so sensed the historic significance of the great agricultural romance which had been enacted without due recognition of its miraculous proportions, that he made some effort to put it down on paper.

At the turn of the present century, John Milne could give my grandfather a first-hand account of his own grand-uncle in the eighteenth century, who was the goadsman of a ten-owsen plough on the farmlands by Maud, as well as being obliged to thresh the corn crop by flail (a murderous task) for the princely wage of twenty-five shillings, or £1.25 today, per half year!

They wore home-made brogues but just as often went bare-footed, even to church, where they would put on their socks and shoes before entering and take them off again when they came out. In those days they made up for a scarcity of food for cattle and horses by crushing whins with a heavy wooden hammer; for their own diet they concocted a dish which Grandpa Barron still enjoyed until his death on New Year's Day of 1948. That was the old-fashioned offering of sowens, made of oat husks and fine meal, steeped and strained and fermented to a solid mass which was eaten like porridge.

That and piz-meal brose were two doubtful delicacies to which he failed to convert me in my childhood days, though I willingly joined in the ritual of 'milk-an'-breid', which amounted to a bowl of milk, into which a corter of oatcakes was broken and supped in hearty spoonfuls by young men who wanted to grow up with mush on their arms.

John Milne's father took on a lease at Atherb in 1836 and embarked on the kind of bare existence which makes you realize that, whatever the hardships and injustices of today, we have much to appreciate when set against the trials of those ancestors who slaved last century. This is the kind of memory John Milne was leaving to people like my grandfather:

> I can remember my father and mother taking but one cup of tea, and that only in the morning, sweetening it with treacle because that was cheaper than sugar. The children got no tea excepting one cup on the Sabbath morning, while tobacco was a luxury not to be thought of.
>
> Being the only boy, I had to work as soon as I was able— and indeed before I was able—and 'tis with sadness that I look back on those early days. My education was curtailed and in-terrupted . . . and even when at school in winter, I had to work morning and evening, plying the flail when I should have been

233

at lessons. My father began his improvement by draining the bogs with stone drains. Part of my first work was to fill the stones into a barrow when the ground was too soft to carry carts, or to hand them to my father as he built the drains. During the lease, we put in about 4,000 yards of those stone drains.

The boulder stones which were later to plague my own father on the neighbouring farm of Honeyneuk were an even greater hazard at Atherb a century earlier.

We began to take out the boulders [said John Milne], and this was the heaviest and most fatiguing work of all. We had no mechanical appliances except long levers and blocks. They were hard to bore for blasting. Four or five feet was all a man could do in a day. Many a time have I set up a box barrow to shelter me from the drifting snow or the sleety shower and drilled a hole. Once we got them loose and free from earth all round, we put on a fire which broke them up. Bluestone splits readily when exposed to heat. In winter the boulders were dirty and wore the skin off our hands. Often after a hard day's work among these stones, with tired muscles and aching hands, I have been unable to enjoy refreshing sleep at night, but in a feverish dream repeated the work of the day.

That farm of Atherb had further intrigued my grandfather because it was where they had dug up a cairn known as 'The Fear'd Place', for the purpose of making a road, and found large quantities of human bones and flint arrowheads. The bones were mixed with charred oak and covered to a depth of three feet by stones showing signs of having been subjected to heat. There were circular and semi-circular cavities nearby. Whether it was a mass burial ground from some long-forgotten battle or the remains of a fort, with the occupants burned out by their enemies, will remain for ever a mystery.

So much for the recollections of a Buchan loon in the mid-rig of the last century, a time when the name of Maud would hardly have been known. There was just the hamlet of Bank, called after the farm of Bank of Behitch, where horse-carriers between Aberdeen and the lesser towns of Peterhead and Fraserburgh would unhitch their animals for food and rest at the parting of the ways. The name of Behitch had nothing to do with the unhitching of the horses but merely meant the Bank of the Birch Tree.

That Y-shaped route between the three North-East towns became further emphasized in the middle of last century by the building of the Buchan and Formartin railway line when, once again, the village now known as Maud was to be the parting of the ways for the Aberdeen train as it split into two halves, which wended their separate ways to Peterhead and Fraserburgh.

With such a junction springing up around 1865, the original village of Bank, situated in the parish of Old Deer, was destined to spread over the Old Maud Burn and into the adjoining parish of New Deer to form a larger village, which came to be known as New Maud.

The convenience of the railway turned it into a natural meeting point for district councillors and Presbyterian parsons alike, and in 1866 the twenty-four parishes of the area pooled their resources to build the Buchan Combination Poor's House, still standing today as Maud Hospital.

So a place of 200 or 300 people began to cluster round that railway junction, and in time it grew to more than 700 inhabitants and to have three butchers, three bakers, four grocers, two shoemakers, two watchmakers, joiners, millwrights, cabinetmakers, a saddler, a druggist, dressmakers and a corn merchant, not to mention a Post Office, two hotels, a station refreshment room and Lizzie Allan's sweetie shop. The village sloped downwards past the station to the old Bank Village, which nestled at the foot of Bank's Hill and contains to this day the kirk and the hospital and a single streetful of douce dwellings.

CHAPTER FOUR

ROAR LIKE A DOVE

Having travelled around the world in my years as a journalist, I have paused at many an unlikely corner between Honeyneuk and Hong Kong, Maud and Moscow, and wondered what prompted enough people in that particular location to find a reason for permanent settlement. Why not closer to the amenities of a city or the warmth of a more hospitable climate?

No doubt there are people who have chanced upon my native land of Buchan and asked themselves the self-same question. So perhaps I have been able to answer my own queries by the same token as I can give a convincing answer to theirs.

It takes only a minor catalytic agent to spark off the spirit of community, just a few people with a common cause, like that cluster which gave rise to the village of New Maud in the middle of the last century. Soon the convenience of the railway commended itself to the agricultural needs of the Buchan area. Where better to build the livestock marts from which the animals could then fan out across the North-East of Scotland and even further to the butchers of the south, finding their way to the tables of the grand hotels in London?

But even without the special circumstances of central convenience, there would still have been a spirit of community, just as there is in other parts of the rural scene not so blessed with amenity. For the people who live by the loneliness of the land develop a sense of responsibility for it, becoming as thirled to its tilth as they are to the flesh and blood of their own breeding.

In the sparseness of population the folk become responsible for one another, dependent on each other, not with an ostentatious display of caring but in a quiet observance of unobtrusive decencies.

From the stability of a rural setting it is not too hard to pick up the strands of ancestry and to gain some sense of the patterns of living which your forefathers were managing to create. You can easily imagine how the surrounding farmers of Clackriach and Atherb and Honeyneuk and Affleck gathered together one night about 1825 and decided to raise enough money to provide a local school, in the shape of a little thackit hoosie, down by the hamlet of Bank. Up at the farm of Honeyneuk, which was later to become my own home, the education of girls was undertaken in a room of the old farmhouse, it seems, by the farmer's daughter, Miss Paterson.

In the second half of the century, they were schooling the boys down the brae at Bank village, in what later became the Masonic Lodge, while the girls were now being educated at the other end of Maud, in what was to become Willie Ogston's smiddy to a later generation.

In 1896 they combined these two inadequate establishments and built a new central school by the picturesque avenue which looks down across the station to the hospital and the kirk and then upwards to the knoll of Bank's Hill with its clump of trees atop.

My great-grandfather, Gavin Greig, the playwright, composer and folk-song collector, was present on that opening day of April, 1896, and it was to that same building exactly forty years later (the Aberdeenshire school year started in April then) that I was led by my mother for my first day at Maud Higher Grade School. The original headmaster, John Law, still lived by the playground wall, as did one of his first teachers, Miss Slessor. One of my primary teachers in those innocent days was none other than Bell Duncan, who had been a pupil at that girls' school in the smiddy away back in 1888 and could bring us the warm reassurance of a life that endured with surprising stability, considering we were now on the other side of that great divide, the First World War, which separated the old order from the new.

In Bell Duncan's schooldays the spiritual life of the village had blossomed from an early mission to a proper *quoad sacra* parish church, which gained for its first minister a former Donside ploughman, William Cowie, who was to seed a highly talented family. Bell Duncan and her sister Jessie became close friends with Mr Cowie's daughters, one of whom was to emerge as a great British playwright of the twentieth century, under her pen-name of Lesley Storm.

With her real name of Mabel Cowie, she graduated at Aberdeen University in the early 1920s and first attracted public attention with novels like *Head in the Wind*, *Small Rain* and *Strange Man's Home*, which shocked the more pious of her father's flock. She married a Dr Clark, who practised from the highly fashionable London address of 25 South Terrace, Kensington, and it was there, on my first visit to the big city in 1950, that I ventured along, knocked at her door and introduced myself as a loon fae Maud. (I can now marvel at the effrontery of it!)

Lesley Storm took me in and entertained me for the afternoon, a delightful hostess, still recognizable as a bonny lassie from Maud but now with the overtones of sophistication that had come with living among the literati of London and being dined and wined by men like Lord Beaverbrook, who was among her greatest admirers. (He included her picture on the front page when he produced his very first edition of the *Scottish Daily Express* in 1928.)

She recalled with affection her childhood in Maud, the school, the people, the pranks, the boy-friends, the Forces who had passed by during the First World War. When she asked what I had been doing in London, I told her of a splendid film I had seen the previous evening. It was called *Tony Draws a Horse*, a humorous psychological film about a boy who, when asked at school to draw a horse, gave exaggerated embellishments to its most potent anatomical features! She smiled at me warmly. 'I wrote that story in 1939,' she said.

Lesley Storm had also written the screenplay of Graham

Greene's *The Fallen Idol* and was on the point of giving us some of her own finest masterpieces, plays like *Black Chiffon*, *The Day's Mischief*, *Roar Like a Dove* and *Time and Yellow Roses*. From the film rights of just three of her plays she had earned £150,000, a sizeable sum in any age but a fortune in the 1950s.

Once I had established myself in journalism, many years later, I was able to meet her again and to interview her for none other than Lord Beaverbrook's *Daily Express*. She also returned to Maud in 1961 to visit her old friends, the Miss Duncans, while *Time and Yellow Roses* was having its world première at His Majesty's Theatre in Aberdeen.

But the reputation for laying the foundations of notable citizens was not confined to Mr Cowie, who remained as minister at Maud for thirty-five years. Round the hill, at the farm of Mains of Clackriach, one of the workers had a daughter, Jean Minty, who grew up to be the mother of Lady Isabel Barnett, distinguished as a television personality in programmes like *What's My Line*, alongside the memorable Gilbert Harding. Young Isabel used to come back to Buchan, where her favourite playmate was Mona Low, now Mrs Dawson of Coronation Cottages, Maud.

Further down the road, at the Aden Estate by Old Deer, Colonel Russell was rearing a daughter who was to become the mother of Lord Whitelaw, the familiar Willie Whitelaw of Mrs Thatcher's governments.

CHAPTER FIVE

LIKE ROBBIE BURNS

That panorama of local history had passed vividly before my eyes that July morning of my fiftieth birthday as I stood at the doorway of Fedderate Cottages, Maud, and tried to encompass the half century that had flitted by since first I saw light in what was then a but-and-ben.

My parents had begun their married life more modestly in a rat-infested hovel at Mill of Bruxie, two miles from Maud, where my father stood guard by the cottage door, firing off his double-barrel gun at the invading vermin. My mother was already pregnant, but before the birth of their only child they would move into the village, to the greater comfort of Fedderate Cottages, a stone-and-lime block of eight flats between Kitchie's Dam and the school, which would seem like Paradise after Bruxie, even if it was not yet blessed with inside toilets.

And there, as I stood by the doorway of my birth, I had clear recollections of living there, though we had moved to a council house at 2 Park Crescent, less than a hundred yards away, by the time I was three years and four months old.

Now I was striving to separate the fact from childhood fantasy and to flesh out the skeleton of memory which had followed me through the 1930s into the dark excitement of the Second World War and out again to the bleakness of a post-war youth.

So many changes and so many different standpoints, bewildering enough in themselves without nature's own hazardous journey from boy to man. How much is ever real?

Well, for a start, I remember that flitting of November, 1934, when I was three, in which I was entrusted with the task of carrying the biscuit tins from Fedderate Cottages up the back lane and past the midden to Park Crescent. Neighbours like John Craig and Jimmy Pyper helped my father to carry the furniture. Around that same time, I recall my aunt's wedding in the village hall at the neighbouring New Pitsligo. Even before that, I have vague impressions of two local lads, Charlie Hunter and my mother's favourite message-boy, Sandy Dyer, a chubby rascal in freckles, dirding my pram round Fedderate Cottages as part of their lorry-driving fantasies, all the while terrorizing the infant into bewildered silence.

In that decade of the thirties I can trace a pattern of awakening to the joys and excitements of a big wide world: the feein markets, when farm servants were engaged for the term; the skirl of the recruiting pipe bands for those who didn't find a fee; the general tenor of a rural way of life with its sights and sounds and scents.

I can still hear the mellow saxophones of Roy Fox and Lew Stone on the national wireless, the gloom of King George V's funeral and the stir of Abdication for his son, the Prince of Wales, which had us riveted round the sets for a sombre speech of which I had only the vaguest understanding.

It was in that year of the old king's death that I was welcomed into the fold of Maud School by the kindly Miss Catto, who had come from her native Aberdeen in the year of the General Strike, a decade earlier. What a different world it had seemed that April day of 1936 when a tearful mother delivered me unwillingly into the care of the infant class. With a motherly manner, the golden-haired Miss Catto had set us down to a routine of slates and plasticine and counting beads, in front of a roaring fire enclosed by a sturdy guard-rail.

In that warm and happy atmosphere the foundations of life were well and truly laid, the Three Rs of reading, writing and 'rithmetic well and truly taught, and, if the truth be known, the first flickerings of love well and truly stirred. Across the passage sat Doris Symon, dark ringlets dangling against her lily-white skin, so clean and neat and gently perfumed, fine-boned and truly beautiful. Prompted surely by nature, we would reach out a touching hand and blush in the bewilderment of alien forces. Ah, for the tingling beauty of innocence!

Innocent, too, we were of that Depression which must have been raging outby in the thirties, though it did not seem to intrude overmuch on our rural life with its hot summers and dramatic winters (or so they seemed) which blocked us in for weeks on end and turned the Christmas card of the artist's brush into a picturesque reality.

The North-East childhood of the 1930s seemed as smooth and golden as Miss Catto's hair, uncomplicated by the gathering troubles of an outside world, the insanity of which was conveyed to us by means of the wireless (but then only if Bob Sangster had charged your wet batteries). Up and beyond Bank's Hill lay the foreign lands that folk spoke about; but our little universe was safe in the folding arms of the River Ugie as it flowed down from Bonnykelly, past Brucklay and Honeyneuk on the way to Old Deer and the North Sea beyond; safely defined it was by the railway lines which curled around our perimeter.

Within the limits of that universe we knew contentment and excitement in agreeable proportions, the hard work of country folk still lightened by an active and home-made social relief. With Aikey Fair and the feein markets came the hawkers and pedlars, selling preens, pints and bars of soap, fishwives from the Broch bearing heavy creels on their backs; the visiting circuses of Dick's and Pinder's, modest enough when you look back but major events in their time. Among those pedlars was old Geordie Robertson, whose mathematics were simple. When my grandmother remonstrated with him about the price of a small item, he had a ready answer: 'Na na, Mrs Barron, I buy them for a penny and sell them for tippence— just one per cent profit, ye see.'

There was croquet and crumpets, and the unforgettable waft of hot cheese-cakes from the fresh ovens of Morrison's Bakery. Not the least of it was the excitement of the yellow van appearing round the Hill o' Clackriach from Peterhead to herald the arrival of Luigi Zanre, who made the finest ice-cream in all Christendom. But more of Luigi later.

In front of a roaring fire in the infant classroom, Miss Catto served lunchtime cocoa for country bairns who had brought their 'piece' in a bag, and she rounded off a perfect week with her Friday afternoon caramel. So she fed the bodies and nurtured the child mind with the basics of a sound education. By the time we moved up school from Miss Catto to Miss Duncan and Miss Morrison we were already benefiting from a thorough grounding. For amusement, I still keep my dictation book of 1938, from which I discover that 'A little mouse has made its home within my house' and 'The pilot had a leather coat, also goggles' at the Croydon Aerodrome which was the focal point of all flying interest in those early days of Biggles.

Those thoughts of Maud School were revolving freely in my head on that anniversary visit when I was striding out towards a rendezvous with two very special ladies. There they were, coming towards me, just as they had crossed the playground at Maud all those years ago—none other than Miss Catto and Miss Morrison, looking little different from the impressions I had guarded for nearly half a century. Miss Catto was the senior by quite a number of years, having taught at Maud from 1926 until 1942, but happily she survives in good health into 1987, living at Seafield Gardens, Aberdeen. Miss Morrison is an active citizen of Banchory, where she is now Mrs Reith of Glassel Road. Having arrived at Maud in 1939, she remained throughout the war years before moving to Kittybrewster School in Aberdeen, which was to count among its former pupils such diverse talents as Denis Law, the footballer, and Lord Armstrong, former Head of the Civil Service and Chairman of the Midland Bank.

So we chatted over old times and rekindled the sense of a bygone age which had slipped so quickly and elusively out of our reach. As time creeps upon us, quiet and unnoticed, the mundane things of life which seem scarcely to merit a mention take on the gloss of history.

We remembered a rural enclosure of contented people, unconcerned with class or creed and forging for themselves a steady rhythm of honest toil and simple pleasure which produced a happiness beyond analysis. We remembered the names and the faces, the laughter in the still country air, and the dreaded scourge of consumption and diphtheria which regularly stalked our village classrooms to bear away another innocent child in the sorrow of a little white coffin.

Miss Catto remembered that I had stated an ambition to be 'jist like Robbie Burns' and that she had re-told it in the staffroom, expressing the hope that I would not become too much like Robbie Burns!

We remembered the new arrival in the infant room, a farm boy who sat all day just gazing up at the ventilation grille in the ceiling. At the end of the day he affected an adult posture and asked the teacher 'Are ye ill wi rottens?' which, translated into English, means 'Are you troubled with rats?' The boy, who grew up to be a solid farmer, was clearly more concerned with rodent infestation than primary education.

There was also Miss Duncan's story about the day she was giving a lesson on children's pets when one boy announced that his dog was called 'Moreover'. When she expressed doubts about such a name, the little chap assured her of his authority: 'Ay Miss, it says it in the Bible. "Moreover the dog came and licked his sores."'

Imagine the chagrin of discovering that, in the 1930s, these noble ladies were being rewarded with the princely salary of £180 a year if they were graduates and £130 if they were not. Out of that came 18s. a week (ninety pence) which they paid for digs to Ma Smith at Woodville, not to mention those caramels and assorted sundries which came out of their own pockets without thought of recompense.

Their multifarious duties included the unpaid care and collection of our pennies for that same Aberdeen Savings Bank account which, in 1986, gave me preferential treatment for buying shares in the flotation of the TSB! But the service of such ladies could not be measured in pounds, shillings and pence. Their contribution to human happiness and well-being, helping people to make the most of what they were given, is reflected in the lives of their former pupils, countless hundreds who have gone forth into a busy world, cautious and respectful to a fault, only to find to their surprise that the primary grounding in schools like Maud had already fitted them for comparison with more senior levels elsewhere.

It does not surprise me to learn now that students of such matters have come to the conclusion that, during the last century at least, the North-East was the best educated part of Scotland and had the highest literacy rate in all Britain.

That has been the achievement and the reward of all the Miss Cattos and Miss Morrisons and Miss Duncans who have graced our Scottish schools down the years.

CHAPTER SIX

GREIG AND GRIEG

I have never been impressed by, nor even fully understood, the notion of the 'old-established family', since it must surely follow from the plain facts of life that all families stretch back to the same kind of genesis, whether you believe in the phenomenon of Adam and Eve or not.

But the likelihood that we are all much of an age does not occlude the fact that there are branches and twigs of the old hereditary oak which produce much more colour than others. At my grandmother's knee I was given an early lesson on how there came to be a touch of blossom in the forestry of my own family, not through any sense of braggadocio but by the simple duty of passing on the story.

On three sides of my grandparentage, the Websters, Watsons and Barrons, we were fairly plain and predictable country folk, striving to make two corns grow where one grew before and plodding our way through the various travails that beset the Scottish peasantry those few generations ago. Even the fourth strand of the grandparent base, the Greigs, began in similar fashion in the Fraserburgh district, towards Rathen, Lonmay and Cairnbulg, but the even tenor of that heredity was somewhat diverted by the injection of less mundane elements.

For a start, those Greigs claimed earlier cousinship with the Alexander Greig who left Mosstown of Cairnbulg in 1770 to settle in Bergen, where he became the great-grandfather of Edvard Grieg, national composer of Norway and one of the most creative talents in musical history.

Whatever the closeness of the family link, there was certainly a strong resemblance between Edvard Grieg and a corresponding member of the Greig family who stayed in

Scotland—Gavin Greig, who not only looked like his 'distant cousin' but had developed a powerful talent for music, to the point that he too became a composer, brilliant organist, poet and playwright, but known best of all perhaps for his famous collection of folk songs, claimed by those who know about such matters to be the best of its kind in the world.

All of that, incidentally, was achieved while he pursued his bread-and-butter occupation as headmaster of a rural school in the Buchan district of Aberdeenshire. By coincidence, however, the person of Gavin Greig was further enhanced by a more clear-cut relationship, which arrived through his mother, Mary Moir, who came directly from the same Burness family, near Stonehaven, which produced Robert Burns, the National Bard of Scotland.

Gavin Greig himself was brought up at Parkhill of Dyce (not far from the present Aberdeen Airport), where his father was forester on the estate. I have said much about him in my earlier book, *A Grain of Truth*, so for the moment let me condense him to being the classic example of a Scottish lad o' pairts, graduating from Aberdeen University and settling at Whitehill of New Deer, where he became headmaster at the age of twenty-two. There he began to father his nine children, the eldest of whom was Edith, the same grandmother who was telling me this story at her knee in the 1930s.

The route of those Greigs who left the shores of Buchan for the fjords of Norway, however, needs further explanation. With the long-standing links between Scotland and Scandinavia, it was not surprising that a certain Mr Wallace from Banff became the British Consul in Bergen. He happened to be a friend of the Greig family from Mosstown of Cairnbulg and it was to work in Mr Wallace's office that Alexander Greig left home in 1770, at the age of thirty-one.

He settled so well in that role that he eventually succeeded Mr Wallace as British Consul, while never surrendering one whit of his Scottishness. Twice a year, in fact, he used to cross the North Sea in a little boat just to attend communion in the kirk back home! By the time he was followed in the Consul's job by his son and grandson, they had conformed to the continental style of spelling and transposed the vowels to turn Greig into Grieg.

None of that would have gained much attention, and indeed the North-East of Scotland might have bothered very little about claiming their origins, had it not been for the genius who turned up in the next generation. Edvard Grieg, born in Bergen in 1843, was soon establishing himself as one of the greatest living composers, bringing the mountains and fjords alive with the power and passion of his music.

His compositions for Ibsen's *Peer Gynt* and the Piano Concerto in A Minor were just two of the creations in an illustrious career which brought him into contact with everyone from Liszt to Hans Christian Andersen. Significantly perhaps, the intense awareness of the folk heritage was a prime characteristic of Edvard Grieg, just as it was in his distant relative in Scotland, Gavin Greig, who was born just thirteen years after the composer.

The two men never met, but my grandmother did remember her father leaving home one day on a long journey to hear Edvard Grieg giving a piano recital. She thought he went to Edinburgh; but being of such a retiring nature, he apparently did not go backstage to introduce himself. Some have expressed doubts about Grieg ever having visited Scotland, on the grounds that he was a very bad sailor, but the man himself put the record straight in a remarkable conversation which is recorded by the late John Cranna, former harbour treasurer of Fraserburgh, who undertook a great deal of research in these matters of local history. Cranna told us about a Morayshire minister, the Rev. W. A. Gray, who was visiting Norway and who gave this account of the surprise which came upon him in a Laerdal hotel:

> Scarcely had I taken my place in the hotel porch after supper for a smoke in the cool night air when Grieg stood beside

me alone and lit his cigar. His figure was even shorter and slighter than I first imagined it to be.

Everyone speaks to everyone in a Norwegian hotel. I accosted him, introducing myself briefly and any doubt I had as to the character of my reception was at once set at rest. Off went the hat with a courteous Scandinavian sweep; the clear blue eyes glanced keenly into my face; the attitude was of frank and friendly attention. The talk (Grieg speaks fluent English, only now and again interjecting a Norsk word) turned first upon Scotland. The musician asked in what part of Scotland I lived and I answered 'Not very far from the home of your forefathers.'

'Then,' said Herr Grieg, 'you live near Fraserburgh. Alexander Greig, my great-grandfather, who afterwards changed his name to Grieg, emigrated from Fraserburgh last century. See,' he said, displaying the seal at the end of his watch chain, with the figure of a ship among stormy waves, and the motto *Ad spes infracta*, 'here is our crest; it is the same as that of the Scottish Greigs. Yes,' he continued, 'I have various ties in Scotland. I have Scottish friends; my godmother was Scottish—Mrs Stirling; she lived near the town of the same name. I know something of your Scottish writers too, especially Carlyle. I am fond of reading Carlyle; in what part of Scotland was he born? And I admire Edinburgh—Princes Street, the gardens, the old town, the castle—ah, they are beautiful, beautiful. Edinburgh people are very kind.

'They have asked me repeatedly to visit them and to play and I would do so willingly if it were not for the sea. I am the very worst of sailors. Once, some years ago, I crossed from Bergen to Aberdeen. I shall never forget that night of horrors, never!'

We turned to the subject of Scottish music. 'I admire it greatly,' said Herr Grieg, 'and I find a similarity between your Scottish melodies and our Norwegian ones, especially when the sentiment is—what do you call it—*alvorlig*, grave, serious.'

The Reverend Mr Gray did well with his near-verbatim

account of a rare meeting, giving some hint of what a marvellous occasion it would have been if only Gavin Greig and Edvard Grieg had found each other's company.

CHAPTER SEVEN

ON MORMOND HILL

From Granny Barron I gained a perspective of our family history, brought alive by first-hand tales from the last century; tales like the visits of that greatest of fiddlers, J. Scott Skinner, King of Strathspey, to the family home at the Schoolhouse of Whitehill, where he and Gavin Greig cemented their friendship and collaborated in musical works, not least the famous *Harp and Claymore* volume.

Gavin Greig, a tall, lean, scholarly man whose name brought light to the eyes of those who remembered him, had become one of the most loved and revered of the North-East sons, as far away as the academic cloisters of Edinburgh and even on the continent, where they found it hard to understand why a man of such international calibre should closet himself in what seemed to them the backwater of rural Aberdeenshire.

But that was where he belonged and where he was at his happiest, a brilliant conversationalist as naturally and uncondescendingly at ease with the farm servants of his beloved Buchan as with the erudite professors who came to seek him out from distant parts. They were all the same to him.

As a child I knew little about his novels, which were often published in the serialized fashion of the last century (*Logie o' Buchan* was re-published by Bisset's of Aberdeen in 1986). But I was well aware of his musical plays, like *Mains's Wooin'* and *Mains Again*, which have remained in production for nearly a century, from that opening night at New Deer in 1894, when the leading lady was the Buchan beauty of her day, Nellie Metcalfe, who later married the well-known local farmer, athlete and writer Archie Campbell of Auchmunziel, by whom she bore that distinguished Scottish poetess of modern times,

251

Flora Garry.

So I would be taken to productions of those Doric classics in town and village halls around the country and, in the fullness of adulthood, would find myself invited to say a few words, as the great-grandson of the author.

I became deeply aware, too, of his presidential part in a rather special body of people, the Buchan Field Club, a collection of the best brains in the North-East of Scotland who met for the purpose of studying the natural sciences, archaeology, history and literature of Buchan and to interest the young in such studies. Happily, the public interest in that local background, which was strong in Gavin Greig's day, is stronger again in the last quarter of the twentieth century than it was in the middle portion, with the activities of the Buchan Field Club extended by a Buchan Heritage Society.

There is now an annual festival of local speech and music and a splendid heritage centre at Lord Whitelaw's ancestral home of Aden, by Old Deer, where my father's old harvest binder from Honeyneuk has been among the latest exhibits of traditional hardware, still in use for the cutting of oats.

While public speaking has never been a strength of mine, I was nevertheless prevailed upon to address the Buchan Field Club at the annual dinner in Strichen in 1983, held in the same Freemasons' Hotel where they used to meet in the days of Gavin Greig. Such an engagement compelled me to some rewarding research before facing so distinguished a gathering and the results enabled me to place my own lifetime more securely into the context of local history.

This is a summary of what I said at Strichen that night, with some embellishments from what I had intended to say:

On an August day of 1904, this very club gathered here in the village of Strichen and went on an excursion up Mormond Hill, under the leadership of my great-grandfather, Gavin Greig, who was even then on the way to fame as a playwright and composer but more so as the man who collected the folk songs of the North-East. He had to travel only from the Schoolhouse of Whitehill, a few miles from here, but others that day came from as far as London and Kent. They assembled on the arrival of the afternoon train and drove up the hill as far as Brans Farm and thereafter the ascent was accomplished on foot. They visited the Resting Cairns, the Hunt Stone, Rob Gibb's Lodge, the White Horse and the Deer.

Having enjoyed the view from the summit and cast their eyes over Buchan, they descended to hold a meeting in the Freemasons' Hotel where we sit now. After speeches a good deal more scholarly than you are going to hear now, the company sat down to an excellent tea, purveyed by Mrs Mackay.

In a world which seems to change at a bewildering rate, it may be difficult for us in the 1980s to imagine what it was like all those years ago. It is a common fault to believe that the people were stiff and quaint and not so alert as ourselves, but a glance at the quality of address produced in your own transactions shows how scholarly and perceptive and humorous they really were in those days.

As a preliminary to coming here tonight I did not engage in the worthwhile pursuit of climbing Mormond; if I had, I certainly could not have roamed so freely as our forefathers and I might even have come across a group of demonstrators protesting about the NATO base on the hill.

No, I was to be found instead this afternoon at Pittodrie football park, watching Aberdeen, a club which was just one year old at the time of that meeting in 1904. If Gavin Greig had gone to Pittodrie that afternoon he could at least have caught a train to Strichen in time for his meeting. But that main artery has been cut away by Doctor Beeching and we are the poorer for it.

Gavin Greig was indeed a great scholar and it does seem extraordinary that a man of that calibre—and he was not alone in rural Scotland—remained as headmaster of a country school like Whitehill. No wonder Scottish education gained such a high reputation.

I was lucky enough to have a first-hand account of life in

Gavin Greig's household from my grandmother, eldest of his nine children, who lived on to her nineties and died not so long ago. It was a house of discipline but it was also a house of good conversation, good music and good fun, all that despite the hardship and tragedy of tuberculosis and so on. Four of his children died in early life.

At that meeting in this hotel one of his daughters, Mary Jane, sang 'Mormond Braes' and he himself had composed an ode for the occasion, called 'On Mormond Hill', which would flow effortlessly from his quill and which ended like this:

> But now the gloaming hour is come
> The breeze dies down; and in the vale beneath
> All by the crooning stream
> The Lammas fields stand deep and dumb
> The shadows deepen over moss and heath
> And far along the shore the great lights gleam
> Downward we take our way till, dark and still,
> The long ridge looms behind. Farewell to Mormond Hill.

At an earlier meeting of this club the members gathered in my native village of Maud, and before they went off to have a look at Brucklay Castle and the ruins of the old Fedderate Castle, associated with Robert the Bruce, they adjourned to my old school (then brand new), where Gavin Greig was again in evidence with a talk which he called 'Lease of Life in Buchan'.

In it he was giving his observations on how life had changed in the Buchan district during the last twenty years of the nineteenth century. Even then he was saying that the old customs were becoming obsolete and the superstitions dying. Within that period, concerts were on the increase but the unaccompanied singer had almost disappeared. Now there was the piano for accompaniment.

In the kirk, the precentor with his pitchfork had been replaced by the pipe organ and full-blooded choir—and the minister's sermon had been shrinking at the rate of about a minute per year until, in 1899 in the more advanced churches, it was down to about twenty minutes!

Many influences had been at work but perhaps the bicycle had as much to do with it as anything; in fact, he said the innocent looking thing was revolutionizing the conditions of modern life and, among other effects, producing a new type of woman with whom man would have to reckon in the near future.

He was greatly struck by the fact that, within that twenty-year period, the Buchan schoolboy had enhanced his capacity for understanding and appreciating wit and humour. He himself, of course, had encouraged self-awareness and further education through his Mutual Improvement Association classes which were so popular in the North-East of Scotland. He used to tell a story of one such meeting where he would give a talk and prompt discussion. That night he asked Jimmy Paterson from Aulfat to start the discussion.

'What's your opinion, Jimmy?' he asked of one who had not been the most diligent of members that evening.

'Weel,' said Jimmy, making a promising start, 'I think . . . (changing tone) . . . I think . . . (changing tone again) . . . Damn it, Maister Greig, I dinna ken fit tae think!'

In a fastly changing world, Gavin Greig noticed that Buchan was retaining its individuality better than most districts of the North-East, and he credited the club with having achieved so much in that direction. With the influences which spread across society today, making for a uniformity of life, it is hard enough to detect differences between one part of Scotland and another, let alone parts of Aberdeenshire. Even today, despite the assault of change on the surface of our lives, it seems to me they make a slower impression on the deeper character of the Buchan folk.

As I say, Gavin Greig was observing change in that period from 1880 to 1900. That great North-East writer, Lewis Grassic Gibbon, born in 1901, believed that the rural Scotland of his childhood—and many childhoods before him—disappeared with the First World War. Yet when I read of the North-East he describes, it seems to me very much the world I remember in the 1930s. Whereas Grassic Gibbon thought it went out with the First World War, I thought it disappeared with the Second.

The people had certainly drained away from the land. The tractor and bogie now cleared stooks once gathered by the horse and cart of the thirties, and soon the combine harvester was to put the binder into the pages of history. I suppose children of today would hardly know a binder if they saw one.

My early Buchan was of hairst parks at leading time, trailing on as a child, more of a hindrance than a help no doubt but carrying the basket with the piece for my granny, plain loaf and baps with butter and home-made raspberry jam and a kettle of tea. We travelled to the moss, too, in the lea of a cart and brought home the peats from Cowbog, through the long straggle of New Pitsligo, or Kyak as we called it, down the Gairdner's Brae and round by Mac's Yard to Mains of Whitehill.

It seemed like a golden age of school picnics at the Broch Beach, warm days at Aikey Fair, beer tents and bargains and the excitement of a thousand horses on that brae of a July Wednesday, when we savoured the sweet smell of peace before the deluge of war that swept away my young illusions, just as that earlier war had swept away Grassic Gibbon's.

In a lively social scene of the 1930s, I can still remember my mother dressing up in her evening gown, screwing ear-rings into her lobes, dabbing scent around her person, adjusting her suspenders, turning this way and that before a mirror, in preparation for the Buchan Bachelors' Ball or the Mintlaw Ladies' Dance.

Meanwhile my father was struggling to fix a thrawn stud in a stiff collar, with the damned thing skiting across the floor to the accompaniment of an oath, for which my father had a particularly rich and colourful vocabulary. I can still hear their voices in late-night laughter at solo parties, long after I was in bed. I can hear the call of 'Abundance', 'Cop', 'Prop' and 'Misere' and the explosions of disbelief when some incredible coincidence of cards befell.

But soon my golden age of the thirties was tarnished by the black-out of war, a legislation which dimmed all lights but the moon, the glow of the lunar lamp revealing the silhouette of great convoys passing up our coast in the night. The odd ship would sink and we scrambled to Rattray Head beach to gather up tins of sardines, lumps of coal and sheets of cork. From the aerodrome at Longside gigantic bombers took off into the mystery of the night and lent an added air of excitement to a boy's war. Soldiers passed by and billeted themselves in places like Brucklay Castle and Strichen House and the village halls and hotels around Buchan.

In the midst of that war my father came home from the Broch, having kept his regular contact with farmers there, to say he had done something that day he had not done for years. Whereas he preferred to keep his dram till evening, he had joined some farmers for a drink in the Commercial Bar, along the main street of Fraserburgh, that afternoon; a crowded place it was, with the customary bustle of darts and drinking.

After tea that evening, a glow arose in the sky and word soon spread that Benzie and Miller's shop in Fraserburgh was on fire. As it happened, German bombers were over the Forth Bridge and they too saw the glow. Normally hampered by the black-out, they were not slow to accept an easy target for to-night. Up they came, clean over the rooftops of Maud as we cowered beneath the eaves of Park Crescent and trembled at the bumble-bee note which distinguished German planes from our own. On they went towards that glow which lit up the whole town of Fraserburgh and dropped a land-mine—right on that Commercial Bar where my father had broken his rule and imbibed that day. Some of the thirty-one dead had been there since a darts match in the afternoon. Ironically, it was Guy Fawkes Night.

When that conflict was finally over, I found that the childhood innocence had peeled away—no more the safe caress of a steadfast world—but it was hard to apportion blame between war and puberty. The old feein markets had gone and the horses of Aikey Fair too. I believed that the old Scots ways, the songs and the speech and the customs, had gone with the wind of war; but I may have been wrong.

I hear younger people today talking nostalgically about their childhood in the fifties and sixties, mentioning features of life which I thought had gone with the Second World War and which Lewis Grassic Gibbon thought had gone with the First.

For certain, the young of today are more interested in folk song than we were in my own youth, and the renaissance in our culture is undeniable.

So the links remain and I am reminded of a letter I received in the aftermath of writing *A Grain of Truth*. It came from an oil-rig in the North Sea and it was written, in beautiful hand, by a man who had unearthed from a drawer at his home in the Braidsea of Fraserburgh the reminiscences of his grandmother. He told me of their content and I gave some encouragement towards their publication. (They were accepted by my own publisher at the time, Paul Harris.) How delighted I was when they eventually came alive in the form of a book, *The Christian Watt Papers*, the diaries and papers of a fisher lassie, describing with skill and sensitivity the life of this area when she would carry her creel up through Buchan and on to Balmoral, where she would meet Queen Victoria and Prince Albert.

It is a story of such hardship and tragedy, ending with forty-seven years in Cornhill Mental Hospital in Aberdeen, as to be almost too much to take. Yet what an inspiring tale of courage and determination, of kindliness and good humour. It is the type of story which helped to forge the Buchan character.

Those of you who have read *The Christian Watt Papers* may have been haunted, as I certainly was, by her description of working in the hairst parks of Strichen House in the days when it was owned by Lord Lovat. There they were, a hundred workers in the field, binding sheaves in the still of a summer's evening, when they suddenly broke into the singing of 'The Lord is my Shepherd'. Can't you just imagine it? A spontaneous choir of hairsting folk, raising a heavenly voice which would filter down over the rooftops of Strichen and up towards the hoosie at the top of Mormond.

It could have been a sound to meet Gavin Greig and his Buchan Field Club members as they descended that August evening for their meeting here in the Freemasons' Hotel. So much changes but so much more remains the same; for we are no more than the children of the children of those people who were here in this hotel those eighty years ago.

Whatever the changes, I believe we are basically the same

Buchan folk whose individuality is to be found buried deep in the mysteries of that life in the hairst parks of Strichen House and far beyond. Buried, too, in the ethereal beauty of those voices which rose and wept over Strichen so many years ago.

CHAPTER EIGHT

THE GARDEN OF BUCHAN

In an eventful newspaper career I have wandered far and wide across the world, but the farther I roamed from my native Scotland and the deeper the dimensions that were added to my life, the more I was thinking of Buchan, of the mart at Maud and Aikey Fair and New Deer Show; of the folk who would be swinging up the spring drills or tyauvin' among neeps or silage or redding up a sotter of dubs in the farm close. I could smell the hot dung of cattle in the byre, hear the rustle of the cornyard and sense the melancholy peace of the farmstead on a warm summer's day when a strutting cockerel kept toun and all life seemed to lie somewhere else.

This Buchan which had found its way into the marrow of my bones was an elusive substance to crystallize. On the face of it, Buchan was Mormond Hill and Windyheads, Peterhead and Rattray Head, beef and barley, brose and bannocks; Buchan was Robert Boothby and Aikey Fair, cattle floats and feein markets, wild sprees at the Baron's Hotel, rowdy dances at Mintlaw Station. Drop down the cliffs at Pennan (where they made the film *Local Hero*) or comb the beach at Aberdour and Buchan was the poetry of J. C. Milne, a whisper in the wind that mixed the tang of the land with the gentle odours of the sea; it was psalms at Crimond and acres of golden sand at Cruden Bay, where Bram Stoker came to create swatches of his famous *Dracula*.

Closer to my own particular focal point, Maud was a lady all douce and respectable on the one hand yet lying in a shameless troilism between her Old Deer and her New Deer. New Deer was the village two miles to the west, higher in its elevation but lower in its tone, a Maud man might tell you, with just a hint of superiority. The main street of New Deer was long and sloped, downwards to the Howe of Hell, you might think, and upwards on a path to the foothills of Heaven, passing through the granite gates of Culsh, where my forebears are to be found in their celestial peace.

Though New Deer in my early days had a fair spattering of folk who were not beyond breaking the peace after a night with John Barleycorn, a native would nevertheless be capable of saying to a Maud man: 'Of course you need three cells in your police station at Maud.'

'Ay, fairly that,' would come the reply. 'But that's only for haudin' folk from New Deer and Pitsligo and tink places like that.'

If New Deer was little more than one long street, New Pitsligo, or Kyak as we preferred to call it, was an even longer worm of a place, home for masons, souters and hawkers, peats from the Moss o' Cowbog, biscuits from Smith's bakery and paraffin and petrol from the kenspeckle figure of Dorothy Park, a lady of ample girth who bothered nobody yet was found one day most brutally and callously done to death. (They never did find the murderer.)

Round yet and you came to Byth, a quaint little rickle of a place with a sense of inferiority, perhaps arising from the fact that a succession of nobility from the seventeenth century onwards, with high-sounding names like Sir John Baird, Member of Parliament, Lord of Session and a Lord of Justiciary, kept disposing of it to each other as if nobody really wanted it. Even up to the twentieth century Byth tended to be represented in the public mind for backwardness, broken down thackit houses, illegitimate bairns and God-forsakenness, a fair sotter of a reputation but a fine bit place for all that.

Not far away, at Slacks of Cairnbanno, my maternal grandfather, Arthur Barron, grew up as a fine, upstanding young man, tall and lean in the mould of Gavin Greig and with so much of a similar interest in local culture that he not only became a willing assistant in Greig's folk-song collecting but an equally willing suitor for the hand of his eldest daughter, Edith.

Together they moved into the tenantry of Mains of Whitehill, just a mile from the Schoolhouse home of Greig, and started their own family of five, of whom my mother was the eldest.

Within the Barron family, my grandfather had a beautiful sister, Betty, married to Willie Park, who took on the lease of Newlandshill of Maud towards the end of last century, and there they raised a large family in the impoverished circumstances of small farming at that time. There was barely enough to meet the essentials of living and certainly not to provide for anything in the way of education. Yet those children of Betty Barron and Willie Park were a highly gifted collection, whose mettle can be gauged from the fact that the eldest son, George, lent the money to put sister Anna through as a teacher; Anna then gave the financial help which put Jessie through as a nurse (she later owned a beautiful nursing home in Edinburgh); the two of them helped Bessie to become a teacher and brother Wilson to become a doctor. And so it went on until the whole family had been given the opportunity to make the most of their talents.

It is not a responsibility that one would advocate for youngsters today, but for those who found the strength and determination to meet the deprivations of poverty in that particular way, there was almost bound to be a reward of character and satisfaction and some measure of success in their subsequent lives.

Perhaps the most interesting story of the Park family was that of Anna. First married to Tom Smith, schoolmaster at Kilspindie in Perthshire, she was left an early widow. Then she married the general practitioner at the ancient village of Old Deer, Dr Ritchie. The marriage took place on the Saturday and on the Monday morning my mother was hanging out her washing when a neighbour, knowing that my mother was a cousin of Anna, came out to say: 'That's very sad about Dr Ritchie. I see his death in the papers this morning.'

'No, no,' said my mother. 'It's his wedding announcement in the papers. They were married on Saturday.'

'Ay,' said Mrs Craig. 'His wedding announcement is there—but his death announcement is there too!'

Dr Ritchie had indeed died within a day of his marriage and poor Anna was a widow for the second time. By then she had become not only a teacher but a preacher as well, destined to be a legend in the Episcopal Church of Scotland as its first Deaconess, embracing that brand of faith like many more North-East people who felt John Knox went too far.

She found home with her mother in an eerie, rambling house upon a shelf of land opposite the gates of the historic Abbey of Deer, and there we would drive down from Maud on family visits, which I viewed with a mixture of fear and excitement. High among the trees their secluded house, called Newlands, was surely the perfect setting for a Victorian novel, a place of long shadows and weird wails of wind. Sweeping through the corridors of the house in full-length black dress with high collar, Mrs Park still had the bearing and remnants of beauty from her days as Betty Barron.

Still in black, with the white-collared assimilation of a minister, Anna did nothing to detract from that ghostly air, at least to the impressionable child. Her soft, caressing rattle of a voice and gentle demeanour somehow combined the authority of Heaven with the covert mystery of darker places.

She was the ideal voice of Victorian story-telling and by now, as Deaconess Anna, she was spreading her influence throughout the Episcopal Church, among other things conducting a uniquely imaginative postal Sunday School for children in remote areas. She corrected the homework of hundreds and corresponded with them individually. She became the leader of education in the North-East of Scotland, her power and influence standing in inverse ratio to the noise she made about it.

In time they built a new school in Peterhead, dedicated to the care of handicapped children, and they could hardly have done better than to name it the Anna Ritchie School, a tribute to a quite remarkable woman, though I had never regarded her as anything other than my mother's cousin, a quaint relative who was for ever the Woman in Black.

Tending upon Deaconess Anna, and completing the whole setting of that Victorian novel, was a feeble and faded maid-servant called Isobel, a character straight from Dickens, with straggly hair, streaks of red in her cheeks and eye sockets that were gaunt and mysterious and gave rise to the thought that here was a gentle soul outwith the touch of everyday life.

As if all that were not enough, my childhood visits to Newlands were marked by a most extraordinary event which used to take place on an annual summer day in that picturesque strath which spread itself beneath Deaconess Anna's house, by the Abbey of Deer and the babble of the River Ugie, as it wended its way from Maud and onwards to Peterhead.

Called from our ramblings around the terraced greens and outhouses of Newlands, we would freeze into an awed silence at the sight of a great procession as the Buchan train braked and screeched for its once-a-year halt at a little wooden platform by the foot of Aikey Brae. There it disgorged a teaming array of chanting, white-robed figures who promptly arranged themselves into a parade of the Roman Catholic priesthood, complete with mitre headgear, poised like gaping jaws to the heavens above, before moving off in a prayerful wail of incantation which aroused the tingle of fear and imprinted itself indelibly on the tenderness of the child mind.

This religious pomp in the heart of Presbyterian Buchan needs some kind of explanation. If we think the ruined Abbey of Deer belongs to antiquity, we must stretch the imagination back still further to an earlier Abbey of Deer, which stood by the site of the present Church of Scotland in the village of Old Deer, less than a mile away.

That early monastery was founded by St Columba and his disciple, St Drostan, who came, we are told by legend, on a mission to the Celtic people of Buchan in the sixth century. It was here that the highly-prized Book of Deir was written, now preciously guarded in Cambridge University and containing a splendid record of life in Buchan around the ninth and tenth centuries, with such fascinating details as the shopping-lists of the day.

The present Abbey of Deer nearby was founded by the Earl of Buchan in 1219, as a subordinate house to Kinloss, and flourished for more than 300 years until just before the Reformation. It was run by fourteen Cistercian monks. Two of them came from the south but one couldn't stand the Buchan weather, cauldrif cratur that he was, and the other couldn't bear the uncouth manners of the people.

It may be hard for us today to understand the place which these monasteries occupied in community life, but they were, to all intents and purposes, the local inns, the safest place for a traveller to seek a bed at a time when the highway robbers of Scotland had nothing to learn from the muggers of the twentieth century. In the best traditions of the inn, the monks had a close liaison with a local brewery and were said to be over-fond of the beverage themselves.

The Abbey was in decline before the Reformation, which broke the dominance of the Roman Catholic Church, and some of it had been pulled down by 1560, with local folk carting away the stones. The Abbey contained a church with a nave of five arches in length, transept and choir; that remained standing until 1848 when the proprietor, Admiral Ferguson of Pitfour, the local laird, demolished it and built a mausoleum. That remained until 1930, when the Roman Catholic Church repossessed the ancient property, demolished Ferguson's mausoleum and handed over the ruins of the Abbey to the Ministry of Works for its preservation.

It was this re-establishing of the links with the Roman Catholic Church which brought forth that pride of prelates in the 1930s, to fix the gaze of Buchan folk, not least the young, in the posture of mesmerized rabbits. Their annual procession was soon to be interrupted by the Second World War, however, and it was not until 1981 that they came again to the lush valley of the Ugie in the Garden of Buchan.

Mercifully, the trouble between Catholics and Protestants, which ravages the beauty of Ireland and simmers bitterly in the West of Scotland, has no place in the life of the North-East. The 700 Roman Catholics in that stretch between Peterhead and Ellon live with their Protestant neighbours in an atmosphere of goodwill.

On the eve of Pentecost, Father Alistair Doyle of Peterhead invited non-Catholic clergy to join the 200 people who gathered in 1981. As a measure of an important occasion, the Abbots of the three Scottish monasteries were there—Abbot Spencer of Pluscarden, Abbot Holman of Fort Augustus and Abbot McGlynn from Nunraw, men of such strict religious orders that they seldom wander from their cloisters.

For me there was a particularly intriguing character involved in that ceremony of 1981. Dom Basil Robinson, a monk of Pluscarden, near Elgin, might have passed unnoticed if I had not discovered that he was none other than the son of the famous Heath Robinson, the English artist whose draughtsmanship poked fun at the machine age, with his hilariously absurd contraptions for such simple tasks as raising your hat, shuffling and dealing a pack of cards or retrieving a stud which has slipped down the back of the neck.

Dom Basil Robinson had devoted himself more seriously to the cloisters of religion, and his artistry included the carving of a plaque for that ceremony, to be erected at the Abbey of Deer.

In the Deanery of St Mary's, which officially describes the North-East corner of Catholicism, what better place for people to share their Christianity than in the Garden of Buchan, with the terraced trees of Pitfour as a theatrical backcloth and the gurgle of the sparkling Ugie for musical accompaniment?

Here, overlooking the ruins from her lawn above, Deaconess Anna once gripped my arm and told me in that voice which seemed to echo from the heavenly places: 'When I waken every morning, I look out on the ruins of the abbey and feel that I must do my best before the day is ended.'

Here indeed, as I gaze upon it now in the latter years of the twentieth century, lies a haven of peace and harmony still, where history seems to linger and listen, as if for the eternal voice of a bygone age.

CHAPTER NINE

A GERMAN PROVOST

Some of my earliest memories of the 1930s consist of gazing hopefully from the top of the Bobby's Brae in Maud and wondering if today would bring the sight and sound of a man whose name added the ring of magic to my childhood.

If the prayers were answered he would suddenly appear in the distance, coming round the Hill of Clackriach from the direction of Peterhead on his motor-bike and yellow side-car. The very thought of Luigi Zanre (we pronounced his name as Louis) stirred dreams of heaven in my young mind, for his ice-cream was a smooth velvet of vanilla, sheer poetry to the palate, and it cost no more than an old ha'penny for a cone.

Luigi's round, smiling face, topped off by jet black hair, brought us the sunshine of his native Italy, from which he had come to Peterhead in 1915 as a lad of just sixteen. And when the long days of summer had shortened to bleak winter, we would travel to Peterhead to the pictures on a Saturday night, to the Playhouse in Queen Street or round the corner to the new Regal, and there we would lose ourselves in the Hollywood fantasy of Clark Gable and Deanna Durbin, Nelson Eddy and Jeanette Macdonald, Fred Astaire and Ginger Rogers. When we eventually emerged to the cold reality of a North-East night, the scent of cinema still fragrant in our nostrils and the balm of Beverly Hills having massaged the imagination, we would call in at the chip shop in Queen Street for a fish supper to last us the journey home to Maud, and there, behind the counter, I would see again that appealing figure of the warm summer days, now in his other role of fish-and-chip man but for ever to be remembered as King of the Cones, Wizard of the Wafer, Lord of the Slider, Luigi Zanre himself.

But soon those safe and comforting days of childhood, re-assured by the cushion of two or three generations above, were shattered by the on-ding of war, a mixed emotion of fear and excitement which took time to unravel its bewilderment.

One of the earliest lessons to be learned, however, was that there would be no more ice-cream, not only because the commodities of luxury were now rationed but because the Government, in its precaution of interning all citizens who sprang from enemy origin, had thrown poor old Luigi in prison. We were at war with Mussolini's Italy as well as Hitler's Germany and Luigi was carted off to the barbed-wire captivity of the Palace Camp on the Isle of Man, where he wallowed with others who had failed to change their nationality, including another restaurateur who would later become famous as Charles Forte.

The injustice of imprisoning a harmless friend like Luigi was all the more resented when that same fishing town of Peterhead continued to sport, as its civic provost at the beginning of the Second World War, none other than a German by the name of Max Schultze. The provost had certainly had the good sense to change his nationality—but more of his story later.

In due time the Government felt safe enough to release Luigi and his seventeen-year-old son Joe, who returned quietly to Peterhead and made what kind of business was possible until the end of food rationing.

When I returned to Buchan to mark my half-century, it was one of the true delights to discover that Luigi Zanre was not only alive and well at the age of eighty-two but still battering up the fish in the Queen Street chip shop at weekends, though he no longer ran the business himself. (At the time of writing this book, he is still going strong at eighty-eight.) Nothing less than a rendezvous would do that time in 1981, so we met up in warm reunion at his home in Queen Street, Peterhead, where at long last I caught up with the details of his background. The face, the smile and the shape of the man were unchanged from the 1930s, only the mellowing of jet-black hair revealing that time had not stood still completely.

Though the name Zanre is more French than Italian, Luigi came from the Bologna district to settle in Peterhead when the First World War was only a year old. Some members of his family were already here, as part of that Italian exodus which went in search of a better living outwith their own long-legged land of sunshine.

As Luigi explained to me: 'My uncle started the ice-cream and they sent me out to the country districts to sell it. There was more money in the country than the town at that time.' By 1921 he was taking the ice-cream as far as the New Pitsligo Games, twenty miles away, with a horse-drawn vehicle. In 1926 he graduated to an open car, and the motor-bike of my early memory was to follow in 1930.

'I was happy going out to the country,' said Luigi in accents which reminded me that he was always better at making ice-cream than speaking English. 'People used to wait for me coming.'

At my own home village of Maud each summer there would be a special delivery for the dazzling Madam Morrison, a French lady who arrived to enliven our sober scene at the end of the First World War, having met our village baker and leading citizen, Captain John Morrison, during battle-torn days in France. When fashionable guests came to visit her from Paris, the glamorous Madam held parties in the luxuriant Morrison gardens, down the back from the bakehouse, and these were not regarded as complete without Luigi's ice-cream, in return for which he recalled being given a handsome glass of champagne.

Madam Morrison, whom I visited in Aberdeen when she was a very old lady but still a vivacious beauty, brought a whiff of Parisian style which gave them something to talk about in the matter-of-fact community of Maud, where you were less likely to encounter French fragrance than the pungent scent of a skittery coo.

So Luigi brought the Madam's order and he never failed to gift his ice-cream to the hospitals in Maud and Peterhead at Christmas and New Year. Then came that war of 1939 when he and young Joe were spirited off to the Isle of Man and, while my favourite Italian did not much like to talk about his internment, he did remember thinking in his captivity that it would have been a specially good summer for selling ice-cream! While his father returned to the scarcities and restrictions which persisted from then till well after the war, Joe went on to join the British Army and serve his family's adopted country with pride.

Quietly in the background of all this, Mrs Zanre, a woman of fine beauty, brought in the coffee and recalled that she had never seen ice-cream until she came to Peterhead. She had previously been Flora Ferrari, aunt of the well-known Ron Ferrari, who departed from his family's traditional livelihood in Peterhead at the news of North Sea discoveries and became one of the modern millionaires of the oil business.

Luigi Zanre had been back to sunny Italy three times in the course of his lifetime in Scotland but always found himself longing for home, which was now in the cold bare blast of Peterhead. Despite the devotion to his adopted homeland, however, Luigi had still retained his Italian nationality. As for that delicious ice-cream, he maintained there was no trade secret beyond the best of ingredients and a great deal of time spent on its creation. Alas, I know of only one ice-cream man in Scotland today who can stand any kind of comparison with Luigi's talents. Happily, his shop is in my neighbourhood on the south side of Glasgow.

To that extent, this permanent tribute to Luigi Zanre can be taken as a kind of requiem for a departed slider, while being at the same time a celebration of the fact that I was able to find its creator still a cheerful and lively citizen of Peterhead more than sixty years after he first tickled the palate of Buchan children.

But what of the German-born Provost of Peterhead? As a

271

young journalist running the Buchan office of *The Press and Journal* in the early 1950s, I was finally able to make the acquaintance of Max Schultze, who had been a name on my horizon since those early war days when he became a figure of sharp controversy over the civic position he held at a time when Britain was at war with his country of origin.

The Buchan folk were keenly divided on the question of Schultze, some refusing to see him as anything but a symbol of the Germany which was now the enemy of Britain and a threat to the peace of the world, others defending a man who had done much for the trade and civic life of the area and was as well established a citizen of Peterhead as any foreigner can be. (Even folk from other parts of Buchan have faced difficulty in being accepted in the Blue Toun!)

In the anti-German feeling of the time, I can recall that my childhood instincts favoured the former view, so it was all the more intriguing to meet the man in person when I arrived as a journalist to live and work in Peterhead. While he had been the Provost in 1939, he was still the town's treasurer more than a decade later, and here, at town council meetings, I found this foxy little figure in John Lennon spectacles, white hair and with a distinctive German guttural in his voice, now well into his seventies but still motivated by a razor-sharp mind which could cut to ribbons the more pedestrian councillors whose stature was purely of the local variety. Schultze, by now calling himself Saunders, was a figure who could have taken his place in the broader arenas of European politics.

I soon learned that he was a capitalist with strong left-wing views, indeed the first Labour Provost to be elected in Scotland, or so I was told.

I engaged him in as much conversation as possible and learned even more about him from that great Victorian presence, Allan Taylor, editor of the *Buchan Observer*, an adversary who once 'chased the little bugger up Queen Street with my stick' but was the first to acknowledge the depth of his culture and the brilliance of his intellect, embodied in which was an impish mischief.

Piece by piece I learned the story of Max Schultze, who was born in Stettin, which was then in Germany but is now in Poland. His father so disliked Prussian militarism that he uprooted himself and two small children, Max and Charlotte (he was by then a widower), and moved to Britain in 1885, settling in the North-East of Scotland, which had strong trading links with the Baltic. From being a herring importer in Germany, he became an exporter in Peterhead, but they were a family of great substance, well beyond what you might have expected from alien people arriving unknown on the Buchan coast.

Young Max's grand-aunt was the German poetess, Malvinia von Meysenbug, friend of Richard Wagner and the only woman, apart from Frau Wagner, who attended the dress rehearsal of *Tannhäuser*, her account of which was later published in a documentary study of the composer. Malvinia was finally buried beside two more of her friends, the immortal Keats and Shelley.

Max and his sister grew up in Peterhead, Charlotte proceeding to Aberdeen University where she was among the first women to become medical students, gaining a gold medal for excellence in anatomy and physiology. There she met another medical student who was not faring so well in his medical studies, presumably because he was devoting his energies to other matters.

Frank Pearce Sturm, who had family origins in Dufftown, Banffshire, as well as in Sweden, did reach eminence as a physician in due course but later repudiated his success in favour of a life as a poet and mystic, a talented and controversial writer who became the friend and confidant of W. B. Yeats, the Irish poet and dramatist with whom he shared a fascination for the occult.

Sturm, who stirred up fierce controversy in his writings for that memorable North-East publication, the *Bon Accord*, was certainly one of life's extraordinary characters, a writer of such gift that Yeats was moved to write of 'his lovely lines', adding this well-balanced assessment: 'A very delicate sense of rhythm, strange and vivid metaphor. The defect is that the parts are generally so much better than the whole.' He died of a cerebral haemorrhage and coronary attack in 1942, two years after Charlotte had died, aged fifty-six, of cancer.

Meanwhile Max Schultze developed a career in the family shipbroking and herring exporting business, a capitalist interest which would not have seemed to Buchan folk to match up with his passion for socialism; that particular leaning took him to the chairmanship of the East Aberdeenshire Constituency Labour Party and to a position of influence in the wider movement.

At those meetings of Peterhead Town Council where Allan Taylor, a brilliant cartoonist as well as writer, would sit drawing caricatures of local pomposity around the table, Schultze was to be heard cutting through hypocrisy with a rapier for a tongue. Even at his own farewell he rather mischievously rejected the laudatory tributes by refusing to separate public service from private vanity—but that was Max Schultze, lively politician with a wit as sharp as a Prussian helmet and a heart that was so much warmer than he was generally prepared to display.

His son Max volunteered for the Forces soon after the outbreak of the Second World War but felt it would be embarrassing to serve in the British Army with a German name like Schultze; so he changed it to Saunders and his father and the rest of the family followed suit.

Son Max died in 1980, the same year as his mother, but his brother Rudi retains a warm affection for Peterhead from the distance of Bedford, where he is a distinguished gynaecologist.

They lent much colour and variety to our North-East life, these foreign people who came among us around the end of the last century and the earlier part of this. With admirable enterprise, they merged into an alien society and made their mark, whether it was a spirited contribution to the civic life of the area or the sheer gastronomic joy of a slider, for which a little boy in Maud would wait patiently for hours, longing for the sight of that yellow motor-bike.

CHAPTER TEN

FROM ABERDOUR TO ITN

The humour of Buchan has long been rich and dry, an essential safety valve born of dreich days when not all the drudgery in Christendom could dim the shrewd observation of human behaviour or blunt the fine edge of wit. The unconscious variety was often the best.

I never forgot the minister who was trying to persuade Sandy the Joiner to become an elder of the Kirk. Since Buchan folk are notoriously inclined to accept a modest station in life, Sandy was full of protest. 'Na na, meenister, I'm just a humble joiner.'

'But that's the very point,' said the cleric. 'Just think of it, Jesus himself was a carpenter, exactly like you.'

A new light dawned on his rugged face as Sandy forgot himself and exclaimed, 'Christ, so he wis!'

While I had grown up with the humour and took it for granted, those years as the Buchan reporter of *The Press and Journal* were a rewarding reminder of my heritage. I recall the story of the Peterhead solicitor who went to pay his respects on the death of one of his clients, old John Smith, who had expired after some weeks in Aberdeen Royal Infirmary, on the heights of Foresterhill.

In the customary way of Buchan folk, he was shown through to the parlour to view the corpse and stood in that embarrassed silence which descends on such occasions. Leaving the room with Mrs Smith, he sought to ease the embarrassment with a few faltering words. 'John's lookin' affa like himsel, Mrs Smith, real bonny and peaceful like.'

'Ay,' said Mrs Smith. 'I just said—that last fortnicht in Foresterhill did him a world o' good!'

Further inland, they laughed about Geordie, the Buchan

farmer, whose steading went on fire one night. Neighbours rushed to free the cattle and drive them out of byre and bigging, forming a human chain with pails of water until the arrival of the fire brigades.

At the height of his major drama Geordie paused to wipe the sweat from his brow, suddenly observing a member of the Fraserburgh Fire Brigade with a skin too dark for Buchan. Raising the man's helmet for a closer inspection, he said, 'Faar the hell div ye come fae, min?'

'Oh I am coming from Pakistan,' said the alien fireman in his native lilt.

'Man, ye've deen nae bad,' said Geordie. 'The Peterheid boys are nae here yet!'

Rich humour to accompany a dram on a wild winter's night.

In those days as a Buchan journalist in the early 1950s I unearthed unconscious humour of another variety when, without the usual preliminaries, I was conducted through the gates of the notorious Peterhead Prison, where I spent a week observing and recording the life inside the most forbidding walls in all Scotland.

The Governor of the day, an enlightened man called Major Heron-Watson, gave me a remarkable amount of freedom to talk to prisoners, whose varied reactions to my presence were an interesting study in themselves. Some well-known murderers of the day were frank and friendly, others slunk away with dark looks.

Among the prisoners in Peterhead at that time was a dark, stocky young man serving a sentence for rape, a name which was yet to reach the criminal history books for a series of events which made him the most notorious killer that Scotland has ever known. When they finally caught up with Peter Manuel in his trail of murders from High Burnside, Glasgow, through East Kilbride and Uddingston, slaughtering the Watt family and the Smarts and so many more, there was no second chance of life in Peterhead. They hanged him in Barlinnie Prison, Glasgow, in 1958. (Ironically, while Buchan was playing host to

Manuel, a little boy called Dennis Nilsen was growing up in Fraserburgh and Strichen, later to move to London where he admitted the wilful murder of fifteen men, making him the biggest multiple killer in British criminal history.)

In Peterhead Prison the more likeable residents who engaged me in conversation included another legend of Scottish criminal history, the incomparable safe-blower, Johnny Ramensky, of central European origin but brought up in the Gorbals of Glasgow.

Ramensky was such a craftsman in the art of opening the big steel box that detectives were never in any doubt when they came upon the work of the master! So he spent the majority of his years in Peterhead, except during the Second World War when someone in Whitehall had the wit to divert him to more fruitful purpose. Parachuting him behind enemy lines in Italy, they gave him the dangerous mission of bursting open Mussolini's strongroom and stealing vital documents. John accomplished his mission with customary perfection, was honoured for his services to his country—and promptly returned to a life which brought him back time and again to the North-East of Scotland, over-staying his welcome as the guest of Her Majesty.

But if Ramensky (he later changed his name to Ramsay) was a specialist at breaking in, he was equally skilled at breaking out and my childhood days in Maud were punctuated by periodic police activity, as the word went round that Ramensky had again escaped from Peterhead. On one famous occasion, with road-blocks over the River Ythan at Ellon, he speiled hand over hand on the under-side of the bridge as the police checked cars a few feet above. But he would always return, until one felt, on meeting him in Peterhead Prison, that that was his natural habitat.

I was sitting in front of him at a prisoners' concert one evening when a friend of his tapped me on the shoulder and asked if I was the reporter. 'Well, remember that big robbery at the Palace Cinema in Aberdeen?' When I confirmed that I did remember the event quite well, he beamed with pride and added, 'Well, that was me!'

I refrained from offering the hand of congratulation, which he clearly expected, but turned instead to a magnificent rendering of 'Blue Moon' which was coming from the familiar voice of a newcomer to Peterhead, a crooner with a well-known dance band of the day.

The unconscious humour which led me to this topic in the first place came when I was welcomed to the prisoners' discussion group, a lively forum chaired by a former headmaster gone wrong, and sometimes dominated by extremist views which ran from the political to the plain grudge against society. Subjects of discussion included 'Crime in Society' and 'The Problems of Juvenile Delinquency Today', no less!

Perusing the minute book of the group, I was amused to find such items as a welcome for Mr So-and-So; they were sorry that Mr X had now left—but they were delighted to welcome back Mr Y!

The Buchan humour was of a vastly different texture from what those inmates would have known from their homeland in Glasgow and the West of Scotland, where most of them originated. The Glasgow humour always seems to me beautifully encapsulated in the story of the two Glesca Johnnies waiting for a bus in the Gorbals. When it finally arrived, the little conductress called out 'Wan passenger only—the bus is full up.'

The two men pleaded with her to let them both aboard but the wee clippie stood her ground and pressed the bell. As the bus moved away, one of the Glesca men shouted, 'Ach, awa an shove yer bus up yer arse!'

'Naw,' replied the clippie. 'But if you shove yer pal up yours, ye'll baith get oan this bus!'

From the stark walls of Peterhead Prison, which overlooks the spacious Harbour of Refuge constructed last century by a previous generation of convicts, I would drive back round the bay into Peterhead, pondering the weird events of the night and the forces which lead a proportion of the human race to spend the best years of their lives behind bars.

From the office in Broad Street, opposite the illuminated town clock, I would munch into a bag of Luigi Zanre chips, listen to the late-night background of Radio Luxembourg and phone off my reports for next morning's issue of *The Press and Journal*. The head office in Broad Street, Aberdeen, was staffed by as skilled and colourful an array of journalists as has ever graced a British newspaper, many of whom I have already described in *A Grain of Truth*.

One of the brightest lights in that galaxy was George Fraser, whose delightful prose was being offered to North-East folk in a regular column as far back as the First World War. Imagine my delight, when I went north to tidy up the loose ends of this book in 1987, to find that the same George Fraser was still writing his regular column all of seventy years later!

So I sat down with George at his home in King's Gate, Aberdeen, and caught up with the background of the kind of young man who was liable to become a journalist in those far-off days. Born at Newmachar, where his father was the railway signalman, George was soon flitting north to Buchan, where his father became stationmaster at Longhaven, near Boddam. Peterhead granite was the main export from the local station but the Frasers were on the move once more, first to Drum, on Deeside, and then to Kinaldie, near Kintore. In those days it was left to wise headmasters to persuade parents that a gifted child had to be given the chance of further education. So it was that young George Fraser went from Hatton of Fintry School to Inverurie Academy and then to Aberdeen University, where he graduated MA.

He was marking time for the teacher-training college when he ran into Alexander Keith, a former student friend who would later gain prominence as journalist and author of such books as *A Thousand Years of Aberdeen*.

The persuasive tongue of A.K. diverted George Fraser to thoughts of journalism and that chance meeting in Union Street took him to the office of Sir William Maxwell, editor of the old *Daily Journal*, who told him prophetically: 'Journalists live to be a ripe old age.' George was remembering it well—when he told me the story at the age of ninety-two!

With the First World War at its height, he was one of only four sub-editors turning out the daily paper, handling in particular the foreign news which arrived in the almost unmanageable form of 'flimsy', hand-written and brought down from the Post Office rather like the old-fashioned telegrams.

'The most exciting time,' said George, 'was when we began to get messages about revolution breaking out all over Germany. We knew they were cracking up.'

He was already writing a weekly column when he sub-edited the news of Armistice in 1918. Four years later, when the *Daily Journal* amalgamated with the *Free Press* to become *The Press and Journal*, George became the first chief sub-editor of the new title, the oldest surviving newspaper in Scotland today, with its ancestry dating back to 5 January 1748, and the aftermath of Culloden.

Before George Fraser took up his senior position in 1922 (at the astronomical wage of £9 a week), he had his eye on a girl in the cashier's office.

Young Peggy was already being wooed by a young reporter who wrote her loving verses during his late shifts, but the chief cashier advised her, 'Dinna waste yer time wi' him.'

George Fraser won the hand of pretty Peggy but conceded that the poetry of his rival suitor was powerful stuff, not all that surprising when you find the young reporter was James Leslie Mitchell, destined to become the North-East's greatest-ever writer, Lewis Grassic Gibbon.

When I visited them at King's Gate, George was still rising at 6.30 a.m. and cultivating his garden with the same exquisite care that shaped his weekly column in *The Press and Journal*. Peggy, a charming lady of eighty-eight, could still produce with pride the hand-written verses of Grassic Gibbon.

On that same week, George Fraser had been regaling his

readers about the origins of that first column in 1918 and how he had been cajoled by Sir William Maxwell. He concluded his article with these beautifully-honed words, themselves a tribute to the sharpness of a man in his nineties:

Happily for me it established to the satisfaction of my mentor the fact that I was capable of putting words reasonably together and of conveying something of what I knew and what I got to know on the long trail ahead.

In time came diversification and a broadening of the harvest field. Some grains of truth, one hopes, have emerged from the preponderance of chaff, winnowed by those favourable winds of chance that have kept me going all these years.

Among the others who had worked away at that same subeditor's desk in Broad Street, burning the midnight oil as he wrote headlines for my humble offerings from Peterhead, was a man much younger than George Fraser, a fellow-Aberdonian who was destined to be better known in the years ahead.

His name was Sandy Gall, a typical Buchan name, but it was much later before he and I sorted out our common heritage, which extended as far as some common ground in the kirkyard of New Aberdour, where many of our ancestors came finally to rest.

Our rendezvous was far from the sweeping plains of Buchan or the granite sparkle of Aberdeen. It was, in fact, high up in ITN House, a rather unimpressive building tucked away behind Oxford Circus in the heart of London, from which Sandy would come beaming into our living-rooms with *News at Ten* most nights, following those introductory booms from Big Ben.

From the craggy, likeable face, you could almost tell he was a man from New Aberdour, that little village round the corner of the Moray Firth from Fraserburgh, where the beach remains free of commercial influence and the sea gives off that rich tang of dilse I have never experienced on any other coast.

News at Ten was still four hours away as Sandy and I sat in his office raking over our careers and keeping one eye on the teatime news bulletin so he could begin to gather the flavour of what was going on in the world that particular day.

For generations back the Galls were mainly farming folk in the district of New Aberdour, but Sandy's father, the youngest of a large family, went off to be a tea planter in Malaya, where Sandy was born. His father retired to Banchory, sending his son to the prestigious Glenalmond School. In 1945, at the age of eighteen, he became a National Serviceman in the RAF, having just missed the war. Back home in 1948, he embarked on an honours degree course in French and German at Aberdeen University, which preceded his time in the Broad Street headquarters of *The Press and Journal*. From Aberdeen he went off to be a trainee foreign correspondent with Reuters news agency and extended that experience when he joined ITN, all of which brought a wealth of memories, from the pleasurable to the downright dangerous.

It was trying enough to be covering the Congo War, but imagine his feelings when he was thrown into jail by the soldiers of the notorious Idi Amin and later forced across the jail compound with a sub-machine gun stuck in his back. Mercifully Sandy survived to tell the tale on ITN and to write a book called *Gold Scoop*, which was based on his Ugandan experience.

The horrors of Vietnam and the Middle East War of 1967 were just two more of his adventures before Sandy settled behind the newscaster's desk at Oxford Circus. His routine, I discovered, was to arrive at the ITN studios at three o'clock for a conference fifteen minutes later. His job was then to study film reports arriving in the office and to prepare his mind for writing one or two of the night's stories himself. There was a break between six and seven for a snack or a drink and thereafter the *News at Ten* operation slipped into top gear.

Everyone was busy writing and checking scripts for the various news items and at half-past-nine, with the adrenalin flowing, they settled to a rehearsal. The final pattern of the bulletin was still being thrashed out till the last minute, always making room for announcements like, 'We have just heard that a bomb has exploded in the West End of London. We hope to bring you fuller details in part two.' The uncertainty added up to a real testing of the nerves in one of the few pieces of live television we ever see nowadays.

Before the tension of that evening began to mount, Sandy and I had fair taken Buchan through hand. By then he was Rector of Aberdeen University, an honour which impressed him immensely, as did the maturity of the students and the way the university was run.

'When I went back to Aberdeen I didn't see much change,' he told me. 'But again, I was impressed by Old Aberdeen and the way the university had done so much to preserve the old buildings. Old Aberdeen is really very beautiful and in much better condition than when I was there.'

Every month he took time off to fly to Aberdeen to chair the University Court before handing over to the Principal, Sir Fraser Noble, whose elder brother Donald was my editor on the *Turriff Advertiser* in 1948. By the end of that evening in the ITN studios, the dramas had been performed, the nerves tested and the sweat had run before the closing chords heralded the fade-out and the two announcers exchanged those waggish comments of relief. A chauffeur-driven car was waiting to drive Sandy Gall on the thirty-mile journey to his wife and four children in Penshurst, Kent, a far cry from the gunfire of the Congo and Vietnam and the Middle East, and maybe just as far from the bare braes of Buchan and that rich tang which stirs the nostrils as you comb along the beach at Aberdour.

CHAPTER ELEVEN

AULD MEG POM

On my sentimental visits back to Maud, I would be regaled with stories from older folk which would stir vivid pictures of life in a bygone age. Old Jimmy Spence had tales of his boyhood days in Maud in the early part of the century and remembered being home during the First World War and taking a dander across the railway line, down through the Low Village and up Bank's Hill. It was a fine clear day and everything was so quiet and peaceful. Yet away down there, far beyond the Hill o' Jock and beneath that same blue ceiling, there were men killing each other by the thousand.

In that same youth, Jimmy Spence, who later settled in Kintore, was walking home with some friends from a dance at New Deer when suddenly there was a loud yell. Somebody had trampled on Meg Pom, asleep by the roadside but soon roused to fill the air with words of blue.

His story sent shivers down my spine, for Meg Pom was still a sight to frighten little children in my own early memories of the 1930s. She and her nomadic brother, Jock Pom o' Leeds (the village of New Leeds in Buchan), went roaming far and wide, Jock with his little cairtie and Meg wrapped in rags and puffing at her clay pipe.

There were few people of the time who did not have a story of coming upon a bundle by the roadside, distinguishable as Meg by the wisp of smoke and the mumblings of one who has had too much to drink. To hear these stories from people like Jimmy Spence and Myra Thow, who grew up at Mid Culsh of New Deer, was not surprising in the context of Buchan life, but the name of Meg Pom (her real name was Park) was liable to crop up in the most unexpected places.

When I left the *Daily Express* in 1980, after twenty years as a sub-editor and feature writer, I spent some time in California, absorbing the life of Hollywood and strolling on the beaches of Santa Monica. A dinner party in Beverly Hills would almost certainly arouse a picture of soft lights and sophisticated conversation, but, lo and behold, I found that my discussion with the lady across the table was about none other than the notorious Meg Pom!

I had met up with long-lost relatives from the North-East, Dr Billy Coutts and his wife Nora, who hailed from Inverurie and Premnay respectively and were visiting their daughter Jennifer, a lady then making a name for herself as the British Airways boss for the whole West Coast of America. The Coutts family were well known for their music on Donside, and once we had given the piano a good dirl, the conversation turned to the vagrant characters who roamed the country roads before the Second World War.

It turned out that Nora Coutts, living nearer the Don, was just as well acquainted with Meg Pom as the Buchan folk who were closer to her origins by the shadow of Mormond Hill. Nora had been so moved by her memories of old Meg that she once wrote a poem, which she recited across that Beverly Hills dinner table and which I am delighted to reproduce here:

> D'ye mind o' AULD MEG POM
> A wifie we wad see
> Lyin' roon the roadsides
> At the back o' Benachie
>
> Like an orra birn o' rags
> That had jist been tummelt doon
> An lookin' oot a facie
> That was ever barkit broon
>
> She'd petticoats an' shawls
> Frae her chin doon tae her feet

I never saw her lauchin
But I aften saw her greet

She had anither bunnle
I suppose that was her lot
Row'd in an auld print apron
Tied wi' a muckle knot

Her hair was kind o' tooslie
An' never had a wash
She could hae been rale bonny
But ach, she didna fash

Her auld clay pipe she sookit
'Twas ever in her moo
She lay sae still I winnert
Gin she were deid or foo

In a ditch doon by the railway
Sae quaitly there she'd lie
An' never move a muscle
Fan trains gaed roarin by

But we were richt coorse nickums
We'd creep up tae MEG'S lug
An' roar a' we were able
'AULD TINKIE TARRY BUG'

In a trice the auld rags shivert
Her airms cam flailin' oot
She ca'ed us a' the vratches
Ye'd ever heard aboot

Her een noo shone like glaissers
As she tried tae heist hersel
By grabbin' at a breem bus
But back again she fell

We kent she couldna catch us
But feart kine a' the same
We turned an' ran like rabbits
On the lang lang trek for hame

We didna tell oor Mither
We'd roared TINKIE TARRY BUGS
If she had only kent o't
She'd gien us richt het lugs

We winnert faur MEG cam fae
Faurever did she gang
Fan North winds started howlin'
An' nichts grew cauld an' lang

But then cam roon ae Springtime
MEG wasna there ava
Maybe her ain Creator
Had cairtit her awa

Whaur'er she be, I'll wadger
Gin ye speirt fat she wad like
She'd say 'Green grass tae lie on
An' a sook o' my auld clay pipe.'

Versifying about Meg Pom would not have made much sense
to the American ear, passing only for the quaint expression of
some rustic culture. Yet I knew in my heart of hearts that we
were talking about real life and real people.

I knew that, much as I warm to the Americans, the folk of
rural Buchan had more true wit and wisdom, downright common sense and sheer smeddum than those pampered floozies
of California, so bereft of real problems that they seemed hell-
bent on lolling on a psychiatrist's couch and acquiring some.

When I heard them posing such questions as: 'Who am I?
Do I know my real identity?' I was tempted to tell them, if they
had been capable of understanding Buchan logic, that the Scot-

288

tish farm workers I had known down the years, pulling turnips in the frosty dead of winter with an ache in the back and
a drip at the nose, had no such crisis of identity. They knew
damned well that they were Wullie or Dod or Davie, working
so long and eident-like that there was little time left to dream
up imaginary problems on a psychiatrist's couch. They knew
there was a wife and bairns to feed and rig for winter and if
they had enough left over for a dram on a Saturday night they
thanked the Lord that, for another week at least, they had
managed to make their frayed ends meet.

Fate may seem to deal out a hand that is uneven and unjust,
yet I doubt if the Buchan folk have any real cause to envy the
schizophrenic life-style of Tinsel-Town, where constant sun
can bake your brain and separate you from reality by the
breadth of a dozen Grand Canyons.

I doubt if auld Meg Pom would have chosen the Califor-
nian fantasy in preference to her orra birn o' rags and her auld
clay pipe.

289

CHAPTER TWELVE

THE BUCHAN TONGUE

The tongue of North-East Scotland, often mistakenly called the Doric, is indeed a language and a law unto itself, broad in its vowels, subtle in its grammar, rich and rollicking in the depth and rhythm of its expression and quite unmistakable in its accent.

It follows the general pattern of what is known as Lowland Scots, as distinct from, and having very little in common with, Gaelic, but it takes the basis of that Scots language and not only broadens everything at least one stage further but has confounded the critics by the fact that it is still in regular use as an every-day speech long after its demise was expected to have been completed.

Well before the days of Robert Burns, the Scots tongue was said to be dying out. More than a century later, Robert Louis Stevenson did not expect it to survive his lifetime yet, in the year of his premature death, 1894, my great-grandfather wrote his most popular vernacular play, *Mains's Wooin'*, which is still performed, understood and enjoyed nearly a hundred years after Stevenson was dead and gone.

Of course no one could pretend that the vocabulary has been totally preserved or that there has not been a dilution of the quality of speech, but the fact remains that it is still there in daily use, nurtured with care and loyalty by the North-East folk themselves and a subject of fascination for the Americans, Russians and Japanese and other nations nearer home.

As far as its culture is concerned, the fact that Aberdeenshire is a wholly lowland region comes as a surprise to many people, even Scots in the southern half of the country, who glibly refer to Aberdonians as Highlanders without realizing there is very little of that culture in the North-East. They themselves, if they happen to live in Glasgow, are much more likely to have Highland origins.

That lowland tongue of North-East Scotland is frequently condensed to a description of 'the Buchan dialect', perhaps because that particular corner of the region typifies its most extreme elements. Of the overseas people who have been intrigued by the Aberdeenshire tongue, the Americans who came by the thousand to participate in the oil bonanza during the seventies had the most practical reason for trying to unravel its mysteries. Once I found myself trying to write a simple explanation for an American oilman who was totally baffled by the niceties.

If he had already learned, for example, that the standard Scots word for 'stone' is 'stane', I then had to complicate life by explaining that Aberdonians further broadened the vowel to make it 'steen'. Similarly, 'bone' to 'bane' became 'been'. That was fairly elementary stuff, just as I assumed the gent had already learned that a 'quine' was a girl and a 'loonie' was a little boy and not a lunatic.

It was more difficult to explain that 'ging' and 'gyang' were subtly different uses of 'go' and that 'gyan' meant 'going'. For example: 'Will ye gyang [go] doon tae the shoppie?' But 'Are ye gyan [going] doon tae the shoppie?'

The English language settles for the single word 'have' but no such simplicity will do in the North-East of Scotland. 'Hae' and 'hiv' are just two of your choices according to the form of sentence. Where an Englishman would say 'You have to have something in your stomach', the Buchan man would say 'Ye hiv tae hae something in yer stamack.' Transposing these two forms of 'have' would sound a nonsense. Yet, change the same sentence into the future tense and it becomes, 'Ye'll hae tae hae something. . .'

When President Eisenhower (commonly known as Ike) came to Balmoral to visit the Queen in the late 1950s, he was greeted by a local newspaper headline which summed up the North-

East greeting to perfection: FIT LIKE, IKE?

A North-East response to such an inquiry after one's health could cause some problems to the foreigner, ranging from the understandable 'Nae bad, min' (Not bad, man) to the more puzzling 'Tyauvin awa' or 'Warslin throu' or 'Knypin on', all three of which indicate that you are working away or struggling along, with the first two giving hint of a harder struggle than the third. Oh, the subtleties of that North-East tongue!

A hard day's work is liable to leave you 'fair ferfochen' (exhausted) and a heavy meal will make you 'fair stappit fou'. If your toe becomes your 'tae', it will be just as painless as your ankles becoming your 'queets'. A knowledge of the German language can be as useful as English when coming to terms with the Buchan dialect. In my childhood, the language of counting was 'een, twa, three, fower, five, sax, seiven, acht'. Aberdonians follow the Germans in telling the time. Whereas 'half-two' in Glasgow or London is just a slovenly way of saying 'half-past-two', the corresponding 'half-twa' means half-past one in Buchan—half-two being one half of the second hour, exactly as in the German 'halb-zwei'.

On top of all that, Buchan folk possess an absolute genius for diminutives, managing to turn semantics into gymnastics with examples such as 'Little wee bit wifikie', which actually produces five diminutives in a four-word sentence!

And what would the outsider make of this particular conversation in an Aberdeen wool shop, conducted entirely in vowel sounds? The customer is inquiring if her prospective purchase is real wool and all from the same cut:

Customer: Oo?

Assistant: Ay, oo.

Customer: Aa oo?

Assistant: Ay, aa oo.

Customer: Aa ae oo?

Assistant: Oh ay, aa ae oo.

So much for a sketchy background of what the language is all about, a language which lives and breathes as much through its every-day speech as in the richness of its literature. From William Alexander's *Johnny Gibb o' Gushetneuk* through Gavin Greig's novels and plays to the poetry of people like Charles Murray, the life and language of the North-East have been enshrined for generations to come.

Add to that the unique contribution of Lewis Grassic Gibbon, the North-East's greatest writer, who managed to mould the rhythms of his native corner to the cadences of the English language, and you begin to understand why the special nature of one part of Scotland is becoming more fully understood and appreciated by that wider world outby.

CHAPTER THIRTEEN

THERE'S AYE A SOMETHING

If you have an ear for the so-called Doric of North-East Scotland and have ever pursued it through verse, you will inevitably have come across the works of Charles Murray, more commonly known as Hamewith.

Murray was the lad from Alford, in the Donside valley of Aberdeenshire, who rose to become secretary for public works in the Union of South Africa in the early part of this century and spent much of his time nostalgically thinking and writing about the place of his roots.

He wrote in that rich and rollicking style which characterizes the speech of the North-East, with a keen eye for the quirks as well as the qualities of the people. He is remembered for poems like 'The Whistle that the Wee Herd Made' and 'It Wisna His Wyte', and there are purists who will tell you that his technique maintains a higher level than that of Burns.

Certainly his cameos of description are priceless. Just consider the poem 'Dockens Afore his Peers', in which the small farmer is appearing before the labour exemption tribunal in the First World War, seeking dispensation for his son and showing how badly off he is for workers.

He describes the kitchie deem:

> She's big and brosy, reid and roch an' swippert as she's stoot
> Gie her a kilt instead o' cotts, an' thon's the gran' recruit.

For those with doubts about translation, the first line is 'Big and robust, red and rough and nimble as she's stout'. In the next line, 'cotts' are petticoats.

Then old Dockens describes another of his work-force

liabilities, the makeshift cattleman:

> The baillie syne, a peerhoose geet, nae better than a feel
> He slivvers an' has sic a mant, an ae clog fit as weel
> He's barely sense tae muck the byre an' cairry in the scull
> An' park the kye an' clogue the caur an' scutter wi' the bull.

The 'peerhoose geet' is a creature from the poor's house, such a common institution in those days; to 'slivver' is to drool and to 'mant' is to stammer. 'Clogue the caur' means to feed the calves milk from a pail.

Such was the power of Charles Murray. He came back to the North-East from South Africa to retire, and lived there until his death in 1941. Among those who got to know him well was the late Dr Nan Shepherd from Cults, herself a distinguished writer and teacher, who met Murray first when he visited her parents and again when she went to South Africa to see her brother's grave.

Nan Shepherd, who is said to have had a strong affection for the poet (they used to be seen in public holding hands), gave us this description of him in her later life:

> Charles Murray was a man one could not miss in a company. He had presence; not self-assertive but dynamic—one felt more alive from being with him. When he spoke he had compulsive listeners. Droll, witty, solemn, seemingly nonchalant but with a delightful relish in what he related, he was a raconteur of genius. He was company for a duke or ditcher and imperturbably himself with both. His lean, hawk face was warm with interest—sheer simple interest in people, what they were, what they did, how they did it.

In an introduction to Murray's *Last Poems*, Nan Shepherd perhaps summed up her feelings when she wrote: 'The seed of Charles Murray's power is that he said yes to life.'

Not everyone was so bowled over by Murray. That other

notable North-East writer, John R. Allan, had certain reservations about him, taking the view that his work was more observed than felt.

But few would argue with the appeal of such memorable verse as 'There's Aye a Something', which tells of Sandy, the farmer whose wife is town-bred and genteel and come of folk who thought him 'an unco come doon'. This graphic description of Sandy must surely commend itself even to the most un-Scottish of ears:

> He's roch an' oonshaven till Sunday comes roon
> A drap at his nose and his pints hingin' doon
> His weskit is skirpit wi' dribbles o' kail
> He drinks fae his saucer and rifts ower his ale.

For the uninitiated, his 'pints' in North-East parlance are his bootlaces.

Sandy's offspring have had to take pot luck in drawing genetic elements from their genteel mother and uncouth father, a gamble which Murray sums up in this little gem:

> They're like her in looks as a podfu' o' piz
> But dam't, there's aye something—their mainners are his.

Charles Murray spent those last years in the North-East in the company of a few friends who formed the Sit Siccar Society, with a motto which he penned as a delicious condensation of native caution:

> Be wise an' sit siccar—
> Ye're safe on your doup!

CHAPTER FOURTEEN

A GREAT SCOT

No mention of Scottish language can pass decently without reference to a man who is still hale and hearty at the writing of this book but who will no doubt have passed on to his Elysian pastures before he is properly recognized as one of the great Scots of the twentieth century. Such is our neglect of those around us.

It was all the more essential that I beat a path to the doorway in Dennyduff Road, Fraserburgh, where I would meet David Murison, a local lad o' pairts whose smallish stature and modest manner tend to belie the greatness within him.

Yet this son of a Buchan joiner went from local schooling to take on the might of Cambridge, gain a double first in the classics and proceed to spend most of his working life in creating for his beloved land that colossal and definitive fount of its language, the *Scottish National Dictionary*. It was a daunting task which called for a scholastic giant with a heart that beat strongly to the rhythms of the traditional Scottish speech, and it was to the eternal good fortune of this nation that such a rare creature emerged in the form of David Murison.

Having achieved his lifetime's work in the same George Square of Edinburgh where Sir Walter Scott had spent his early years, David Murison was now home for retirement in his native corner of Scotland, and there, in his den at Dennyduff Road, I heard again those warm tones of his Buchan tongue, untouched by a life-long barrage from alien forces. David Murison was the same couthy chiel he had always been, as proud as ever of his mother tongue and exercising it with natural ease.

His family came from Wellhowe of Brucklay, apparently

ordinary like folk with a genetic streak that was far from ordinary, having previously produced at least one genius, Alexander Murison, who became Professor of Roman Law in London and a famous jurist of his day. He died in the 1920s and a plaque to his memory is to be found at the Brucklay house where he was born.

David Murison's father was a joiner who went to Fraserburgh to find work. His mother's family came from my own native village of Maud and the boy went to Fraserburgh Infant and Central Schools before his father moved to Aberdeen, again in search of work. After the Grammar School and Aberdeen University, he moved on to his distinguished career at Cambridge before returning to be a lecturer in Greek at King's College, Aberdeen.

The idea of a *Scottish National Dictionary* had first been mooted as far back as 1907 and was eventually taken up by Dr William Grant of Aberdeen. By the end of the Second World War the dictionary was in need of a new and full-time editor and fresh inspiration—and that was where David Murison became the man of destiny for the preservation of the Scots language.

It was a task which was to absorb all his energies for the next thirty years or more. Countless thousands of words dating from 1700 had to be gathered, sifted, checked and double-checked for shades of meaning and usage in different parts of the country before finding their way into the definitive dictionary of the land.

Now that he had reached the final Z, put his *Scottish National Dictionary* to the printer's bed and retired to his native corner, I was interested to know what he had rediscovered about the life and language of the place where he grew up. This was David Murison's view of his return:

> I wanted to come back and end my days here and now that I am re-establishing my roots, I have picked up some threads and see faces that are familiar to me, though I cannot put a

Above: My two grandmothers, Granny Barron & Granny Webster.
Right: My father with Paddy.
Below: My father in the sale ring at Maud Mart.

above: Perhaps the first photograph ever taken in Buchan—at Inverugie around 1860—the work of Joseph Collier from New Byth, who became a famous photographer in America.

below: The legendary Lizzie Allan (both legs amputated after a bad childhood inoculation) who ran her sweetie shop from a wheelchair and excited my interest in life.

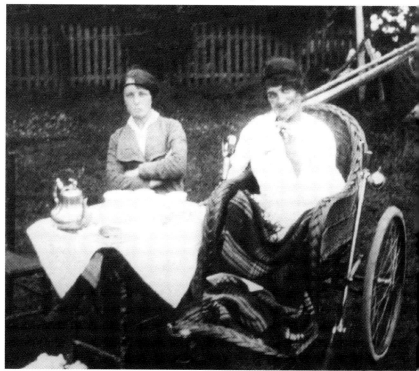

above: A rare picture of Strichen's controversial novelist, Lorna Moon.

above: James Duthie,
St Combs fisherman
turned television playwright.

right: David Toulmin,
genuine son of the soil.

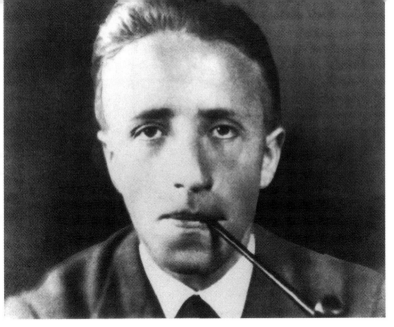

above: Lewis Grassic Gibbon, a unique talent.

below: Rhea Martin, gifted daughter of Grassic Gibbon.

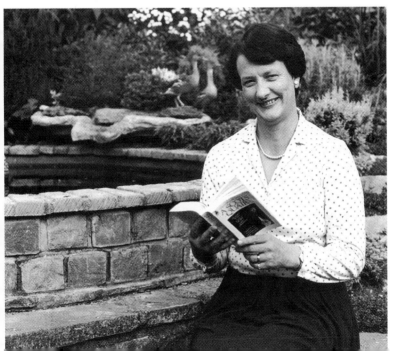

above: Fifty-three years later, I meet up again with Luigi Zan[...] still going strong at eighty-eight.

above right: As a *Daily Express* feature writer, in the company [...] Sophia Loren.

below right: Four generations; with my grandmother (Gavin Greig's eldest child), mother and my eldest son Geo[...]

above: With Bertie Forbes, the New York millionaire who encouraged me into journalism, w
he returned for his Whitehill picnic.
below: A generation later, with his famous son, Malcom Forbes, who resumed the picnic in

name to them. But it is sad to come up a street and remember that so-and-so used to live there but is now long gone. The people have not changed. I see the same types. I can remember Fraserburgh just after the First World War when there was a great burst of affluence and a sense of euphoria. Now that has repeated itself with North Sea oil and I am experiencing the same thing twice over.

But the Brochers have not had their heads turned. They have kept an even keel, are still pretty canny and take a sober and serious view of things. They are friendly and still say 'How d'you do?' in the street, even if they don't know you. There are, of course, the unpleasant things, like vandalism, but that is universal. In my day there was harmless mischief but now there is more coarseness in it.

I find that people are alert—they always were—tumbling to what you are getting at with great celerity. They are critical and can size up a situation or an argument and find a flaw in it. Their own speech has changed not very much, with a lot of Scots still spoken, though not so rich. A lot of the vocabulary has gone and there are more anglicisms and American slang picked up from the wireless and television.

But the timbre of the voice is still fundamentally Buchan and I can hear some of the older fisher folk speaking an older-fashioned Scots. The vocabulary does get less, however. Just look at *Johnny Gibb o' Gushetneuk* and you will find words that you never hear nowadays. It was reckoned that, between the end of last century and 1926, about one-third of the vocabulary had gone from our speech. Another third must have gone since then and the deterioration is increasing with television. The trouble is that, with TV and radio, the sound is coming across to affect pronunciation so it reaches you even if you are living in the Moss o' Byth.

Against that, however, it is true that people getting older tend to revert to the speech of their childhood. Just as old memories come back, they remember the speech of their grandmothers and will begin to use the words again. So there is a compensatory swing. But with the trends as they are, our Scots will vanish completely one day unless people consciously and deliberately try to preserve it.

The schools have not helped the position. The educational system has been geared to the furtherance of English and not very successfully, especially now that grammar has gone by the board. There is a great snobbery attached to the use of English in Scotland. Scots has lost social prestige and until you get people out of this fear of dropping social bricks, there is not much hope for it. It was intended to make the *Scottish National Dictionary* available to schools but there has been very little sign of this being taken up. Teachers are apathetic if not antagonistic and only the occasional enthusiast here or there tries to introduce Scots into the culture.

In George Square, where I worked in Edinburgh, the gentry were speaking Scots in the eighteenth century. Then the judges and advocates began imitating the English; the Select Society was formed to acquire standard English and Scots speech had moved to the middle classes.

The rot had set in. The intonations will last for a long time—the vowel sounds and so on. Of course I am a born pessimist; that way I can get only pleasant surprises. But I must admit that, at times, I see a glimmer of hope. It may yet come back into use, as a fashion.

David Murison believes that the so-called inarticulateness of Buchan folk is due to the fact that their speech has been repressed. In the formation of the *Scottish National Dictionary*, however, his own native corner ranked in the top bracket of source material, maintaining a good literary tradition which is still producing its prose and poetry. Other areas which have held to their local speech include the Borders, Galloway, Angus and the Shetlands.

It was David Murison who convinced me that we are mis-using the word 'Doric' when we adopt it as a label for our North-East speech. Being the Greek scholar that he is, he reminded me that Doric was the dialect of the Spartans and had to do with roughness and coarseness. The word found its way into the English language bringing the same connotation, and was used by Milton. How it arrived in the North-East of Scotland is something of a mystery, but we seemed to imagine that it applied to us because of our characteristic dialect. This hint of coarseness perhaps explains why so many well-intentioned people talk about 'lapsing into the dialect'. Is it really a lapse?

David Murison spoke it richly and naturally as we sat in his Fraserburgh home and looked across to the Infant School which first set him on his road to Cambridge. The question in his mind was whether or not his life's work would prove to be of lasting value.

Leaving the presence of such a remarkable man, I wondered if Fraserburgh had any notion of the calibre of human being who had come amongst them. Here was such a fount of knowledge about the Scottish tongue as we would certainly never see again. We shall put him on a pedestal one day and say, when it is too late for him to hear it, that we had a truly great Scot in David Murison.

CHAPTER FIFTEEN

DAUGHTER OF GRASSIC GIBBON

For many years of my youth, it would be fair to say, I trod my native scene with little eye or ear for the things around me. It was plain and familiar and generally to be taken for granted. People went about their daily darg with steady gait in a life which seemed dictated more by the bite of drudgery than the soul of inspiration.

Then it happened that, within a matter of days, the whole familiar scene had gained new meaning: the plodding ploughman suddenly symbolized a deeper life that had eluded me; the land that lay still and secretive was adding to its yield of oats and turnips and potatoes a whole new harvest of heritage that was rich and bountiful and nourishing. At last my ears were opened to the voice of that land in which my own ancestral roots were buried, and for all this I had to thank a man called Mitchell—James Leslie Mitchell, better known to the world as Lewis Grassic Gibbon.

I had just read his trilogy of novels called *A Scots Quair*, a remarkable piece of literature which gets at the heart of Scottish rural life and character and expresses it so the whole English-speaking world can understand. The rare technique is that, in order to reach that wider audience, he used a minimum of Scots words which might turn away the outside reader, yet produced a rhythm of Scottishness which left the impression that he had been writing in Scots all the time. It was a language and a feat which belonged to no one but himself.

Mitchell was born and raised in his early years on the very edge of Buchan, at the modest holding of Hill of Seggat at Auchterless, before the family moved diagonally south-eastward to the Mearns, that red-clay district below Stonehaven from which Robert Burns's father had, in his day, moved southward to find work and to settle in Ayrshire.

While his father and mother worked the croft of Bloomfield, young Leslie was travelling down the road to Arbuthnott School, where he was fortunate in the calibre of his headmaster, Alexander Gray. In *A Grain of Truth* I told the story of how he went on to be a journalist in Aberdeen and Glasgow, to spend obscure years in the Army and the Air Force during the 1920s and finally to settle to a life of authorship in Welwyn Garden City, north of London, where he produced sixteen books in less than seven years.

His feverish pattern took its toll, and what should have been a routine stomach operation turned into tragedy when he did not regain consciousness from the operating table that February day of 1935. Lewis Grassic Gibbon was dead before his thirty-fourth birthday, leaving his wife Rebecca, herself from a neighbouring croft in the Mearns, with two young children, Rhea and Daryll. The funeral service was at Golders Green Crematorium and his ashes were brought back to the kirkyard of Arbuthnott, a great light dimmed for ever but not to be extinguished.

The struggle and hardship of the crofting life had raised rebellion within him, but through his anger came an abiding love of the land and the folk whose honest toil had turned it into the fertile base of a decent society. At the same time he could be critical of nearby places like Aberdeen and Stonehaven, and indeed his essay on the Granite City contains such amusing gems as this:

> Aberdeen is the cleanest city in Britain; it makes you long for good, wholesome dirt, littered roadways and ramshackle buildings leaning in all directions, projecting warm, brown sins and rich smutty reds through an enticing, grimy smile . . .
>
> Where Union Terrace breaks in upon Union Street there is an attempt at a public garden. But the flowers come up and take one glance at the lour of the solicitors' offices which man

Union Terrace and scramble back into the earth again, seeking the Antipodes.

From that base of Welwyn Garden City, Lewis Grassic Gibbon had nevertheless sighed for his beloved North-East, and it was to those leafy lanes of Hertfordshire that I betook myself one day to satisfy a curiosity about the effect of an English upbringing on the children of a great Scottish writer. And there, in the alien tones of a refined English which would have been fair the speak of Kinraddie, Rhea Martin opened up her heart on the subject of her famous father, a man she was really too young to know.

For long, I discovered, she had wrestled with the torment of a memory which lay just beyond her reach and sought to unravel the conflict which made her proud of a distinguished father on the one hand and impatient with some of the consequences on the other. With all the independence and thrawn nature of her ancestral North-East of Scotland, she was determined to be known for herself and not as the daughter of . . .

She need have had no fears on that score. As Rhea Mitchell, brilliant scholar, she studied law at London University, was called to the Bar and became dean of the School of Business and Social Studies at Hatfield Polytechnic, as well as a distinguished legal figure serving on bodies like the Lord Chancellor's Advisory Committee on Legal Aid.

By the time I met her she was already in her fifties, a formidable, good-looking wife and mother to three grown-up sons, one of whom was a Fleet Street journalist.

But to the purpose of my visit: What was it like to grow up as an Englishwoman far removed from the source of her father's life and inspiration in North-East Scotland, with little chance of encountering its language and culture? Could a child of that great novelist perhaps fail to recognize and appreciate Chris Guthrie, his memorable and symbolic character who runs through the trilogy of *A Scots Quair*?

In the calm of that garden city, not far from the house where

Grassic Gibbon lived, Rhea turned it all over in her mind and surprised me with some of her revelations:

> Do you know, the idea that I was the daughter of a famous author did not materialize as a general proposition in my life until the BBC televised *Sunset Song* in 1970, when I was forty. Other people, including my mother, had told me so but it was not a personal experience for me.
>
> After the television serial, people down here were saying, 'Is it true that you are the daughter of Grassic Gibbon?' When I said it was, their next question was, 'Why didn't you tell us?' But I had no inclination to tell people.

Irked by what she took to be sycophancy, she explained:

> I dislike when people enjoy the artificially reflected glory of having been close to someone related to the famous. I find that experience very difficult to respond to because I have such fragile recollection of the things they are being so admiring about. It is a painful vacuum in my life but I have learned to adjust my emotions, to blank it out—not to ignore it—because you have to get on with living your own life.

That fragile recollection arises from the fact that Rhea Mitchell was barely five when her father died on that operating table. So what did she remember?

> I have a recollection of sitting scribbling in his study while he was at work in our house at 107 Handside Lane, here in Welwyn Garden, but I have no memory of his voice. I still wonder what his speech was like.
>
> When you have been told anecdotes so many times they become part of your memory, so it is difficult to know what I do actually remember about him. I have a recollection of my mother telling me something very solemnly and I can only imagine she was breaking the news of his death.
>
> I first read *A Scots Quair* when I was about fifteen or six-

teen but found it difficult because I felt under an obligation to read it. However, I still take the view that the emotions expressed are very hard to understand at fifteen, and I am not sure it should be O-grade material in the Scottish schools. I think it is too early.

I don't think I knew the character of Chris Guthrie and I found I had absolutely nothing in common with her. Yet some people say she was modelled on my mother and that made it difficult for me to read about her objectively. So there was a long time I didn't read the books at all. But last year I wanted to take a fresh look at them. They were doing a musical version of *Sunset Song* at the Edinburgh Festival and I took a paperback version of *A Scots Quair* up with me and read it again and enjoyed it best of all this time.

I wondered if any of Grassic Gibbon's writing urge had been passed on to his offspring.

People say I have a talent with words but I use it more in speech than in writing. I used to cringe when people asked me if I was going to grow up and write books like my father. It was very inhibiting and I didn't know what the hell they were talking about! I had no interest in writing novels, partly because I had turned my back on it all. I was being asked to emulate someone I didn't know and was always suspicious of that since I am very much my own person.

Struggling as a young widow with two children to bring up, Rebecca Mitchell (she came to be known as Ray) went back to the Civil Service and young Rhea was sent to Christ Hospital, the charity school which kept some places for the children of deceased people who had had some distinction in life. Compton Mackenzie and Ivor Brown had a hand in the matter. She remembered arriving there in September, 1939, at the outbreak of war, and tucking her gym slip into navy knickers for the very first job of filling sandbags.

Brother Daryll was sent to the famous A. S. Neil's free discipline school at Summerhill, but they were re-united with their mother at holiday times, when they headed for Scotland.

My mother had to breathe her native air so we stayed with relatives and I had to go out to play with cousins I could hardly understand—and they couldn't understand me.

There was a slight resentment about the Mitchells who had gone off to live in England, almost as if we had manufactured airs and graces to which we had no claim.

On one of our visits to Scotland we stayed with a family called Crawford in Dundee. We went into a tea-shop one day and Mr Crawford, who had known my father, called over another man and introduced me as Lewis Grassic Gibbon's daughter. What I received from this man was a tirade which made it clear he was not an admirer of my father. It was the first time I had heard anyone speak against him. Mr Crawford then told me he had done that deliberately because he felt I should know that not the whole world was pro-Grassic Gibbon.

Whatever the charity of that, it was of course true that many people, unable or unwilling to appreciate the poetic genius of the man, were ready to take umbrage at his forthright observations. Had not his own mother been tempted to ask what he was writing all that 'muck' for?

What of the Scottishness which must surely have lurked somewhere in the genes of Rhea Mitchell's Pictish parentage?

When my father died, a number of people encouraged my mother to take us back to have a Scottish upbringing but she was not prepared to move. My own view about being Scottish is, I suppose, much the same as that of people who emigrate to Canada. Once you are out of Scotland, the distance doesn't matter. People are glad to say they come from Scottish parentage. It is nothing to hide but it is nothing deeper than just that.

Since the death of her mother in 1978, I suspect that Rhea Mitchell, married to a delightful Englishman, Gill Martin, an engineer who gave up work early through ill health, has found herself with the new responsibility of keeping the ancestral threads intact. She acknowledged that there was a basic instinct to do that.

Just as her father was cremated at Golders Green and his ashes taken back to Arbuthnott in 1935, she followed the same routine for her mother, placing the ashes under the same headstone which bears those moving words from the closing passage of *Sunset Song*:

> The kindness of friends
> The warmth of toil
> The peace of rest

Ray Mitchell had been bitter about losing her life's partner so young, feeling his death could have been prevented. Her own life was spent in furthering his name, when publishers and public were in shameful neglect of him. (In the 1950s I joined with her in badgering publishers about bringing his work back into print.) Now they were together again, back in the red clay of the Mearns which had given them both roots and an early contact with each other.

That noted Aberdonian poetess, Nan Shepherd, mentioned in a recent chapter, was present in 1978, as she had been for Grassic Gibbon's own funeral in 1935, remarking on how completely similar the two services had been.

They played 'The Lord's my Shepherd' and closed the service with 'The Flowers o' the Forest', just as Grassic Gibbon had closed *Sunset Song* with the piper playing the lament up there by Blawearie Loch.

That same day, Rhea's journalist son Alister, from Fleet Street, found himself gazing at the land and its people and appreciating for the very first time what his grandmother had been speaking about throughout the years.

Rhea herself came back to that Edinburgh Festival with no intention of visiting the Mearns. Then a strange thing happened:

> When I was there I suddenly felt a strong requirement, not an obligation, just a 'requirement' within myself to go back. So I drove up from Edinburgh and back again without speaking to a single soul. And I wondered why I had gone because there was no one left to visit. But it is a peaceable place and it satisfied something within me.

Her face glowed warmly, like the rich soil of the Mearns, as she spoke of it. It was the tug of a tradition which had ensnared her father without yield and produced great literature from the distance of Welwyn Garden City. There she stood alone at Arbuthnott, like Chris Guthrie at the standing stones of ancient times, listening to the grey North Sea as it rumbled beneath the cliffs.

The gaze of Grassic Gibbon's daughter spread across the Mearns, with its red clay soil and modest crofts, reaching to the foothills of the Grampians and rising into the western horizon of a summer's evening; rising into the glow of a Sunset Song which echoes like a distant melody in the human heart.

CHAPTER SIXTEEN

TRAUCHLE AND TRIUMPH OF TOULMIN

My joyous ramble over Buchan revisited was bringing me, more than I had intended, into the company of people who were expressing themselves in words of one kind or another.

But the contact was as rewarding as it was inevitable, especially on such an occasion when I crossed outwards from the Buchan boundary to renew acquaintance with an exile who had gone to the city of Aberdeen. Driving down one of the streets which lead to the Pittodrie Stadium of Aberdeen Football Club, I found myself at the fireside of a man who could be described as a unique figure on the Scottish literary scene.

I had come to visit David Toulmin, an old-time farm servant who was thrust into publication when approaching his sixtieth birthday, with a book of stories from his observations of country life. Not that his projection into the limelight of acclaim was resisted by any means; indeed it was something that might have belonged to his private dreams, but, with the curse of self-effacement which besets the Buchan breed, the transfer to reality would have seemed an unlikely proposition.

For here was no phoney farm labourer who might be concealing some university background. Here was a genuine, 100-per-cent son of the soil, a ploughman born into an Aberdeenshire cottar house and sired by a father who could not sign his own name.

It was a bare childhood in the grey, dreich setting which had been the farm servant's lot for generations, moving from school to school in the Buchan area according to his father's latest 'fee'.

But David Toulmin, whose real name is John Reid, had a sensitivity of soul which stirred dreams of a romantic world beyond the fairm-toun, with its dubs and drudgery and siccar code of unrelenting hard work. Even if that other world were not a haven to which he could readily escape, there was at least nothing to stop the humblest human from entertaining his flights of fancy. At the Playhouse Cinema in Peterhead he absorbed the glitter of early Hollywood and proceeded to write his own little stories, passing them cautiously round the chaumer where he and his fellow farm servants bothied.

There was little privacy to continue his writing but, merci-fully, the bite of the turnip field in winter and the numbing thistles of the cornyard at harvest time did nothing to blunt the sensitivities of David Toulmin, who worked on the farms of Aberdeenshire from the day he left school at fourteen. He kept a diary and recorded not only the life and work of the fairm-toun but the thoughts and feelings of one who might have come to be regarded as a bit of an oddity had he revealed to his fellow workers the true extent of his delicate pursuit. Such tenderness might have seemed out of place amid the tang of sharny cattle and the earthy talk which characterized rural life.

However, he still managed to adorn the chaumer walls with pictures of Marlene Dietrich and Greta Garbo, a custom qui-etly noted by Margaret, the kitchie deem at Newton of Kinmundy, near Peterhead, when she went to make the men's beds. Margaret was maybe no Garbo or Dietrich but neither would Garbo or Dietrich have been much of a Margaret when it came to milking kye or baking scones or reddin' oot the chaumer. So Toulmin put his celluloid fantasies to one side and married her and they settled in a cottar house at Newseat of Peterhead, where his daily labours as a dairyman produced those same little bottles of milk which we awaited so eagerly at Maud School when Duncan Davidson's van arrived at 11 o'clock.

With privacy thus restored in a home of his own, settled in marriage in 1934 at the age of twenty-one, he could write again, and in time the *Farmer and Stockbreeder* accepted his

311

modest offerings on animal husbandry and paid him five guineas, which was a good deal more than you were paid for mucking nowt in a byre.

But the prospects of a writing career remained fairly remote for a man at the hard end of the working scale, without any contacts in the distant realms of literature. He read his way through the whole of Shakespeare (except *Love's Labour's Lost*), then chanced upon the wonder of Lewis Grassic Gibbon, whose books inspired in him a fresh burst of activity. But Toulmin was approaching fifty before his stories and recollections, expressed in the native rhythms of Buchan, saw the light of day, even in his own local newspaper in Peterhead, the *Buchan Observer*.

From there they were spotted by a Buchan man at the BBC, Arthur Argo, who arranged for them to be broadcast. Then, in 1972, the imaginative young publisher, Paul Harris, then functioning in Aberdeen through his Impulse Publications, brought out that first collection as a book called *Hard Shining Corn*. It was so well received as to send some critics into comparisons with Grassic Gibbon himself. If that was stretching it too far, it did at least help to spawn a successor, *Straw into Gold*, and then, at the age of sixty-three, Toulmin wrote his first full-scale novel, *Blown Seed*, in which the talented farm servant wrote passages like this:

> Now the soft wind carried the seed over the parks, tiny motes in the sunhaze, each one its parachute of lighted down, blown seed in the wind, showering over the crofts and the farms like snow in summer, sprouting in a year or two where folk scythed and hoed to keep their crops clean.

The paperback rights were sold before the hardback edition was even published and, as we sat by his homely fireside that day in Aberdeen, Toulmin regaled me with the story of how he was feted by the London paperback people at the Station Hotel, Aberdeen:

They took us to dinner but before we sat down the chief salesman went away to check up on the latest figures. He came back to announce that, in less than three weeks, they had sold 16,000 copies. They had to bring me a chair till I recovered!

Toulmin, now roused like a frisky stirk by the revelation of his own potential, began to harbour thoughts of blockbusting success, and he and Margaret, a fine, homely body of plain dignity and charm, wondered quietly if he had made it at last to the best-seller bracket. Since *Blown Seed* unveiled some of the sexual life of the countryside, had Scotland perhaps produced a Harold Robbins in tackety boots?

That early selling promise was not exactly fulfilled but the paperback company came back for his next book, *Harvest Home*. In 1980 he parodied Robert Louis Stevenson and wrote *Travels Without a Donkey*, an account of the journeys which he and Margaret had made around Britain since the day he was able to afford a motor car. During a decade of literary success, David Toulmin left the trauchle of farm life and moved to the refinement of landscape gardening in Aberdeen, settling himself in that street where the football crowds stream past to Pittodrie. And there he continued his writing, with more time and comfort at his disposal, till he retired from all kinds of manual labour. He suffered periods of deep depression for which he sought treatment, and by the age of seventy he was telling me that he had written his last book. With rural matter-of-factness, he said: 'Tae tell ye the truth, I'm scunnert o' writin'. It's gettin' tae be a trauchle. Fin I sit doon at the typewriter it's like sendin' me tae pu' neeps.' Mercifully he survived that state of mind and has since produced other books.

In 1986 his appetite was sufficiently revived to give us more sketches of life and characters from his native corner, under the title *The Clyack Sheaf*. In farming terms, the clyack was the last-bound sheaf but not the end of harvest altogether, and therein lay the hope that we had not seen the last of Toulmin. His writing has retained that ingenuous touch you would expect from a man who has riven with nature all his days, facing the hard facts of a demanding life without any expectation of a favour.

Some might hint at early deprivation and say a man like Toulmin would have gone further with more schooling, but I suspect that his raw talent might well have been impaired. In the Scottish system of his day, rural children were remarkably well educated by the age of fourteen (Grassic Gibbon had no more favourable a start) and Toulmin made it his business to acquire books which took him well beyond that level.

In *The Clyack Sheaf*, he went back to visit some of the places he knew as a young farm servant. As a starting point he returned to Greystone farm, near Peterhead, and was met there by farmer Willie McIntosh, on the very spot where Willie's father had engaged him as a loon to work the orra beast and sort the nowt fifty-six years earlier. He took us on through the country life of his younger days resuscitating characters like the flamboyant Baillie Booth, Buchan farmer and butcher and the man who went north to the Orkney sales of 1923, bringing back a piece of livestock with a difference—Robert Boothby, who would spend the rest of his career as Tory Member of Parliament for East Aberdeenshire.

Though firmly on the other side of the fence, Toulmin was not short on his fascination with local lairds like Doctor Bruce of Inverquhomery, who happened to be one of the most eminent medical men of his day, pioneering the study of psychiatry, neurology and multiple sclerosis. He reminded us (if ever we knew) that Rafael Carlos Gordon, laird of Wardhouse, at the back o' Benachie, was so closely involved in the affairs of Spain that he practically ruled the country in 1931, when King Alfonso was dethroned. He was then forced to flee from Franco.

He touched on the living poet of Peterhead, Peter Buchan, and the dreaded Miss Mackenzie of Foveran House, who lived reclusively in her mansion until 1973, having once studied music in Germany and frequently had tea with Hitler at Berchtesgaden. But he never strayed too far from grubbing the

314

hill park or hyowin the neeps, mixing his English with Buchan phrases which came as naturally as his stride down the greip with turnips for his beloved cattle.

David Toulmin saw his first tractor at work in 1928 and a decade later it was intruding upon the domain of the work-horse. In time the machine made obsolete his own labours of nearly half a century, and it was then that he withdrew gracefully to that job as a landscape gardener in Aberdeen, 'where I was privileged to finish my working life in pleasant surroundings, which made a gentle art of my former agricul-tural experience.

'I got out of farming at the right time,' he said as we looked back on his life and times. The years had not softened his dis-taste for the grey pleiter of farm work; yet, ironically, he could say in all honesty: 'I'm glad I did live in that manual era in-stead of working with those new-fangled tractors. There was more camaraderie and the world was a happier place.'

So Toulmin found himself in the same predicament as Grassic Gibbon and many others—writing about a life of drudgery and sometimes despair, yet doing so with not a little affection. That land still tore at him like a nagging love, so deep and abiding that you could rail against it with the full force of your vigour, in the certain knowledge that you could not bear to be free of it.

CHAPTER SEVENTEEN

THE SCRIBE OF ST COMBS

The beach by St Combs stretched like gold against the clear blue sky, punctuated by that column of cement blocks which still stood poised in anticipation of Hitler's tanks.

My mission as I drove towards that cluster of fishing villages on the Buchan coast was to find a man who had intrigued me in recent years, a man just born as that German crisis was reaching its height. James Duthie had been a fisherman from the day he left school in Fraserburgh in 1957, steaming first to the herring grounds and later to more distant waters where they fish for pilchards or whatever comes their way. While plying those varied waters this typical Buchan fisherman who claims, without boast, to having been 'rale thick' at school was scribbling in the dead of night and giving shape to a most extraordinary play for television.

When he took his courage in his hands and marched up to the BBC with his script, they blinked with new respect for a man who scarcely looked the part. They did indeed make it into a strangely haunting and beautiful television play called *Donal and Sally*, which dared to tread on the sensitive ground of two mentally retarded youngsters falling in love. That was followed by a shorter but no less perceptive piece of television drama, *The Drystane Dyker*.

What sort of a man, I wondered, was producing those delicately observed dramas while pursuing the harvest of the sea as a means of livelihood? James Duthie was already at the door of his house to greet me as I drove into St Combs, looking every inch the rough-hewn, weather-beaten fisherman and much less the playwright. It was a reassuring start. The lean and angular appearance and lilting fisher tongue were reminiscent of Fraserburgh fishermen I remembered from as far back as those days when we boarded the train at Maud Station with an unbearable anticipation of the school picnic which would take us to that magnificent beach stretching round from the Broch towards the point at Cairnbulg.

James Duthie was born in 1942 of a Fraserburgh father and Cairnbulg mother and brought up in Watermill Road, though his actual birth took place in the aristocratic setting of Haddo House, family seat of Lord Aberdeen, which was turned into a hospital during the war. At the age of fifteen he followed the tradition of the sea as tenth man on a fishing boat, remaining there for twenty-three unbroken years until he said goodbye to his mates of the *Sedulous* and came ashore in 1980.

The years between reveal a classic tale of what can be achieved when your heart has set its objective. For James Duthie was no academic. Grammatic writing, as he said himself, was beyond his capability. To him a dangling participle was something which needed surgical attention. But he did have the urge to be a writer.

Claiming that he shared a birthday with Shakespeare, he was soon testing me out with his solemn-faced wit: 'I think I'm better than Shakespeare. He couldna write for television. Of course, the English will tell you there wisna television in his day but the English will use anything as an excuse.'

Jokes apart, James Duthie knew that, in the absence of grammar, his concentration must be on the dialogue of drama, where very little grammar is expected. So he sat down to write his play, all the time wondering who there might be to advise him. That was where fate took a hand. While unloading catches at Shields, in the north of England, he discovered that a gentleman who often came to collect fish at the market was Tom Hadaway, one of the writers then engaged on that popular television serial *When the Boat Comes In.*

'I introduced myself and said I could write better plays than you see on television,' said James Duthie. It was the kind of stray remark we all make after some dismal drivel on television but Hadaway knew that Duthie really meant it.

'He advised me to write in the dialect and to pick a subject I knew something about, a situation I had seen for myself. Well, there was a woman who used to live beside us in the Broch and she was handicapped and her boy-friend was the same. He would come up to see her, swinging round the lamp-posts as he came, but she would let him in only if he had a bag of sweeties.'

Thus the seeds of *Donal and Sally* were sown, with Duthie developing his personal observations through visits to the Willowbank centre for handicapped people in Peterhead, where the play was eventually filmed, using a mixture of professional actors and handicapped people. The actual script took only two or three days to write; then Tom Hadaway lent his advice and put him in touch with the appropriate producer at the BBC in London. What seemed like a risky undertaking ended up as a memorable piece of television drama.

James Duthie hovered behind the cameras as they filmed, bemused that the brainchild of a working fisherman was actually receiving this kind of attention from actors, producers, camera crews and so many more. He regarded the fee of £950 as proof in his hand that he had made it as a writer, albeit without any knowledge of technicalities like grammar.

An encounter with an old-fashioned drystane dyker on Deeside was the inspiration for his next attempt at television drama, and that survived a period of cold storage to become another success on screen. What finally brought James Duthie ashore was a commission from the BBC to write a major television series which was intended to do for the North-East of Scotland much the same as Tom Hadaway and *When the Boat Comes In* had done for the North-East of England. He gave it the title *The Buchans of Buchan*, the story of a fishing family with a look at the traditional values, set alongside the values of the modern day.

'We have lost a lot on the way,' he laments. 'The fishing community today is not so close-knit as it used to be. The great god money has taken over.'

But there is still a recognizable way of life in places like Inverallochy, Cairnbulg and St Combs, an atmosphere of the true fisher folk, with faces that are etched from the experience of a fickle fate, triumphant one moment, tragic the next, calmly resigned to whatever the gods may decree. James Duthie's grandmother was one of those people, living in the last house in Cairnbulg to acquire electricity and still carrying water when she was in her eighties, not so long ago.

The BBC paid him for his first six episodes of *The Buchans of Buchan* but, paradoxically, the commission which brought him ashore to the life of a full-time writer was later shelved and has not yet seen the light of day. James Duthie conducts his correspondence with the BBC in the Buchan dialect and has been known to storm the sophisticated Television Centre in London with a splendid disregard for the language and sensitivities of the English. As a left-over from his days of reading and writing while the boats were searching the fishing grounds or heading back to port, I discovered when I intruded on his routine on that bare Buchan coast that he had still retained the nocturnal habits of working. Nowadays he was catching words instead of fishes and wandering along that lonely shore by day, dreaming up his dramas.

His wife, Margaret, and children, James and Margaret, know him better as a fisherman but seemed to attend respectfully on his new career. They are all fisher folk from St Combs who have been going to sea in little ships for generations. No matter what height of literary success may be achieved—and he deserves so much—that is where James Duthie and his family will always belong.

CHAPTER EIGHTEEN

MOON OVER MORMOND

Motoring through Buchan on this mission of rediscovery, I was turning over in my mind some of the great worthies I remembered from childhood days, people like Sandy Wilson, the Strichen horse dealer; John Dickie Dempster, rugged farmer and calf dealer who regaled us with the gossip of the district in our house at Park Crescent, Maud; Johnny Robson, the Carrot King who could fair make the melodeon dance and was better known as Johnny Naeman, from his quaint habit of muttering to himself 'Nae man, nae man'.

Most warmly of all, perhaps, I remember Lizzie Allan, who ran the sweetie and tobacco shop in Timmer Street, Maud, from the seat of her old-fashioned wheelchair, having suffered amputation of both legs as a little girl. As I described in *A Grain of Truth*, Lizzie dispensed politics with peppermints, philosophy with fags, a powerful magnet of a woman who held court in the paraffin-dim bleakness of her timber-built shop, mesmerizing with the clarity of her mind, the whiplash of her tongue. To me she was Boadicea in a bathchair, riding through life with a rare majesty when all the forces of humiliation were ranged against her. She excited my interest in life but it was only recently, when acquiring some early photographs from her half-sister, Ada Stott, that I realized what a truly beautiful woman poor Lizzie had been in her day.

The modern propensity for self-examination and the exposure of every quirk in human nature militates against eccentric behaviour, so we resign ourselves to the fact that the great characters belong to another day and age. Yet I was meeting people of my own generation who had developed strengths of character and powers of personality which could not have been foreseen when I knew them as youngsters. Perhaps we need to reach a certain level of age and experience before those added layers begin to come through; indeed it would be astonishing if the processes which have survived the long history of human development came suddenly to a halt in our own generation. So there are still eccentrics in our midst today (or worthies, as they call them in the North-East), and the destination of my drive that day would set me down at the door of one of them.

Bob Bandeen of Strichen had survived two coronary attacks, a cerebral haemorrhage, a major stomach operation and goodness knows what else, but was still in such good fettle as to joke about the fact that there is a lot of killing in a kyaard. The Bandeen home was The Cloisters in Strichen, a house as unusual as the man himself inasmuch as it used to be the Roman Catholic chapel of the aristocratic Fraser family, who later became the Lovats. His living-room rose in steps to the altar and there was even a pedal organ to round off an atmosphere of peace and contentment.

I had first known Bob Bandeen at the end of the Second World War, when he came to make a kilted skirt for my mother; but then Bob was always making something. He had made breeks and waistcoats for the Duke of Windsor in his days as a tailor in Insch. Though he left school at the customary age of fourteen, he had been in his time a teacher, tailor, soldier, preacher, dance-band pianist, toolworker, librarian and anything else you cared to ask of him. Bob was never stuck, and what he didn't know, folk said, he would damned soon make up. During the Depression of the 1930s he worked as a navvy while perfecting his knowledge of Latin, Greek and Hebrew at the same time.

They used to tell some wonderful tales about Bob, some of them apocryphal but most of them perfectly true; like the day he was on his way to play the organ at Insch and fell off his bike on the ice, ending up with a wet backside. Hurrying on to the kirk, he sought to hasten the drying process by leaving his shirt tails flapping outside his trousers to gain benefit from the wind. As the minister waited anxiously for his organist, a breathless Bob arrived at the kirk, proceeded to march straight through from the vestry—and convulsed the congregation with the sight of his sark tails still flapping behind him!

On another occasion, he was accompanying a much-remembered Strichen minister to a social gathering where his reverence commented upon the early physical development of young girls in the modern world.

'Ay, minister,' Bob is alleged to have replied, 'there's mair uplift in yon lassies than in maist o' your sermons!'

Bob acknowledged the stories, and took me back to his early days in Aberdeen, where he attended Westfield School, at the corner of Esslemont Avenue and Whitehall Road. Being 'the feel o' the faimily', as he liked to describe himself, he served his apprenticeship with his father, who had a tailor's shop in Leadside Road and one in Skene Square. But Bob got the dirty jobs to do, so, as soon as his time was served, he moved out to that rural tailor of great renown, Russell of Insch, who served royalty and millionaires as well as local folk.

'The Royal Family would come over tae Russell's on a coorse day when they couldna get oot an' aboot,' Bob recalled. 'Queen Mary used tae come and the Lascelles family and the Duke o' Windsor; but nae Mrs Simpson. They used tae hae a glorious rake roon and they aye bocht something.'

But there were long periods of unemployment in the winter months and Bob navvied and played the piano in a dance band, taking lessons in his spare time from a Highland schoolmaster who sharpened up his knowledge of Latin and Greek.

Greater security came with the offer of a job as dairyman at Nether Cortes of Lonmay, but it was 1939 and the war was on. Bob remembered it well: 'I joined the Home Guard with the laird and big Norman Murray, the heavyweight athlete, and we were stationed on the edge o' Cortes Lake. But we couldna live for midgies so we decided tae gie Hitler a scare and jine up. We gaed tae Saltoun Place in the Broch but didna expect tae be called up. Inside a week, however, the laird was awa tae the Air Force, Norman Murray was in the Navy and I was in the Army.'

I have long been convinced that the magnetism of personality attracts experience so it was no surprise to find that Bob Bandeen was seconded to Intelligence and drafted into that extraordinary emergency when Hitler's deputy, Rudolf Hess, landed in a field at Eaglesham, near Glasgow, in 1941, on the eve of Germany's attack on Russia. Hess had come to plead the cause of a negotiated Anglo-German peace, prompting Churchill's comment: 'The maggot is in the apple.'

Back in Buchan after the war, Bob went to the Training Centre in Aberdeen to gain a teaching qualification, meeting up with J. C. Milne, the lecturer who wrote *The Orra Loon*, and who told him 'We never turn onybody awa fae the troch.'

Bob Bandeen was appointed librarian at the village of Strichen with the princely salary of £156 a year, with £20 a year for an assistant and £20 for a cleaner. His wife became both and, while he regarded it all as a matter of genteel poverty, it was at least a job in which the Bandeens could be completely happy.

That howe of Strichen which was home to Bob and his family had produced many fascinating tales in its time and I was particularly interested to know what part he had played in the modern reprinting of the novel *Dark Star*, which was written by a famous daughter of Strichen, Lorna Moon.

Lorna Moon was the pen-name of Nora Low, whose father was Charlie Low, a well-known Strichen personality and one of the early Socialists who used to organize meetings of the Fabian Society on the market-stance. The Lows had the Temperance Hotel in Strichen and it was a commercial traveller who happened to pass that way, a William Hebditch from Selby in Yorkshire, who fell in love with one of the daughters of the inn, Nora Low. The pair eloped to be married by special licence in Aberdeen on Christmas Eve of 1907 before emigrating to rural Canada. Nora had one child by Hebditch but the restless spirit of the budding writer was soon on the move; she left home for the city life, met up with a man called Moon (the source of her pen name), by whom she had a daughter. But that liaison was no more enduring than the first and she was on her way again. This time she gravitated towards Hollywood and became a script-writer, gaining fame for such films as *Mr Wu*, starring Lon Chaney, and working with directors like Cecil B. de Mille. It was in 1929 that she wrote *Dark Star*, a deeply moving novel about her beloved Buchan but one which appalled the local populace by describing some folk of the Strichen district with unmistakable clarity. Among them was Billy Fraser, described in the book, in the way he was in real life, as a man of stunted growth who was the local librarian. Ignoring the fact that a girl from their own backyard had written a literary masterpiece, Strichen folk fumed with rage, by which time Lorna Moon was well established in America.

Her own father had been outraged by her previous book of short stories, *Doorways in Drumorty*, in which he recognized himself (from a period of working in Africa) as the man who left his family struggling at home while he lived in some style abroad.

To lessen the embarrassment of Billy Fraser, who was still alive at the time, the local library committee decided not to stock Lorna Moon, and that situation persisted throughout Bob Bandeen's years as librarian. But old Charlie Low did ask if he would accept *Dark Star* and *Doorways in Drumorty* as gifts, and Bob readily accepted and lent them privately to those who were especially interested.

When David Toulmin wanted to reissue Lorna Moon's books with Gourdas House, the Aberdeen publishers, he went in search of copies and it was evidently Bob Bandeen who produced them.

Her *Dark Star* had no sooner appeared in 1929 than Lorna Moon was dying of consumption, a woman in her prime at barely forty-four, possessed of that delicate beauty which so often accompanied tuberculosis. By then her fame in America was such that newspapers carried regular bulletins about her health. When she died in Albuquerque, New Mexico, in 1930 they brought her ashes home to be scattered on Mormond Hill, in accordance with her dying wish, and that story became one of the local legends which enlivened my childhood. Strichen had indeed produced a novelist of world class, whatever offence might have been taken at the way she highlighted local foibles.

As a bizarre postscript to that sad tale, my father-in-law, Nelson Keith, was passing Charlie Low's house one day when he found him cementing the doorstep.

'Man, that's a gey fancy troch ye've got, Charlie,' said Nelson Keith.

'Oh ay,' said Charlie. 'It's the boxie they brocht Nora's ashes hame in!'

There is another postscript to this strange story, offering further proof that we live in a funny old world. Into the village of Strichen in 1984 came an American gent whose presence turned a few inquisitive heads, especially when it became known that his surname was de Mille. Word went round that he was a son of the famous Cecil B., Hollywood creator of such Biblical epics as *Samson and Delilah* and *The Ten Commandments*.

Richard de Mille was accompanied on this very personal mission by David Clark, a medical sociologist at Aberdeen Royal Infirmary who was living on a croft at New Deer at the time and who had been engaged by de Mille to undertake research on the background of his mother. The name of his mother? Lorna Moon. During his visit, Richard de Mille was saying nothing about the identity of his father and, when I later wrote to him in California seeking confirmation of his parentage, he wrote back to say: 'I am currently writing in an autobiographical vein and I hope to prepare a volume about Lorna, which will answer the questions you have asked. I do not expect to have a manuscript for several years. In the meantime I think it would be prudent not to discuss details of the story . . .'

He had also written to David Toulmin pointing out that he holds the rights to Lorna Moon's two well-known books. And there, for the moment, this intriguing story must rest.

Bob Bandeen was delighted with the modern interest in the work of Lorna Moon, just as he was delighted to be enjoying the privilege of being alive that day we met at The Cloisters. Among his five children, he too had produced some rare talents, including a brilliant son Robert, who went to work for ICI, and a daughter, Alicia, who followed the missionary trail to the Mary Slessor Hospital in Africa and was feared lost in the Nigerian troubles of some years ago. Happily she survived to become health visitor at Aboyne, on Royal Deeside, while another daughter, Irene, was similarly engaged in her home village of Strichen.

Since our joyous meeting that day, when we took people and places through hand in a well-worn Buchan tradition, Bob Bandeen has passed on to higher plains, taking with him the guarantee that there will be laughter unlimited even in the dullest corners of Heaven. His last words to me were by way of a thanksgiving for the fact that he managed to find something new to celebrate on every morning of his life. Each day was a new adventure, a fresh cause for joy in the experience of this rugged Buchan individualist. Can you think of a better philosophy with which to face the daily darg?

CHAPTER NINETEEN

GOLD AND SILVER

There is an unusual story behind the common bond which I share with a Dutch schoolmaster, Hans Tuyman by name, who was growing up in Holland as a boy of exactly the same age as myself, no more aware of a Scottish village called Maud than I would have known about his native town of Flushing.

While we were lamenting the black-out and food rationing, the absence of oranges, melons, bananas and Cow Candy, Hans had something more serious to worry about, when the innocence of his childhood was invaded by the German armies, storming towards the English Channel to complete their occupation of Western Europe.

To a youngster on the plains of Buchan there was full compensation for the deprivations when a more friendly invasion of soldiers came to occupy our village halls and hotel. We ran from our local school that October day of 1942, filled with excitement as the caterpillar tracks of bren-gun carriers and lorry-loads of the King's Own Scottish Borderers came thundering upon our quiet village of 500 souls and trebled the population within an hour. They had come to prepare for the Second Front which was on everyone's lips, the inevitable attempt to regain a foothold on the European soil from which we had been unceremoniously driven into the waters of Dunkirk in 1940.

The wider strategy of their presence was of less importance to the child mind than the fact that they brought their parades and pipe bands, their swinging kilts and flying maces. It was the stuff of schoolboy dreams as I marched alongside them, the self-appointed mascot, lengthening my stride on tiring route marches, worshipping those big, friendly Borderers like the heroes they were soon to become—and accepting the tuition of that legendary Kelso piper, Jock Gray, who turned me into a fair little player before he disappeared on the road to D-Day.

The KOSB inspired a new level of life in our sober little village of Maud, as well as bringing us our one and only royal visitor, the Duchess of Gloucester (their colonel-in-chief then as now), to inspect her troops and meet the village folk who were inviting them into their homes and providing a canteen in the Pleasure Park Pavilion. In the nearby woods of Brucklay that evening, the military band played Franz Lehar's 'Gold and Silver' waltz, a haunting melody which filtered through the trees to the lazy village below, a scene of blissful serenity in marked contrast to the war which was raging outby. That melody invaded my tender soul and has lived there ever since. For I knew, in the still of that April evening, that here was one of those precious moments in life to distil and to store away for ever, before time untethers it and casts away the fragrance. I knew too that my Border heroes would soon be gone, off to the uncertainties of a war which grown-up people said, in tones of doom, would last for ten years.

When the dreaded day came, I filed in and marched alongside as the whole village turned out to bid a fond farewell. Seeds of friendship and some of love had been sown by these men who now marched off to their next billet at Hayton Camp, Aberdeen, on that route which would take them, step by step, to the south coast of England. Several miles on, they fell out for a rest and Jock Gray put a hand on my shoulder and turned me back, lest my mother was worried.

There I stood, biting a silent lip and fighting back the tears as my heroes went off to war, that vision of the rhythmic mass now blurring like a mirage and leaving me alone to nurse a broken heart. While that heart marched onwards, the rest of me came back to a village now ringing with the hollow sound of a place deserted, the involuntary gasp of a sigh suggesting that life might never be the same again. Mercifully in this wonderful world, the healing property of the broken heart is one of nature's daily miracles.

Long after the Second World War was over and my surviving heroes came home to the mill towns of the Scottish Borders, they began to invite me to their annual reunions—and I have been going there periodically ever since. They are now past the stage of their fortieth anniversary dinner, but when I join them in the Town Hall of Hawick on an October night it is the custom to say a few words, and there, as I rise to face their elderly ranks, I can still feel that hot sting in my throat, as if it were 1942 all over again.

But we laugh and sing and drink together and damned near cry as well. Some come along with wives they met along the way, people like our own Peggy Ellis from Maud, who lived at the West Lodge of Brucklay Castle, where her father was on the staff, before marrying big Alex McLean on his way to France.

One of the most moving aspects of those memorial evenings in Hawick is the presence of a party from Holland and Belgium, people who never fail to come all that distance to reiterate their gratitude to the men who freed them from that Nazi tyranny one day in 1944.

That was how I came to meet Hans Tuyman, the Dutch schoolmaster who was my counterpart in the town of Flushing. Just as I had seen them off to the liberation of Europe from our little community in Scotland, so did young Hans welcome them at the other end of their mission as the men of the King's Own Scottish Borderers went storming ashore at Flushing. To heighten the drama of that evening at Hawick, Hans Tuyman brought with him not only his heartfelt gratitude but some amateur cine-film which showed the actual landing of those men from Hawick and Selkirk and Galashiels and many miles around. From behind the backs of the Germans you could see them advancing to meet the defence. Flushing people, shooting with cameras instead of guns, were recording a piece of priceless, historic film of their liberators' arrival, all the more natural for the mediocrity of its quality.

329

As we watched in rapt attention, I was conscious of a poignant moment for the man who sat beside me. The stocky frame of Ken Rust gripped the arm of his wheelchair, looked down at his legless body and told me: 'That's where it happened—as we landed there at the docks.' As those Borderers charged ashore, a burst of German gunfire blew off most of Ken's right leg. With remarkable courage, he grabbed a knife and cut away the part which still hung loose. So they put him on a stretcher and were rushing him for treatment, the white flag flying, when another burst of fire got his left leg. And there we were, seeing the mayhem at the very moment it happened.

But Ken doesn't complain. From the standpoint of two short stumps he gives us all a lesson in getting on with life and making the best of it. As an Englishman who now lives in Folkestone, he never misses a reunion in Hawick and regards his Scottish connection with bursting pride when you might expect that he would want to forget it. Between times, he hurtles over to the Continent to see that they are looking after the graves of those who were even less fortunate than himself. As they all agree, Ken is one helluva fellow and none pays him greater tribute than Brigadier Frank Coutts, a young KOSB officer when I knew him in Maud but later Colonel of the Regiment, a Scottish international rugby player and joint secretary of the Earl Haig Fund and the British Legion, Scotland.

It was Frank Coutts who drew my attention to the brevity of contact with those Dutch and Belgian people who were liberated by the Scots. While the Borderers had spent seven months in our Aberdeenshire village, they met those Continentals for only a matter of hours on a particular day of 1944. There was no time to linger for pleasantries when the Hun had still to be defeated. But they did pick up the names of people like Adri Van Wyngen, an Underground worker who sped them on their way to victory. Adri comes back to speak at Hawick, as a result of those very few hours in which he forged bonds which would last for ever.

Back home in Holland and Belgium they tend the graves

and tell the children about the courageous Scottish soldiers who came to save the lives of their forefathers. Where windmills tilt, they are determined that they should never forget those men. Enjoying the glorious good humour of the heroic Ken Rust and watching as he happily propels himself in his wheelchair, I know why I must wear my Flanders poppy on Armistice Day each year, as a symbol of a debt that can never be repaid.

CHAPTER TWENTY

A SPURT OF OIL

Drive down that final sweep from the south into the city of Aberdeen and the glint of grey granite in the morning sunlight confirms that here is one of the most beautiful places on God's earth.

Shielded from a wicked world in its Grampian cocoon, this northern citadel has long maintained a sturdy independence which gave it a distinctive character when so much else of society had slithered down the drain of uniformity. Aberdeen and its agricultural hinterland went their own determined way, riving at a grudging soil, hewing a desirable stone and facing stormy seas to bring home the harvest of the sea. In the process, they moulded their own nature, fashioned their own standards and honed their own dry, biting sense of humour.

But who would have guessed there was oil? All the shrewdness of the Aberdonian became no more than a plaything of fate as she suddenly revealed that a fortune of liquid gold had been lying beneath the offshore doorstop for seventy-five million years or more, leaving the affronted native to call out 'We didna ken, we didna ken'. But they damned well ken noo. If it took foreigners to charm the elusive lubricant from the bowels of the North Sea, the locals were not slow to cotton on to a technology which soon brought them unprecedented wealth.

Millionaires became numerous as Aberdeen floated off on a tide of affluence, heady from the experience and prepared to let the ebb take care of itself.

It is always hard to come to terms with a zenith of history but there is little doubt that, through 1,000 years of Aberdeen, the city reached an all-time peak of experience in that period from the mid-seventies to the mid-eighties, throbbing with a prosperity as the oil capital of Europe which brought no fewer than 50,000 jobs related to that one industry.

But how did it all begin? The historian seeking to pinpoint the first signs of an oil industry in the North Sea would probably find his way to the desk of Ted Strachan, a former colleague of mine on *The Press and Journal* who, when short of a story one day in the sixties, pursued a vague reference to what might possibly lie under the sea bed. And there he produced for his newspaper the very first hint of what could be in store.

Another who remembered the early vibrations was Lord Kirkhill who, as plain John Smith, was a year ahead of me at Robert Gordon's College but was a Labour Lord Provost of the city by the time I talked to him about the coming of oil. He recalled it like this: 'During the sixties I had known geologists who told me there was oil but what they did not know was whether or not its extraction would be commercially viable.'

Big oil companies play their hands close to the chest, but soon there were courtesy knocks on the Lord Provost's door; Shell came to say they had established an office in the old tramcar depot at North Esplanade West; British Petroleum was heading towards a discovery in the Forties Field. Lord Kirkhill's excitement at what was about to break over Aberdeen and the North-East was not shared by all his colleagues on the Town Council, many of whom suffered from Labour's traditional distrust of big business.

'Some felt that big international companies would be in and out for a quick buck, exploiting local people in the process,' said Lord Kirkhill. 'Indeed there are still people in Aberdeen today who don't consider the discovery of oil as of great consequence to the over-all well-being of the city. They think it puts an over-reliance on the relatively easy way of making money and that there will be greater unemployment in the long run. My attitude was to accept the prosperity while it was there; any problem beyond that would be something for our grandchildren to solve. Without doubt this is the most important thing that has happened to our city this century;

just as it was granite last century, it is oil in this one.'

By the first stirrings of that oil industry I had long since left for the south, but I suppose I was a natural choice of Beaver-brook newspapers to go back and report on what I found on my native heath.

I headed first for the Cromarty Firth and the shelter of Nigg Bay, where they were scooping out a dock in which they would build the first gigantic oil platform to be towed out to the Forties Field, off the North-East coast of Scotland. From there I drove along the Moray Firth coast by Elgin, Banff, Fraserburgh and Peterhead to the village of Cruden Bay, a golfing resort once sporting a swanky railway hotel like a lesser Gleneagles, which was served by a branch line from Ellon, on the Buchan route of the London and North-Eastern Railway Company.

It was there we used to picnic on warm summer days and ponder the blood-curdling fact that we were on the same spot where the Irish writer, Bram Stoker, used to come visiting when he was creating his horror tales of Dracula. Now it was oil, not blood, they were planning to suck from the depths of the great North Sea, and farmer Jimmy Cantlay had sold fifty acres of Nether Broadmuir which was earmarked as the gathering point for the oil that would gush ashore from its seabed pipe before starting another remarkable journey to the BP refinery at Grangemouth, 140 miles away.

On one of my early despatches to the *Daily Express* in 1971 I wrote:

The whole vibrating atmosphere of a prosperity just round the corner is there to be absorbed in Aberdeen, whether you are walking down the grey granite splendour of Union Street, breathing in the fishy smell of Market Street, joining in the football enthusiasm of Pittodrie Park or relaxing with a pint in a cocktail bar.

Aberdeen has never been a dull city. But now, apart from its own lively social life, with an abundance of cinemas, dance halls, pub entertainment and concerts, the present week's diversions include the Stanley Baxter Show at His Majesty's and Dickie Henderson's All-Star Show, not to mention the regular draw of the roulette tables at the Blue Chip, the Cheval or the Maverick.

Even before the promise of oil, Aberdeen's unemployment was running at only 3.6 per cent, against the Scottish average of 6.3. As the regional capital, it has always been more of a servicing than an industrial centre, a hub of financial operation which includes an incredible total of nearly two hundred insurance offices. But, with a population of 180,000, it had slipped below Dundee to become the fourth city in Scotland, a situation which will soon be reversed.

As to how long the bonanza will last, Lord Provost John Smith says: 'People guess at all kinds of figures but we are assured by the oil companies that, whatever the final outcome, there is twenty-five or thirty years of production lying out there in the Forties. So we see it as a matter of continuing job opportunity. The marine servicing industry, for example, will play an increasing role with renewal work. Light industry is bound to benefit from what they now call spin-off work. The hotels, restaurants and pubs as well as the whole food and drinks industry will benefit.'

Outside, as the November sunlight catches the grey granite from the spires of Marischal College right uptown to the posh dwellings of Queen's Road and Rubislaw Den, the tangible signs of oil begin to mushroom.

One telling sign was the decision of British European Airways to move the headquarters of its entire helicopter service from Gatwick to Aberdeen Airport because of the volume of work now involved in carrying personnel to and from oil rigs and bases. Around the local folklore names like Fittie and Point Law and up by Old Torry to Girdleness, the wider names like 'Global' and 'Transcontinental' appear on modest shore bases, announcing that the big oil men are here to probe but do not wish to make too much noise about it until they are sure the liquid is gonna gush.

Crowds gather to gaze at the rig-ship in port, while divers

and roughnecks of sundry nationality come and go in a buzz of activity.

Across in Torry you will find a long, lean Texan, name of Calvin Seidensticker, draping himself over a desk and drawling words like 'gee' and 'mighty fine' into a telephone. Actually things are not so fine as they might have been for Mr Seidensticker. As drilling supervisor for Mobil exploration in Aberdeen, he says 'Yeah, I guess you could say we are a little disappointed that we have not so far found oil. It has been costing us £10,000 a day but we are not giving up . . .'

Other companies, like British Petroleum, have found oil all right and it is now mainly a question of how many of the giants strike it lucky enough to make a final decision to go ahead.

Not everyone in Aberdeen wants oil. There are fishermen who fear it will alter the eating habits of the fish as well as provide difficulty for their nets. There are sectional business interests which don't particularly relish the rising demand on harbour accommodation, nor the rising level of wages that an oil bonanza will bring.

But these are minor considerations. Aberdeen is on the march as the centre of a prosperity which will stretch right down the east coast from Orkney to Dundee and beyond.

So there is oil and business and finance and research; there is still a substantial fishing industry as well as papermaking and granite and a vast agricultural hinterland creating its own industrial structure.

Inevitably there are the camp followers, the women whose nose for an opportunity is as sure as their profession is old. Taxi-drivers are already well versed on the habits and the hangouts, whether they be in downtown dockland bars or the more plush surroundings of a West End cocktail bar.

One luscious lady from London was reporting that she was doing business in Aberdeen which surpassed her achievements in the metropolis. And her pad is not in a seamy backstreet but in a swanky Deeside suburb where ladies play golf and bridge and raise teacups with pinky held high. All part of the business of prospecting for prosperity, I suppose, the only difference being that, unlike the ladies of easy virtue, Aberdeen has been sitting primly on a fortune all those years—and didn't know it!

Thus I recorded the growing excitement about oil in the North-East of Scotland in 1971.

CHAPTER TWENTY-ONE

A ROYAL DAY

Away out there in the Forties Field, 110 miles off the Aberdeenshire coast, a vast reservoir of oil lay awaiting the suction pumps of mankind, several miles beneath the bed of the sea and trapped in impervious layers of rock. It lay not in wells of liquid, as one normally imagined, but rather like water to be extracted from a sponge, marine organisms transforming into gas and oil over that unthinkable period of millions of years.

At last the human race was coming to fetch it as a modern fuel to sustain the circus of civilization, with a technology to baffle the most fertile imagination. Mankind would not only have to build those giant platforms (each one with nearly as much steel as the Forth Railway Bridge) and tow them out to an angry reception from the most inhospitable of waters, but it would also be necessary to drill towards the furnaces of hell to a depth which, if taken upwards instead of downwards, would reach the summit of Mont Blanc in the Alps. Then there would be the pipeline covering hundreds of miles along the seabed to find land at Cruden Bay and continue down the subterranean route to Grangemouth.

Those miracles of technology, perhaps the greatest engineering feat in the story of mankind, were duly completed over the four years from my earlier visit to the North-East, and it was for a very special occasion that the *Daily Express* sent me back to Aberdeenshire on Monday, 3 November 1975.

This was my report of an historic day, not only for my native part of Scotland but for the whole British economy:

> What a glorious occasion it was—a Royal occasion, a Scottish occasion, blessed with sunshine and colour and the

atmosphere of a gala celebration. It was the day when Britain became an oil-producing nation.

The presence of Her Majesty the Queen and the Prime Minister (Harold Wilson), his Cabinet colleagues and a thousand invited guests suddenly crystallized the distant myth of North Sea oil into a living reality. Here at the village of Dyce, on the outskirts of Aberdeen, we were witnessing the creation of that chapter of history which will tell our grandchildren of the new industrial revolution.

From all the talk and argument and barrage of statistics it now came clear, even to the least technically minded, that the miracle had worked. The oil was flowing from the silent depths of the North Sea bed, a hundred miles east of Peterhead, ashore to the Scottish coast and south to the BP refinery at Grangemouth, all symbolized by the pressing of a button by the Queen. Here we were, marking a memorable event with one of the biggest sprees ever seen in Scotland, costing British Petroleum somewhere around £700,000. But what was that compared to the £745 million it has already cost the company to bring the oil ashore?

It was all in sharp contrast to the pastoral scene twenty-five miles to the north of this Royal occasion—at Cruden Bay, where the great pipeline comes rising out of the North Sea like a monster from the depths of hell. The oil which had lain there for seventy-five million years or more was being sucked from that sponge-like substance below the seabed of the Forties Field and, as it struck land at Hay Farm, Cruden Bay, there was hardly a hint of this great day in Britain's history. For the pipe goes almost immediately underground, buried in the fields of farmer Geordie Carnie, who has already grown and harvested a crop of oats on the restored soil. Yesterday he went off to plough his stubble field, little aware of the golden wealth which flowed under his feet on its way to the lubrication of the national economy. 'I'll jist ploo awa,' said Geordie. 'I dinna expect the Queen will bother comin oot this wye.'

Significantly perhaps, the pipeline comes ashore in the political constituency of East Aberdeenshire, a Tory stronghold until last year but now part of that North-East shoulder of

Buchan, Banff and the Moray coast which has gone solidly over to Scottish Nationalism. Douglas Henderson, the Nationalist Member for East Aberdeenshire, was at Dyce yesterday declaring to all who would listen that this was a great day for 'Scotland's oil'. Undoubtedly Mr Henderson and the people of his constituency, whose close contact with the activity of oil has sharpened their awareness of the new-found wealth, echo a broader cry across Scotland for a greater say in the running of their own affairs.

Today, however, the oil and the running of Scotland belonged to Westminster, symbolized by the full array of first-team members, making it plain to those who had any doubts about the matter that this was a British occasion.

Mr Wilson was here to greet the Queen and speak about this milestone in Britain's economic history. Mr Callaghan, the Foreign Secretary, and Mr Benn, the Energy Minister, were here and so was Mr Ross, the Scottish Secretary, and his Tory predecessor, Lord Campbell of Croy, the Liberal leader, Jeremy Thorpe, the Nationalist chairman, Willie Wolfe, Shadow Energy Minister Patrick Jenkin, Reginald Maudling and so on.

Aberdeen had never seen a gathering like it. Whoever owns the oil, the main function of this day was to rejoice in the fact that it was flowing in quantities which would soon reach 400,000 barrels per day, a statistic which can be meaningless until you calculate that each barrel carries nearly forty gallons. (This field alone will provide a quarter of Britain's oil needs.)

So we rejoiced in a £48,000 tent which was reminiscent of Bertram Mills Circus, with its dais of radiant red and muted blue, with concealed television sets to show the spectators what they might be missing in the flesh.

Television's Donny B. MacLeod compered the show and jollied the audience into a warm-up session before the Queen arrived.

The Grampian Police pipe band skirled a real Scottish welcome and the regimental band of the Gordon Highlanders, flown home specially from Singapore, were given a heroes' reception in the land where they belong.

Then came the Queen in emerald green, serene and thoughtful, turning to face the audience as they joined in the National Anthem. Prince Philip looked on tenderly and Prince Andrew stood straight as a guardsman. Among those presented to Her Majesty was Mr Matt Linning, the engineer who masterminded the North Sea operation. The Royal Family met other BP workers and walked out among the flag-waving children from local schools before the Queen moved into the main BP operations centre from which the whole flow of oil from the Forties Field is controlled.

There she pressed the button which inaugurated, with ridiculous simplicity, a whole new age for Britain. We awoke from the technological dream and finally accepted the fact that it was all for real. The battle to wrest the liquid gold from the vaults of nature had been won against heavy odds. 'Oil Strike North' was no longer just a series on television; as from this moment, Britain was now an oil-producing country, its citizens the blue-eyed Arabs of North-West Europe.

In the words of Her Majesty, it was a story of excitement and romance. And, as she drove out of the tented arena on her way to the nearby airport, the crowd rose and cheered, waved and rejoiced. The band struck up 'God Save the Queen'. In such a setting of historic splendour, it would have been a hard man who did not have a lump in his throat.

Less than three years later the Queen was back on the Buchan coast, some miles further north, to perform a similar ceremony for the arrival of gas. That took place at the unpretentious village of St Fergus, where nothing very much had ever happened before, though the district gained its name from an early Christian preacher who is said to have wrought miracles in the Buchan area. As far as we know, the creation of gas was not one of them.

CHAPTER TWENTY-TWO

GOLDEN AGE OF ABERDEEN

The modern romance of oil, with all its reputed gains and losses, was not readily discernible on the face of Aberdeen as I returned to the granite canyon of Union Street in the 1980s, seeking proof that extraordinary things had been happening these last ten years.

Exiles like myself could still find the reassurance of familiar landmarks. Robert Burns, as ever pigeon-encrusted, still brooded in Union Terrace while the mighty sword of William Wallace remained poised in a gesture of unjustifiable threat towards the magnificence of His Majesty's Theatre. Floodlit spires still rose like Northern Lights in the deepening melancholy of an evening sky.

The native tongue, as heard in city restaurants, was little different from days gone by, except for an occasional slickness of phrase and the alien ring as it curled round subjects once unheard of: 'Ach, I dinna like praans wi ma avocado!'

But the veneer was so thin you could be tempted to think the North-East was much the same place as it was in my childhood, when we came stumping in from rural Buchan to savour the excitements of city life. I could still re-create the adrenalin of the young boy arriving from our village of Maud to be schooled at Robert Gordon's College.

Bombs may have been falling in the wartime black-out but tramcars still clanked their way up a Union Street bustling with crowds in their utility coats; a scent of coffee still wafted from Collie's delicatessen; and the dreichness of a grey day could soon be forgotten in the celluloid magic of the picture houses.

On this sentimental journey of mine there was still a lingering image of broth and butteries, though no longer an Isaac Benzies in George Street in which to sample them. It was only when you ventured up Albyn Place and Queen's Road that you began to notice those miniature palaces of residence now converted into offices. Great blocks of headquarters proclaiming the names of Conoco, Marathon or Britoil stood on the edge of the old Rubislaw Quarry, that legendary hole in the ground just off Queen's Road, from which the bulk of Aberdeen's grey granite was hewn.

Driving out to Altens or the Bridge of Don you would find industrial estates where once the contented cow would chew her cud. Walking down by the harbour of an evening you marvelled at the floodlit spectacle of ships with names like *Seismic Explorer*, *Cromarty Service*, *Lido Supplier*. Mosey into one of the plush hotels and hairy roustabouts with names like Rick and Chuck were mighty glad to meet you, sir. There too you could be subtly propositioned by that new breed of sophisticate who operated discreetly, in contrast to the old-fashioned Aberdeen whore who plied her trade overtly along the harbour area.

Any suggestion of a red-light district, however, was without foundation, a fact of the oil boom which bewildered a visiting investigative reporter from Fleet Street who refused to believe that a major oil capital could be so lacking in immoral purpose.

Piece by piece, the modern reality of Aberdeen began to dawn. A gnawing sense of having missed out crept over the exile, a feeling of coming home and finding that a stranger has been enjoying too well the hospitality of your house. Not all, of course, were strangers. Charles Skene, who took our wedding photographs as a member of the family which owned Studio Morgan, had long since wearied of arranging bridal groups and had turned instead to property, a major investor with his base in Queen's Gardens, an address at which three of his adjoining properties had a market value of nearly a million pounds. That was typical of what had happened to the housing market in Aberdeen as a result of the inflationary effect of an oil boom. As a young journalist I had stayed in lodgings just off Carden Place, a pleasant enough suburban street but not in the top bracket of residential properties in the city. Yet houses costing £5,000 in 1964 were changing hands for an unthinkable £250,000 by 1984, popular with companies which converted them into offices and were drawn by the spacious front gardens which became valuable as private car-parking spaces.

Inevitably, the housing market created its own problems. Though average wages in Aberdeen were high, the modest artisan was struggling to survive and companies were finding it difficult to recruit from other parts of the country because of the gap between home-selling prices elsewhere and buying prices in Aberdeen.

Businessmen, complaining of high rates, were not all prospering from oil. Retailers were feeling the pinch and even hotels, apparently well cushioned by the block bookings of oil companies, were running into trouble with loan interest. The plush American-style Huntly Hotel and the Victoria (formerly the Douglas, where we used to dance on Saturday nights to Fred Cowie and his orchestra) were among companies to land in the hands of the receiver. By 1986 the rush of bankruptcies and list of unsellable houses had reached alarming proportions, in the wake of falling oil prices—and just as the prophets of doom had forewarned—but long before that, Aberdeen had spawned its own new breed of multi-millionaires, leaping like the salmon of the nearby River Ythan.

From my own village of Maud, young George Simpson, the joiner's son, had moved to Aberdeen to be a draughtsman when oil arrived, deciding to take a mortgage on a flat instead of paying for lodgings. He then saw the prospect of buying for let another flat, and another, self-financing projects which soon turned modest little George into the boss of his own multi-million property company, Kildonan Investments of Queen's Road.

The most dramatic story of all the entrepreneurs, perhaps, belonged to another man in his early forties, Ian Wood, son of a ship-repairing family who turned away from a brilliant academic career to pick up his business heritage and extend it into the age of oil. While most local business people seeking a share of the new prosperity had contented themselves with a servicing role, lucrative enough in itself, Ian Wood joined the big international brigade of people who actually drilled and produced the oil.

The result was an overturn of £90 million, with 2,300 employees and a type of business which could be taken wherever they were drilling around the world, long after the North Sea days were over.

Wood had shown himself to be a young man with the insight of a visionary, anxious to take advantage of the heaven-sent opportunities of oil yet never losing sight of the indigenous industries which would one day be called upon again to provide a living for the North-East of Scotland. He harboured a secret fear that his grandchildren might look upon his generation as the one which took the benefits to themselves and failed to preserve the heritage.

Not everyone made the millions of a Wood or a Simpson or countless others, but there were also more modest stories of enterprise which warmed the heart of the returning exile. I met Denny Morrice and his wife, Margaret, who ran a little newsagent's shop in Thistle Street. Seeking his own crumb of comfort from the oil boom, the jovial Denny went knocking on the doors of big oil companies offering to supply newspapers to the men on the rigs. Happily, they responded to his enterprise and Denny soon found himself heading for the whole-saler's depot at 4 a.m. with a number of assistants, bringing back the papers to the wee shop in Thistle Street and preparing them in bundles to be delivered to the helicopters at Aberdeen Airport. With just a little bit of thought, life had never been so sweet for Denny and Margaret Morrice.

Into the fabric of local life had come whole communities

of itinerant oilmen and their families, to the extent that there were both a French and an American school in Aberdeen. Accustomed to exploring in less civilized surroundings, these people had a history of depending on themselves, which had rather come apart in the North-East of Scotland. Though they still held their own house parties, with bridge a favourite pastime, the Americans had integrated with local life so well that one of their sons became school captain of Robert Gordon's College.

As I wandered on through the back ways I turned into Exchange Street and was faced by an illuminated sign on a pub which proclaimed 'Willie Miller's', a reminder that all was not oil in Aberdeen. Was it indeed a coincidence that the high mark of the city's history had run parallel with a similar peak in the football fortunes, of which the illustrious name of Willie Miller, greatest player and captain in the entire history of Aberdeen Football Club, was a shining symbol?

Blossoming within that period of oil, Aberdeen FC had succeeded in doing what all others had failed to achieve during the whole of the twentieth century, namely breaking the tiresome monopoly of the two Glasgow giants of Scottish football, Rangers and Celtic. The Dons became the dominant force in Scottish football from the late seventies to the mid-eighties, carrying all before them, even to the point of becoming the top team in Europe in 1983, when they not only beat the legendary Real Madrid for the European Cup Winners' Cup, but clinched the honour by beating Hamburg in the final of the European Super Cup.

The late Chris Anderson, that fine innovator of football ideas who played for the club before becoming its vice-chairman, refused to separate that success from the presence of oil. It had given the whole city a new belief in itself, he claimed. Taking a cue from the Americans, local people walked tall as Texans in their new-found confidence.

Side by side with oil and football, I concluded, there had been a curious upswing in cultural fortunes, as if fate were getting its act together. The industrial prosperity had undoubtedly brought a new awareness of North-East Scotland, which had so often been by-passed by the touring public in favour of more rugged wilderness to the west. There were minor matters, like David Puttnam discovering the picturesque hamlet of Pennan, near Fraserburgh, as a location for filming *Local Hero*, starring Burt Lancaster. But even before the focus came fully upon Aberdeen and its hinterland, there was already a pattern of fate developing in tandem with oil.

In that watershed year of 1970 the BBC finally released the distinctive dialect of Aberdeenshire on the nation's network through the televised version of Grassic Gibbon's novels, which were found to be intelligible even in the United States. So there followed the works of Jessie Kesson and James Duthie and suddenly Aberdeen found there was a renaissance of local culture and a new level of acceptance in the outside world, where the life and the speech of the area were now more freely understood .

Within the same period, that rare phenomenon of satirical entertainment, which questions the bravado of 'Scotland the Brave' by calling itself 'Scotland the What?', had spread its fame throughout the world; while that other form of entertainment, television's Jim and George of the BBC's *Beechgrove Garden*, also played its part in focusing attention on an area long regarded as eccentrically apart.

On this pilgrimage to Aberdeenshire I found myself caught up in local festivals of poetry, music and drama, with more youngsters capable of playing a fine tune on the fiddle than could ever have been said of my own day. And if the new recognition needed an international ambassador, it materialized in the form of Annie Lennox, a North-East girl who not only became the world's greatest female Rock star of the eighties but never forgot to come back and see her granny, Mrs Dora Ferguson in Maud!

On reflection, this renaissance of culture may well have sprung from an instinctive fear that alien forces were insidiously at work and that local tradition had better be redefined and preserved before it was too late.

So you could walk down the length of Union Street in the age of oil and sense the pride and prosperity of it all. There were bigger cars, well-stocked shops and plush hotels serving sophisticated dishes where once the Aberdonians would have contented themselves with a plate of stovies or skirlie or mince and tatties.

Grassic Gibbon used to complain of a certain bleakness in the Aberdonian character but his short life was devoted to that early part of this century which included the First World War, the poverty of the twenties and Depression of the early thirties. If only he could have accompanied me on that walk down Union Street in the eighties I think he would have tempered his assessment with elements like confidence and buoyancy, perhaps at times a shade of arrogance.

I concluded this particular part of the pilgrimage with an evening walk and came upon the old Tivoli Theatre in Guild Street, down by the Joint Station, suddenly remembering that I had taken Charlie Chaplin on a nostalgic visit to the Tivoli in 1970 (yes, that watershed year again). By then the boom of burlesque had long since given way to the call of 'Bingo!' but the scent of a bygone day still lingered in doorway signs which said 'Grand Circle' and 'Fauteuils Stalls'. Chaplin had recalled for me vividly his early days when he came to Aberdeen as a boy to clown with Fred Karno. We were already a world away from the baggy pants of a legendary clown but, as we looked back to some good old days, who could have guessed in 1970 that better ones lay ahead? How could we possibly have known that the Golden Age of Aberdeen was lurking round the corner?

CHAPTER TWENTY-THREE

GRANITE CITY GROWL

If Aberdeen was riding on a zenith of historical experience, affluent and vibrant as never before, it was not everyone who took a favourable view of its current state. Indeed there were inevitably criticisms which were valid and which had already been freely voiced.

None of that, however, prepared Aberdonians for the assault which came their way on the morning of 7 August 1983, when those who opened the *Sunday Times* were confronted with an article by the distinguished American writer, Paul Theroux, in which he poured out the most vitriolic verbiage on the subject of Aberdeen. Mr Theroux, who had written in most entertaining fashion about many parts of the world, had been living in London for ten years without ever venturing outwards to Wales or Scotland or even to many parts of England you might have expected him to have visited.

Suddenly he tired of London and set out on a whistle-stop tour of Britain, which would result not just in a series of articles but in a full-scale book, called *The Kingdom by the Sea*, from which the *Sunday Times* was printing extracts. Mr Theroux's declared hate of Aberdeen would have been bad enough in the transience of a morning paper, but to give it a hardback permanence which would be read by an international audience for years to come seemed like a gross injustice to the North-East.

Of course Mr Theroux was entitled to his opinion (our native humour makes us fairly tolerant of those who fail to discern our intrinsic worth), but a writer of his reputation was under some obligation to seek out the other side of the story. That newspaper extract infuriated many people, including myself, and I immediately phoned Frank Giles, editor of the *Sunday Times*, to ask for the right of reply on behalf of my fellow-Aberdonians. That was duly granted, and my article appeared in the *Sunday Times* on the following week, under the headline of 'Granite City Growl'. With the permission of Mr Theroux's agents, I am now quoting that part of *The Kingdom by the Sea* which applied to Aberdeen, followed by the text of my own response. Mr Theroux had travelled from Glasgow up the west coast to Cape Wrath and down to Inverness. From there he came by train to Aberdeen and this, in his own words, is what he found during his fleeting visit:

We reached the coast. Offshore, a four-legged oil-rig looked like a mechanical sea monster defecating in shallow water. It was like a symbol of this part of Scotland. Aberdeen was the most prosperous city on the British coast. It had the healthiest finances, the brightest future, the cleanest buildings, the briskest traders. But that was not the whole of it. I came to hate Aberdeen more than any other place I saw. Yes, yes, the streets were clean; but it was an awful city.

Perhaps it had been made awful and was not naturally that way. It had certainly been affected by the influx of money and foreigners. I guessed that in the face of such an onslaught the Aberdonians had found protection and solace by retreating into the most unbearable Scottish stereotypes. It was only in Aberdeen that I saw kilts and eightsome reels and the sort of tartan tight-fistedness that made me think of the average Aberdonian as a person who would gladly pick a halfpenny out of a dunghill with his teeth.

Most British cities were plagued by unemployed people. Aberdeen was plagued by workers. It made me think that work created more stress in a city than unemployment. At any rate, this sort of work. The oil industry had the peculiar social disadvantage of being almost entirely manned by young single men with no hobbies. The city was swamped with them. They were lonely. They prowled twilit streets in groups, miserably looking for something to do. They were far away from home.

They were like soldiers in a strange place. There was nothing for them to do in Aberdeen but drink. I had the impression that the Aberdonians hated and feared them.

These men had seen worse places. Was there in the whole world an oil-producing country that was easy-going and economical? 'You should see Kuwait,' a welder told me, 'you should see Qatar.' For such a man Aberdeen was civilization. It was better than suffering on an oil-rig a hundred miles offshore. And everyone who had been in the Persian Gulf had presumably learned to do without a red-light district. Apart from drinking and dancing Scottish reels there was not a single healthy vice available in Aberdeen.

It had all the extortionate high prices of a boom town but none of the compensating vulgarity. It was a cold, stony-faced city. It did not even look prosperous. That was some measure of the city's mean spirit—its wealth remained hidden. It looked over-cautious, unwelcoming and smug, and a bit overweight like a rich uncle in dull sensible clothes, smelling of mildew and ledgers, who keeps his wealth in an iron chest in the basement. The windows and doors of Aberdeen were especially solid and unyielding; it was a city of barred windows and burglar alarms, of hasps and padlocks and Scottish nightmares.

The boom town soon discovers that it is possible to make money out of nothing. It was true of the Klondike where, because women were scarce, hags came to regard themselves as great beauties and demanded gold dust for their grunting favours; in Saudi Arabia today a gallon of water costs more than a gallon of motor oil. In Aberdeen it was hotel rooms. The Station Hotel, a dreary place on the dockside road across from the railway station, charged £48 a night for a single room, which was more than its equivalent would have cost at The Plaza in New York City. Most of the other hotels charged between £25 and £35 a night, and the rooms did not have toilets. I went from place to place with a sense of mounting incredulity, for the amazing thing was not the high prices or their sleazy condition but rather the fact that there were no spare rooms.

For £25 I found a hotel room that was like a jail cell, nar-

351

row and dark, with a dim light fifteen feet high on the ceiling. There was no bathroom. The bed was the size of a camp cot. Perhaps if I had just spent three months on an oil rig I would not have noticed how dismal it was. But I had been in other parts of Scotland, where they did things differently, and I knew I was being fleeced.

To cheer myself up I decided to go out of the town. I found a joint called 'Happy Valley'—loud music and screams. I thought: Just the ticket.

But the doorman blocked my path and said, 'Sorry, you can't go in.'

Behind him were jumping people and the occasional splash of breaking glass.

'You've not got a jacket and tie,' he said.

I could not believe this. I looked past him into the pandemonium.

'There's a man in there with no shirt,' I said.

'You'll have to go, mate.'

I suspected that it was my oily hiker's shoes that he really objected to, and I hated him for it.

I said, 'At least I'm wearing a shirt.'

He made a monkey noise and shortened his neck. 'I'm telling you for the last time.'

'Okay, I'm going. I just want to say one thing,' I said, 'You're wearing one of the ugliest neckties I've ever seen in my life.'

Up the street another joint was advertising 'Country and Western Night'. I hurried up the stairs, towards the fiddling.

'Ye canna go in,' the doorman said. 'It's too full.'

'I see people going in,' I said. They were drifting past me.

'And we're closing in a wee munnit.'

I said, 'I don't mind.'

'And you're wearing blue jeans,' he said.

'And you're wearing a wrinkled jacket,' I said. 'And what's that, a gravy stain?'

'Ye canna wear blue jeans here. Regulations.'

'Are you serious? I can't wear blue jeans to an evening of country and western music?'

352

'Ye canna.'

I said, 'How do you know I'm not Willie Nelson?'

He jabbed me hard with his stubby finger and said, 'You're nae Wullie Nullson, now piss off!'

And so I began to think that Aberdeen was not my kind of place. But was it anybody's kind of place? It was fully-employed and tidy and virtuous, but it was just as bad as any of the poverty-stricken places I had seen—worse, really, because it had no excuses. The food was disgusting, the hotels overpriced and indifferent, the spit-and-sawdust pubs were full of drunken and bad-tempered men—well, who wouldn't be bad-tempered? And it was not merely that it was expensive and dull; much worse was its selfishness. Again it was the boom town ego. Nothing else mattered but its municipal affairs. The newspapers ignored the Israeli invasion of Lebanon and the United Nations' initiative on the Falklands and the new Space Shuttle. Instead, their headlines concentrated on the local money-making stuff—the new industries, the North Sea Pipeline about to be laid, the latest oil-rigs. The world hardly existed, but financial news, used cars and property took up seven pages of the daily paper.

The *Aberdeen American*, a fortnightly paper, had the self-conscious gusto of a church newsletter. It was a hotchpotch of news about barbecues, schools, American primary elections and features with an Anglo-American connection. It was a reminder that the American community in Aberdeen was large. The American School had three premises. I heard American voices on the buses. And I was certain that it was the Americans who patronized the new health clubs—weight-loss emporiums and gymnasiums with wall-to-wall carpets. A lovely granite church had been gutted and turned into 'The Nautilus Total Fitness Centre'.

On a quiet street in the western part of the city was The American Foodstore. I went there out of curiosity, wondering what sort of food Americans viewed as essential to their well-being on this savage shore. My findings were: Crisco, Thousand Island Dressing, Skippy Peanut Butter, Cheerios,

Pepperidge Farm Frozen Blueberry Muffins, Bama Brand Grape Jelly, Mama's Frozen Pizza, Swanson's Frozen Turkey TV Dinner, Chef Boyardee Spaghetti Sauce, El Paso Taco Sauce and Vermont Pancake Syrup. I also noted stacks of Charmin Toilet Paper, Budweiser Beer and twenty-five pound bags of Purina Dog Chow.

None of it was good food and it was all vastly inferior to the food obtained locally, which cost less than half as much. But my experience of Aberdeen had shown me that foreigners were treated with suspicion, and it was quite understandable that there was a sense of solidarity to be had from being brand-loyal. Crisco and Skippy were part of being an American—and, in the end, so was Charmin Toilet Paper. I imagined that, to an American in Aberdeen, imported frozen pizza was more than cultural necessity—it was also a form of revenge.

'Isn't there *anything* you like about Aberdeen?' Mr Muir asked imploringly, as we waited on the platform at Guild Street Station for the train to Dundee. I had spent ten minutes enumerating my objections, and I had finished by saying that I never wanted to see another boom town again. What about the Cathedral, the University, the Museum—hadn't I thought the world of them?

'No,' I said.

He looked appalled.

I said, 'But I liked the bakeries. The fresh fish. The cheese.'

'The bakeries,' Mr Muir said sadly.

I did not go on. He thought there was something wrong with me. But what I liked in Aberdeen was what I liked generally in Britain; the bread, the fish, the cheese, the flower gardens, the apples, the clouds, the newspapers, the beer, the woollen cloth, the radio programmes, the parks, the Indian restaurants and amateur dramatics, the postal service, the fresh vegetables, the trains, and the modesty and truthfulness of people. And I liked the way Aberdeen's streets were frequently full of seagulls.

Under that heading of 'Granite City Growl', the *Sunday Times* carried my reply, as follows, in the following week's edition:

Whatever it lacked in Christian charity, if Paul Theroux's Epistle to the Aberdonians had been no more than the provocative prose of a passing journalist, it might have been dismissed for its transparent shallowness. But Mr Theroux has presumed to write a permanent record, which will spread across the world an impression of Aberdeen and Aberdonians which does, at the very least, beg correction.

An 'awful city' which he came to hate? Stony-faced, smug and unwelcoming and not even offering the compensation of vulgarity? Dear dear.

There is, of course, a strong element of impertinence in passing through a strange place, snatching at a few random experiences and coming up with a snap judgement which some might mistake for responsible study.

Let me give you another side of Aberdeen, through the eyes of someone who has regularly returned to his native corner of Aberdeenshire to conclude that the Granite City remains one of the truly civilized cities in the world.

Imperfections? No city which becomes the oil capital of Europe can escape the scars of prosperity. Where there's oil there tends to be a veneer of vulgarity, loud bar talk from a set of roustabouts more intent upon cocktail chrome and hovering whore than local culture.

And culture is there in abundance. Aberdeen, city of fish and flowers and good humour, is currently on an upswing of local writing and music, not to boast about its art gallery, concerts and theatre which Mr Theroux failed miserably to unearth. For those who insist on pursuing the sweaty disco, an encounter with a clutch of Kentucky dudes should come as no surprise.

Seek further, Mr Theroux, and you will find an Aberdeen inextricably bound up with its rural hinterland, a race of those same honest, hard-working and independent folk who so impressed you on the wilds of Cape Wrath.

While sheep and resignation continued to rule in the bare-

355

ness of the Highlands, the Aberdonians got down to transforming a sour and grudging soil into a land of high production, turning out the best of British beef, with oats to make the porridge and barley to fill the whisky vats.

A dozen generations have bent their backs in an agricultural conversion which ranks with the greatest achievements of mankind. Such drudgery in an inhospitable climate may have left them short of time to develop superficial courtesies but it brought them many a useful trait instead.

In a Grampian cocoon they move with the gait of their beloved Clydesdales, slow to impress or flatter yet sure and loyal when friendship has been earned. Clearly Mr Theroux did not linger long enough to find out.

He could have learned too about their dry, piercing humour, expressed with an economy of words and typified in the tale of the English commercial traveller, arriving early for his train and placing his umbrella and briefcase on a seat before retiring to the buffet.

When he returned the carriage was filled with ruddy Aberdeenshire farmers going home from market and deeply engrossed in their short-stemmed pipes. 'Excuse me, gentlemen,' said the traveller, 'but when one puts one's umbrella and briefcase on a seat it rather indicates that one has reserved that seat . . . at least in the part of the world where I come from.'

Whereupon one rosy farmer piped up: 'Ah weel, my mannie, in this pairt o' the world, it's erses that coont!'

Here then, Mr Theroux, is no sunny California of swimming pools and nasal brats with too much money and too little discipline. But need we apologize for it? Here is a breed of worthwhile men and women, the like of whom you will find in your own American land, in places like North Dakota, where I have downed a soothing dram with toothless cowboys who still conclude big cattle deals by the old Scots custom of slapping the hand, declaring that a man's word is his bond.

Such men had never been in New York or Los Angeles and were appalled that I might judge their great country by the human assortment I might find there. To those fine American people, these cities seemed like the most God-awful holes in

Christendom. I wouldn't have gone that far, not even about the soulless wastes of Detroit which, now that Mr Theroux tempts me, might well lay claim to some of his extravagances about Aberdeen.

There is one final treat I would have reserved for Mr Theroux had I been able to steer him around this northern citadel. In Britain's first all-seated, all-covered stadium, he could have sampled the delights of a football team, new champions of Europe, whose skills might have stirred his aesthetic instincts.

These are not, of course, your great lumbering hulks with padded shoulders and steel helmets where their heads ought to be, but men of balletic artistry.

If such delicacies were not too far removed from the din of disco Mr Theroux would surely, given time, have begun to understand the subtlety of it all.

CHAPTER TWENTY-FOUR

THE AULD HOOSE

On a winter's day not so long ago I drove, from the south, through a snowstorm which would certainly make me late for a very important dinner at the New Marcliffe Hotel in Aberdeen. In treacherous road conditions, vehicles were being abandoned by the roadside and the car radio was bringing me police reports of no fewer than fifty accidents in the stretch between Glasgow and Stirling, a situation which filled me with anxiety.

Good manners dictated that I should arrive on time for this auspicious occasion, all the more so since the Gordonian Association, the former pupils of Robert Gordon's College, had invited me to be their Guest of Honour and principal speaker: Gordonian of the Year, 1986! What would they have called me in 1946? The irony of the situation helped to divert me from the chaos of the road conditions. For was it not exactly forty years ago that I had walked out through the vaulted gateway of Gordon's College in Schoolhill, Aberdeen, with the tears of remorse streaming down my cheeks, the ring of failure resounding in my ears? Would Gordonians now recognize the pale-faced lad of fourteen, nervously going home to face an irate father in Maud with nothing much more to show for three years of academic misadventure than the certificate of a shattered confidence?

In retrospect, it seemed far too tender an age for any human being to be set on the motorway of life in such a state of depression. Yet too many good things had happened since then to leave any balance of bitterness.

Despite serious illness, which followed very soon, I had recovered in time to carve a reasonable niche of my own and there was still room in my heart for a reservoir of good feeling about the Auld Hoose. The beginnings had been quite promising. On the May morning of that entrance examination in 1943, as I arrived from Maud with the odd straw sticking out of my lugs, a smart young city lad came forward on the steps of the MacRobert Hall and offered to relieve my mother of the burden. He would see that I was all right. That was the start of a friendship with Stanley Shivas, as suave and debonair at eleven as he was later to be known in his role as a distinguished journalist, indulging himself in the casinos and caverns of nocturnal opulence, in the service of those who read the *Daily Record*.

In his longing to peer beyond the drystane dykes of Buchan, the shy loon from Maud had regarded a glimpse of the swimming pool at Tarlair or the boating pond at the Cooper Park in Elgin as symbols of a more glamorous world outby. Now he was joining the throng in the big city of Aberdeen which, though essentially an agricultural market town with an odour of fish, seemed to the innocent mind to have all the deliciously wicked trappings of a cosmopolitan centre.

As I settled into digs with Miss Stott at 14 Elm Place, I was vaguely conscious that this majestic city of grey eminence had already wound itself into the fabric of my emotional being. Was it not here, at Kittybrewster, that my father would unload us from our little Austin motor on Friday mart days, during the school holidays, to join a tram-car down George Street towards 'The Queen' at Union Street?

That excitement of a day in town would be rounded off with an hour in the Astoria Cinema before returning to the car-park at the mart, where the withered gypsy face of Madame Veitch, in her caravan by the corner, stirred the trembles of mystery in the child breast.

Was it not here, in the faded pink of a June evening in 1940, that I stood on the beach esplanade and gazed with a queer mixture of emotion towards the south where, for the purposes of my imagination at least, a distant rumbling brought eerie echoes of the Dunkirk evacuation and filled me with a sense of narrowly missing out on the action of history? We had just had a happy day attending my Aunt Betty's wedding in the Palace Hotel and rounding off the occasion with a visit to Harry Gordon's show at his famous Beach Pavilion on the promenade.

Then we drove home the twenty-eight miles to Maud, out by the double-road at Bridge of Don and on to Balmedie, Ellon and Auchnagatt, back to an uneasy co-existence with 200 evacuee children from the Dowanhill and Hyndland Schools of Glasgow, with whom we would plod to Maud School, complete with gas-masks over our shoulders, and find excitement in the periodic air-raid drills when we would dash home in response to the dominie's whistle. The dominie was Donald Murray, who had come to Maud School in 1937, having been headmaster at Skene, where he made such an impression on an orphan child called Jessie Kesson that she later dedicated to him her memorable book *The White Bird Passes*, with that quotation from R. L. Stevenson:

> Bright is the ring of words
> When the right man rings them
> And the maid remembers

Donald Murray, who used to regale us with great tales of meeting Lord Baden-Powell when a young Boy Scout, conducted the kind of local school which made Scotland famous for its education; yet the exquisite nature of my seven years there did not reveal itself until much later. How strange it is to look back on childhood and find that the actual number of years involved seem far too few to embrace the wealth of compacted experience which lingers with you for the rest of your life. Either time has played a clever trick, or the child mind, in its response to new experience, has absorbed and lent importance to an inordinate amount of detail.

Whatever the case, in the midst of that war to end all wars I was moving to Aberdeen, where the emergency was heightened by the existence of an air-raid shelter in Elm Place, into which we all crowded one fearful night when the German bombers came bumbling over like angry bees. There were air-raid shelters, too, in the fore-lawns of Gordon's College, bringing overtones of twentieth-century warfare to the very place where Butcher Cumberland stationed his troops on the way north to Culloden and again on his victorious way home.

His plundering soldiers were billeted right there in the main building of the school, in those ancient rooms up well-worn stairs, where people like Long Tom made brave attempts to teach us mathematics. When that lofty gentleman lost his temper and brought down the leather strap from a great height, you could have sworn that some of Cumberland's aggression had affected him.

Long Tom came to school on a double-barred bicycle, upon which he balanced in a most precarious fashion, and it was the special joy of pupils to greet him with the obligatory salute and to watch as he tried to return the courtesy while wobbling with only one hand on the handlebars.

Boys were always boys, sometimes to cruel effect, as in the case of another teacher of mathematics, known as Knockers, a kindly and sensitive man who had been shell-shocked in the First World War as I remember, and who could be goaded into a frothing fury when boys would blockade his room or pay an organ-grinder to play in the lane beneath his classroom window. The poor man collapsed and died in the staff-room on the first morning of the new session, 1945-6, perhaps unable to face another year of torment and leaving many a Gordonian with a hint of conscience about his part in the destruction of a fine human being.

So there was an array of notable personalities on the teaching staff of Gordon's College, saddled with such names as Fat Bill, Hooter, Frosty, Pudner, Johnny Mac and Greasy Bob. Many of the able-bodied were away to war, which increased the scope for women, some of whom had been there since the similar emergency of the First World War. With a warm irreverence we called them Moosie, Squeezy, Bunty and Skinny Liz, spinster ladies of a lost generation, dedicated teachers who epitomized that fondness for sound education which gave the North-East of Scotland the highest adult literacy rate in all Britain during Victorian times.

To a wide-eyed innocent from the country, however, that road to literacy stood little chance against the bright lights which beckoned from every corner. For educational purposes we had been taken to hear Sir John Barbirolli and the Hallé Orchestra at the Music Hall and to see Shakespearians like Donald Wolfit playing Shylock in *The Merchant of Venice*. I had already had the privilege of hearing the incomparable Richard Tauber at His Majesty's, that gem of theatrical creation designed by Frank Matcham in 1906, during the reign of King Edward VII, and would later revel in the peerless repertory of the Wilson Barrett Company and the Whatmore Players. They brought every notable performer of the day, from Stewart Granger (earning £10 a week, I have discovered) to Michael Denison and his wife, Dulcie Gray, alternating with grand opera, ballet, pantomime and the summer seasons of every Scots comedian from Dave Willis to Rikki Fulton.

At the matinee performances in His Majesty's I used to be intrigued by the fact that you could be served with afternoon tea, brought to your seat if you were in the Orchestra Stalls, the Parterre Stalls or Dress Circle. After that, I have discovered, Jimmy Donald ran short of cups! I was just as likely, however, to be found in the less salubrious setting of the Tivoli Theatre in Guild Street, where vaudeville survived and you were liable to be entertained by a mixture of trick cyclists, bawdy comics, dancing girls in fish-net stockings and a boy soprano who went on for so many years and became so broad in the hips that dark rumour suggested he might well be a soprano but had never been a real boy!

On light evenings I would be found at Linksfield Stadium, just off King Street, supporting the St Clement's football team which included a dashing right-winger called Martin Buchan, who would later father a son of the same name to captain both Aberdeen and Manchester United in the respective Cup Finals of Scotland and England, the only footballer ever to do so.

After school on a Friday I would buy my *Evening Express* from Patsy Gallacher at the corner of Union Street and Union Terrace and head down Bridge Street towards the Joint Station, past the site of the Palace Hotel, which had been burned down in 1941, the year after we had attended my aunt's wedding.

Back home in Maud at weekends I would play the drums in my Uncle Gavin's dance band for ten shillings a night, touring the village halls and having my eyes opened by an adult world where men away at war were sometimes replaced in their wives' affections by passing soldiers. The child mind was quick to sense the liaisons, even as I caressed the brushes round my little drum to the beat of our signature tune, which was 'All the World is Waiting for the Sunrise', symbolizing perhaps our yearning for a youth now sadly stunted by Hitler's holocaust. When that monster finally perished in his Berlin bunker we lit the bonfires of Victory-in-Europe Night, 8 May 1945, and waited for the sunrise of a brave new world. Somehow it was all too late for the flowering of a proper teenage, and the world we saw, when the lights went up again, stood poor comparison with the childhood memory of the 1930s.

Despite its Depression, that earlier decade still beckoned like a golden glow as it filtered through the hideous ruins of the Second World War and came to torment us on the other side. Winston Churchill, architect of victory, came driving up Union Street in an open car that April day of 1946 to receive the acclaim of an electorate which had already, paradoxically, consigned him to the Opposition benches. That seemed to me like foul ingratitude as I ran alongside his car and reached out to touch him, with cries of 'Good old Winnie!' In the same week I was innocently making my stage début on the boards of that same MacRobert Hall where I had sat the entrance examination, now playing a minor role in *The Auld Hoose*, the story of Robert Gordon and his college.

I still have the programme, which shows that I was engaged in a scene with a certain contemporary called William D. Hardie, taking his own first steps towards fame on the stage under the name of Buff Hardie, a contraction of his childhood nickname which was 'Buffalo Bill'. A brilliant student, Buff not only went on to mastermind the student shows at Aberdeen University but gained a scholarship to Cambridge in those satirical days when Jonathan Miller had just gone and Peter Cook was soon to arrive. Returning to Aberdeen, where he later became Secretary of the Grampian Health Board, he teamed up with two other student performers, Stephen Robertson, who had become a city solicitor, and George Donald from Huntly, a schoolmaster who was to become deputy headmaster of Perth Academy. Performing through the 1960s, they decided to devote more time to their young families and planned a farewell appearance at the Edinburgh Festival of 1969.

There they were seen by Neville Garden, then a colleague of mine on the *Scottish Daily Express* (he was related to the famous Aberdeen opera singer, Mary Garden), who wrote that this was the funniest show at the festival. The crowds flocked in and, instead of a farewell, those three Aberdonians who called themselves 'Scotland the What?' found that their career was just beginning. By public demand they extended their appearances from Aberdeen as far as London's West End and from stage shows to records and cassettes. Their name became legendary in a role which could be described as a modern satirical extension of the mood portrayed by the great Aberdeen comedian Harry Gordon, with a humour rooted every bit as firmly in their native culture. By the 1980s, in the prime of middle age, they gave up their secure and well-paid careers to cast themselves into the more precarious but also more lucrative realm of full-time show business, three delightfully natural and humorous men whose friendship I have long enjoyed.

So these were some of the thoughts which occupied my

mind as I ploughed through a snowstorm on the way to the Gordonian dinner in Aberdeen. Fortunately the weather improved the further north I drove and the company was just finishing its meal when I breezed breathlessly in to snatch at the main course before facing the most important audience of my life.

Just twenty-four hours earlier I had seen my Honeyneuk film beaten on a casting vote for the Special Programme prize at the Television Awards and now, in rather inauspicious circumstances, I was gathering my thoughts and trying to unjangle the nerves for a speech which needed to go some way towards disproving the events of forty years earlier. After a eulogy from the distinguished psychiatrist, Dr Robert Davidson of Glasgow, I rose to respond. Burdened with a stammer, I could never claim public speaking as one of my strengths but there are moments in life when the Lord comes suddenly on your side. After the turmoil of a troubled day, anxiety drained miraculously out of my system and I spoke for twenty-five minutes without a written note or a moment of hesitation. I knew what I wanted to say and said it. By my own mediocre standards, it was by far the best speech I have ever made. The Auld Hoose, which had despatched me from its vaulted gateway with a heavy heart in 1946, had welcomed me back into the fold, the academic failure now acclaimed for whatever he had made of himself.

It was a night of revelry extending from hotel to the Queen's Road home of the president, Ian Edward, where I rounded off a rather important occasion in my life with a company which included those good friends, Steve Robertson and the same Buff Hardie with whom I had shared that theatrical stage oh so many years ago.

CHAPTER TWENTY-FIVE

THE QUEEN AND JOHN BROWN

Deeside looked just as serene and beautiful as Queen Victoria always said it did when I drove westward to Braemar and Glenshee beyond. Indeed the old Queen herself was much in my thoughts as the spectacle of her beloved Aberdeenshire home came closer, mile by mile, and the intriguing question of her association with John Brown, the Balmoral manservant, began to engage my mind.

It was a perfect springtime day on which to follow the silver thread of the river as it wove its picturesque pattern through a valley of rich foliage. At Dinnet, just forty miles from Aberdeen, a granite slab was telling me that I was 'now in the Highlands', which seemed to me like a bit of a liberty. I can never imagine my native county as having much in common with the Highlands since Aberdeen itself is such a lowland city in character and outlook. Surely there is more to the Highlands than high lands. It is a whole separate culture and language, stretching down the western half of Scotland as far as Glasgow and Argyll and quite distinctly different from the North-East corner. Soon I had reached Ballater, where Dark Lochnagar frowned down disapprovingly from its lofty perch, white-capped and haloed in a ring of spring cloud.

So I sped on past Balmoral and drew in for lunch at the Inver Hotel, where Jack Crawford was dispensing beer with bonhomie and his wife, Frances, cooked Sunday lunches in the heat of the kitchen.

While her skill in the creation of a steak pie delighted my palate, it was her other claim to fame which occupied our discussion. When Jack took over the burned-out shell of the old Inver Inn and set about reconstructing it in the seventies,

Frances opened up in business as a hairdresser to eke out the family living. With an old shed at the back as her salon, there was nothing more basic to be found in all the land, nothing further removed from the high coiffure of London fashion. Imagine, then, the surprise when the telephone rang one day with a call from Miss MacDonald, a lady-in-waiting to the Queen. She was calling with a royal request: that Mrs Crawford should come to Balmoral to do the Queen's hair! Once she had recovered from disbelief, the homely Mrs Crawford left the confines of her portable shed and drove across the River Dee to the majesty of Balmoral Castle en route to her first royal appointment.

'On that first occasion I was so nervous that, when I came back, I could only remember seeing the figure of the Queen,' she told me. 'I could not have told you what was in the room or anything else I saw.'

But the result of her efforts must have been just fine because Frances Crawford has since become Her Majesty's regular hairdresser when she comes north. Promptly at 3.45 on a Wednesday, a chauffeur picks her up and drives her the three miles to Balmoral where she enwraps Her Majesty in a gown like any other customer in a salon, tilts the head of the Head of State over the basin and gives her a good old wash-and-set.

'I am still nervous on the first visit each year,' Frances told me, 'but the Queen soon puts me at ease and after that I really look forward to the weekly visit. I wait for Her Majesty to lead the conversation. When Princess Grace of Monaco was killed, for example, she spoke about the tragedy and I could see that she knew her very well and was most upset about it.'

On another tragic day, Frances was present when the Queen opened up to her on the assassination of Lord Mountbatten, on whom she laid such store. Far away from the uncertainties of London, the Queen is very much at home with the folks of Deeside, who are the solid, dependable salt of the earth so beloved by Queen Victoria.

'She knows all that is going on in the district,' said Frances

Crawford whose father was a blacksmith on Deeside, called in on occasion to shoe the horses at Balmoral. 'When my husband was rebuilding the hotel from a burned-out shell, she knew all about it. On the day of Braemar Gathering last year I was outside with a coachload of people who had been having their afternoon tea here, when the Royal car came past on the way to the Gathering. The Queen spotted me and waved, much to the delight of the day trippers. I feel I know her better now and she seems more relaxed with me. We are invited to the annual Ghillies Ball and what a lovely atmosphere there is in the ballroom, with Charles and Di there and the Queen Mother dancing away as usual.'

Jack and Frances Crawford have recently left the Inver but have remained in Crathie, from which the royal hair appointment is still kept every Wednesday.

As I was saying, the mystery of Queen Victoria's connection with John Brown had been occupying my mind on that Deeside adventure, heightened by an evening I once spent with Elizabeth Byrd, the American authoress who based herself in Edinburgh and was so fascinated by the subject that she wrote a historical novel about it.

In Victoria's own day, the magazines went as far as to report (quite daringly for the period) that the Queen and her manservant were secretly married and that she had gone abroad to have Brown's baby. The reports were nonsense but Victoria's own reaction to the baby story was merely to laugh. To say the least of it, she was indiscreet in her connection with John Brown and, according to Elizabeth Byrd, she was almost certainly in love with him.

John Brown's father was schoolmaster at Crathie, near Balmoral, and the basic facts of the story are that the teenage Brown, who was eight years younger than the Queen, was a stableman at Balmoral, even before Victoria bought it. He became a ghillie and a great favourite of Prince Albert, who asked him to lead the Queen's pony when they went on their safaris into the hills. John Brown was a tall, good-looking man with red beard and hypnotic eyes, according to all reports, and Victoria herself became very fond of him.

But there was nothing untoward in their relationship until after Albert's death in 1861, when the Queen was in her early forties. She then appointed him her personal attendant, on constant call, and gradually their association became much more intimate, according to Miss Byrd. The evidence apparently is that, when the Queen went to pieces and began the long mourning, John Brown had to lift her from couch to bed and back again; he was in and out of her room without knocking and could sit down in her presence and smoke and even drink if he liked—and he did. He was a heavy drinker and taught the Queen to drink whisky.

John Brown seems to have accompanied Queen Victoria everywhere, including tours abroad, becoming devoted and protecting her from all that bored her, including her own family and the Prime Minister of the day, William Ewart Gladstone, whom she never liked. There was an evening at Balmoral when Brown, who was honest, sincere but very blunt, was standing behind the Queen at dinner as Gladstone was going on and on about something. He could see clearly that she was bored and that some action had to be taken, so he tapped the Prime Minister on the shoulder and said sternly 'That's enough, that's enough!' The great Gladstone had to shut up.

This is how Miss Byrd answered my question about the actual evidence of Queen Victoria's love for John Brown:

When a woman loves a man, she cannot stop talking about him. And Victoria talked a great deal about him in her leaves. When Brown died at Windsor in 1883, at the age of fifty-six, nobody could bring himself to tell her. The shock paralysed her legs and for days she would not see anyone or put her signature to anything.

She even wanted to write a biography of John Brown but was finally dissuaded by the Dean of Windsor. She also wanted to publish his diaries but was persuaded to have them destroyed.

Whether or not the affair was sexually consummated is likely to remain a mystery for ever. Though Victoria was prim, pious and prudish in some respects she was also regarded as a very passionate woman sexually and is said to have worn out poor Albert, who did not exactly relish his role as royal stud.

No love was lost between Brown and Victoria's son Bertie, later to be King Edward VII. In fact the future king loathed the servant's bluntness. One day, it is said, he came into Balmoral demanding to see his mother but Brown told him she was having her nap. When the Prince insisted, he was told in no uncertain manner what to do with himself!

After Victoria's death, he destroyed almost every statue and cairn the Queen had raised for Brown but did not dare tamper with the loving inscription which she had placed on his gravestone at Crathie churchyard. It spoke of 'that friend on whose fidelity you count, that friend given you by circumstances over which you have no control. This stone is erected in affectionate and grateful remembrance of John Brown, the devoted, faithful personal attendant of Queen Victoria, in whose service he has been for 34 years . . . enter thou into the joy of thy Lord.'

There is also a statue to Brown within the grounds of Balmoral Castle, lauding him as friend more than servant, loyal and brave. He was born at Crathie on 8 December 1826 and died at Windsor on 27 March 1883.

From the widespread researches of Elizabeth Byrd Victoria seemed to emerge as more of a red-blooded being than her stony portraits suggest. She used to appal titled ladies by encouraging the tradition of the ghillies ball at Balmoral, where they had to dance with 'uncouth, sweaty, drunken servants'.

It is perhaps a measure of the lady who reigned for those sixty glorious years that such earthy experience did nothing to blunt the feminine appetites which evidently burned so fiercely beneath those skirted folds.

CHAPTER TWENTY-SIX

THE MIGHTY MONTY

That old winding gramophone which skraiched in protest under the heavy metal of a muscular arm and needed a new needle for every record was our symbol of modern entertainment before the Second World War.

You could go to the pictures at Peterhead or tune into the wireless, which were other novelties of that decade, but there was a special excitement about hauling out the heavy box from under the bed, setting it upon the kitchen table and cranking it up in anticipation of the first selection. With the sentimentalist's weakness for hoarding, I still have many of those old records which spun round at seventy-eight revolutions per minute under the Beltona label and cost half-a-crown, which translates into twelve-and-a-half pence in modern language, a greater proportion of a wage-packet in the thirties than a long-player would cost today; and you were getting only seven or eight minutes for your money.

The records we turned out in those innocent days had titles like 'Red Sails in the Sunset', Will Fyffe's 'I Belong to Glasgow' and 'I'm 94 Today', as well as our own Harry Gordon's popular songs of the time, 'Hilly's Man', 'I Wish I were Single Again' and 'The Auldest Aiberdonian'. But the mixture also included melodies like 'Trees', played by Henry Hall and his Gleneagles Hotel Band, 'Ave Maria' by John McCormack, 'O sole mio' by Enrico Caruso and 'Drink to Me Only' by Lawrence Tibbett.

While the essential Scottishness of our existence seemed stronger before the war than ever it did afterwards, the music of the time was not given over exclusively to bothy ballads and old Scots songs. The wireless and cinema had made their mark, bringing in the Charleston of the flapper era and the syncopated rhythms of the thirties which fascinated me immensely. To discover the occasional Lew Stone record among the antiquity of our household collection was always a delight which sent me on my first faltering steps of ballroom dancing.

One of the highlights of those childhood days in Maud was the weekly visit of a continental dancing teacher who lived in Aberdeen, Marguerite Feltges by name, who taught us eurhythmics and introduced us to the modern waltz. Whatever rhythms eluded me in my speech were made good in the body and Miss Feltges wanted to take me under her wing for some professional training. But the rural distance of Maud was not the ideal location for budding Fred Astaires. Browsing through that record collection, I find the changing mood of the times reflected in the appearance of Benny Goodman with 'Lady Be Good', Glenn Miller with 'In the Mood' and Joe Loss with 'Perfidia'.

With the Second World War behind us, it is interesting to see what a teenager of the late forties and early fifties was gathering in his record collection, as the popular tunes of the day, before the blast of Rock 'n' Roll and subsequent events came to change the face of contemporary music, not to mention the pattern of human behaviour itself.

Far from adhering to the uniformity and slavish dictates of puppeteers in London, my collection ranged from the orchestras of Harry Roy and André Kostelanetz, Cyril Stapleton and Victor Sylvester to the solo arpeggios of the incomparable Freddie Gardiner and his mellow saxophone and the warmth of Steve Conway's crooning. In covers marked 'Jack Webster, 2 Park Crescent, Maud, 25th September, 1947', I still have 'J'attendrai' sung by Tino Rossi, 'La Ronde' by Anton Wallbrook, 'A Beggar in Love' by Guy Mitchell, followed by 'Island in the Sun' from Harry Belafonte and 'In a Shady Nook' by Donald Peers. In the affections of an Aberdeenshire teenager in that post-war period, however, there was also room for a full range of music from Ivor Novello, George Gershwin, Richard Rodgers and singers like Richard Tauber. Heaven preserve us, there was even a place for the tenor tones of Jimmy Young.

Just as our musical horizons had expanded, there was an increasing movement of people, not that the Scots were ever lacking in enterprise when it came to turning up in distant parts. Two of my father's aunts, Sophie and Babs Watson, had been typical of the young Scots girls who went south at the turn of the century to provide the service of the aristocratic households of England. With a high standard of expectation ingrained in their very nature, they served as cooks to people like Admiral Beatty, hero of the Battle of Jutland in 1916, and the Cayzer shipping family, in stately homes where the guests would include King Edward VII.

Sophie would come home to Buchan to tell us great tales of her service in the London home of a prominent Egyptian, whose handsome young son was completing his English education by chasing maids around the house. That apprenticeship in hedonism was later to produce a bloated monarch affectionately remembered by dear old Sophie as the young King Farouk of Egypt. Good advice from influential employers enabled these thrifty Scots lasses to invest their wages in valuable stocks, and long before they retired, Sophie and Babs had established a home in Stanmore, Middlesex, to which they could repair in their time off. That home, in which those truly gentle spinster ladies eventually settled, also became my London base when I first went south to explore the excitements of the metropolis, laden with butter and cheese and oatcakes and anything my mother could produce to remind them of home.

On at least one occasion during those visits the dutiful grand-nephew would take the ladies to the West End to see an Ivor Novello musical, and there they would recall bygone days in the theatreland of London, giving me a fine sense of the atmosphere in Edwardian times.

In 1949 I was merely passing through London en route to Paris for the first time, boarding the express for Newhaven and Dieppe and savouring a flavour of the French capital which still lingered from pre-war days. It was not so long ago that jack-booted Nazis had goose-stepped down this same Champs Elysées but now the lights were bright once more, the Folies Bergère was restored to former glory, with Josephine Baker to entertain, the Lido had opened up again and Montmartre was beckoning with all the lurid promise of a naughty madame.

Four years later I was back in Paris, this time en route to the Balkans with my journalist friend John Lodge, from *The Press and Journal* in Aberdeen, with whom I was to explore the Communist state of Yugoslavia. We joined the Orient Express at 8.30 on a Saturday night and arrived in Belgrade at the dawn of Monday, cold and hungry and miserable, without a word of the language in a country which was not then geared for tourism. Soon we fled over the Dinaric Alps to the greater warmth of Dubrovnik which, in 1953, did not even have an airport. The old Pionair plane came bumping down on a grazing field where cattle and horses were programmed to scatter for the daily arrival.

In his more liberal way, President Tito had permitted a measure of private enterprise and around the arrival shed women pushed forward young daughters as bait if only we would come to lodge in their homes. In that rather pathetic scene we found a distinguished gent who spoke English and turned out to be the boss of telephones in Dubrovnik. Back at his council house his wife, Dusanka, proved to be an equally distinguished looking lady, a pre-war friend of the king who now found herself in the more straitened circumstances of a Communist regime. In that year of Queen Elizabeth's Coronation, Dubrovnik was not yet a holiday resort for overseas visitors so we explored the ancient, walled city and the modern spread beyond and suddenly found ourselves intrigued by a villa which stood aloof, its lawns sloping down in terraced steps to the waters of the Adriatic below.

'It's the Villa Sheherazade,' they told us, 'where President Tito entertains his foreign guests. Princess Margaret comes there but your war hero . . . Field Marshal Montgomery, yes? . . . he stays there at present.'

The instinct of two keen young journalists led them to the heavy gates of Villa Sheherazade where we negotiated with an armed guard and left a rather presumptuous request for an interview with Field Marshal Montgomery of Alamein. He would hand it in and deliver the reply if we presented ourselves at his guard-room at 6 o'clock that evening. The tones were perfunctory and far from encouraging.

However, we duly presented ourselves at 6 p.m. for the anticipated rebuff. Instead, the gates of Sheherazade swung open and a military guard ordered us to march this way, down through terraced gardens and trees and fairy-lights and across the lawn to a table in front of the villa. A small figure rose to greet us: 'What can I do for you, gentlemen?'

It was the unmistakable figure of Monty, sitting out in the warm, balmy September evening. We explained our mission and he invited us to join him at the table. Remembering his own teetotal habits, we hesitated over an offer of drinks till he saved us the bother and called for two glasses of vermouth. A man in dark suit arrived with silver tray and handsome glasses and placed them before us. We acknowledged him momentarily; but the 'waiter' who had obeyed Montgomery's instruction then pulled up his chair to join us—and turned out to be none other than M. Popovic, the Yugoslav Foreign Minister!

We may have imagined we were there to interview Montgomery but he used the occasion to question us about our own experiences which lay outwith his own itinerary. How were the people in their own homes? What was the state of the agriculture?

We talked about Alamein and his contacts with Churchill. ('Last weekend, when I was visiting Winston, he was telling me what he was backing in the St Leger.')

John Lodge and I were then the employees of Lord Kemsley, who owned the vast newspaper empire later to be acquired by Lord Thomson of Fleet, stretching all the way from London to Aberdeen, where Kemsley's daughter married the Marquis of

Huntly. As the lights glistened from the trees above on a cascade of waterfalls, Monty showed us out and left us with a parting message: 'Do tell my friend, Lord Kemsley, that I was passing on my regards.'

Did he really mean it? Was it just the kind of thing people say? Lord Kemsley was well beyond the orbit of a couple of juniors but we decided to take no chances. Back in Aberdeen, we rather sheepishly sent him a message with the Field Marshal's regards. A few days later another message arrived on Lord Kemsley's desk. It was a letter which said:

My Dear Kemsley,

I was in Yugoslavia recently, as you may have seen, and while there I met two young men from the Aberdeen Press of your group, John Lodge and Jack Webster. They asked if they could come and see me and they came to my villa that evening.

I thought they were both extremely nice young men, very courteous and interested in everything. They told me all about their experiences and they had, without doubt, displayed great initiative in making the journey on a limited amount of foreign currency. They gave me the impression of being two very fine types of young journalists, keen and alert, and proud of being in the Kemsley Group. I told them that they were to send you personally my good wishes—and I hope they did so . . .

Montgomery of Alamein

How glad we were that we took the trouble! Whatever else we learned that memorable night, we could now understand more fully the mind of a great soldier in his attention to detail. No wonder he routed Rommel in North Africa.

CHAPTER TWENTY-SEVEN

GOD BLESS AMERICA

That encounter with Montgomery of Alamein was the first in a long list of major interviews I was to conduct in the years ahead. Though my career in journalism is not the subject of this book, I should perhaps explain that that was what took me away from the North-East after I had learned my craft as a reporter with the *Turriff Advertiser*, the *Evening Express* and *The Press and Journal*, for whom I was the resident Buchan staff man, based in Peterhead and Fraserburgh between 1951 and 1954.

A move to the *Scottish Daily Express* in Glasgow on Leap Year Night of 1960 was the first step towards a career as a features writer which brought to fruition all the romantic dreams I had ever nursed about being a journalist. Each year became a greater excitement than the last as I found myself in the company of people like Charlie Chaplin, Bob Hope and Bing Crosby, Mohammed Ali and Stanley Matthews, Paul Getty and Sophia Loren, even Margaret Thatcher and the notorious Christine Keeler, with whom I conducted an interview in the not inappropriate setting of a bedroom.

Glancing over the diary of 1972, for example, I find I started the year in Northern Ireland, being caught up in an ambush with an army patrol in the Turf Lodge district of Belfast. By April I was accompanying crippled children in the candle-lit procession of the sick at Lourdes. In May I was shaking off my Russian shadow and roaming freely in the streets of Moscow (only to be apprehended at the airport and questioned about my movements), discovering, among other things, what a potentially capitalist nation the Soviets really are. That summer was spent in Germany and by September I was flying off to

Singapore, sampling life in the jungles of Malaya and landing at a party in the company of Princess Margaret. Restoring a sense of unreality to life, I ended the year back in the mayhem of Northern Ireland, where it had all started in January.

Among other experiences of the 1970s, I found myself one day in the London home of Lord Mountbatten, father figure of the British Royal Family, who was giving me what turned out to be a rather poignant interview. The man who fought gallantly in two world wars and took the surrender of the Japanese in 1945 was fighting an even greater battle to bring the youth of the world together. It was an idealistic scheme called the United World Colleges, the brainchild of Kurt Hahn, founder of Gordonstoun School in Morayshire, where Lord Mountbatten's nephew, Prince Philip, was a pupil before sending all three of his sons there. By now Mountbatten was head of the organization and there we sat talking about the future of civilization in general and the role of his favourite grand-nephew, Prince Charles, in particular.

Suddenly he remembered I worked for the newspaper empire of Lord Beaverbrook, a man well known to have a black-list of public figures. As we relaxed in that London drawing-room, he broke into a smile and told me the story of Anthony Eden, Britain's debonair Foreign Secretary in the days of Churchill and a man high on Beaverbrook's blacklist.

Apparently, when Churchill was standing down and Eden was offered the Premiership in the Spring of 1955, he consulted Mountbatten on the wisdom of accepting, referring in particular to Lord Beaverbrook, whose power in those days could go a long way to making or breaking a politician.

'I'm right at the top of Beaverbrook's shit-list, you know,' he told Mountbatten. 'He'll crucify me.'

'No, you're wrong there, Anthony,' Mountbatten countered. 'I'm the one who heads the Beaver's shit-list!' And from all accounts, he was probably right.

We were able to laugh about it a generation later. What we did not know as we sat in the calm of that London town-house, to which I had been admitted with a minimum of security vetting, was that, much more sinister than being high on Lord Beaverbrook's shit-list, Mountbatten was also figuring in the IRA's hit-list. During his next annual visit to Classieburn Castle in County Sligo, he was on a family boating trip from Mullaghmore Harbour when an IRA man detonated a planted bomb by remote control. A great man was blown to smithereens, along with three more of his party, including his fourteen-year-old grandson.

Before I leave my journalism of the 1970s, there is some relevance in recalling my assignment in the United States in 1976, when the *Express* sent me to describe how that extraordinary nation was celebrating its 200 years of independence.

This is what I wrote about a rather special Fourth of July, a day when I also renewed acquaintance with a colourful Scots-American who will warrant a later chapter of his own:

> They are dancing in the streets of America tonight. The bands are playing, majorettes are marching and the biggest-ever display of fireworks is exploding around the pious head of George Washington on that majestic sweep before the White House.
>
> The Viking spacecraft may be hovering for the final touchdown on Mars, 200 million miles away, but the action for tonight is here on Mother Earth, from New York to San Francisco, from the Custer battlefields of Montana to the jazzbands of New Orleans. For this is the 200th birthday of the most remarkable nation in man's history and they are not going to let it pass unnoticed.
>
> This is America, loud but lovable, of Hollywood and hamburgers, baseball, Bing and Broadway, of Dallas, Deadwood and the Almighty Dollar. It is good old star-spangled, bible-belting, corny-as-Kansas America, baring its soul and seeking to exorcize the nightmare of a devilish decade or more.
>
> And this is the day when you want to embrace it all. Personally, I settled for a drive down from New York to Washington, passing through Philadelphia, where they signed the Declaration of Independence 200 years ago today and cut the Ameri-

can people loose from the apron strings of Mother Britain.

New York had to be seen to be believed. As if by deliberate contrast to the magic of a spacecraft on Mars, this great city surrendered itself to the charms of the windjammers, or tall ships as John Masefield called them.

An armada of 225 sailed up the Hudson River at nature's pace, under the Verazanno Bridge and past the upraised arm of Liberty's Statue, watched by a crowd estimated in millions and including President Ford. A big American beside me threw away his cigar and said, gee, that sure was the most touching sight he had ever seen.

The man with the finest view of all was multi-millionaire Malcolm Forbes, the publisher whose father was a poor country boy from Whitehill in the parish of New Deer, Aberdeenshire.

Mr Forbes's magnificent yacht, the *Highlander*, was berthed in the 79th Street basin and he was holding a party for his distinguished guests, some of America's top business people.

Having sampled the caviar and venison of the Forbes party, I headed for Washington with its history stretching from the original George, who couldn't tell a lie, to the shady men of Watergate, who couldn't tell the difference. In this capital city, which rivals Paris for its wide-avenued splendour, they had come from the morning church services to join in the celebrations. Among the simple words which Thomas Jefferson wrote down in the Declaration of Independence was the fact that everyone had the right to enjoy 'life, liberty and the pursuit of happiness'. And that is a pretty fair description of tonight's activities.

Two hundred years ago these words were tantamount to a kick in the pants for the British but the bitterness of the past had melted in the warmth of friendship. They welcomed the pipes and drums of the Scottish infantry as they beat Retreat tonight at Quantico, outside Washington.

I bumped into Miss Duncan MacDonald, who was preparing to head off to the Scottish Highland Games in North Carolina, which attracts a crowd of 40,000 over two days. Miss MacDonald runs the Scottish-American Heritage body and told me: 'In this age of computerized living we have found that young people in particular are trying to trace their ethnic roots. Those of Scottish descent all want to know what clan they belong to. It is as if they are seeking the strength of personal identity in this anonymous age.'

As the summer winds blew gently down the plains of Oklahoma, the Americans are thus consolidating their past before turning to face a new century. Whatever terrors that may hold are deep in the lap of the gods. It is enough to raise a glass tonight, to join in the singing of 'God Bless America'—and leave the rest to fate.

CHAPTER TWENTY-EIGHT

FAIRY-TALE OF FORBES

Exactly ten years later, the man who welcomed his guests aboard the yacht on that memorable day of American history was stepping up the aisle of the Mitchell Hall at Marischal College, Aberdeen, complete with gown and hood and sustained by a procession of solemn academics.

Malcolm Stevenson Forbes had come back to receive the honorary degree of LLD from Aberdeen University in recognition of his outstanding achievements as publisher, writer and adventurer and one of America's most colourful and influential characters, who owed his origins to the plain, unpretentious land of Buchan.

Somewhere built into that honour was a tacit recognition of his father, the late Bertie Charles Forbes, whose story I recounted in *A Grain of Truth*. Briefly, he was one of the ten children of a poor country tailor at Whitehill of New Deer who became a pupil of my great-grandfather, Gavin Greig, a man he came to idolize. Gavin Greig helped him on the road to a newspaper career, via the *Peterhead Sentinel* and the *Dundee Courier* to the *Rand Daily Mail* in Johannesburg, which he helped to establish with Edgar Wallace, the thriller writer. The financial markets fascinated him and in 1904, at the age of twenty-four, he sailed for New York, passing under the mighty arm of Liberty who called upon the world to 'give me your tired, your poor, your huddled masses, yearning to breathe free'.

Without money, job or influence he soon took the outrageous step of renting a room in the old Waldorf Astoria, for the purpose of gaining proximity to famous men like John D. Rockefeller, Henry Ford and Frank Woolworth. It worked exactly as he had planned and the story of Bertie Forbes has now passed into business legend. Not only did the world's most powerful newspaper owner, William Randolph Hearst, offer him a blank cheque to write his own salary but he started his own business magazine which stands today as the most influential journal of its kind in America.

Appropriately, it is called simply *Forbes*, a fortnightly publication which runs to the length of a novel on most issues, a businessman's bible which lands on 77,000 desks and is reckoned to have one millionaire in every ten of its readers.

Bertie returned to his native corner of Buchan every two years to entertain the local folk to a picnic, bringing his beautiful wife and five sons to stay at the old railway hotel at Cruden Bay. As a great-grandson of Gavin Greig, I gained more than my share of his attention, as if he were repaying a back debt of gratitude. It was there at Cruden Bay during the 1930s that I first remember young Malcolm and his brothers. When Bertie dropped dead at his Manhattan desk in 1954 it was the eldest son, Bruce, who first took over the reins, but he developed cancer and died in his forties, at which point the mantle fell to Malcolm.

After Princeton University and a distinguished war career, in which he was badly wounded at the Normandy landings, his calling seemed to be for politics. In the 1950s he was seen as the Republicans' answer to the up-and-coming John F. Kennedy and was widely tipped as a future President of the United States. A bad defeat for the Governorship of New Jersey ('I was nosed out—by a landslide!' he joked later) gave him second thoughts about politics and diverted him back to the family business in time to take over Bruce's role. By the mid-sixties he was the sole owner and autocratic head of the multi-million enterprise and remains so today, making him something of a rarity in an age of corporations and limited liability.

In his plush headquarters on Fifth Avenue he reigns like a king, entertaining top people at his adjoining town-house or on the fabulous *Highlander* which plies between the Hudson River and Florida. Intimate photographs with people like Presidents Eisenhower, Nixon and Kennedy and the Rockefellers abound, and Malcolm Forbes will tell you about the politician who came to visit him one day and made so little impression that he wasn't even invited to sign the visitors' book. His familiar face turned up later in the White House—as President Jimmy Carter!

Defying that tradition of sons who are never the men their fathers were, Malcolm took the silver spoon out of his mouth and used it to expand Bertie's successful enterprise out of all recognition, moving from publishing into real estate and counting among his personal properties the Governor's Palace in Morocco, the magnificent Château Balleroy in France, an island in the South Pacific, a private Boeing 727 decked out as a flying mansion and, perhaps most valued of all, more Fabergé eggs than the whole priceless collection within the Kremlin of Moscow.

When he is not flying in that Boeing or sailing on the *Highlander*, you will find him chalking up more records for hot-air ballooning across America or riding his motor-bike (he owns the company) to Moscow or Peking. But if any of that gives an impression of a spend-thrift playboy then nothing could be further from the truth. Malcolm Forbes is a shrewd financial adviser with a genius for making money, believing in the philosophy that you must spend a lot to make more.

The financial ear of his magazine is close to the ground and the authority of its writers commands enormous attention. Malcolm Forbes himself is not prepared to stop short of a practical example. He once bought 250 square miles of Colorado, intending to turn it into a game reserve for the state. But the Attorney General put so many obstacles in his path that he eventually gave up the idea and sold off 30 per cent of it for twenty million pounds.

His idyllic island in the South Pacific, called Laucala, is not only a splendid retreat where the natives line up to welcome him but is also an island of copra, the seed which gives us coconut oil. (Needless to say, he bought the place when copra was at a low price.)

With his son Christopher—there are four sons and a daughter—he set out to build a collection of Victorian paintings when they were out of fashion. Today, when they are back in vogue, he has the largest private collection in the world.

To reach Malcolm Forbes in that Fifth Avenue building you pass bullet-proof displays of those priceless Fabergé eggs, as well as Abraham Lincoln's lum-hat, the opera glasses which fell from his hands at Ford's Theatre, Washington in 1865, when he was assassinated by the actor John Wilkes Booth, and a piece of towel they used to wipe away the President's blood.

But acquisition does nothing to divert his central philosophy that life has to be fun. 'When you're alive—LIVE' is one of his favourite sayings, incorporated in a book of epigrams which he once published under the tongue-in-cheek title *The Sayings of Chairman Malcolm*. Though his father came more and more to Scotland in his latter years, Malcolm's own connection became fairly tenuous in the post-war period, such was his involvement with life in the United States.

In time, however, I began to sense that advancing years were turning his thoughts more and more to his father's homeland, arousing a greater appreciation of the character and determination it must have taken to follow that route from a lowly cottage near New Deer to the skyscrapers of New York.

He has been known to slip quietly across Scotland on his motor-bike, and just a few years ago he flew into Aberdeen Airport hoping to buy Castle Forbes, which lies at the other end of Aberdeenshire from where his own humble father had grown up and which was then available for purchase. He failed to do business with Lord Forbes but links were nevertheless re-established.

In the mid-seventies his daughter Moira came to spend two years at Aberdeen University, living at the halls of residence at

Seaton and visiting Whitehill, where she met some of the people who still remembered her grandfather.

Whatever his thoughts about strengthening the ties with his father's native land, however, Malcolm Forbes had been dicing with death too often for the comfort of his insurance advisers, whether at war, at sea or in his beloved balloons, where he twice came within seconds of being killed. But his closest shave of all came on Sunday, 10 July 1971, when the King of Morocco invited him, as owner of the Governor's Palace, to his birthday party. King Hassan and his guests were about to start lunch when 1,200 military cadets came hurtling up the Casablanca road and swung into the palace gates, automatics ablaze with gunfire. Malcolm Forbes thought the fireworks display had started a little prematurely. Little did he know it was the beginning of an attempted *coup d'état*. Soon there was a bedlam of gunfire, screams and spurting blood and, by the time the dust had settled, 100 people lay slaughtered in the courtyard. The Belgian ambassador died in the arms of the French ambassador and the famous French cardiologist, Jean Himbert, was callously machine-gunned to death as he tried to crawl to the aid of the wounded.

The King had escaped and the resourceful Malcolm Forbes leaped over a wall to the sand and crawled away on his belly. Eventually he was found by the soldiers, marched back to the palace and forced to lie among the others, in fear and doubt about the future of his existence.

Providence, it seemed, was on his side and the horrifying experience did not deter him from making plans for the Arab world. In fact he followed up by printing an edition of *Forbes* in Arabic. There were only a few hundred potential readers but those few were worth so many tens of billions that there was an absolute rush to buy advertising space.

Perhaps it was the smeddum of an Aberdeenshire parentage that saw him through that emergency in Morocco, along with many others, proving him not only a winner but a survivor in the most literal sense. For him it is all a great adventure.

These thoughts were passing through my head that July afternoon of 1986 as I sat in the balcony of the Mitchell Hall and watched a graduation ceremony which would have filled Bertie Forbes with pride. Just as he had gone forth to make his mark on America and to be feted and honoured by the University of Southern California, his own son was now back in the home corner of the Forbeses, just thirty miles from that Cunnyknowe cottage at Whitehill of New Deer. When the ceremony had spilled out into the quadrangle of Marischal College and the greetings and congratulations had been well and truly bestowed, Malcolm Forbes took me aside and asked if I would help to fulfil a wish which had been welling up inside him.

More than thirty years after the death of his father, he wanted to revive the tradition of 'Bertie's Picnic', out there at Whitehill where the old school was now converted into a dwelling house but where there was still a recognizable community of local families, with children now attending the village schools at New Deer, Maud and New Pitsligo.

I contacted Mrs Glennie and her parents' committee at Whitehill and they were delighted to make the local arrangements. So it was, in the summer of 1987, that Malcolm Forbes set out from his office on Fifth Avenue, New York, to board his luxurious Boeing 727 at Newark Airport for the flight to Scotland. From Aberdeen he drove out into the Buchan territory of the North-East, wending his way to that rural corner of Whitehill, in the parish of New Deer, where the children of his father's old homeland were waiting to greet him with their own special song of welcome. Bertie's Picnic had now become Malcolm's Picnic.

The man whose personal wealth is counted in hundreds of millions of pounds, who grew to be one of America's most fabulous characters and might well have been one of its finest Presidents, had brought the story full circle; back to the neep parks of Buchan and the humble cottage of the Cunnyknowe where, once upon a time, this fairy-tale began.

CHAPTER TWENTY-NINE

MY HERITAGE TRAIL

So life wears on, and in the early spring of '87 I went for a drive around Buchan, as if to redefine my boundaries and confirm in my own mind that the land of my begetting was still there in all its rich tang of expression.

As I drove out from the Saplinbrae House Hotel I paused along the road at the Abbey of Deer, spiritual heart of Buchan with its ancient stones still clinging together after eight centuries, the foundations laid out in the form of a cross, its spruce and beech and ancient elms standing stiff as guardsmen o'er their historic keep. Then I wandered across the burn and up through the gorse and heather of Aikey Brae, the hillside much quarried by uncaring councils, the trees now legally vandalized by some visiting woodchopper.

By an even stretch an old tinker's wagon seemed poised for the Sunday fair while, on brown carpets of spring soil, tractors laid the seed of a new growth, trailing a procession of gulls over there by the shelter of Pitfour estate. Spring cattle dotted the greensward in shades of black and brown while the sheep munched happily near by and the burn went warbling on its way to the great North Sea, to a counterpoint of gentle breeze.

Up through Maud I drove, and out by the old Brucklay road, where daffodils spread their bloom against beech hedge.

On I went by my grandfather's former tenancy at Mains of Whitehill, down Pisga, along by Mac's Yard, past the moss and up the Gairdner's Brae into New Pitsligo, or Kyak as I knew it; at the far end of the village, little hoosies which once had thackit roofs now sheltered under brittle slate. So the road marched high by Windyheads, where the Civil Aviation Authority has an air traffic control, a bare hill that gives sight of

Troup Head then dips towards Pennan, where weekend crowds now flock to view the setting of David Puttnam's popular film, *Local Hero*.

On by New Aberdour, where the sea wafts up with its own rich tang of dilse, and round to that magnificent stretch of golden sand at Fraserburgh, where two prancing horses materialized like magic and were ridden headlong into the sea to cool their heated hooves. Even David Puttnam could not have produced a more timely and picturesque scene. Round by the rocky foreshore, towards the harbour, I remembered the lifeboat disaster of February, 1953, just nine days after the Great Gale which devastated the North-East in that Coronation year. There we had stood, helpless, as Coxswain Andrew Ritchie thrashed his way towards survival, only to be beaten at the last minute by a piece of flotsam which finally tore out his strength.

Along by Crimond, two siccar chiels leaned defiantly on a gate-post, wondering no doubt who the stranger might be as I tarried and remembered my father-in-law, Nelson Keith, and his brother Norman, products of the crofting community here between the shadows of Mormond Hill and the shores of St Combs. In this parish kirk of Crimond, their father had sung as a young lad with Jessie Seymour Irvine, the local minister's daughter who wrote the famous psalm tune for the twenty-third that spread the name of Crimond around the world.

You could hear it now, rich and mellow in its choral cry, lingering long past the generation that heard it first but coming from the past as a voice that will endure and tell us of the universal faith and hope that sustains mankind through the trauchles of the daily darg.

CHAPTER THIRTY

BACK TO CULSH

Yes, the land was still there all right, deep and abiding in the regeneration of its tilth, serving one generation after another, furrow upon furrow of the human flesh. The landscapes are undeniably the same as we remember from our childhood days, yet you could swear there was a difference in substance; for sure there is a difference in the emotions they evoke within the human breast. The transformation, we must conclude, is within ourselves.

Layers of experience which build themselves into the fabric of a human life will alter our standpoint one way or another. Time will edge us onward upon that long and winding road, each mile and bend of the way producing its own glint of sunlight or cast of cloud, arousing in the human soul a subtle change of feeling.

Even along this short, absorbing tour of Buchan, by the time I had reached the sandy shores of Cruden Bay, the bleak Hills of Fisherie were already a world away in my emotional experience, dim in the mists of an antiquity which is eerie to behold and impossible to explain.

Driving in through Longside, Mintlaw and Old Deer, I came round the Hill of Clackriach from Aikey Brae once more, as the valley of Maud unrolled itself before my wondering gaze.

Across the howe lay Honeyneuk, now in the hands of Jim and Belinda Muir, who ran the place themselves, eident, hardworking folk. The Websters were now taking their place alongside the Pauls and the Raes and the Galls and all the forgotten folk who had farmed down the years at Honeyneuk, each in their day regarding the place as a home and living and way of life vital unto that moment and familiar in every neuk, little anticipating that one day they would be consigned, like all the others, to a faded name on a title deed.

There stood the cottar houses, no longer providing the labour of the land, bare grey relics of a rural life now lacking an authentic core. Gone, it seemed to me, was the warmth of the farming community I had known; gone the structure that made it so. If all the world were truly a stage, as the Bard maintained, then gone were the cast of this particular rural drama, exit left and right, to leave a proscenium that echoed still with the sounds of a performance long faded into the wings and never to be repeated.

I was remembering about folk like old Jimmy Park, the bailie at Honeyneuk when my father took on the place, a man who spent his days in undistinguished bliss and typified as well as any the kind of folk who vrocht the grudging acres of Buchan. Old Jimmy lived in the cottar house with the 'aul 'umman', which was I suppose the nearest he ever came to an endearment; but it had a good deal more depth than all the 'dears' and 'darlings' that fall so loosely from smarter lips. Jimmy and the aul 'umman raised five strapping sons and taught them nothing very much to catch the modern fancy.

But they showed them by example how to be thrifty, hardworking, honest, decent members of society, and two of them grew up to be fine, reliable farm servants like their father while two more solid lads became prison warders and the fifth boy died in the heat of the Second War. I doubt if Jimmy and his wife ever got over it but the sorrow was not for public viewing. A quiet tear was wiped away and at yokin' time he was down the greip as usual to muck out and feed the nowt, with a spit or a curse about the pipe that wouldn't draw and, in time, the deep rumble of a laugh.

Jimmy Park was Santa Claus with the robes off, a finely creased face of good humour and character and above all kindliness, a man untroubled by education and not much the worse for it as far as I could see. With steady gait he roamed free among those nowt in the fields and found that rare peace which comes of being at one with nature. About Hogmanay his gait was less steady for Jimmy would repair to the local 'Refresh' at the railway station, where Lil and Lena would serve his celebration 'fusky' and at closing time his fellow servants would prop him up to face a world that had gone damnably off balance. He would wipe the bree from his big moustache and reflect on the pleasures of simply being alive. The taste was as plain as the Moss o' Byth and the gratitude and satisfaction as deep as the wreath of snow by the windmill at Honeyneuk.

There are folk who would scoff at such human beings but they had a wealth of their own which eluded the more sophisticated; not the affluence of material things but just the priceless currency of a generous humanity.

I doubt if Jimmy Park knew much about the inside of a kirk but the faith of the man was there in his eyes. And as his image springs unaccountably to mind at this particular moment, I have little doubt that he found his eternity in the corner of some Elysian Field where he tends the Lord's cattle and puffs out yoams of satisfaction from the short stem of his Steenhive.

From Honeyneuk I took the scenic route by the Fishfir Brae and the Brucklay policies to the West Lodge, turning left and then right to mount the gentle Hill of Culsh, where I find myself drawn time and time again in a manner which might suggest my eventual destination. There I stood pondering by the gravestone of my great-grandfather, Gavin Greig, the outstanding Buchan figure of his day, whose obituary notice in 1914 filled whole text-size pages of the local papers.

The departure from this earthly scene while still in his fifties brought an agonized cry from the heart of his many admirers.

'Gavin Greig dead. That was the news and it struck his friends like the announcement of a lost battle,' was how the editor of the *Peterhead Sentinel* began his seven long columns. I still have a copy of the paper. He eulogized a man who, from the remoteness of Buchan, had not only written plays, poetry and music which reached the far corners of the country but had gathered the folk songs of the land to a degree which gained the recognition of professors in Berlin.

All the time, while he and Granny Greig were bringing up their nine children, he was also managing to turn learning in the classrooms of Whitehill School into a joyous adventure. Ill health was bearing in upon him but the editor of the *Sentinel* gave us some hint of the man through his letters, which are often a reliable guide to the inner self:

Mr Greig caused his pupils to love himself and to love learning. When illness and weakness came upon him it was very unwillingly that he abandoned the various helpful agencies in which he had been engaged. This was touchingly revealed to me in the letter which he wrote from Deeside announcing his inability to continue his articles on the Bards. 'This I regret very much indeed; but I have found it necessary to lighten the ship and have been laying down one task after another, to see if vacuity will help me to recover tone and form.'

The letter is almost too sacred for quotation; but in order that our readers may see the noble spirit in which this man laboured in our midst let me extract one paragraph. 'Of course, though thus in a way driven to discontinue the series meantime on the account of the state of my health, I should like very much to resume the task at some future date . . . I do trust you will see how I am placed and grant me kindly indulgence. Believe me, my dear friend, the will remains as strong as ever. If the flesh is weak I must e'en submit. Honestly, when I breathe a wish for restored vigour, it is that I may be able to do a little more work in our little world and I should think we ought to be ashamed to put forward any other plea.'

The versatility of the man was most amazing. And what a companion he was! If his oratory at times touched the sublime it could also at other times be full of exquisite humour. The best instance of this I can recall is the speech he gave at the complimentary dinner to Dr James F. Tocher on the occasion of his leaving Peterhead to take up the post of county analyst. There was much good oratory on that occasion and, as I remarked at the time, the speech of Mr Greig was the speech of the evening. He was entrusted with the toast of 'Peterhead'. Such a blending of fine feeling with delightful humour is seldom found and it was no wonder that those of us favoured to listen were quite enraptured.

CHAPTER THIRTY-ONE

ROCK OF AGES

As I stood by Gavin Greig's gravestone now I tried to conjure up the scene of his funeral day, on Thursday, 3 September 1914, assisted once more by the pages of the *Sentinel*, whose editor gave this account of that sad occasion, improving our under-standing of what a country funeral was like in those distant days:

It was indeed a Buchan funeral. From far and near the mourners had gathered. Almost every mode of conveyance had been called into requisition. Of course the country gig pre-dominated; but there was a strong representation of motor cars, big and small. The service was specially impressive by its simplicity. The benches [of the school] were filled with adult mourners and many others could only get standing room. From the schoolhouse near at hand the coffin had been carried and was placed on a white-covered table. Handsome in polished oak and brass, it was unusually long for our departed friend was a tall man. The drawing back of the glass partition ena-bled the school to be used as a single meeting hall. In such a place on such an occasion one could not help musing. This was where he had reigned. For so many years this had been the centre of his beneficent activities. Here his kindly guidance had started many a scholar on the acquisition of knowledge, bring-ing them later on to see that wisdom was greater than knowl-edge.

A poor building to look at, yes, but it had been ennobled by the life of him that laboured in it so long. It had, too, deep and tender and sacred memories. Today's funeral was not the first that had set forth from this place. There was an occasion when a smaller coffin had been carried forth after a service which, even now, years later, was recalled with hushed voices by those who had been present at it. Then a daughter of the school-house had been cut off in youthful charm and he whose weary frame now lay in that oaken casket had himself played the accompaniment to the funeral hymn.

The hymn now sung was 'Rock of Ages'. Could a better choice have been made? Most popular of the sacred songs in our tongue, it linked us to many a hallowed memory. And he whom we had come to lay to rest was skilled above most in sacred music and familiar with the songs of Zion. It was fitting too that the scripture passages should have been read by the Rev. J. B. Duncan of Lynturk, who has been so closely associated with Mr Greig in the work of collecting and editing the Folk Songs of the North-East.

Some of the words of Sacred Writ sent our minds off at a tangent. 'The days of our years are three score years and ten.' Alas, if only this had been true of our departed friend, would our regret have been so great? What might he not have accomplished if another dozen years had been vouchsafed to him? But the wise Taskmaster had ordered it otherwise and He doeth all things well.

The Rev. William Beveridge's prayer had some beautiful touches. We rendered God thanks for what our friend had been and for the faithfulness to the gift bestowed upon him. It was a short service but simple and telling.

The accompaniment to the hymn was played by Miss Dingwall-Fordyce of Brucklay Castle. The cortège set forth on its slow funeral way to the Churchyard of Culsh, New Deer. In the school playground we left the mourning scholars, drawn up in one long line, under the supervision of Mr A. R. Dunbar, the comrade of Mr Greig in many a venture, the prototype of 'Mains' in the plays which bid fair to do most to perpetuate his literary fame and now, by a strange coincidence, the *locum tenens* to take up the work of teaching, which death has compelled his friend to close.

Before the eulogies and colourful descriptions were completed, we had read that two well-known local farmers, Mr

James Brebner of Hillhead of Ironside and Mr William Shirras, Upper Ironside, had an alarming experience while attending the funeral. When descending the brae at Weetingshill, the horse in their trap slipped and fell. It rose with such force that the shafts and part of the trap broke away. Mr Brebner jumped on to the bank at the roadside but Mr Shirras was precipitated with great violence under the vehicle quite close to the horse's feet. The animal took fright and bolted along the road, dragging with it part of the trap. The vehicles in front were now in danger and several of the occupants jumped on to the road and were successful in turning the horse to the side.

The animal made a dash for the wire paling but got entangled and was captured. Except for cuts and bruises, Mr Shirras escaped what could have been a tragic accident.

The pall-bearers included my grandfather, Arthur Barron, Mains of Whitehill (Gavin Greig's son-in-law), Tom Rodger from Crimond (son-in-law), Ernest Coutts from Port Elphinstone (another son-in-law, soon to be killed in the First World War), James Ferguson of Glasgow (brother-in-law), A. W. Simpson of Monymusk (brother-in-law) and James Will, schoolmaster at New Pitsligo.

I make no apology for reproducing the list of mourners, which not only testifies to the diligence of the reporting journalist but gives an interesting picture of the names which constituted the Buchan scene at the outbreak of the First World War. More than seventy years later those same names still survive in their descendants and, if this book is read in another seventy years, it should be of some interest to see how well the indigenous families of Buchan have adhered to their roots.

Here then is that catalogue of country folk who followed my great-grandfather to the Hill of Culsh at the outbreak of a war, the prospect of which so depressed him as to further dim the flame which flickered precariously between life and death:

W. F. Anton, schoolmaster, Crimond; James Angus, Queen Street, Peterhead; A. Adams, merchant, New Deer; James

Alexander, Affath; A. J. Allan, banker, Maud; Rev. W. Beveridge, New Deer; Joseph Blake, New Pitsligo; James Brebner, Hillhead of Ironside; John Barron, Cabra, Mintlaw.

George Brebner, Mill of Whitehill; Mr Blake, Fyvie; W. Barron, Whitehill; Alex Barron, Whitehill; Rev. Wm Cowie, Maud; Henry Cowie, Schoolhouse, New Deer; George Cruickshank, factor, Fyvie Estates; P. Creighton, banker, New Deer; Archibald Campbell, Auchmunziel, New Deer; George Calvert, roads superintendent, Maud; Mr Catto, Mains of Culsh; George Corbett, Weetingshill; James Cruickshank, Grassiehill; B. Cheyne, South Culsh; Mr Corsie, Peterhead; L. Cruden, Brucklay Castle; Rev. J. B. Duncan, Lynturk; D. C. Dundas, schoolmaster, Inverallochy; Adam R. Dunbar, retired schoolmaster, New Deer; Mr Davidson, Gaval; John Duffus, New Pitsligo; Charles Davidson, Waulkmill.

Ex-Baillie George Duncan, Peterhead; James Elrick, Aucheoch; George Fowlie, Mains of Auchreddie; J. Fowlie, Millhill; J. Ferguson, Aberdeen; John Fowlie, Loanhead; John Forbes, Mill of Fedderate; James Findlay, Kirkhill; W. Findlay, Peterhead; Rev. D. Grigor, Congregational Church, New Deer; Mr Giles, Fyvie; Keith Gray, Brucklay Castle; A. Gillespie, New Deer; Mr Gordon, Middlemuir, Methlick; Rev. J. Halliday, Peterhead; William Hadden, schoolmaster, Knaven; William Halkett, Peterhead; Edward P. Horne, New Deer; Alex Horne, New Deer; James Ironside, Brunthill; Mr Ironside, schoolmaster, Fetternear; John Innes, Port Elphinstone; John Jack, Rathen; James Johnston, Mill of Allathan; Joseph Johnston, Fridayhill; James Knox, Peterhead; M. Keith, Aberdour House, factor Brucklay estates; Alex Keith, Burnshangie; R. Murdoch Lawrence, Aberdeen; Rev. W. M. Meston, UF Church, New Pitsligo; Captain J. Morrison, 5th Battalion, Gordon Highlanders, Maud; Frank Metcalfe, Cachar, India; Wm Mitchell, New Deer; John Mitchell, Millbrex; John Mowat, Craigmaud; James Morrison, schoolmaster, Oldwhat.

William Murison, Upper Aucheoch; William Mitchell, Whitecairns; Dr Mitchell, New Deer; Alex Milne, Maud; J. Michie, Maud; Alex Murray, Hillhead, Bonnykelly; James Moir, Fedderate; James Macpherson, schoolmaster, Cairnbanno;

James McAllan, Whitebog; Rev. R. MacKinlay, Congregational Church, New Pitsligo; J. McBoyle, Fyvie; Alex R. McFarlane, editor, *Peterhead Sentinel*; J. Pettie, Port Elphinstone; C. D. Rice, rector, Peterhead Academy; Mr Ritchie, retired schoolmaster, Port Elphinstone; John Reid, Colliegard; George Robertson, clerk to school board, New Pitsligo; A. Robb, Brucklay Castle; William Shirras, Upper Ironside; Dufton Scott, Inverurie; J. Stephen, schoolmaster, New Deer; George Stewart, Auchmaleddie; Mr Smith, Burnshangie; A. Smith, banker, Inverurie; J. Boyes Sinclair, merchant, New Pitsligo; J. Sim, New Deer; A. MacDonald Reid, Central School, Peterhead; J. F. Tocher, County Analyst, Aberdeen; R. Topping, HM Inspector of Schools; William Turner, butler, Brucklay Castle; James Will, schoolmaster, New Pitsligo; George Watt, Whinhill; David Will, Alehousehill; Charles S. Walker, Brucklay; William Walker, 65 Argyll Place, Aberdeen; Dr Wood, Longside; James Walker, Brucklay Castle.

CHAPTER THIRTY-TWO

END OF THE DAY

That solid body of menfolk—for women did not follow the hearse in those departed days—came round from the School of Whitehill, down past Weetingshill and along by Mains of Fedderate, turning right, as I had done that very day, to ascend the slopes of Culsh. In their solemn ranks, they gathered round the spot where now I stood alone contemplating the fact that each one of them, in their appointed time, had since come down the same road, or one like it. As far as I know, the last survivor of that vast cortège was Jimmy Moir, who died a centenarian not so long ago, having been blacksmith at Whitehill and a cousin of the same Bertie Forbes who went to America and became a millionaire.

As I paid homage at Gavin Greig's grave, I remembered again those newspapers which carried not only detailed accounts of his remarkable career but even swatches of poetry composed on the spur of the moment in his honour. One which appeared in the *Aberdeen Daily Journal* perhaps summed up what the others were trying to say:

> Gone from our gaze; but never lost, thy work
> Abides, diffusing like the sun its rays
> Of light and strength to all that can receive
> Its powerful influence. On great and small
> Thy varied gifts were showered with lavish hand
>
> In music's art thou showed'st a master's hand
> Uniting both the gifts of sight and sound
> In later days the folk-song of the swain
> In thousand songs and tunes obeyed thy spell
> Detracting from our rush and love of gain

Thou broughtest back to mind the freer life
Of old, the happy childlike days of men
And settings, too, in book-form thou did'st give
And realistic placed the deeds of men
Dramatically in 'Mains' and 'Mains Again'.

Athletic body first and mind always
Endued with genius rare; thy facile pen
Has left its mark embedded in our hearts
Another tree branch lopped from Scotia's bard*
Like him thou'st lived too much and died too soon

High up here on the Hill of Culsh the nights are stretching their arms to embrace the fledgling spring; the seeds of a life renewed are sprouting in the virgin soil of those Buchan fields spread out before me now. Though the years have cast their shadows and borne away those people who inhabited the childhood dream, I am strangely at one with the world on this lonely hillside; just as I was not so long ago on the heights of Mount Nebo, where Moses came to die, and I could look across the Jordan Valley to the Dead Sea and the Judean Hills beyond, with Jericho brooding in the middle distance, all still and timeless and unchanged from long before the days of the Lord.

This twentieth century itself may be running into old age, but at the first melodious call of an April evening the heart still stirs with the eternal hope of youth—and the sheer privilege and joy of being alive to partake of this mystifying and glorious adventure.

* The allusion here is to Greig's family kinship with Burns.

401